Mary B. Cassata
State University of New York at Buffalo

Molefi K. Asante
State University of New York at Buffalo

Mass Communication

Principles and Practices

Macmillan Publishing Co., Inc.
New York

Collier Macmillan Publishers
London

Macmillan Publishing Co., Inc.
866 Third Avenue, New York, New York 10022

Collier Macmillan Canada, Ltd.

Library of Congress Cataloging in Publication Data

Cassata, Mary B.   (date)
  Mass communication.

  Includes bibliographies and index.
  1. Communication—Social aspects.   2. Communication
—Psychological aspects.   3. Mass media—Social aspects.
4. Mass media—Psychological aspects.   5. Mass media—
Political aspects.   6. Mass media—Law and legislation.
I. Asante, Molefi K., (date)   joint author.
II. Title.
HM258.C397   301.16   77-27121
ISBN 0-02-320010-3

Printing: 2 3 4 5 6 7 8   Year: 9 0 1 2 3 4 5

ACKNOWLEDGMENTS

Permissions

Addison-Wesley Publishing Company. For figure, "Types of Models." From Han-
    neman and McEwen, *Communication Behavior* (1975). Reprinted by permission.
American Academy of Arts and Sciences, Boston, Massachusetts. For Rosten, "The
    Intellectual and the Mass Media: Some Rigorously Random Remarks" (1960).
    Reprinted by permission.
American Society of Newspaper Editors. For "Canons of Journalism" (1923). Re-
    printed by permission.
———. For "A Statement of Principles" (1975). Reprinted by permission.
Audio-Visual Communication Review. For figure, "A Graphic Model of Com-
    munication." From Gerbner, "Towards a General Model of Communication,"
    1956. Reprinted by permission.
Harvey Bondar. For "The Reality of TV Violence: The Violence of TV Reality" writ-
    ten in collaboration with Mary B. Cassata. By permission.
Comics Magazine Association of America, Inc. For "Code of the Comics Magazine
    Association of America, Inc." Reprinted by permission.
Jules Feiffer. For cartoons. Reprinted by permission.
Information Handling Services. For table, "Inventory of Mass Communication
    Theories, According to Components of the Mass Communication Process."
    From Cassata and Palmer, *Reader in Library Communication* (1976).

Journalism Quarterly. For figure, "Mass Communication Model." From Westley and Mac Lean, "A Conceptual Model for Communication Research" (1957). Reprinted by permission.

Emanuel J. Levy. For "Canada/United States: The Limits of Media," written in collaboration with Mary B. Cassata. By permission.

Longman, Inc. For figure, "Mass Communication System." From DeFleur, *Theories of Mass Communication*. (David McKay Co., 1966). Reprinted by permission.

Motion Picture Association of America, Inc. For "The Motion Picture Production Code" (1930). Reprinted by permission.

———. For "Code of Self-Regulation" (1966). Reprinted by permission.

———. For "The Movie Rating System" (1968) by Jack Valenti, president, Motion Picture Association of America. Reprinted by permission.

National Association of Broadcasters. For "The Radio Code" (Twentieth Edition, 1976). Reprinted by permission.

———. For "The Television Code" (Nineteenth Edition, 1976). Reprinted by permission.

Public Relations Society of America. For "Code of Professional Standards" (1977). Reprinted by permission.

Radio Television News Directors Association. For "Code of Broadcast News Ethics" (1973). Reprinted by permission.

Niki Scher. For "You've Come a Long Way, Baby . . . From Minnie Mouse to Wonder Woman," written in collaboration with Mary B. Cassata. By permission.

The Society of Professional Journalists, Sigma Delta Chi. For "Code of Ethics" (1973). Reprinted by permission.

The University of Illinois Press. For figure, "The Shannon-Weaver Model of Communication." From Shannon and Weaver, *The Mathematical Theory of Communication* (1949). Reprinted by permission.

Erika Wenzel Vora. For figure, "Model for Diffusing Concepts." From Vora, *The Development of Concept Diffusion Models and Their Application to the Diffusion of the Social Concept of Race*. Ph.D dissertation, State University of New York at Buffalo, 1978. Reprinted by permission.

Mass Communication Scholars

We acknowledge the contributions of the many mass communication scholars from whom we borrowed freely—Berlo, Carey, DeFleur, Gerbner, Katz, Klapper, Lasswell, Lazarsfeld, McLuhan, Schramm, and Wright, to name a few.

Students

In addition we acknowledge the special assistance given to us by our students—Harvey Bondar, Samuel Boadu, Gary Charney, Emanuel Levy, Erika Wenzel Vora, Lisa Bryant and especially Niki Scher. We also owe a debt of gratitude to the students of Communication 240 on whom we practiced many of the ideas contained in this volume.

Communication Department, SUNY/Buffalo

Our thanks must be expressed to our office staff, who generously and competently typed the many revisions of this manuscript—to Lillie Fryar and Shirley Cady, and most of all to Dorothy Horst and Marilyn Coughlin.

for S. J., Ngena, and Mama

Preface

Never before during the history of *Homo sapiens* has one person been able to communicate to so many. Daniel Webster, famed for his ceremonial orations to thousands, had an audience of perhaps 20,000 at the dedication of the Bunker Hill Monument. Billy Graham, a leading evangelist, addressed over 60,000 in the Los Angeles Coliseum. On December 8, 1941, 60 million people listened on the radio to President Franklin D. Roosevelt asking Congress for a declaration of war. By contrast, over 100 million persons heard and saw President Richard M. Nixon resign. Thus we have seen a multiplication not only of listeners but also of viewers. Technology has given communicators vast audiences never dreamed of by the Demosthenes or by Chaka, the eloquent Zulu chieftain.

The twentieth century more than any other is the age of human communication. We are not quite sure what to do with the abundance of information or how to make good use of the speed with which it can be transmitted. Yet we seek more information and demand it with even greater speed, and we want to have the transmitting instruments at our own disposal. We are living in an age of senders as well as mere receivers.

What we have discovered in our rush to enter the information age is that our technology has brought us a greater accuracy in transmission. We can hope to be able to get along better with our neighbors, perhaps better communicate interculturally because what we say can be transmitted with fidelity. The media bring visual and vocal symbols into the homes of people who have difficulty reading books and newspapers, thus greatly enlarging the numbers who receive the message. Seeing and hearing allow more sensory participation than either one by itself, which can make the message more accurate.

The study of mass communication is particularly concerned with how communication serves to *create*, *animate*, and *influence* human societies. Wilbur Schramm is right when he calls communication the tool that makes human societies possible;[1] every human endeavor implies communication at some level. Definitions of communication abound, and we could survey the field from Edward Sapir to Marshall McLuhan in a fruitless search for the all-inclusive definition. Basically, most authors agree that communication involves the process of sharing information.

Mass communication, in the sense of communication mediated to reach extended audiences, creates territories of its own. It isolates audiences, defines boundaries, and caters to the needs it has created. Thus the instrument becomes a creator of human societies, organizing groups around similarities and dissimilarities. During World War II Winston Churchill speaking for the Allies and Adolf Hitler speaking for the Axis used the radio to shape vastly different societies. Certainly there were economic and political questions that aggravated the conflict, but it was the rhetoric of these spokesmen broadcast throughout the world that polarized the warring groups.

Societies can be animated by external forces. Mass communication does this by raising issues that fuel further discussion and debate. The diffusion process prompts inquiry and interest. This is not to say that without mass communication human societies would disintegrate. Rather, our point is to emphasize the stimulative function of mediated messages. The Watergate hearings clearly demonstrated the ability of mass-communicated messages to animate a society. Discussions of public policy, ways and means, war and peace are intensified in the body politic when the issues are broadcast.

The debate over media influence has been raging at least from the time that Plato recommended exclusion of Homer's epics from his ideal republic. Scholars may tug over attitude change, but there is little doubt that media do influence audiences. In Buffalo, New York, a 10-year-old boy tried the latest Kung Fu fighting technique from a movie on his 7-year-old brother to see if it

[1] Wilbur Schramm, *Men, Messages, and Media* (New York: Harper & Row, 1973), p. 2.

would work. While the German Army was gearing up in Europe in 1938, Orson Welles created panic in America with his radio adaptation of H. G. Wells's novel *The War of the Worlds;* convinced that an invasion of Martians had begun, many people in the eastern United States left their homes in search of safer locations. Television's impact on children, blacks, women, and older people is massively documented. Magazines and newspapers are influential as disseminators of ideas as well as shapers of attitudes.

In this book we seek to present theories and practices of mass communication in order to explain how the various media influence society.

Mary B. Cassata
Molefi K. Asante

Contents

Part One
Mass Communication:
Fundamentals

Chapter 1. Introduction 5
The Process of Communication 6
Elements of the Process Model 7
Interpersonal and Mass Communication 9
Immediate Theme Control 11
Emphasis and Restatement 11
Sensory Stimulation 12
Feedback 12
The Multiplicative Factor 13
The System Concept 14

Chapter 2. Roots 19
The Communication Revolution 19
Summary of Significant Events 40

Chapter 3. Mass Communication Constituents 43
Reproduction 44
Circulation 46
Feedback 49
Support 51
Ownership 54

Part One Readings 57

Part Two
Theoretical Dimensions

Chapter 4. Mass Communication
Models and Theories 63
Verbal Models 65

Diagrammatic or Graphic Models 66

Mathematical Models 72

Relationship Between Models and Theories 72

The Communicator Component 73
Authoritarian Theory
Libertarian Theory
Social Responsibility Theory
Soviet-Communist Theory
Power of the Press Theory, Bullet Theory, Hypodermic Needle Theory
A Final Word

The Message Component 80
Cultural Indicators
Agenda-Setting Hypotheses

The Channel Component 82
McLuhan's Theories
The N-Step Flow Models

The Audience Component 84
Individual Differences Perspective
Social Categories and Social Relationships Theories
Cultural Norms Theory
Ludenic Theory: Play
Summary

The Effects Component 87
Uses and Gratification Approach
Social Learning Theory
Theory of Effects and No-Effects Theory

Theories of Violence 89

Summary 95

Chapter 5. Mass Communication Effects 97

Audience Saturation/Impact Studies 97

Functions of Mass Communication 99

Mass Media Accessibility 100

General Considerations 102

Dramatic Effects 104
Case History 1
Case History 2
Case History 3

Learning Without Involvement 106

Modeling and Imitation 106

Uses and Gratifications Studies 107

Conclusion 109

Part Two Readings 111

**Part Three
National and
International Systems**

**Chapter 6. Mass Communication: National
and International Perspectives** 117
International News-Gathering
Agencies 117
How Does an Agency Function? 122
Contrasting Media Systems 125
*United States
The Soviet System
Federal Republic of Germany
Japan
Nigeria*

Chapter 7. International Satellite Systems 135
Capabilities of Satellites 135
Uses of Communication Satellites 136
Characteristics 137
Educational Television 140
International Satellite Systems 140
*Substitute Satellites
Intelsat*

Chapter 8. Film: an International Medium 143
Beginnings 146
The Rise of the Narrative Film 147
The Documentary Film 148
The Naturalist 149
The Realist 149
The Newsreel 150
The Propagandist 150
Cinema Verité 151
The Entertainment Film 155
The Stars Are Born 157
Hollywood in Decline 159

Part Three Readings 162

**Part Four
Mass Communication:
Controls and Challenges**

**Chapter 9. Mass Communication

Regulations and Control** 169
Regulation 169

Legal 169
The Fairness Doctrine
The FCC and Its Muscles
FCC Operation
Programming Categories
The FCC and the News
The Federal Trade Commission and the Food and Drug Administration
The Copyright Law
Obtaining a Copyright
Ascertaining Copyright Status

Economic 182
The Advertising Factor

Social 184
The Good
The Presentation of Truth
The Revelation of Error
The Education of the Public
The Basis of Broadcasting
The Means-End Controversy

Investigatory Bodies 187
Commission on the Freedom of the Press
National Advisory Commission on Civil Disorders
Carnegie Commission on Educational Television
National Commission on the Causes and Prevention of Violence
Surgeon General's Scientific Advisory Committee on Television and
Social Behavior
Carnegie Commission on the Future of Public Broadcasting
Summary

Chapter 10. Minorities: Coloring the Media 195
Minorities 195
The Black Press Audience 196
Black Broadcasting 198
Functions 199
Employment of Minorities 200
The Looking Glass 202

Chapter 11. You've Come a Long Way, Baby . . .
from Minnie Mouse to Wonder Woman 203
Socialization of Children: Sex Role Stereotypes 208
Advertising and the American Woman 210
Women in the Daytime Soaps 212
Women in Prime Time 214
Women Employed in the Industry 216

**Chapter 12. The Reality of TV Violence
The Violence of TV Reality** 219
TV News and Violence 223
Televised War and Social Values 223
Television as a Major Societal Force 224
Conclusion 228

Chapter 13. Canada/United States: the Limits of Media 233
The Canadian Struggle for National Identity 233
The Role of Broadcasting 237
Looking Through the Looking Glass—Darkly? 240

Chapter 14. Mass Communication: Prospects and Directions 245
Technology 245
The News 247
Entertainment 248
Consumer Awareness Training 249
Research Instruments 249
Content Analysis
Likert Scale
Depth Interview
Questionnaires
Case Methods
Semantic Differential
Other Tools
UNESCO Communication Activities 254

Part Four Readings 256

Appendixes   **Appendix A. The Codes** 259
Codes of Ethics 259
Journalism Codes 259
Canons of Journalism
A Statement of Principles
Code of Ethics
Motion Picture Codes 265
The Motion Picture Production Code
Code of Self Regulation—Motion Picture Association of America
The Movie Rating System
Broadcasting Codes 292
Code of Broadcast News Ethics
The Radio Code
The Television Code

Code of the Comics Magazine Association of America, Inc. 333

PRSA's Code of Professional Standards 337

Appendix B. Glossary of Mass Communication Concepts 339

Appendix C. Referenced Bibliography 343

Index of Names 351

Index of Subjects 355

Part One

I AM LOVED.

PEOPLE NEED ME, WORSHIP ME, CAN'T LIVE WITHOUT ME—

GO CRAZY WHEN I DON'T COME ACROSS WITH WHAT THEY WANT.

I SHAPE LIVES. I TEACH: HOW TO SHOOT. WHAT TO BUY.

I DRAIN EMPTINESS FROM LIVES. FILL THE VOID WITH JUNK. PEOPLE ARE GRATEFUL.

I AM THE GIVER OF NEWS. OPINIONS DON'T EXIST WITHOUT ME.

I AM THE INSIDES OF YOUR HEAD.

IF YOU WANTED A GROSS NATIONAL PRODUCT, YOU GOT IT.

Messages are the medium in which human beings exist.
Precisely how human behavior and attitudes are shaped by
the multifarious forms of mass communication is now
beginning to be investigated.
George Gerbner, "Communication
and Social Environment," 1972

Mass Communication: Fundamentals

Chapter 1
Introduction

When people respond to symbols instead of the realities
represented by the symbols, semanticists call this the
"Fallacy of Misplaced Concreteness." This situation can
have great significance in mass communication, for the
mass media create a symbolic world which may or may not
correspond to the real world.
Ronald Hicks, *A Survey of Mass Communication*

The history of the world may well be the history of the development of mass communication. In this light, the development of the printing press marked a critical juncture in human history. Soon communicators were capable of sending a message to an extended audience without the need of their physical presence. Like the mass production of the automobile hundreds of years later, the invention of the printing press revolutionized the essential process of how human beings relate to each other. What a person said to one could now be said to many; private thoughts could be circulated to the farthest reaches of the earth.

Throughout the last hundred-odd years we have seen an explosion of new techniques and mechanisms for the delivery of messages: the postal service, the telegraph, the linotype, the telephone, the rotary press, the radar, television, satellite transmission, and now laser communication beyond the experimental stage. Gutenberg could not have dreamed of the scientific advances made since the fifteenth century in the delivery of information. In a radical sense it could be argued that all technological advances are delivery systems. The attaché case, the television set, the locomotive, and the Saturn rocket are parts of the same technological revolution.

It is almost a cliché to speak about the communication revolution. Some skillful writers have measured the extent of the revolution, not only pointing out the current phase but also projecting what we can expect in the years ahead.

We talk so much about communication that the nature of the process has often been obscured. It is indeed multidimensional. When Lagos, the booming metropolis of Nigeria, gets an efficient telephone system it will serve to reduce the traffic problems that tie up the city for hours. A large percentage of the automobiles on the streets are driven by messengers delivering messages and replies for their superiors. Modern societies tend to have less interpersonal contact than this, because of the intervention of technology. Perhaps the revolution to come in communication will be back to basic, face-to-face interaction. Nevertheless, at present the process of communication has numerous technological dimensions. We can speak of it as telephone, telegraph, video, or satellite communication. Even more, computers can read millions of bits of information back to a user in a striking display of speed and memory. We are like children sitting on edge waiting for the next surprise, one that is sure to come.

The Process of Communication

Our most natural attribute is the need and ability to communicate. What is communication? We define it as the transmission of information with the purpose of influencing audiences. In the landmark volume *The Process of Communication*, David K. Berlo popularized the source-message-channel-receiver model of communication. Despite numerous attempts to supplant the SMCR model, it remains one of the most useful interpretations of the process of communication.

Berlo introduces six constituents of the communication model: [1]

1. The communication source.
2. The encoder.
3. The message.
4. The channel.

---

[1] David K. Berlo, *The Process of Communication* (New York: Holt, Rinehart and Winston, 1960), p. 32.

5. The decoder.
6. The communication receiver.

Actually, for Berlo, the source and encoder are the same, as are the receiver and decoder. After all, a human being can never be a source of verbal information if he or she never encodes—i.e., translates thoughts into words or other symbols that an audience will understand. Similarly, receiving a message is, by definition, decoding that message.

The idea of communication as process is central to the new conception of how humans interact with each other through messages. Berlo writes:

> Five hundred years before the birth of Christ, Heraclitus pointed out the importance of the concept of process when he stated that a man can never step in the same river twice; the man is different and so is the river.[2]

Thus the constituent elements of communication—source, message, channel, and receiver—are interrelated in a particular situation that can never again have precisely the same configuration.

Elements of the Process Model

When we attempt to find the meaning of the basic constituents of a communication situation, it becomes clear that *process* is the key to how humans communicate. For example, you are in a large assembly hall awaiting the arrival of a featured speaker. You turn to the person next to you and begin to converse. In this situation you have immediately established a *dyadic* ("two-way") communication relationship, with the source and receiver interdependent. One defines the other. You may be the immediate source whereas the other person serves as receiver or vice versa. An interpersonal communication situation is set up between the two of you.

Suppose you want to establish communication contact with your neighbor. You feel the need; the message is transmitted by your central nervous system to your speech mechanism. At that point the part of the brain responsible for speech produces a message that expresses

[2] Ibid., p. 23.

your purpose. You say, "Hello, my name is Sam." Once this message has been transmitted through time and space (the only way, so far, that we can adequately communicate with each other), the receiver's decoder goes to work. In a sense, this may be viewed as the reverse operation by the speech mechanism in the brain. Thus, if there is no interference at the hearing level and none at the decoding level, the response should be indicative that the expression "Hello, my name is Sam" had a social-contact meaning for the receiver. A typical response might be "And I'm Susan." The miracle of communication has occurred again. Analytically we notice in this example that the constituents were all present in the process—the source, the message, the channel, and the receiver. Although the source and receiver alternated and the messages from the two communicators were different, the channel—sound waves through the air—remained the same. Conceivably, one or both of the communicators could have written the message in a note rather than have spoken it.

Communication worked in this instance, but it does not work in all instances. For example, if you do not know what you want to say, your encoding mechanism cannot be instructed to transmit a message. A further difficulty may arise from the way you perceive another individual in relation to yourself. Suppose you thought that you held a higher social or economic status. Your encoder might transmit something like "Good day, I am Dr. Manners." Suppose you wanted to lay the groundwork for future contact. Your encoder might transmit "Hi, I'm Sam," a less intimidating statement than the preceding one.

Another problem inherent in the communication process is the possibility that the encoder, deficient in some way, might substitute the wrong sounds in the process of transmission. Your message could come out, "Hello, my game is Ham." This could lead to embarrassment. But if the receiver's decoding system were faulty, she might hear, "Hello, my what a dame!" Or the communication channel might be overloaded with hundreds of other people speaking simultaneously throughout the assembly hall, and Susan would not hear you. One other possibility is that the cultural norms of Susan's society might not permit her to respond to a stranger. Your communication would be ineffective.

Although we have discussed a fairly uncomplicated situation, the process analysis approach to communication provides a frame of reference for looking at the most complex communication situations, whether interpersonal or mass.

Interpersonal and Mass Communication

The basic model for communication processes just described

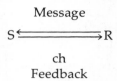

may be applied to all forms of communication. However, although the
essential differences between interpersonal and mass communication
are usually cited as being quantitative,[3] the vastness of those differences itself often constitutes a major qualitative difference. In interpersonal communication the source is usually concerned with one
other person or a small group, whereas mass communication from the
time of George Whitefield and before has been defined by its multiple
receivers. A message is widely and rapidly distributed. The capacity
of mass media constantly grows so that audiences expand endlessly.
Over 200 million people throughout the world were believed to have
watched the Apollo-Soyuz joint space flight on television. Some scholarly journals have no more than a few hundred receivers; a preacher or
rabbi may have from 25 to 5,000; a popular book several hundred
thousands; and a top-ten record, millions. To account for this significant difference in range of receivers and differences in channels, one
might consider the receivers as *audiences,* the channels (i.e., magazines, television, newspapers, radio, movies, and books) as *media.* In
this way it becomes obvious that society uses mass media to achieve
mass communication.

   Although differences exist in terms of the multiple receivers of a
mass medium as opposed to the few receivers of an interpersonal communication, other differences are not always so clear. Wilbur Schramm
understood the difficulty extremely well when he wrote:

> When we speak of a mass medium, we usually mean a channel of com-
> munication in which a machine (to duplicate and distribute the informa-
> tion signs) and a communicating organization (like the staff of a news-
> paper or broadcasting station) has been interposed. When we speak of
> an interpersonal channel, we mean a channel that reaches from person to
> person, without such things interposed. As we have seen, the distinc-

[3] Frederick C. Whitney, *Mass Media and Mass Communications in Society* (Dubuque, Ia.:
W. C. Brown, 1975), p. 6.

**Table 1-1. Key Differences in
Communication Modes**

	Interpersonal	*Mass*	*Medio*
Communicator	Independent	Complex organization	Individual or organization
Message	Private or restricted	Public	Private or restricted
Channel	Vocal	Electronic and print	Vocal and electronic
Audience	Individual or small group	Mass	Individual, small group, or mass
Feedback	Immediate	Delayed	Immediate or delayed
Contact	Primary	Secondary	Primary or secondary
Example	Family discussions	Television news	Telephone

tion blurs. For example, on which side of the fence does the telephone fit?[4]

In their book, *A Taxonomy of Concepts in Communication,* Blake and Haroldsen attempt to answer Schramm's question about whether the telephone can be classified as belonging to the interpersonal or the mass communication mode by introducing a third area of communication study called *medio communication.*[5] Medio communication "lies in the interface between face to face and mass communication." (*Medio* is from Latin and means "middle.") It is distinguished by the use of technology, takes place under special conditions, and involves identifiable participants. Hence the message's recipients are few in number and are known to the communicator. Further, unlike in mass communication, the message is not public. Examples of medio communication are point-to-point telecommunications (telephone, teletype, CB radio); surveillance communication (radar, supermarket monitors); closed-circuit TV (occupational, educational); and home movies.

Leaving medio communication aside, we will now discuss the

[4] Wilbur Schramm, *Men, Messages, and Media: A Look at Human Communication* (New York: Harper & Row, 1973), p. 115.
[5] Reed H. Blake and Edwin O. Haroldsen, *A Taxonomy of Concepts in Communication* (New York: Hastings House, 1975), pp. 32–33.

clear-cut distinctions that do exist between interpersonal and mass communication.

Immediate Theme Control

During a conversation, either one of the parties has the liberty to change the topic. All of us are familiar with the expression "Not to change the subject, but . . . ," which has become a part of American English etiquette for when one desires to move on to another topic of discussion. This amenity is not possible in most mass media communications. Topics and themes are controlled by the producer of the primary message and the audiences have no immediate control over topics. It could be argued that the choice in mass media is inherent in the multiplicity of sources. For example, an audience dissatisfied with one talk show may switch to another talk show. Or a reader who dislikes the editorials of one newspaper may change newspapers. In this way the audience makes a choice, but this choosing cannot be compared with what happens in an interpersonal interaction where an individual initiates a change in the discussion. The mass media assume all control over the topic; the viewer or subscriber must change information sources in order to alter the topic.

Emphasis and Restatement

Interpersonal communication thrives on emphasis and restatement. The participants have the opportunity to make statements, to emphasize points by verbal and visual action, and to ask questions of each other. The pace of the communication is thus controlled by the immediate participants. There are, however, different levels of emphasis and restatement depending on the medium. For example, the written medium allows the reader to reread, to lay the material aside for a few minutes or days, to underline sentences or paragraphs, and to write notes in the margin. Similar extended input into the pace of a communication is not normally afforded the radio, film, or television audience. However, in the last decade television has perfected the "instant replay" sequence for certain live athletic events. The viewer is able to get a second look at the action. But the viewer has no effective control over what events will be repeated. A person may certainly leave the set, turn it off, or change channels, but when it comes to regulating the information flow the viewer is helpless.

Control of the information flow by the sender makes for more effective persuasion, whereas control exercised by the audience makes for more effective learning. Because technology has not been able to make an inexpensive system that combines the central distribution of information with an efficient mechanism for receiver control of the information flow, emphasis and restatement in mediated communication will continue to be dictated by the source.[6]

Sensory Stimulation

Human beings are capable of communicating as total organisms. Thus we may experience a communication via the five senses—*visual, tactile, auditory, olfactory, gustatory*. Interpersonal communication allows the participants much more opportunity to be stimulated through all the senses than does print, film, radio, or television. However, although a person who engages in face-to-face communication may have the possibility of all his or her senses being stimulated, there do exist sometimes physical and biological limitations. Interpersonal communication allows participants to communicate more completely because of the advantage of simultaneously hearing, seeing, touching, and so on. We usually think of hearing and seeing as the primary communication senses, yet touching and smelling are equally significant in communicating intimate messages. Experiments in film with the olfactory sense have so far proved to be difficult to manage. One of the problems has been how to provide just the proper amount of aroma at the proper time and how to make it go away once it has served its purpose.

Feedback

It should be understood that in any communication situation information flows in a reciprocal fashion from the initiating source to the receiver, who in turn becomes an initiator. In this way feedback

[6] Schramm, op. cit., p. 117.

occurs between the communicators.[7] One is able to monitor the message of the other and to send impressions that indicate how the message was received. In a typical communication situation this process occurs almost simultaneously with the sending of the message. However, in many mass media situations it is impossible for the audience to send simultaneous feedback to the source, a clear disadvantage for programmers, producers, and advertisers who use television and radio.

Large numbers of television and radio broadcasters use write-ins and phone-ins to test audience feedback to programs and advertisement. Such feedback is necessarily incomplete because the audience's physical reaction, i.e., facial, gestural, or postural reaction, cannot be received and interpreted. Many media organizations have used what might be coined "feedfront" when they want to have audience reactions. In feedfront the producers and programmers pretest their materials on a group of experts or on a select audience who may be asked to respond verbally to the test segment, indicating what did and what did not appeal to them. *Sesame Street*, the popular children's show on public broadcasting stations, is usually pretested. In this limited way the media organizations are able to get some idea of what reaction to expect from audiences.

The Multiplicative Factor

The ability to multiply the number of recipients of a message is the most fundamental invention in the last 500 years. The crowds of 200,000 that Premier Fidel Castro speaks to in Havana Plaza can scarcely compare with the 50 to 100 million who hear a United States President's news conference. The media greatly multiply the audience. In such situations the speaker gives up control over the quality of the audience. Although it may be possible to prepare a message for a specific audience, even as large as 200,000, it becomes an extremely delicate task to develop a message for 100 million. Within that audience are ardent believers, ardent disbelievers, and persons who don't care one way or the other. Nevertheless, media's multiplicative possibil-

[7] Arthur L. Smith, *Transracial Communication* (Englewood Cliffs, N.J.: Prentice-Hall, 1973).

ities if used properly vastly increase the user's ability to influence other people.

The foregoing discussion has centered on some distinctions between interpersonal and mediated communication. However, there are no hard and fast rules in this regard; the boundaries between those two forms of human communication are less exclusive than one might believe. The differences pointed out simply represent the areas where broad distinctions can be made.

The System Concept

Several analogies may be used to discuss what happens in a communicative situation. One approach is the system concept.

Communication theory is indeed the great crossroads of scholars. Authors from anthropology, psychology, and other disciplines have come into it only to go back to the central interests of their own disciplines. Two of the more influential passers-by were Claude Shannon from engineering and his coauthor, Warren Weaver. Their book, *The Mathematical Theory of Communication*, has been an important documents in the reformulation of communication theory, i.e., it is one of the works that bridged the chasm between early go-no-go models and modern communication theories. Osmo Wiio, the Finnish communicationist, has argued that Shannon's theory of signal transmission cannot be called information theory; rather, it is one of the few likely candidates for a communication theory, because Shannon understood communication as the transfer process for information.[8]

An employee of Bell Laboratories, Shannon was concerned with radio and telephone technology and with the derivation of a physical model for communications via those channels. *The Mathematical Theory of Communication* was the forerunner of David Berlo's process model.[9] Shannon's work expands the vocabulary of communication theory to include terms such as *entropy, redundancy, bit, feedback, channel, capacity, noise,* and *feedback.*[10]

The two-step flow model (Fig. 1-2) pioneered by Lazarsfeld,

---

[8] Osmo A. Wiio, "Contingency Views of Human Communication" (paper presented at the International Communication Association Conference, Chicago, April 1975), p. 2.
[9] Berlo, op. cit., p. 72.
[10] Wiio, op. cit., p. 3.

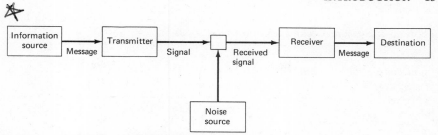

Figure 1-1. Shannon and Weaver's model of communication.

Berelson, and Gaudet and later expanded and perfected by Elihu Katz
was the immediate precursor of mass communication models. This
model emphasized the opinion leader as a significant factor in mass
communication. It has been applied to numerous national systems of
mass communication; however, its validity has been questioned in
many of the developing nations. One of the major problems has to do
with the identification of opinion leaders, a task that can prove difficult. In some societies the traditional leaders may be assumed to be
the opinion leaders, yet elsewhere the erosion of traditional leaders'
authority by outsiders may have made their titles meaningless.

Communication methods employing forms indigenous to the so-

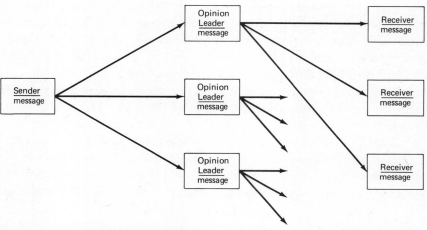

Figure 1-2. Two-step flow model.

Table 1-2. System Closedness and Openness

Correlation Between the Input and the Throughput of a System	Degree of System Openness	Type of System
0.0	Completely open	Social systems Man
Low correlation	Relatively open	Monkey Amoeba
High	Relatively closed	Computers Complex machines Subway
1.0	Closed system	A switch

ciety are necessary to improve interactions with people of another culture, and popular beliefs, methods, and products may be utilized in an effort to communicate. Finding the cultural keys to a society is one of the first steps toward establishing effective communication.

Another direction for research has been the general systems school, a movement initially connected with biological theory. In this approach the researcher seeks to view systems as functional wholes. *A system is usually thought of as a group of constituents plus the relationship between them plus their attributes.* Such systems may be closed or open in the sense that they may be isolated from external influences or integrated with the environment. Closed systems do not exist in human communication; the concept is useful for research in the physical sciences, but a closed system is extremely difficult to isolate. Theoretically, the functions of a closed system are predictable whereas the functions of open systems are unpredictable. Information, energy, matter (input) enters the open system and is processed and exported (output) in different forms into the environment from which it came. Feedback is a regulatory device whereby open systems receive information from the environment to regulate the input and output of the system.

Wiio developed a practical systems model for mass communication.[11] Starting from the position that all communication systems are relatively open, he developed a model that included four broad systems in a suprasystem: political, social, economic, and social

[11] Osmo A. Wiio, "System Models of Information and Communication," *The Finnish Journal of Business Economics*, 1, 1974.

institutional. This suprasystem defines the sender's input; the sender, in this case media technology, processes the information in close conjunction with the receiver system to produce the output. According to Wiio, feedback, direct and indirect, goes into both input and output, with the output reciprocating. The final control of the product, however, depends on laws, public opinion, decisions by the owners of media, and other forces interacting with the suprasystem.

Concurrent with the rise of general systems models in communication has been the emergence of the critical school. Proponents of the critical school argue that other communication researchers, particularly positivist-empiricists, have simply established and supported one-sided, atomistic empiricism. The critical school attempts to introduce values into the discussion of mass communication. The normative goal becomes to make people aware of the enormity of the pain that can be inflicted by the wielders of power. Critical schoolers want to make mass communication the servant of humanitarian interests. Values are introduced into every discussion of communication and are constantly assessed in terms of their relationship to human progress.

The systems concept in communication provides one way to view mass communication, the critical school another. Both of these approaches provide a useful framework for analysis.

(1) BERLO'S MODEL - 6

(2) DYADIC - 7

(3) DIFFERENCE BETWEEN MASS & INTERPERSONAL - 9, 10, 11

(4) THEME CONTROL - 11

(5) EMPHASIS & SENSORY - 12

(6) FEEBACK - "FEEDFRONT" - 13

(7) SHANNON & WEAVERS SYSTEM MODEL - 14, 15

(8) OPEN & CLOSED SYSTEMS - 16

(9) CRITICAL SCHOOL - 17

Chapter 2
Roots

*Why'd You choose such a backward time and such a
strange land? If You'd come today You would have reached
a whole nation. Israel in 4 B.C. had no mass
communication.*
Judas to Jesus, in *Jesus Christ Superstar*

The Communication Revolution

Of the numerous revolutions that have punctuated history, only two
are generally conceded by social historians to be worthy of note. Although each of these has varied from country to country in terms of
timing and extensiveness, nevertheless everywhere a remarkable
samness has been felt in terms of their impact on the social change
and the social progress of a particular nation.

These two revolutions, which have completely transformed the
quality of life, are, of course, the industrial revolution and the communication revolution. Whereas the first was manifested in the mass
production of goods, the second was manifested in the mass production of symbols. And whereas some social historians choose to regard
these revolutions as separate events, others see them more as cause
and effect, as sequential steps in the same process.

One communication researcher, James W. Carey—deliberately
failing to describe the two revolutions in more universal terms—has
admitted his proclivity for dwelling on the American experience, citing as justification "Gertrude Stein's wry observation that the United
States is, in fact the oldest nation since it came first into the 20th century and has been there the longest." [1]

[1] James W. Carey, "The Communications Revolution and the Professional Communicator," in Paul Halmos (ed.), *The Sociology of Mass-Media Communicators*, Monograph 13, *The Sociological Review*, January 1969, 23.

Carey believes that the industrial and communication revolutions in the United States occurred within a period of some 30 to 50 years or so of one another; between 1840 and 1860 was when the "full tide of industrialisation struck" and the 1890s marked the decisive beginnings of present-day mass communication "with the birth of the national magazine, the development of the modern mass newspaper, the domination of news dissemination by the press services, and the creation of primitive electronic forms of communication."[2] The developments in both revolutions were so rapid and the technological improvements so wondrous that many people today can scarcely imagine life without the benefits they have wrought. However, in terms of the communication revolution, a substantial number of Americans can recall life without the motion picture theater, the radio, or television. Even the mass newspaper is not that old. All things considered, our modern-day communication devices, without which life would be different if not unbearable, have been with us for only a brief time when it is considered that the development of speaking and writing claimed human efforts for a million years or more.

Most historians, of course, place the beginnings of mass communications sometime during the fifteenth century, when printing was invented. We have decided to develop a chronology of mass communication events, beginning early in the fifteenth century when the Koreans made cast metal type using punches and matrices and ending in the year 1975. As the reader will later discover, we do venture beyond 1975 into the future in the closing chapter of this book, but perhaps the most distinctive feature of our chronology is that we have cast it within a historical perspective so that the reader might easily place a mass communication event. We advise the student to read through the entire chronology at this point for the fun of it—for we do believe that what it reveals is intriguing. Later, as more dates and events are encountered, it might be of further benefit to refer again to the chronology to gain a more complete perspective on the developments in mass communication.

[2] Ibid., p. 24.

Table 2-1. A Chronology of Mass Communications (Cast within a Historical Perspective)

Mass Communication Event	Date	Historical Perspective
By 1403, the Koreans make cast metal type, using punches and matrices.	1400 to 1410	Leipzig University is founded by German emigrants from Prague. Baluba Kingdom of the Congo emerges and eventually controls Katanga and Kivu Provinces.
✶ Johannes Gutenberg invents movable type, using a converted winepress, to usher in the era of print. (1450) Vatican Library is founded by Pope Nicholas V. (1450) Mazarin Bible is completed in Mainz, Germany. (1456)	1450 to 1460	Mohammed II takes Constantinople and makes it the capital of the Byzantine Empire. (1453) Hundred Years' War ends. (1453) Prince Henry of Portugal dies. (1460)
Henry VII censors certain books and requires all English printers to obtain royal licenses. (1529–1530) ✶ Authoritarian control over the press is enforced. (1529–1530)	1520 to 1530	Martin Luther is declared a heretic by Pope Leo X; Edict of Worms formally excommunicates him. (1520) Magellan completes circumnavigation of the globe. (1522) Verazzano explores Canada and the New England coast. (1524) Peasants' War in Germany erupts over Lutheran religious ideas. (1524–1525) Somali War begins in Ethiopia.
The Gregorian Calendar is introduced by Pope Gregory XIII. (1582)	1580 to 1590	Raleigh sends expeditions to colonize Roanoke Island. (1585–1587) The Spanish Armada is defeated. (1588)
✶ First printing press in America is established by the Puritans at Harvard College. (1638) *Bay Psalm Book* is printed. (1638) John Milton publishes *Aeropagitica*, as advocate a free marketplace of ideas; urges an end to press licensing. (1644)	1635 to 1645	Harvard College is founded. (1636) Settlements are founded in Massachusetts, Rhode Island, Connecticut, Maryland, and Delaware. (1630–1640) Civil War breaks out in England. (1642) French establish base on Madagascar. (1642)

Table 2-1. (continued)

Mass Communication Event	Date	Historical Perspective
England enacts first modern copyright law. (1709) England places Stamp Tax on newspapers and other publications. (1712) Steele, Addison, and Defoe produce *The Tattler,* *The Spectator,* and *Mist's Journal.* (1709–1720)	1705 to 1715	Great Britain is formed by union of England and Scotland. (1707) The Age of Enlightenment (Age of Reason) begins. (1715)
Benjamin Franklin begins publishing *Poor Richard's Almanac.* (1733) John Peter Zenger, *New York Weekly Journal* publisher, is acquitted on charges of seditious libel—landmark decision in assuring freedom of the press. (1735) The Great Awakening, a series of religious revivals, begins in the Colonies. (1740)	1725 to 1735	Last of the Thirteen Colonies is settled at Savannah, Georgia. (1733) War of the Polish Succession begins as Russia and Austria defeat Spain: Augustus III is placed on Polish throne. (1733) Reign of Emperor Ch'ien Lung begins, during which Chinese Empire greatly expands its territorial holdings. (1735)
Handel's *Messiah* is performed in New York for the first time. (1770) First edition of the *Encyclopaedia Britannica* is published. (1771) Sam Adams organizes the Committees of Correspondence. (1772) Thomas Paine writes *Common Sense,* which is widely circulated. (1776) Paul Revere's midnight ride from Charlestown to Lexington gives warning that British troops are approaching from Boston. (April 18–19, 1775)	1770 to 1780	First public restaurant opens in Paris. (1770) Boston Tea Party—Patriots dressed as Indians dump tea into Boston Harbor. (1773) First Continental Congress of the Thirteen Colonies meets at Philadelphia. (1774) Joseph Priestley discovers oxygen. (1774) First American submarine is built. (1775) James Watt invents the steam engine. (1775) War of American Independence begins. (April 19, 1775) Nathan Hale is executed as American spy by British. (1776) Declaration of Independence is signed. (1776)

Table 2-1. (continued)

Mass Communication Event	Date	Historical Perspective
		Articles of Confederation are submitted to the States. (1777) Rousseau and Voltaire die. (1778) France defends Senegal, West Africa, against British attack. (1779)
Alessandro Volta expounds on the nature of electricity after Aloisio Galvani infers that the muscular contraction of dead frogs was caused electrically. (1789) The First Amendment to the Constitution, guaranteeing freedom of the press, is ratified. (1791) Special low rates for newspapers are granted by Post Office Act. (1792) Claude Chappe invents semaphore. (1793) Lithography is invented by Alois Senefelder. (1798) The Rosetta Stone is discovered, supplying the missing link to the deciphering of the Egyptian hieroglyphics, by Jean Champollion, French scholar, in 1822. (1799)	1789 to 1799	George Washington becomes first President of the United States. (1789) French Revolution begins with the storming of the Bastille. (1789) First census records U.S. population. Records American population as 3,929,214. (1790) Bill of Rights becomes part of the Constitution. (1791) U.S. Mint opens at Philadelphia, introducing dollar coinage in the United States. (1792) Fugitive Slave Act passed. (1793) Eli Whitney invents cotton gin. (1793) Louis XVI and Marie Antoinette are beheaded. (1793) Smallpox vaccine is developed. (1796) Washington dies at Mount Vernon. (1799) By 1799, Portuguese, French, Spanish, Danes, Dutch, Swedes hold trading posts along West African coast and engage in slave trade.
Iron printing press is invented by Earl of Stanhope, permitting printers to make up to 250 impressions per hour. French government suppresses many newspapers.	1800	Jefferson elected President of the United States. (1800) Socialism develops in Europe as reaction to deplorable industrial conditions. Washington, D.C., becomes nation's capitol.

Table 2-1. (continued)

Mass Communication Event	Date	Historical Perspective
First photograph by Nicephore Niepce, who later works with Jacques Daguerre. New press law in France prohibits sale of newspapers unless approved by government and enforces punishment for offenders. Franz Schubert composes his "unfinished" symphony (symphony No. 8 in B Minor).	1822	Turks massacre Greeks on Island of Chios or sell them as slaves. Brazil gains independence from Portugal. Liberia is founded as a colony for freed American slaves.
Principle of motion pictures is discovered: human eye retains an image briefly after the picture is gone. Sequoyah invents the Cherokee alphabet.	1824	John Quincy Adams is designated President of the United States by the House of Representatives when presidential election fails to show a clear majority for any of the four candidates. Lord Byron dies at Missolonghi aiding Greeks against Turkey. Crete is captured by Egyptians.
First Black newspaper, *Freedom's Journal,* is published in New York City. The Society for the Diffusion of Useful Knowledge is founded by Henry Brougham.	1827	Civil War is waged in Portugal. Friction matches ("lucifers") introduced.
Benjamin Day publishes the *New York Sun,* the first of the penny papers.	1833	Jackson begins second term as President.
Talbot produces a photographic negative. Daguerre perfects the "daguerrotype." Photographs appear in journals.	1839	Charles Goodyear vulcanizes rubber. Baseball game first played at Cooperstown, New York. Opium War begins; British provoke war with China, acquire commercial concessions and Hong Kong.

Table 2-1. (continued)

Mass Communication Event	Date	Historical Perspective
Samuel F. B. Morse transmits first message over telegraph from Washington to Baltimore.	1844	James Polk is elected President.
Rotary "lightning" press, producing 20,000 impressions an hour, is invented.	1846	United States declares war on Mexico. Oregon boundary is abolished by treaty with Great Britain. Smithsonian Institution is founded in Washington, D.C. Howe invents sewing machine. Ether is used in surgery.
Associated Press is formed by six New York newspapers to pool telegraph costs. Karl Marx and Friedrich Engels issue *Communist Manifesto*.	1848	Treaty of Guadeloupe Hidalgo is signed by United States and Mexico. First Women's Rights Convention is held at Seneca Falls, New York. Spiritualism grows in importance in the United States. "Gold Rush" is on in California. Taiping Rebellion begins in China.
Henry J. Raymond establishes *New York Times* with an investment of $100,000. Paul Reuter establishes first commercial wire service in Europe.	1851	The man who will later lead the Southern fight for secession, editor of the *Charleston Mercury*, Robert Barnwell Rhett, is elected to the Senate.
Government Printing Office (GPO) is established. Pony Express is instituted.	1860	Abraham Lincoln is elected President. Southern states secede from the Union. Suez Canal is in second year of construction.
Alexander Graham Bell invents the telephone.	1876	Hayes is elected President in disputed election. Southern Reconstruction ends.

Table 2-1. (continued)

Mass Communication Event	Date	Historical Perspective
		Leopold II, with Stanley's aid, sets up organization to exploit Congo.
Thomas Alva Edison develops the first phonograph. David Hughes invents the microphone.	1878	Bland-Allison Bill reintroduces silver standard in the United States. Zulus revolt against the British.
The coherer is invented by Branly, furthering the development of wireless communications. Edison and Dickson develop sprocket system for motion pictures. First regular newspaper comics section is published in *The World*. George Eastman produces a celluloid roll-film.	1889	Oklahoma is opened for settlement. Benjamin Harrison becomes President. Meiji Mutsuhito issues modern constitution for Japan. Menelik II unwittingly signs treaty making Ethiopia a protectorate of Italy. Eiffel Tower is built in Paris.
Thomas Edison's Kinetoscope Parlour opens in New York. Halftone process for printing news photographs is used extensively for the first time.	1894	Jobless ("Coxey's Army") march on Washington to demand public works program. Nicholas II, last czar of Russia, begins reign. Uganda is declared a British protectorate.
Guglielmo Marconi invents wireless telegraphy. Auguste and Louis Lumiere invent the cinematograph, launching the motion picture era.	1895	U.S. income tax is declared unconstitutional. W. Röntgen discovers X-rays. Sigmund Freud founds psychoanalysis. Oscar Wilde sues Marquess of Queensberry for libel, is unsuccessful, and after a sensational trial is found guilty of homosexual charges.
R. A. Fessenden is first to transmit speech by wireless. Associated Press (AP) is reor-	1900	United States expresses its commitment to Chinese Open Door Policy.

Table 2-1. (continued)

Mass Communication Event	Date	Historical Perspective
ganized as we know it today to supply wire news to its client newspapers.		William McKinley becomes President, only to be assassinated 10 months later. U.S. troops assist Peking during Boxer Rebellion. Samoan Islands are divided between the United States and Germany. The cake-walk dance is popular.
Ivy Lee establishes first modern public relations firm in New York. Flemming develops glass-bulb detector of radio waves in England.	1904	Corollary to Monroe Doctrine is cited by Theodore Roosevelt in annual message. United States has responsibility of maintaining order in Latin America. Russo-Japanese War breaks out. Work begins on Panama Canal. French West Africa is reorganized, with capital at Dakar. Safety razor blades are invented.
Vacuum tube is perfected by Lee DeForest, making possible radio voice transmissions. Fessenden broadcasts program of music and readings on Christmas Eve.	1906	San Francisco is destroyed by earthquake and fire. Night shift work for women is internationally forbidden. Independence of Abyssinia is guaranteed by Britain, France, and Italy.
Congress passes Radio Act of 1912, requiring broadcasting licenses. David Sarnoff broadcasts news of *Titanic* disaster. Five million Americans attend cinemas, daily. First Pathe newsfilm is produced.	1912	Woodrow Wilson wins three-way presidential race. U.S. Marines land in Nicaragua to protect American interests during revolt. African partition among European powers is completed; only Ethiopia and Liberia remain independent. S.S. *Titanic* is lost on maiden voyage, with a loss of 1513 lives. Cellophane and stainless steel are invented.

Table 2-1. (continued)

Mass Communication Event	Date	Historical Perspective
Long-distance telephone service reaches San Francisco, with vacuum tube amplifiers. *The Birth of a Nation,* produced by Griffith, is longest, most powerful movie to date.	1915	United States is on the brink of war, as German submarine sinks *Lusitania* off the coast of Ireland; 1198 lives are lost. Albert Einstein develops his general theory of relativity.
License for station KDKA in Pittsburgh is obtained by Westinghouse. KDKA broadcasts Harding-Cox election returns. Zworykin and others resume television experiments. Specialized scientific periodicals proliferate. Jazz bands become popular.	1920	Prohibition is enforced in the United States. The League of Nations is established. Women's suffrage amendment is ratified. Harding is elected President; Coolidge, Vice-president. Most of Kenya becomes British Crown Colony.
Station WEAF in New York City begins to sell air time to advertisers. Associated Press refuses to allow broadcasting of AP reports. Movie industry imposes self-regulation to avoid government censorship; establishes a Production Code, sets up the Hays Office. *Reader's Digest* begins publication. More than 500 broadcasting stations are licensed during the year.	1922	Russia becomes the Union of Soviet Socialist Republic, the first Communist state in the world. Benito Mussolini becomes premier of Italy. Main powers at Washington Disarmament Conference agree to limit size of navies. Revival of Ku Klux Klan occurs in the United States. Self-winding wristwatch is invented. U.S. women marrying aliens are granted independent citizenship.
The Canons of Journalism are adopted as an expression of the "social responsibility" of the press. *Time* magazine is founded. The Eveready Battery Company produces and sponsors its own hour-long show on WEAF.	1923	Harding dies, Coolidge becomes President. Teapot Dome scandal brews. Rhodesia is divided into Southern and Northern Rhodesia and is placed under British rule. Continuous hot-strip rolling of steel is invented.

Table 2-1. (continued)

Mass Communication Event	Date	Historical Perspective
Zworykin invents the iconoscope and the kinetoscope, both of which become fundamental for television transmitting and receiving of messages. Hitler's *Mein Kampf* is published.		
The Jazz Singer, starring Al Jolson, is first talking picture. Columbia Broadcasting System is organized to compete with NBC. Radio Act of 1927 establishes commission to license broadcasters and prevent signal interference. AT&T sends closed-circuit television picture from Washington, D.C., to New York City.	1927	International Peace Bridge between the United States and Canada is opened. Chiang Kai-shek organizes government at Nanking. Charles Lindbergh becomes overnight hero with his solo flight from New York to Paris, which takes 37 hours. Foxtrot is popular dance.
Amos n' Andy becomes series on NBC network. Kodak develops 16-mm color film.	1929	The collapse of U.S. stock market signals the beginning of the Great Depression. Chicago gangster wars peak with St. Valentine's Day massacre. Vatican City in Rome becomes an independent state. Richard Byrd flies over the South Pole.
Radio vaudeville era begins with collapse of live vaudeville. Crossley ratings begin, based on telephone calls. Picture telegraphy service opens between Britain and Germany. Photoflash bulb is invented. William Randolph Hearst amasses 33 newspapers, with total circulation of 11 million. Wider screen enhances movie theaters.	1930	Worldwide economic depression develops, causing rise of extremist movements. Mahatma Gandhi begins civil disobedience campaign in India. Emperor Haile Selassie ascends Ethiopian throne.
Federal Communications Commis-	1934	Adolph Hitler becomes Führer.

Table 2-1. (continued)

Mass Communication Event	Date	Historical Perspective
sion (FCC) is established by Communications Act of 1934 to oversee broadcast media. Legion of Decency is established to police movie industry. Wavelengths of chief broadcasting stations in Europe are altered to conform with Lucerne Committee recommendations.		John Dillinger is slain by FBI agents in Chicago. Induced radioactivity is discovered.
The annexation of Austria is described by Edward R. Murrow over CBS. Kaltenborn broadcasts Munich crisis. News programs expand to world news roundup. Orson Welles's *War of the Worlds* broadcast creates panic. Ballpoint pen is invented.	1938	Germany annexes Austria. Munich Pact leads to appeasement of Hitler by France and Britain; allows Germany to occupy Sudetenland. Fair Labor Standards Act sets minimum wage and maximum working week; prohibits child labor. Lambeth walk becomes popular dance.
Paperback books appear on the mass market. RCA gives TV broadcast demonstration at the New York World's Fair. Experimental FM radio station begins in Alpine, New Jersey. RAF begins leaflet raids on Germany.	1939	Germany invades Poland, starting World War II. America pledges neutrality after war breaks out in Europe; but "cash and carry" policy allows for export of arms to belligerent nations. Einstein advises FDR of possibility of developing atom bomb.
FCC decides on FM sound for TV. Democratic and Republican Conventions are telecast; election returns are also telecast for the first time. German army sings *Lili Marlene*. Charlie Chaplin stars in *The Great Dictator*. London Blitz is described by Murrow over CBS radio. BBC radio newsreel begins.	1940	Germans invade Norway and Denmark. Churchill becomes Prime Minister. British forces are evacuated from Dunkirk. France falls. Churchill rallies forces by "Blood and Toil" speech. Britain faces Blitz. Alien Registration Act is enacted in the United States.

Table 2-1. (continued)

Mass Communication Event	Date	Historical Perspective
		United States enacts first peacetime compulsory military service program. F.D.R. is elected for third term. Penicillin is developed by Florey as antibiotic.
FCC issues licenses for commercial TV. Broadcast editorials are outlawed by the Mayflower decision. First·color television picture is introduced.	1941	Lend-Lease Act gives arms without cash to friendly nations. Germany invades Russia. Atlantic Charter—joint statement of postwar aims—is issued by Roosevelt and Churchill. Japanese attack Pearl Harbor; Congress declares war on Japan. Germany and Italy declare war on the United States. Stalin becomes head of the Soviet Government. "Manhattan Project" for atomic research begins.
Manufacture of television sets is halted. Freeze is placed on FM development by FCC. Office of War Information is established. Armed Forces Radio Service is formed. Magnetic tape is invented. *Stars and Stripes*—daily paper for Armed Forces in Europe—is published.	1942	Bataan, Corregidor fall to Japanese. Guadacanal victory won by U.S. Marines. Doolittle leads raid over Tokyo. Twenty-six nations sign UN Pact in Washington, D.C. Fermi splits atom at Chicago. V-2 rocket is launched. Germans reach Stalingrad.
FCC pressures NBC to sell "Blue Chain"; it becomes ABC, the nation's third network. Wire recorders are used on Italian front. Frank Sinatra becomes first pop idol of teenagers.	1943	Germans are driven from North Africa. Mussolini regime collapses. Italy surrenders to Allies and declares war on Germany. Japanese retreat in New Guinea. Roosevelt attends conferences in Casablanca, Quebec, Cairo, and Teheran.

Table 2-1. (continued)

Mass Communication Event	Date	Historical Perspective
		Turning point of war on eastern front is German defeat at Stalingrad by Russian forces. Streptomycin is discovered.
Wire recordings are made describing D-Day landings in Normandy. Program sponsors experiment with TV commercials.	1944	D-Day: Eisenhower becomes Supreme Commander of American expeditionary forces, invades fortress Europe at Normandy, France. Allies liberate France, Belgium, and Luxembourg. V-bombs dropped on England. Roosevelt wins fourth term; Harry S. Truman elected Vice-President. Quinine is synthesized.
Freeze on TV set manufacture ends. AP membership practices are ruled in restraint of trade by Supreme Court; AP service to be made available to all media.	1945	Charles de Gaulle is elected President of France. Yalta Conference is attended by Churchill, Roosevelt, Stalin; agree to form a United Nations. Roosevelt dies (April 12); Truman becomes President. Mussolini is captured by Italian patriots (April 28); he is murdered and his body is mutilated. Hitler commits suicide in Berlin on May 1. Germany surrenders (May 7) unconditionally. Atomic bomb dropped on Hiroshima and Nagasaki; Japan surrenders (August 14). "Bebop" dancing becomes rage in the United States.
FCC obligates broadcasters to include some public affairs programming. TV sets go on sale.	1946	UN establishes permanent headquarters in New York City; Trygvie Lie becomes first secretary-general.

Table 2-1. **(continued)**

Mass Communication Event	Date	Historical Perspective
CBS and NBC demonstrate color TV. Chester Carlson invents xerography. British TV service is resumed (fewer than 12,000 viewers). BBC inaugurates Third Programme (for cultural entertainment).		Philippines gain independence from the United States. Cold War begins with Churchill's Iron Curtain speech. Segregation of blacks on interstate buses is ruled unconstitutional by U.S. Supreme Court. Nazi criminals are sentenced in Nuremberg trials. India and Union of South Africa break diplomatic relations over treatment of Indian minority.
Phenomenal diffusion of television begins in the United States —from 100,000 sets at year's beginning to more than 1 million at year's end. On September 30, FCC freezes all applications for TV broadcast licenses until further study. Bell Telephone Company scientists invent transistor. First FCC woman commissioner is appointed—Frieda Hennock. A. C. Kinsey writes *Sexual Behavior in the Human Male.* Record industry innovations—33⅓ and 45 RPM records appear on the market.	1948	Alger Hiss is accused by Whitaker Chambers of transmitting documents to Russians. Segregation in Armed Forces is outlawed by executive order issued by President Truman. Harry S. Truman scuttles predictions of Thomas E. Dewey landslide in presidential election upset. European Recovery Plan (the Marshall Plan) goes into effect. Gandhi is assassinated by Hindu fanatic. Israel achieves independence after bitter struggle.
Mayflower decision is reversed by FCC; broadcasters may editorialize. Presidential inauguration is telecast for a TV first. Movie companies are ordered by Supreme Court to divest themselves of their theater holdings. Movie attendance reaches 90 million per week.	1949	President Truman presents Point Four Program of Technical Assistance to promote peace in the world. North Atlantic Treaty Organization approved for collective self-defense of United States, Canada, and ten European countries. West Germany and East Germany are formed.

Table 2-1. (continued)

Mass Communication Event	Date	Historical Perspective
		Soviets explode atomic bomb, bringing to an end U.S. monopoly. Communist People's Republic of China is established at Peiping under Mao Tse-tung.
CBS requires all employees to sign loyalty oath. *Red Channels: The Report of Communist Influence in Radio and Television* is distributed to networks. Langsford, Pa., has first community antenna television system. (CATV) Experimental "pay TV" is authorized by FCC. CBS system for color TV is approved by FCC. "Fotosetter" makes offset newspapers possible.	1950	North Korean troops invade South Korea. Truman orders U.S. troops into South Korea. Infiltration into State Department by Communists is charged by Senator McCarthy. Alger Hiss is found guilty of perjury in concealing membership of Communist Party.
Hear It Now becomes *See It Now* as Edward R. Murrow's documentary program leaves radio for television. *Today* show begins on NBC-TV. Movie attendance plunges, theaters close as TV takes over. Coast-to-coast TV hookup occurs in time to broadcast Japanese Peace Conference at San Francisco.	1951	Twenty-second Amendment places two-term limit on Presidency. General McArthur is recalled from Korea by Truman for insubordination. Rising African nationalism achieves first victory with independence of Libya. Fraudulent Medium Act repeals provisions of Witchcraft Act, 1735, in Britain. Electric power is produced from atomic energy.
FCC reserves 70 UHF television channels for nonprofit and educational use. Freeze is lifted as FCC resumes processing of license applications.	1952	Truman's seizure of steel mills during strike is ruled unconstitutional by Supreme Court. Further restrictions on immigration are levied by McCarran-Walter Bill.

Table 2-1. (continued)

Mass Communication Event	Date	Historical Perspective
Nixon delivers "Checkers" speech. Concern is expressed in Britain over "horror comics."		Republicans win first presidential election since 1928 with General Dwight D. Eisenhower as candidate. Queen Elizabeth II of England begins reign upon death of George VI. Mau Mau, secret terrorist organization in Kenya, begins bloody campaign to oust white settlers. Contraceptive tablets are introduced. United States explodes first H-bomb.
University of Houston becomes first to have noncommercial, educational TV station in the United States. *Voice of America* and FCC are attacked by Senator Joseph R. McCarthy. First of the wide-screen cinemascope spectaculars—*The Robe*—is produced by Twentieth Century-Fox.	1953	Stalin dies. Korean armistice ends war. The Rosenbergs are executed. Khrushchev becomes First Secretary of Central Committee of Communist Party. Hillary and Tenzing climb Mount Everest.
Peter Pan makes TV history; reaches audience of 60 million, largest to date. Old movies are sold to TV by major film studios. Universal copyright convention is held. Commercial television begins in Britain. "Rock Around the Clock" heralds the rock and roll craze.	1955	School desegregation is ordered by Supreme Court. Treaty for European Union is ratified. World focuses attention on Cyprus emergency. Winston Churchill resigns; is succeeded by Anthony Eden. Jonas Salk prepares polio vaccine.
Collier's ceases publication; first of mass circulation, general interest magazine to fold. Bell Telephone Company develops "visual telephone."	1956	Boycott in Montgomery, Alabama, upon arrest of black woman when she refuses to give up seat for white man. Eisenhower is reelected President.

Table 2-1. (continued)

Mass Communication Event	Date	Historical Perspective
Mullard image-dissector camera is developed; takes very rapid photographs. Transatlantic telephone service begins.		Tunisia gains independence from France. Cardinal Mindszenty is released. Grace Kelly marries Prince Rainier of Monaco.
Publicly supported TV begins with the establishment of the National Educational Television Network. Britain reduces entertainment duty on live theater and films.	1957	Integration of Little Rock schools controversy brings out federal troops to protect the rights of black students. Civil Rights Act is passed. Sputnik is launched by Soviets, marking the beginning of the space age. U.S. expedition flies to the South Pole.
United Press International (UPI) is formed with the merger of United Press and International News Service. Coronation of Pope John XXIII is telecast. Stereophonic gramophone recordings are developed.	1958	United States launches its first earth satellite. Pope John XXIII is elected. United Arab Republic formed by unification of Egypt and Syria. "Beatnik" movement, originating in California, spreads to Britain.
Khrushchev tour of the United States is widely covered on television. Number of TV sets rises to 36 million in the United States, 10 million in Great Britain, and 1.5 million in France. Quiz scandal breaks out in the United States. South Africa decides against introducing television.	1959	Alaska and Hawaii become forty-ninth and fiftieth states. Fidel Castro becomes Premier of Cuba. China and India begin border wars. USSR sends dogs into orbit; Lunik III photographs the moon.
Nixon and Kennedy meet in the *"Great Debates."* TV sets (in millions): United States, 85; Britain, 10.4; West Germany, 2; France, 1.5.	1960	United States agrees to suspend flights when American U-2 plane is shot down over USSR. Kennedy is elected thirty-fifth President of the United States.

Table 2-1. (continued)

Mass Communication Event	Date	Historical Perspective
Russian astronomers employ computers to decipher Mayan writing.		African nationalism peaks with freedom of sixteen nations that make up one third of UN membership.
President Kennedy okays televising and filming of press conferences without restriction. Edward R. Murrow heads United States Information Agency. Television violence investigation is launched by Senator Thomas J. Dodd. Newton N. Minow, FCC chairman, calls TV "vast wasteland."	1961	Freedom rides in the United States protest segregation. Peace Corps is established by John F. Kennedy. Bay of Pigs invasion fails. First American astronaut in space is Alan B. Shepherd, Jr.; Russian astronaut, Yuri A. Gagarin, is first to orbit earth. Berlin Wall is erected between East and West Germany. Dag Hammarskjold dies in Congo. Union of South Africa becomes a republic.
Live international broadcasting is feasible through Telstar satellite. Kennedy delivers televised ultimatum on Cuban missile crisis. BBC inaugurates TV program, *That Was the Week That Was.*	1962	James H. Meredith becomes first black to enter the University of Mississippi. John Glenn orbits the earth. Soviets dismantle Russian missiles on Cuba after pressure from President John F. Kennedy.
March on Washington telecasts are climaxed by Martin Luther King's speech, "I Have a Dream." Half-hour evening newscasts are inaugurated by networks. World mourns assassination of President Kennedy and attends funeral through TV. Lee Harvey Oswald is murdered live on television. Newspaper dailies set type by computer. Nobel Committee begins inquiry on moral impact of TV on the young.	1963	Birmingham, Alabama, is scene of racial violence. "Hot line" telephone links Washington and Moscow to reduce accidental war. March on Washington by Martin Luther King. President Kennedy is assassinated in Dallas. Lyndon Baines Johnson is sworn in as President. Pope John XXIII dies; Cardinal Montini is elected as Pope Paul XI.

Table 2-1. (continued)

Mass Communication Event	Date	Historical Perspective
Rachel Carson book *The Silent Spring* focuses on dangers of chemical pest control. Beatlemania rocks the world. Capri bans transistor radios.		
FCC assumes cable television control. CBS decision to halt coverage of Senate hearings on Vietnam War causes resignation of Fred W. Friendly, CBS News president.	1966	Surveyor I makes landing on moon. Medicare program goes into effect. Major race riots break out in northern U.S. cities. Communist China initiates "cultural revolution" through ideological conformity of party leaders.
Decision not to be candidate for re-election is broadcast by President Johnson. Martin Luther King funeral is televised. *Hunger in America* television documentary incites wide comment. Robert Kennedy's funeral is televised. Democratic Convention coverage is marred by violence.	1968	*Pueblo* (U.S. Naval Intelligence ship) is seized by North Korea. Martin Luther King and Robert Kennedy are assassinated. Richard Nixon becomes President, Agnew Vice-President. Vietnam ceasefire peace talks open in Paris.
Landings of the Apollo flights are televised. *Sesame Street* begins TV debut. Agnew attacks news media. *Saturday Evening Post* ends publication.	1969	Neil Armstrong and Edwin Aldrin are first men to land on the moon. De Gaulle resigns as President of France. Iraqi Revolutionary Court executes forty persons accused of spying for Israel, the United States, and Iran, despite world condemnation. Pope Paul VI becomes first pope to visit Africa.
FCC encourages local programming and the growth of cable	1970	Four students at Kent State are killed by National Guard and

Table 2-1. (continued)

Mass Communication Event	Date	Historical Perspective
TV by proposing rules to curb multiple ownership of the media.		two students are killed by police at Jackson State, Mississippi, as a result of student protests against the Vietnam War. U.S. and South Vietnamese troops enter Cambodia. West Germany and USSR sign nonaggression pact. Anwar Sadat succeeds Nasser upon his death. Charles de Gaulle dies.
Ban on cigarette advertising goes into effect in broadcasting media. Vietnam War protests are aired; Vietnam becomes first fully televised war in nation's history. *All in the Family* is launched. CBS produces *The Selling of the Pentagon*. *Look* magazine ceases publication.	1971	Eighteen-year-olds are granted voting rights. President Nixon freezes wages and prices. American dollar is devalued by 8.57 per cent. Communist China is admitted to UN.
Life magazine ceases publication. Nixon vetoes public television appropriation.	1972	Governor Wallace is seriously injured in attempted assassination. Nixon visits Russia and China. "Watergate burglars" are caught inside Democratic Party national headquarters. Nixon and Agnew are reelected President and Vice-president. XXth Olympic Games at Munich are disrupted by Arab commandos who take thirteen Israeli athletes hostage. All are killed. Protestant-Catholic conflict continues in Northern Ireland.
Watergate inquiry by Senate committee is televised. White House tape recordings are revealed.	1973	Watergate dominates political scene. Vice-President Agnew resigns. Gerald Ford becomes Vice-President.

Table 2-1. (continued)

Mass Communication Event	Date	Historical Perspective
		Greece abolishes monarchy.
		Energy crisis is caused by Arabs' embargo of oil shipments to the United States, Europe, Japan.
		Greek monarchy abolished for Presidential Parliamentary Republic.
		Juan Peron returns from exile and becomes Argentine President.
		Large-scale fighting between Israel and Arab nations breaks out.
Release of selected, edited tape transcripts is announced by Nixon in telecast.	1974	President Nixon resigns.
Impeachment deliberations by House judiciary committee are telecast.		Gerald Ford becomes President.
✶ Nixon resigns on television.		Juan Peron dies; his wife, Isabel Peron, assumes presidency.
President Ford announces Nixon pardon in telecast.		Willy Brandt resigns as Chancelor of West Germany.
Prime time access rule restricts network programs to three hours per night.	1975	Vietnam War ends.
"Family hour" concept decided on by networks, sets aside first hour of prime time programming for G-rated shows.		U.S. and Soviet astronauts dock in space.
✶ Television violence is more widely called into question.		Unemployment (9.2 per cent) is highest since 1941.
Bicentennial theme in TV is prevalent throughout the season.		

Summary of Significant Events

Although an extended chronology serves the useful purpose of reinforcing the idea that the industrial and communication revolutions are inextricably intertwined and are best viewed against the larger societal panorama, we do not recommend that the reader attempt to commit it to memory. Instead, we have selected a dozen of the more significant events that we believe would provide the student with a useful progression of mass communications history. Rather than beginning with the invention of the printing press in the fifteenth century, we have decided to organize our brief chronology around the concept of human communication attributes and technological storage and transmission devices. Hence the human attributes of vision, movement, and voice are combined in a framework with the camera, telephone, telegraph, and other electronic media.

Brief Chronology of Communication Events

1822	First photograph is developed by Nicephore Niepce, who is later to work with Jacques Daguerre.
1824	The principle of motion pictures is discovered: the human eye retains an image briefly after the picture is gone.
1839	Photographs appear in journals.
1844	Samuel F. B. Morse transmits first message over the telegraph and the rotary "lightning" press, producing 20,000 impressions an hour, is invented.
1876	Alexander Graham Bell invents the telephone.
1895	Marconi invents wireless telegraphy, and the Lumiere brothers invent the cinematograph, which launches the motion picture era.
1906	Radio voice transmission is made possible with the invention of the vacuum tube by Lee DeForest.
1915	D. W. Griffith produces the film *The Birth of a Nation*, which ushers in new cinematographic techniques.
1923	Zworykin invents the iconoscope and the kineoscope, which become basic to television transmission and reception.
1927	The first talking picture is produced (*The Jazz Singer*, starring Al Jolson).
1946	Xerography is invented.
1962	Telstar satellite makes live international broadcasting feasible.

Chapter 3
Mass Communication Constituents

*Isolating one sense from all others calls for enormous
training and self control and is probably never
achieved. . . .*
Edmund Carpenter, *They Became What They Beheld,*
1970

Mass communication is the product of mass media institutions that
have created an enormous knowledge industry. The structure of the
knowledge industry may be classified according to functions: (1) mediators, (2) transmitters, (3) data providers, (4) data gatherers, (5)
maintainers, and (6) supporters. *Mediators* are multipliers of messages.
In this category are all newspapers, radio, television, magazines,
books, and films. *Transmitters* carry messages from one place to another, e.g., telegraph, telephone, and satellite systems. *Data providers,*
such as libraries, computer services, data banks, and abstract services,
serve individual and public needs for information. *Data gatherers*
function to secure opinions, intelligence, and information for research
and action use. *Maintainers* operate as service and installation units in
the knowledge industry. Manufacturers of electronic equipment may
also be considered as maintainers. *Supporters* represent all the agencies that provide service expertise and personnel for the knowledge industry. This category encompasses publicity personnel, financial services, advertisers, unions, and sales departments. In 1962 Fritz
Machlup suggested education as one of the sectors of the knowledge
industry.[1] Although there is logic to his classification because of the

---

[1] Fritz Machlup, *The Production and Distribution of Knowledge* (Princeton, N.J.: Princeton
University Press, 1962).

dominant role played by education in the distribution of knowledge, our view is that the educational sector, by its nature, involves all constituents of the media.

There are five basic constituents in any mass communication institution: (1) reproduction, (2) circulation, (3) feedback, (4) support, and (5) ownership. Evaluation of a mass media institution, whether print or electronic, may be made on the basis of these constituents.

Reproduction

From the most primitive mass communication system to the most advanced, reproduction is a distinguishing factor. Thus the old English town crier, the Ashanti drummer, and the Intelsat have in common some form of reproduction. Information can be mass disseminated only in a reproduced form; if it remains with its source or goes no further than the initial hearer, it is not mass communication. The rapidity of reproduction is critical to better mass communication. Thus the reproduction of information by voice, signs, images, signals, and print constitutes one of the basic elements of a mass media institution. Because mass media make information widely and speedily available, they serve as amplifiers in much the same way as the traditional African drummer. His function was to convey information to the village as soon as he received it. Similarly, the town crier in Europe served to amplify messages he had received. As Xerox and other companies have taught us in the field of photocopy of print, the reproduction of images and symbols can have a revolutionary impact on humans.

Several methods of reproduction are available to the mass disseminator of information. In newsprint, the verbal statement of an individual must be reproduced in type before it can be distributed to the mass audience. Newspapers reproduce verbal information from political, economic, and social leaders to help sell their copies. Radio's reproduction is in terms of mass amplification of the human voice for hundreds or thousands of people at the same time. Television similarly reproduces the human voice and also transmits the human image through space and time.

Technological changes tend to begin at the reproduction stage of mass communication and create vibrations to the other stages. It is doubtful that the increase in the delivery capability of mass com-

Table 3-1. Reproduction Chart

Words	Picture Symbols	Color	Sound	Action
Books	Books	Books	Radio	Movies
Magazines	Magazines	Magazines	Movies	Television
Newspapers	Newspapers	Newspapers	Recordings	
		Movies	Television	
		Television		

munication will ever be hampered by a lack of technology. Paul Baran is correct to assume that "technology is rarely a binding constraint for new communications applications in the future."[2]

✗ Reproduction may be divided into five parts: (1) *words*, the use of an alphabet to reproduce spoken language; (2) *picture symbols*, the use of engravings, woodcuts, and similar devices to depict the original event; (3) *color*, the addition of hues to picture symbols; (4) *sound*, the transmission of music, noises, and voices; and (5) *action*, the transmission of animation.

To a large extent the manufacturers of electronic and printing equipment are the keys to symbol reproduction. Corporations that at one time were exclusively in the electronic media business have more recently become involved in all phases of the print business. Similarly, a number of print companies have long had holdings in the electronic communication industry. This reciprocal proces allows the industry to utilize the best elements of print reproduction for electronic reproduction and vice versa. In 1975 RCA, one of America's largest communications corporations, launched a 2,000-pound satellite, RCA SATCOM, into orbit. The satellite, designed to handle 24,000 one-way circuits or 24 simultaneous television circuits, was a prime example of how technology expands the capacity of human beings to reproduce communications. Western Union's WESTAR, one of the earliest commercial satellite communication systems, has leased channels to other companies for telephone connections since the early 1970s. Telesat, Canada's satellite communication system, has been used to help connect the world's second largest country together.[3] Unquestionably, the need for nations to convey information to their territories will increase

---

[2] Paul Baran, "On the Impact of the New Communications Media upon Social Values," in Alan Casty (ed.), *Mass Media and Mass Man* (New York: Holt, Rinehart and Winston, 1973), p. 12.

[3] *Buffalo Courier-Express*, December 7, 1975, p. 44.

the demand for technological advances in reproduction. New uses for video cassettes, laser systems, television projection systems, and satellites will continue to restructure the way we think about image reproduction.

Circulation

Circulation is more an extension of image reproduction than its equal as a process; however, the ability to reproduce an image or broadcast a signal represents a technological advance, not necessarily reception by a mass audience. In order for any image to be received a receiver must exist. Circulation is the principal means of securing reception of media messages.

During the early days of newspapers it was customary for an editor to seek out subscribers on his own. The first American newspapers depended on advertising for support, and circulated their papers free. A combination of subscription and advertising revenues has ensured the continuation of most papers. After the Civil War newspapers began to rely more heavily on subscribers than they had before. The rise in literacy brought about a demand for news information and wholesome reading materials. Next to the Bible, Americans found newspapers and the *McGuffey Readers* the most desirable printed matter to have in their homes.

The concept of mass circulation has undergone two basic changes since the beginning of the twentieth century. In the early twentieth century, mass circulation meant circulation to those who were literate. This had a profound impact on the history of mass media because the opinion makers and policy determiners were separated from the masses by their ability to read. Although this had also been true in prior times, never before had the discriminatory nature of the printed word been so clearly revealed. The rise of widely circulated magazines further enhanced the difference between those who could read and those who could not. Whereas it was possible to repeat aloud what was in a broadside to someone who could not read, telling someone all that was in a ten-page newspaper or a fifty-page magazine was impossible, and so illiterates were probably worse off than they had been in the nineteenth century.

The second basic change in circulation occurred with the coming of electronic media: radio and television. Print had been a barrier to those who did not read, but oral communication through the radio made world information readily accessible to almost everyone. With the delivery of electricity to almost every community in the United States and the making of batteries and battery radios, it became theoretically possible for President Franklin Roosevelt to speak to everyone in the United States.

Circulation requires a receiver. In the case of electronic signals it is necessary for a person to have a radio or a television in order to receive messages. The message is not circulated until it has reached its receiver.

Increase in circulation usually means an increase in profits either through additional advertising income or through additional subscribers' fees. Circulation is dependent on four key elements: (1) *cultural acceptability*, the society's response to a given medium; (2) *portability*, the ability of the medium to reach the audience; (3) reviewability, the ability of the message to be received and reviewed at the audience's convenience; and (4) *instantaneous transmission*, the delivery of the message to the audience at almost the instant it originates.

Clearly, cultural acceptability of a medium is dependent on national policy. Until recently the white government of South Africa prohibited the circulation of televised images. On the other hand, all of the other media have operated in South Africa without challenge except in matters of policy. Cultural acceptability based on the significance of media for nation building and the unity of a society is a fact in most societies. A nation without a high regard for books, magazines, radio, television, movies, newspapers, and recordings encourages a lack of national consciousness. Since the transistor revolution in 1955, radio has become exceptionally portable, and technology is such

Table 3-2. Circulation Chart

Cultural Acceptability	Portability	Reviewability	Instantaneous Transmission
Books	Books	Books	Television
Magazines	Magazines	Magazines	Radio
Newspapers	Newspapers	Newspapers	
Radio	Radio	Recordings	
Movies			
Recordings			
Television			

that portable televisions operated by powerful transistors will probably be made and distributed rather inexpensively over the next few years. However, our view is that only the print media, radio, and record players can be called truly portable at the present juncture in media history.

Instantaneous transmission came into existence with the electronic media, i.e., radio and television. Prior to this, the newspapers, a basically American phenomenon, attempted to approach simultaneity by printing "extras" promptly after an important newsworthy event had occurred. There were newspaper boys standing on streetcorners shouting "Extra! Extra! Read all about it!" for many years before the electronic media came into being. The practice is almost extinct today. On television, audiences can see many events just as they are happening, and the aftereffects of unexpected events can be captured almost immediately. Thus a television viewer or a radio listener can make almost instantaneous connection with the newsworthy event, act, or person. Furthermore, the event, usually with accompanying commentary, can be repeated on instant replay. All media, except radio and television, have a time lag from the actual happening of an event to the circulation of the news to the subscribing public. Newspapers normally have the shortest time lag, although in special cases book publishers have been able to get out "instant" paperbacks on issues of critical importance.

Books and movies, for different reasons, take the longest time to deliver to the audience. Books normally take anywhere from eight to fifteen months to produce. A typical book manuscript must go through various editing, galley proof, and page proof stages before it is released as a book. Movies involve the assembling and managing of a complex group of talents and personalities to carry out specific projects. Both the production of books and the production of movies are the result of many months of work.

Reviewability depends on the medium. For example, television and radio are relatively less reviewable than a newspaper. Radio may be reviewed by recording a program and listening to it again; television may be videotaped and played back for review. However, these are not practical review systems for the majority of the audiences, and we can conclude that for most purposes radio and television are not reviewable.

Merrill and Lowenstein have referred to what they call "previewability" as a part of reviewability. According to them, "previewability is the quality of permitting the audience to know what they will find inside the total message presentation."[4]

Print media usually accomplish previewability by having tables of contents, indexes, or headlines. Record album dust jackets give the listener some idea of what a recording will sound like. The various television guides try to give week-to-week previews of programming. In addition, some news shows introduce their programs by giving a small glimpse of the stories to come.

Feedback

Feedback is the communicative response of the receiver to the message. Feedback behavior can be (1) continuous, (2) directed toward multiple sources, or (3) not observable to the system that provoked it. In mass communication all of these conditions can exist at the same time. Their strength is dependent in large part on the particular nature of the medium. For example, the purchasing of subscriptions is feedback in the continuous mode.

Unlike interpersonal communication, where people interact face to face and can exchange ideas and reactions immediately, when a newspaper is delivered to someone's home considerable time is required for the reader to respond with a letter to the editor. A television viewer has even more difficulty responding, and it is much more difficult to find out whether the response was received. There are two principal reasons for this. Television stations receive far more mail than they can answer, and they are not economically able to broadcast all the letters received from viewers.

Feedback is frequently misdirected. One reason for this is that mass communication institutions usually consist of many people working together; twenty or more people may be involved in the production of one television program. To whom should the viewer send a letter? Where will it get the fastest results? Because viewers are not sure where to send letters, they may engage in multidirected feedback, i.e., write to several suspected sources of the message.

There is no certain method for determining the extent of feed-

[4] John C. Merrill and Ralph L. Lowenstein, *Media Messages and Men: New Perspectives in Communication* (New York: David McKay, 1971), p. 22.

back. Whatever the medium, it is impossible to identify every effect of media through recipient response except in rare instances where the audience is very small. A widely used concept in media research is *selective exposure*. The term is used extensively by Lazarsfeld, Berelson, and Gaudet in reference to political campaigns.[5] In addition, Sears and Klapper discuss how mass communications never make their maximum persuasive impact because of the effect of selective exposure.[6] Feedback is not only difficult to determine but also suspect if one accepts the principle of selective exposure. *According to the principle of selective exposure, there may be systematic bias in the composition of audiences.* For example, if a message is sent to a group of Democrats, the feedback is expected to reflect the audience's political bias. Most mass communications, however, reach widely diverse groups of people. *All in the Family* consistently reached diverse groups in the United States for 7 years, and reactions to the show came from almost every ethnic group. To a large degree the sender of a message cannot determine from the responses the full extent of the message's audience. Who responds to a message is frequently a matter of leisure time, economics, education, and motivation. Certainly we all have had moments when we felt like calling the radio station or writing a letter to the editor but did not do it. There is no way for the sender to know the audience's displeasure without feedback. More importantly, the audience through its own selective exposure to message predetermines in large measure what the feedback will be.

Theoretically, the type of messages we receive from newspapers, radios, movies, and television is controlled by the kind of feedback we give them. David K. Berlo has stated: "Feedback provides the source with information concerning his success in accomplishing his objective. In doing this, it exerts control over future messages which the source encodes."[7] It is questionable, however, whether the audience can effectively exert control over future messages. Most media regularly invite audiences to write or to telephone their complaints and other comments. Such invited feedback is also often misleading. Talk

[5] Paul F. Lazarsfeld, Bernard Berelson, and Hazel Gaudet, *The People's Choice* (New York: Columbia University Press, 1948).

[6] David O. Sears, "Selective Exposure of Information: A Critical Review," in Thomas Beisecker and Donn Parson (eds.), *The Process of Social Influence* (Englewood Cliffs, N.J.: Prentice-Hall, 1972), and Joseph Klapper, *The Effects of Mass Communication* (New York: Free Press, 1960).

[7] David K. Berlo, *The Process of Communication* (New York: Holt, Rinehart and Winston, 1960), p. 112.

shows are notorious for bringing out loquacity in their listeners, simply because one of their prime functions is to serve as therapy for people who need someone to talk with about important issues. Feedback of this kind is not a good indicator of the station's or the program's appeal. Many media institutions commission pollsters to make independent assessment of their popularity.

Because feedback is fundamentally important to any media institution, its significance must be adequately determined if the media are to increase the effectiveness of their messages. As one of the basic constituents of the mass communication process, feedback permits audiences to react to communication output. Berlo has differentiated among the media in terms of feedback:

> We can separate one communication situation from another by the ease with which feedback is obtained. Clearly, person-to-person communication permits maximum feedback. All available communication channels can operate. The source has an opportunity to change his message on the spot as a result of the feedback he gets. On the other hand, communication forms that we refer to as the public media (newspaper, television, magazines, etc.) have minumum opportunities for feedback. The source and the receiver are separated in time and space. They have little opportunity to get feedback from the responses of the other.[8]

Support

The single most important factor in mass communication is support. Without money to operate, the mass media could not exist. The amount of support, the hierarchy of support, and the values involved in the support system vary from medium to medium and among individual stations, companies, and agencies. Advertisements are the most characteristic form of support for all media.

Advertising is an unsubtle aspect of media institutions. The cost of a half-hour network television show can range up to $250,000, and the most practical system yet designed to handle the costs of high-quality television production is through advertising. There is no attempt on American television to be covert about the relationship between media and advertising. Advertising is defined as a reasonable part of the free enterprise economic order. All media in free enterprise

[8] Ibid., p. 114.

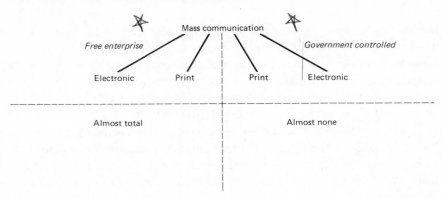

Figure 3-1. Extent of media support from advertisement in two systems.

nations use advertisements to provide part of their financial support.

Figure 3-1 shows the difference between state-controlled econo-

mies and free enterprise economies in the amount of advertising support given to the media. In the United States advertising is big business. Aldrich contends that "at this moment in mass media's history,
they [the media] could not survive without advertising."[9]

Major advertisers spend anywhere from $10 million to $100 million annually; they pay $70,000 for a 30-second commercial on prime
time television.[10] The price for inarticulate guests, high-quality entertainment, sporting events, and the weather report is a huge amount of
advertising dollars. So much for the high cost of television. What about
newspapers?

Newspapers have always depended on advertisers to help fill the
gap between publication costs and subscription revenues. Most newspaper advertisement comes from small individual advertisers; they
provide a fairly constant income for newspapers and simultaneously
provide a service to customers who need to know what they have to
offer.

American newspapers discovered early that they could accommodate more advertising on a page by resorting to smaller print, and so
small print and abbreviations are common in advertisements.

There are two kinds of newspaper advertisements: *classified* and

[9] Pearl Aldrich, *The Impact of Mass Media* (Rochelle Park, N.J.: Hayden Book Company,
1975), p. 34.
[10] Ibid., p. 34.

commercial. Classified ads normally appear at the end of the paper and tend to be individualized expressions of needs and services, plus personals. Commercial advertisements may occur throughout the paper or magazine (except the first page and the editorial page) and usually represent retail outlets' attempts to publicize their goods.

The advent of cable and various other forms of pay television has brought another dimension to the concept of media support. At present, all pay television is either (1) cable-commercial or (2) cable-noncommercial. In the cable-commercial system consumers purchase television programs that they would otherwise not be able to receive at home from a central cable company. These programs are the regular network programs; the cable simply allows customers the opportunity to extend the receptive powers of their sets. Cable-noncommercial is pay television in its pure form. It is completely supported by subscribers to the system, who pay for special movies, sports events, and entertainment programs without having to watch commercial announcements. It is conceivable that pay television will become even more specialized in the future. Stations that show only sports events or live entertainment are possible and probable.

Support for media in controlled economies is not subject to the demands of the market. In other words, programs for television or radio may be aired despite a lack of consumer appeal. The more control present within a society, the less is media support dependent on the consumers. This is true for newspapers and radio as well as for television. In these conditions media systems are often insulated from knowledge of what their standings are.

Merrill and Lowenstein identify the four basic elements of media support as *single sales, subscriptions, advertising,* and *subsidy.*[11] They properly recognize the insignificance of subsidy in the United States and other highly industrialized free enterprise systems, such as Japan and Britain, but they fail to provide a context for understanding the varieties of subsidies. All subisides are not government subsidies. Although it is true, as Merrill and Lowenstein point out, that government subsidies may be outright payments, paid political advertising, or bulk purchases of publications, this does not exhaust the possibilities. In developing nations tending toward less controlled economies the government may well play a major role in subsidizing the young industry; however, most of these nations also receive outright grants

[11] Merrill and Lowenstein, op. cit., p. 25.

from philanthropic foundations and international organizations. Because media ownership is normally controlled by the government, support from foreign foundations and international agencies is usually in the form of grants to the government for media development rather than direct grants to the media system. Wilcox states that 80 per cent of African countries in 1975 had a government-controlled press.[12] Government control of the electronic media in Africa is of even higher percentage for several reasons, the principal one being expense. Another reason is the lack of a private ownership tradition. The control of media by government allows the developing nations to attempt rapid and orderly growth.

What we have said about government support in Africa is generally true for the developing nations of Asia and South America as well. Given the need to communicate with the masses and the limited resources of most developing nations, government support is mandatory if there are to be media.

In this section we have discussed the pervasive influence of advertising on the most highly developed industrial societies. A diversity of industries competing for the public's attention and a technically sophisticated skill pool have created diverse media organizations whose lifeline is the advertisement of goods and services to large numbers of people. As Merrill and Lowenstein have observed, "advertising's impact on media . . . is a result primarily of its concentrated power."[13]

Ownership

Ownership, the guiding influence of the system, usually involves control of message production and direction of the system's programming. There are three basic types of media ownership: *industrial, "biological,"* and *communal*

Industrial ownership, characteristic of most Western media systems, usually operates for the profit of a private corporation. Advertising is its distinguishing characteristic. Private ownership sustains itself by profits made by selling advertising, which implies the

---

[12] Dennis Wilcox, *Mass Media in Black Africa* (New York: Praeger Publishers, 1975), p. 107.

[13] Miller and Lowestein, op. cit., p. 27.

existence of consumers willing to purchase goods as a result of that advertising. The industrial type of media ownership, based in the West on the United States model, is dependent on the public's desire to consume and ability to purchase. Several factors contribute to industrial ownership's resilience: (1) *practicality*, (2) *flexibility*, (3) *relative accessibility*, (4) *efficiency*, and (5) *profitability*.

Industrial ownership is invariably practical because of the competitive nature of industry. Employees compete for jobs, and those who are successful are normally the more experienced and better-qualified ones who can contribute to the overall society or to local and regional interests. Flexibility in industrial ownership derives from the variety of programming that is possible, much of which is done by trial and error. If one program does not attract enough listeners or viewers, it will be replaced with one that does better.

Accessibility to the media is usually relatively simple. A listener or viewer may use the telephone or the mails to achieve accessibility. However, no media system allows its audience absolute accessibility. The newspapers, probably the most accessible of all media in Western societies, select which letters to the editor to print. Letters to the editor and opposing editorials can also be presented on the electronic media, and selection of what and who will appear on the air is a matter of ownership control. In the United States, which has a fairness doctrine, opposition politicians can expect the opportunity to refute political speeches by incumbents. Such accessibility can prove to be a problem for media owners, particularly in trying to determine who should respond to what message and at what time.

The efficiency of industrial owernship is determined by the ratio of useful output to total input. Almost all media systems in Western nations employ an efficiency standard so that the ownership can make certain that the cost of production is not excessive.

Managing a television station is a constant battle to balance the costs of production and the profits from advertising. Television managers must monitor the inflow of dollars and the outflow of programs and services. Too many reporters may mean not enough work to keep everyone busy. Too few may mean that the organization is not able to meet its schedules. Generally television has too many personnel, not too few.

Few television stations go bankrupt in Western nations. The same cannot be said for newspapers. Many newspapers are unable to get the necessary advertising and subscription lists to make them profitable. Overall, however, the media industry in Western nations had demonstrated unusual resilience in its ability to stay financially solvent.

Industrial ownership's achievements in practicality, flexibility, accessibility, efficiency, and profitability must be considered in analyzing the other ownership types. Most media systems seek to achieve these same goals.

The "biological" types of media ownership seeks decentralization of ownership, specialized markets, and perceptual adaptability. Decentralization of ownership, whether private or government, means that the control of the media is redistributed among the users; no "property" claims are made by either government or private investors. Group ownership, i.e., user ownership, substitutes for other possessive arrangements. The cultivation of specialized markets—community, regional, national, or international—is a key element in biological ownership. No attempt is made to teach a mass audience except in terms of all persons in a predetermined market. Perceptual adaptability means the ability of a particular medium to change its market at any time. The market is not fixed; the owners determine it as necessary.

In communal ownership, control resides jointly in user and producer. It differs from biological ownership in cultivating both mass and specialized audiences. Such a system of ownership has rarely been employed, but it appears to offer some advantages over biological ownership.

Whatever the type of ownership, control is intricately tied to support, and ownership is a principal element in media support.

① PARTICIPANTS IN KNOWLEDGE INDUSTRY (6 PARTS)

② REPRODUCTIONS (5 PARTS)

③ CIRCULATION (2 MAIN PHENOMENON)

④ FEEDBACK (3 TYPES)

⑤ SUPPORT (FINANCIAL, ADVERTISING)

⑥ OWNERSHIP DISTINGUISH BETWEEN 3 TYPES

Part One Readings

Bagdikian, Ben H. *The Information Machines: Their Impact on Men and the Media.* New York: Harper & Row, 1971.

Barker, Larry L., and Kibler, Robert J. *Speech Communication Behavior: Perspectives and Principles.* Englewood Cliffs, N.J.: Prentice-Hall, 1971.

Barnouw, Eric. *A Tower in Babel: A History of Broadcasting in the United States Vol. I to 1933.* New York: Oxford University Press, 1968.

Barnouw, Eric. *The Golden Web: A History of Broadcasting in the United States Vol. II 1933–1955.* New York: Oxford University Press, 1968.

Barnouw, Eric. *The Image Empire: A History of Broadcasting in the United States Vol. III from 1955.* New York: Oxford University Press, 1970.

Blake, Reed H., and Haroldson, Edwin O. *Taxonomy of Concepts in Communications.* New York: Hastings House, 1975.

Brown, Les. *Television: The Business Behind the Box.* New York: Harcourt Brace Jovanovich, 1972.

Cantor, Norman F., and Worthman, Michael S. *The History of Popular Culture.* New York: Macmillan Publishing Co., Inc., 1968.

Cassata, Mary B., and Palmer, Roger Cain. *Reader in Library Communication.* Englewood, Colo.: Information Handling Services, 1976.

Casty, Alan. *Mass Media and Mass Man.* New York: Holt, Rinehart and Winston, 1968.

Dexter, Lewis Anthony, and White, David Manning, eds. *People, Society and Mass Communications.* New York: The Free Press, 1964.

Edelstein, Alex S. *Perspectives in Mass Communication.* Copenhagen: Einor Harcks Forlack, 1966.

Emory, Edwin. *The Press and America: An Interpretive History of the Mass Media,* 3rd ed. Englewood Cliffs, N.J.: Prentice-Hall, 1972.

Fabre, M. *A History of Communications: The New Illustrated Library of Science and Inventions,* Vol. 9. New York: Hawthorne Books, 1963.

Farrar, Ronald T., and Stevens, John D., eds. *Mass Media and the National Experience: Essays in Communications History.* New York: Harper & Row, 1971.

Hanneman, Gerhard J., and McEwan, William J. *Communication and Behavior.* Reading, Mass.: Addison-Wesley, 1975.

Kendrick, Alexander. *Prime Time: The Life of Edward R. Morrow.* Boston: Little, Brown, 1969.

Lippmann, Walter. *Public Opinion.* New York: Macmillan Publishing Co., Inc., 1922.

MacNeil, Robert. *The People Machine.* New York: Harper & Row, 1968.

Pool, Ithiel de Sola, and Schramm, Wilbur, et al., eds. *Handbook of Communication.* Chicago: Rand McNally, 1973.

Schramm, Wilbur. *Mass Communication,* 2nd ed. Urbana: University of Illinois Press, 1960.

Schramm, Wilbur, and Wade, Serena. *Knowledge and the Public Mind.* Stanford, Calif.: Institute for Communications Research, 1967.

Schramm, Wilbur, and Roberts, Donald, eds. *The Process and Effects of Mass Communication,* Urbana: University of Illinois Press, 1971.

Sereno, Kenneth K., and Mortensen, David C. *Foundations of Communications Theory.* New York: Harper & Row, 1970.

Part Two

Theoretical Dimensions

Chapter 4
Mass Communication
Models and Theories

*The listener's or viewer's brain is an indispensable
component of the total communication system.*
Tony Schwartz, *The Responsive Chord*, p. 25

In recent years, a good deal of effort has been devoted to the construction of models of the communication process. Communication scholars generally attribute the heightened interest in communication model building to the achievement of a certain sophistication by the field and a general desire on the part of communication scholars to live up to this newly attained status. Perhaps a more scientific explanation, however, lies in the gradual progression of communication research from a nonprocess viewpoint to a communication systems viewpoint, along with the realization that there is a certain economic advantage in the manipulation of symbols rather than objects.

Our discussion of mass communication theory would be somewhat incomplete without some preliminary treatment of mass communication models, despite the fact that we vigorously deny that communication models and communication theory are one and the same, or even that models are prerequisite to the development of theory. Models simply are extremely useful for the beginning student trying to visualize the symbolic (functional) relationship of the objects, components, or forces being investigated.

A good place to begin is with a definition of the term *model*. For our purposes, one of the more appropriate is that formulated by Sereno and Mortensen:

A communication system or model consists of an idealized description of what is necessary for an act of communication to occur. A model rep-

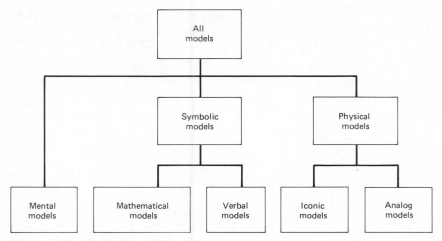

Figure 4-1. Types of models.

From Gerhard J. Hanneman and William J. McEwen, Communication and
Behavior (Reading, Mass.: Addison-Wesley, 1975), p. 426. Reprinted with
permission of the publisher and authors.

resents or *replicates* in abstract terms the essential features and eliminates the unnecessary details of communication in the "real world."[1]

Another source of good definitions of *model* is a recent general
communication textbook such as Hanneman and McEwen's *Communication and Behavior.*[2]

Hanneman presents a taxonomy of models in graphic form (see
Fig. 4-1), in which the degree of abstraction decreases from left to
right. For our purposes we need only be concerned with symbolic and
physical models, noting in passing that Hanneman includes mental
models to represent internal mental processes.

The verbal model is simply the theory stated in words. The verbal models we have chosen to discuss on the pages that follow are the
well-known *"Who* says *what* in which *channel* to *whom* and with *what
effect"* developed by Harold Lasswell, the "general model" of communication developed by George Gerbner, also, later in this chapter,
described in terms of a graphic model, and the SMCR model developed by David Berlo, which some mass communication researchers

[1] Kenneth K. Sereno and C. David Mortensen, *Foundations of Communication Theory*
(New York: Harper & Row, 1970), p. 7.

[2] Gerhard J. Hanneman and William J. McEwen, *Communication and Behavior* (Reading,
Mass.: Addison-Wesley, 1975). See, for example, Hanneman's Chapter 20: "Models and
Model Building in Communication Research," pp. 421–436.

consider to be a simplification of the Shannon and Weaver model. Verbal models are immensely useful, especially in terms of stating hypotheses or presenting the results of a study.

Diagrammatic or graphic models present schematically what verbal models attempt to explain with words alone. These models *do not* look like the subject they attempt to represent. Examples of diagrammatic or graphic models are maps to represent distances on the earth's surface and calendars to represent the divisions of time. In this chapter we shall present several diagrammatic or graphic models of the communication process, namely the schematic of Gerbner's "general model" of communication, Westley and MacLean's *ABC* mass communication model, DeFleur's expansion of Shannon and Weaver's model of the mass communication system, Hiebert, Ungurait, and Bohn's hub model of mass communication, and Vora's model for diffusing concepts.

Iconic models look like what they represent but differ in scale. Photographs, sculptures, and paintings are icons of persons, objects, and scenes. Analog models, on the other hand, bear a defined structural relationship to the subjects they represent but do not look like them. The computer may be described as an analog of the brain.

Mathematical models, although they are the goal of most scientists, are infrequently encountered in the field of communication. Except for graph theory in the analysis of communication networks and the statistical concepts of information processing, communication theories have generally not been expressed in mathematical symbols. We have, however, included a brief discussion later in this chapter of Shannon's formula for information that he developed in 1948.

We shall now turn our attention to the models that we believe the beginning communication student should have at least a passing familiarity with.

Verbal Models

In Table 4-1 are charted the salient points of the verbal models developed by Harold Lasswell, George Gerbner, and David Berlo. All three models describe the first four components of the communication process—source (communicator), message, channel, receiver (audience)—and only Berlo omits the effect or consequence component.

The Lasswell model is perhaps the most widely quoted of all models of the communication process: *"Who* says *what* in which *channel* to *whom* and with *what effect"* captures the essence of the communication process in an economy of words. However, we have slightly changed the order of the sequence of elements in the Gerbner verbal model to accommodate it to our chart, which presents the sequence as it is conceptualized by most communication theorists. The Berlo model as shown in the chart is a verbalized conceptualization of his well-known SMCR diagram, which Barker and Kibler refer to as "a pre-model diagram since it sets forth major variables without performing the function of a model: suggesting specific relationships between the variables."[3] While we are discussing the components of the communication process, we should point out that some authors do not include the "effects" component as being vital to the communication process. They maintain that although "effects" studies have monopolized the attention of mass communication researchers, "effects" are not absolutely essential for the process to work.

Diagrammatic or Graphic Models

The diagrammatic or graphic models that we will now consider are those developed by George Gerbner in 1956, Bruce Westley and Malcolm MacLean in 1957, Melvin DeFleur in 1966, Hiebert, Ungurait, and Bohn in 1974 and Vora in 1978. These diagrams and the simple explanations given for each model in the pages that follow should serve in themselves as an ample introduction. For the student who wishes to pursue a model in greater depth, full bibliographic information is also supplied. Diagrammatic or graphic models, better than any others, show the relationships among their parts, but there are certain disadvantages in relying too heavily on models. In a word, models do not displace theories and they should not be oversimplified or overgeneralized.

The Gerbner model of communication, already presented in verbal form in Table 4-1, is presented graphically in Fig. 4-2. The key to interpreting it is as follows:

[3] See Larry L. Barker and Robert J. Kibler, *Speech Communication Behavior: Perspectives and Principles* (Englewood Cliffs, N.J: Prentice-Hall, 1971), pp. 25–26.

Table 4-1. Verbal Models of Mass Communication

Lasswell* (1948)	Gerbner† (1956)	Berlo‡ (1960)
WHO Communicating organizations, their natures and functions	1. SOMEONE (source, communicator) 2. perceives an event 3. and reacts 4. in a situation	SOURCE Press, publishing research organizations. governments, churches and other social organizations, television, radio, and publishing
says	to make available	
WHAT The nature of the content: informative, entertaining, educative	6. MATERIALS 7. in some form 8. and context 9. conveying content	MESSAGE Words, mathematical symbols, pictorial images
in which	through some	
CHANNEL Print media, audiovisual media, automatic data processing	5. MEANS channels; media; physical engineering; administrative and institutional facilities for distribution and control	CHANNEL Print, electronic media
to		
WHOM The nature and receptivity of the audience	1. SOMEONE (destination, audience) 2. perceives an event 3. and reacts 4. in a situation	RECEIVER General audiences, specialized audiences
and with what	of some	
EFFECT The nature of the effect or response of the audience; the ways in which it *affects* the communicator	10. CONSEQUENCE	

* As described in K. L. McGarry, *Communication, Knowledge, and the Librarian* (Hamden, Conn.: Shoe String Press, 1975), p. 20.
† Adapted from George Gerbner, "Towards a General Model of Communication," *Audio-Visual Communication Review*, 4(3), 1956, 172.
‡ McGarry, op. cit., p. 20.

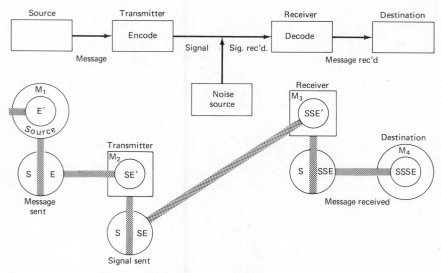

Figure 4-2. George Gerbner's graphic model of communication.

Schematic from George Gerbner, "Towards a General Model of Communication," Audio-Visual Communication Review, 4(3), 1956, 191. Reprinted by permission of the publisher.

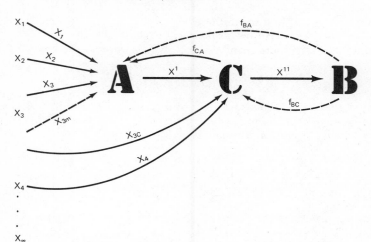

Figure 4-3. Bruce H. Westley and Malcolm S. MacLean's mass communication model.

From Bruce H. Westley and Malcolm S. MacLean, Jr., "A Conceptual Model for Communications Research," Journalism Quarterly, 34, 1957, 31–38. Reprinted by permission of Journalism Quarterly. This schematic appears in Larry L. Barker and Robert J. Kibler, Speech Communication Behavior: Perspectives and Principles (Englewood Cliffs, N.J.: Prentice-Hall, p. 36.)

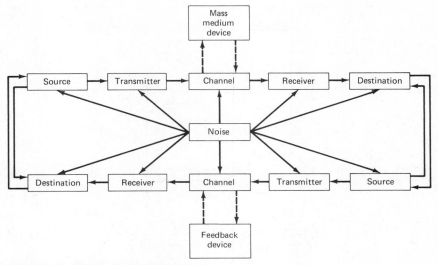

***Figure 4-4. Melvin L. DeFleur's mass
communication system.***

From Melvin L. DeFleur, Theories of Mass Communication. *By
permission of Longman, Inc. Previously published by David McKay Co.
Reprinted by Longman, Inc.*

1. *Someone* is shown as M for "man" or as M if the communication sequence involves mechanical means. M may be
   the originator or the receiver of the message—its role is de-
   noted by its place in the communication sequence.

2. (E′) is the event as perceived by M.

3. (S\E) is the statement about the event.

4. (SSE) is the signal about the statement about the event.

5. (SSSE) is the communicated product.

Thus the Gerbner model shows that someone perceives an event
and sends a message to a transmitter who in turn transmits a signal to
a receiver; in the course of transmission the signal picks up certain
spurious noises and comes out as SSSE to the destination.
The Westley and MacLean model (see Fig. 4-3) expands on Newcomb's *ABX* model (*A* communicates to *B* about topic *X*) with the
inclusion of the concept of the gatekeeper *C* as developed by Lewin.
The *A*'s (communicators representing advocacy roles) select and trans-

GERBNER
TELE-
PHONE
GAME

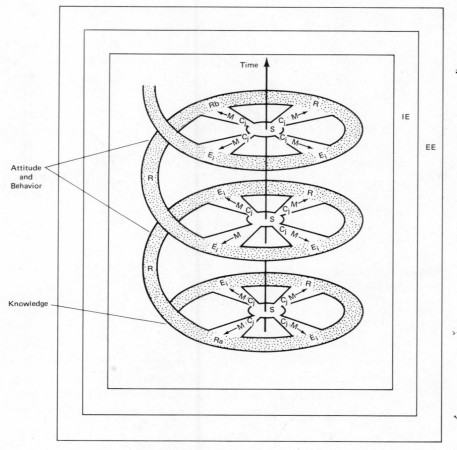

M = Message
R = Receiver, person, group
S = Source, person, committee
EE = External Environment
IE = Internal Environment
C_j = Channels, where j is a subscript representing different types
     of channels; j = 1, 2, 3, 4, ...m. For example, 1, 2, 3, and 4 may
     represent the channels of public speaking, newspapers, radio,
     and television respectively.

E_i = Effect, where i is a subscript representing different types
     of effects; i = 1, 2, 3, 4, ...m. For example, 1, 2, 3, and 4 may
     represent the effects of adopting, rejecting, ignoring, and
     unfreezing respectively.

Ra = Receiver gaining knowledge about a new concept
Rb = Receiver changing attitudes and behavior toward a new concept

Figure 4-5. Vora's model for diffusing concepts.

From Erika Wenzel Vora, "The Development of Concept Diffusion Models
and Their Application to the Diffusion of the Social Concept of Race."
Ph.D. dissertation, State University of New York at Buffalo, 1978.

mit messages purposively to modify the B's perception of X. The B's (receivers—audience members representing behavioral system roles) respond in terms of their needs and requirements for messages as a means of orienting themselves to the environment. The C's (representing channel roles or gatekeepers) are agents of the B's, nonpurposively selecting and transmitting information for them. Feedback is an important component of this model.

The DeFleur model shown in Fig. 4-4 enlarges on the Shannon and Weaver model that we introduced in an earlier chapter of this text. DeFleur pictures the source, transmitter, receiver, and destination each as separate phases of the mass communication process in much the same way that Schramm depicts a source, encoder, decoder, and destination as being distinct phases in his mass communications model:

In his model DeFleur further enlarges on that of Shannon and Weaver by interjecting a mass medium device and a feedback device, the latter to demonstrate that the process is circular. As shown in the DeFleur model, noise may interfere at any stage in the mass communication process.

In the hub model of mass communication, communicationists Hiebert, Ungurait, and Bohn conceive of the communication process as a set of concentric circles much like the waves formed when a pebble is thrown into a pool. The pebble, which is analogous to the communication content, causes ripples that become ever-widening circles until they hit the shore (audience) and bounce back (feedback). The idea is that the initial content goes through a series of actions and reactions that the authors call "the pool of human affairs."

The Vora model, shown in Fig. 4-5, in many ways is the most complex of the models presented. It presents the concepts of diffusion, knowledge, attitude change and behavior change in a dynamic and progressive spiral which utilizes mass communication and interpersonal channels. This model's attention to the mass communication process goes beyond a consideration of the source, message, channel, and receiver components, stressing the external and internal environment factors as well as the effects component. It may be applied to diffusion of concepts in a regional, national or international context.

Mathematical Models

It is in the category of mathematical models that the earliest work as well as the least amount of work has been done in communication research. Although their theory has served as a landmark in communication research for many years, Shannon and Weaver's writings are difficult to understand. For example, Shannon's formula for information (1948) is

$$H = -[p_1 \log p_1 + p_2 \log p_2 + \cdots + p_n \log p_n],$$

or

$$H = -\sum p_i \log p_i .$$

In attempting to describe information as the reduction of uncertainty, Shannon uses the term *entropy*, and in the formula H is the mathematical symbol for entropy, $\sum$ is the symbol for "sum of," p_i is the probability of an event i occurring, and $\log p_i$ is the information needed to predict the occurrence of event i.

Difficult as the applications of the concept of entropy might be, the prospect of applying the mathematical concepts introduced by Shannon and Weaver to human communication excited many communication scholars in the late 1940s. Readers who are similarly intrigued with Shannon's information theory and who would like to come to a closer understanding of it as it applies to mass communication should read Wilbur Schramm's explication.[4]

Relationship Between Models and Theories

Models provide theorists "with a structure for assembling their findings which may subsequently be tested in 'the real world.' "[5] We shall next turn our attention to mass communication theory; however, we caution the student not to be surprised at the extraordinary array (or disarray) of claims, hunches, explanations, perspectives, and myths that abound in the field. The lag in the field in embracing model construction (abstractions) is a clue to the chaos we shall find in theory.

[4] Wilbur Schramm, "Information Theory and Mass Communication," *Journalism Quarterly*, **32,** Spring 1955, 131–146.
[5] Hanneman and McEwen, op. cit., p. 421.

Perhaps the only statement relevant to mass communication theory that has any degree of precision is that so far none of them is complete.

One way to look at mass communication theories is *chronological*—i.e., in terms of their historical development. Another way to look at mass communication theories is through broad *categorical* perspectives, as, for example:

1. Psychological perspectives (e.g., stimulus-response theories).
2. Sociological perspectives (e.g., theories related to broad social categories or group memberships).
3. Theories unique to a single mass medium (e.g., the reflective-projective theory of television).
4. Theories related to function (e.g., utility or gratification theories).

Although either approach—chronological or categorical—would be valid and useful, we believe a more successful way to focus on mass communication theory is to look at the elements or components of the communication process that we have already encountered in our review of models. Our discussion is based on an earlier essay written by Mary Cassata, "Mass Communication and Libraries," in which she developed the "inventory of mass communication theories according to components of the mass communication process"[6] reprinted as Table 4-2. We believe that looking at mass communication theory through the components of the process will enable the student to better visualize the relationship of model to process to theory. We shall also attempt to cast our theories within chronological and categorical frames of reference.

The Communicator Component

Authoritarian Theory. The authoritarian theory of the press can be traced to the very beginning of printing. At that time, truth was thought to reside in those who held power—that is, the governing agency. Thus there was strict control of the press through the licensing

[6] See Mary B. Cassata and Roger Cain Palmer, *Reader in Library Communication* (Englewood, Colo.: Information Handling Services, 1976).

Table 4-2. Inventory of Mass Communication Theories According to Components of the Mass Communication Process

Component	Theory/Perspective	Key Concepts	Researchers/Theorists
COMMUNICATOR (institutional and individual)	Four theories of the press	Authoritarian, Libertarian, Soviet-Communist, Social Responsibilities	Siebert, Peterson, Schramm
	Power of the press theory / Bullet theory / Hypodermic needle theory	Stimulus-response	Tested by various researchers from the World War I period to the late 1940s
	Objective theory of the press	Editors, reporters protect objective character of the media	Flegel, Chaffee
	Information control (gatekeeper)	Communication channels; message selection; censorship; media managers	Lewin, White, Donohur, Tichenor, Olien, Gieber
MESSAGE	Cultural indicators	Content analysis of mass media, message systems; media establish social norms; media set agenda of social issues	Gerbner, Gross
	Agenda setting	Mass media define issues; establish important issues	McCombs and Shaw, Cohen
CHANNEL	McLuhan's theories / The medium is the message; the medium is the massage	Media not only transmit information but also tell us what kind of world exists; media stimulate our senses, alter the ratio of sensory equipment we use, and thus change our character	McLuhan, Innis, Carey

AUDIENCE

Theory	Description	Theorists
"Hot" and "cool" media	"Hot": does not maintain sensory balance; requires little imagination (e.g., print and radio) / "Cool": has sensory balance; requires much imagination (e.g., film and TV)	McLuhan
One-step, two-step, and multistep flow models	Sharing; personal influence; opinion leaders; diffusion of information, and news	Troldahl, Katz, Lazarsfeld, Berelson, Gaudet, Merton, Deutschmann, Danielson
Individual differences theory	Conditioning; selective exposure; selective retention	Hovland, Janis, Kelley, Rosenberg, Festinger, Fleshbach, Klapper, Sears and Freedman
Social categories theory	Media exposure, media preference, and communication effects can be determined according to broad social categories such as education, income, occupation, age, and sex	Lazarsfeld, Schramm, White, Lasswell, DeFleur
Social relationships theory	Informal social relationships impact on audiences	Hovland, Asch, Sherif, Lazarsfeld, Berelson, Gaudet, Katz
Cultural norms theory	Mass media define cultural norms, indirectly influence conduct by reinforcing existing patterns, creating new shared connections, and changing the existing norms	Lazarsfeld, Klapper, Gerbner

Table 4-2. (continued)

Component	Theory/Perspective	Key Concepts	Researchers/Theorists
	Ludenic theory: play	Consumer as producer; distinction between work (information) and play (entertainment); aspects of the mass media; affluence of audience member	Stephenson
	Uses and gratification theory	(see Effects)	
EFFECTS	Media gratification and utility theory	What people do with the mass media	Katz, Lazarsfeld, Davison, Mc-Quail, Blumler, Brown
	Social learning theory	Modeling, imitation, identification	Baran, Meyer, Bandura, Gewirtz
	Theory of effect	Obstinate, self-reliant, active audience; interaction of mass communication with other forces	Bauer, Zimmerman
	"No effects" theory	Reinforcement	Klapper, Lazarsfeld, Merton

From Mary B. Cassata and Roger Cain Palmer, *Reader in Library Communication* (Englewood, Colo.: Information Handling Services, 1976), pp. 212–214. Reprinted by permission of Information Handling Services, a division of Indian Head Inc., and the authors.

of printers by the throne. Censorship was practiced if the ruler thought that information should be withheld from the masses. Therefore, although the press was not necessarily owned by the government, it was looked on as being an advocate of the state.

Today many nations will not admit that their countries are governed according to authoritarian principles; they publicly espouse libertarian concepts, but behind the scenes authoritarian practices are carried out. In a continuum ranging from complete, openly practiced press control to covert discouragement of press opposition we would find the kind of progression charted in Table 4-3.

Libertarian Theory. Today "the open marketplace of ideas" and the "self-righting process" define the conceptual boundaries of the libertarian theory of the press. In the seventeenth century John Milton defended the concepts of reason and the moral integrity of man in telling right from wrong, good from bad, and truth from falsehood in a powerful argument for intellectual freedom (*Aeropagitica*, 1644). Other exponents of this philosophy were John Stuart Mill, Thomas Paine, John Erskine, and Thomas Jefferson. They believed in freedom of expression, rationalism, and natural rights. They saw as the press's function

**Table 4-3. A Continuum of Authoritarian Press
Practices in Modern Governments—1978**

Complete Control ⟶		*to Varying Degrees of Control* ⟶	
Complete press control	Criticism theoretically allowed, but government invokes censorship	Special press laws lead to arrest of editors	Suppression of press opposition is more covert
Soviet Union and satellites			
China		Union of South	Turkey
Yugoslavia		Africa	Argentina
	Colombia	Iran	Indonesia
	Egypt	Pakistan	
	Syria	Iraq	
		Lebanon	

Related theories: Soviet-Communist theory
Power of the press theory
Gatekeeper/information control theory
Agenda-setting theory

to inform, to sell, to entertain, to uphold the truth, and to keep check on the government. Press ownership in countries espousing the libertarian philosophy is likely to be private and should be free from defamation, obscenity, impropriety, and wartime sedition. Countries practicing the libertarian philosophy today are the United States, Great Britain, and other Western European nations. Other theories related to the libertarian theory are the social responsibility theory and the objective theory of the press.

Social Responsibility Theory. The social responsibility theory is an extension of the libertarian theory in that the press recognizes that it has a responsibility to society to carry out its essential functions. The social responsibility theory ascribes basically the same six functions to the press as the libertarian theory: (1) providing information, discussion, and debate on public affairs; (2) instructing and informing the public to make it capable of self-government; (3) protecting the rights of the individual against the government through its watchdog function; (4) maintaining the economic equilibrium of the system by bringing together buyer, seller, and advertiser; (5) providing entertainment; and (6) remaining independent of outside pressures by maintaining its own economic self-sufficiency. The basic principles of the social responsibility theory uphold conflict resolution through discussion; there is a high regard for public opinion, consumer action, and professional ethics and jealous guard over private rights and important social interests. This theory emerged in the United States in the twentieth century, and it is evidenced today in the Anglo-American nations.

Soviet-Communist Theory. Just as the social responsibility theory is an outgrowth of the libertarian theory, Soviety-Communist theory is an outgrowth of the authoritarian theory. However, whereas according to the authoritarian theory the press resides outside the government, in the Soviet-Communist theory the press and the state are held to be one.[7] The main purpose of the Soviet-Communist theory is to ensure the success and continuance of the Soviet Socialist system and to promote the objectives of the Soviet Socialist Party. This system is found mainly in the Soviet Union and other Communist countries. In addition to the authoritarian theory this theory is related to the power

[7]For a scholarly discussion of the evolution of man's thinking on the role of the press vis à vis government, see Fred S. Siebert, Theodore Peterson, and Wilbur Schramm, *Four Theories of the Press* (Urbana: University of Illinois Press, 1956).

of the press, gatekeeping/information control, and agenda-setting theories.

Power of the Press Theory, Bullet Theory, Hypodermic Needle Theory. For years after World War I, popular thinking ascribed powerful influence to the press. The audience was thought of as a sitting target waiting to be shot at. The stimulus was the message carried by the press; the response was the outcome of the audience's complete belief in the press as authority. Something was true because the press said so. This kind of thinking had its roots in behavioristic stimulus-response psychology; furthermore, the years of World War I and immediately after were a time of heavy propaganda campaigns by the Allies and the Central Powers alike. The Nazis and Communists made people afraid to use their powers of reason; gloom, pessimism, and bad news were the order of the day. Thus the theories of mass communication at this time were variously known as the power of the press theory, the bullet theory, and the hypodermic needle theory: the speeding bullet or the magic injection swiftly and efficiently transferred "ideas or feelings or knowledge or motivations almost automatically from one mind to another."[8] The "transportation theory" and the "conveyor belt theory" of mass communication are other appellations for the concept of the transfer of ideas from one mind to another. Contemporary theorists, of course, discount such definitions of the communications process.

A Final Word. A brief comment is in order about the communicator-based theories that relate to the handling of information. In a sense two such theories—the objective theory of the press and the information control theory, which highlights the role of the gatekeeper in society—are antithetical to each other. Whereas the objective theory of the press, which has grown out of the social responsibility theory, stresses the effort that editors and reporters make to protect the objective character of the press, the information control/gatekeeper theory stresses that the media manager takes an active, conscious role in selecting messages, filtering them, and amplifying them for the audience. One has only to consider the various gates through which information must flow in our society to appreciate the magnitude of this problem. In describing gatekeepers, Wilbur Schramm wrote:

[8]Wilbur Schramm, "The Nature of Communications Between Humans," in Wilbur Schramm and Donald F. Roberts, (eds.) *The Process and Effects of Mass Communication*, rev. ed. (Urbana: University of Illinois Press, 1971), p. 8.

Gatekeepers are placed throughout the information network. They include the reporter deciding what facts to put down about a court trial or an accident or a political demonstration, the editor deciding what to print and what to discard from the wire news, the author deciding what kinds of people and events to write about and what view of life to present, the publisher's editor deciding what authors to publish and what to cut out of their manuscripts, the television or film producer deciding where to point his camera, the film editor deciding what to edit out and leave on the cutting-room floor, the librarian deciding what books to purchase, the teacher deciding what textbooks or teaching films to use, the briefing officer deciding what facts to tell his superior, and even the husband at the dinner table deciding what to tell his wife about the day's events at the office.[9]

The picture that one gets of the world is the product of the communicator's bias, whether conscious or not. It has been pointed out by various writers that the symbols employed by the mass media create a pseudoenvironment that stands between people and physical reality. The media deliver to us an incredible number of experiences to react to; it is apparent that our media environment often becomes more important to us than our physical environment in governing what we think and do. We shall discuss this topic in greater depth in the next chapter when we consider the subject of mass media impact.

A number of factors enter into the gatekeeping decision. The time of day a story breaks, the content, subjective value judgments on the part of the gatekeeper, happenstance (i.e., a reporter's being at the right place at the right time), the visual impact of a photograph or film footage, especially if a story is to be telecast—all determine to a greater or lesser degree how a story will be handled, what will be emphasized, changed, modified, or ignored. The gatekeeping theory is related to the agenda-setting theory and the cultural norms theory.

The Message Component

Cultural Indicators.[10] Marshall McLuhan, notwithstanding, many theorists believe that the message and not the medium is the heart of the communication act. George Gerbner and Larry Gross of the An-

---

[9]Wilbur Schramm, *Men, Messages and Media: A Look at Human Communication* (New York: Harper & Row, 1973), pp. 138–139.

[10]For a revealing explication of the cultural indicators approach in studying television content and effects, see George Gerbner and Larry Gross, " 'Living with Television: The Violence Profile," *Journal of Communication*, **26(2)**, Spring 1976, 173–199.

nenberg School of Communication at the University of Pennsylvania have been systematically studying program content since 1967:

> Instead of guessing or assuming the contours and dynamics of that world, message system analysis maps its geography, demography, thematic and action structure, time and space dimensions, personality profiles, occupations, and fates. Message system analysis yields the gross but clear terms of location, action, and characterization discharged into the mainstream of community consciousness. Aggregate viewer interpretation starts with these common terms of basic exposure (pp. 181–182).

Believing that it is not exposure to a single program segment but rather multiple exposures several times a day, seven days a week, that formulate the individual's premises about society, people, and issues, Gerbner and Gross have trained coders to monitor videotaped programs to analyze program content according to carefully constructed measures (cultural indicators). The pattern of their findings strongly suggests that new consideration must be given to Klapper's conclusion of some years ago that mass media exposure is but one of a complex set of variables to be taken into account when determining the strength of media impact.[11]

As a research tool, cultural indicators are related to such communication concepts as gatekeeping, agenda setting, and defining cultural norms.

Agenda-Setting Hypotheses. (Just as program content shapes our perceptions of society by focusing attention on certain types of actions, characters, and issues, the mass media by defining the political issues and the amount of attention to attach to a specific topic set the agenda for public discussion.)The agenda-setting hypothesis assumes that a direct, positive relationship exists between media coverage and the salience of a topic in the public mind. The relationship is stated in causal terms: by conferring status on an issue, the media structure what is important. The Watergate issue is just one of several outstanding modern-day examples of press exposure's impact on the American conscience. As Bernard Cohen succinctly state, "The press may not be successful much of the time in telling people what to think but it is stunningly successful in telling its readers what to think *about.*"[12]

---

[11]See Joseph T. Klapper, *The Effects of Mass Communication* (New York: The Free Press, 1960).

[12]Bernard C. Cohen, *The Press and Foreign Policy* (Princeton, N.J.: Princeton University Press, 1963), p. 13.

The agenda-setting hypothesis has its roots in the power of the press theory (it was called by a different name—"status conferral function"—in 1948 by Lazarsfeld and Merton); it is related to the gatekeeping concept.

The Channel Component

McLuhan's Theories. There has perhaps been no one more controversial in the field of mass communication than Marshall McLuhan, whose writing and probing created a stir in the early 1960s. Perhaps best known for his thesis that the medium of television has usurped the dominant position once held by print, McLuhan, if nothing else, has stimulated people to think more creatively about their place in the world of media technology. McLuhan's probings encourage replacement of the linear thinking mode established by print technology with the multisensory perception mode created by television. The medium of television, according to McLuhan, stimulates our senses, alters the ratio of the sensory equipment we use, and changes our character—all the while altering the environment. "The medium is the message," and the medium is "hot" or it is "cool." A hot medium does not maintain the sensory balance and requires little imagination or involvement on the part of the participant—hence radio, photography, motion pictures, and print, which are highly defined and require little involvement, are hot. Interpersonal conversational exchanges, the telephone, cartoons, and television—which are low in definition and therefore require much involvement of participants—are cool, television being the coolest of all. It is here that McLuhan has received his greatest criticism. What makes one medium "hot" and another medium "cool"? Why is a painting, for example, hot and television cool? Are not both pictures?

First of all, we must bear in mind that when McLuhan refers to "hot" and "cool" he is referring to the number of data present in a medium. Something hot offers many data, something cool few. But does *data* mean "information"? Or does it mean the experience the medium evokes in the receiver? Neither. McLuhan uses *data* in the sense of the physical impact the medium has on the sense organs, nothing more. Thus, according to McLuhan, a medium that is hot requires little effort on the part of the audience, whereas one that is cool requires high participation or completion by the audience. Also ruled from consideration is any evoked recollection of past experience. Completion is simply a matter of physical and tactile action on the part of the audience. In other words, with regard to television, whether viewers know it or not, they are involved to the depths of their being because they must put together the tiny dots that make up the TV picture. McLuhan says that a viewer has 3 million dots per second from which to select to make an image, and from these 3 million dots the viewer selects a few dozen each second.

How much sense does this make? Not very much, we would say! To classify radio, paintings, and motion pictures as hot is to ignore theses facts: (1) the ears of the person listening to a symphony on the radio must put together innumerable wave vibrations that reach them each second; (2) the eyes of the person viewing a painting must put together all the thousands of brushstrokes that make up the picture; and (3) despite the argument that McLuhan uses that the motion picture projector does the work for the viewer, when the frame in the projector changes and the screen is left blank as the shutter closes the aperture, the viewer fills in the blank screen in the same way that he or she connects the dots on the TV screen.

Furthermore, print, according to McLuhan, is hot; the printed word is high in definition and requires little participation on the part of the reader. But consider the senses the reader uses to make the individual letters into words, the words into phrases, and the whole into a comprehensible unit: the combined forces of eye and brain as well as the inner ear and the speech muscles.

However, despite his liberal use of overstatement and his failure to document his pronouncements with scientific evidence, we must agree that McLuhan deserves a special place among media's greats. For, more than any other, McLuhan has stimulated creative thought about the mass media of communication.

The N-Step Flow Models. In the early 1940's and 1950s researchers were studying the diffusion of political information. It was found that personal contact and personal persuasion were often more important in influencing decisions than the mass media. A two-step flow of information was hypothesized: "Ideas often flow from radio and print to opinion leaders and from these opinion leaders to the less active sections of the population."[13]

[13]Paul F. Lazarsfeld, Bernard Berelson, and Hazel Gaudet, *The People's Choice* (New York: Columbia University Press, 1948), p. 151.

When this concept was initially introduced it was widely accepted by communication scholars; later, however, it underwent reevaluation as being too narrow, although its significant contribution to understanding the dissemination process was still appreciated. Along the way communication researchers suggested a one-step flow of information as well as multistep flows. One critic, Wilbur Schramm, faulted the hypothesis on several counts, among them: (1) often information flows from the media to the user without the need of a negotiator; (2) opinion leaders often have opinion leaders of their own to seek advice from, hence the concept of opinion leaders and followers is not necessarily supportable; and (3) there are initial information-seeking stages, multistep intermediary stages for reaffirmation, and later dissonance reduction stages adding up to a whole that is much greater than the sum of the parts of the two-step flow.[14]

The apparent value of the two-step flow hypothesis lay in the amount of research it generated and in the refinement of concepts concerning the flow of information. Information diffusion theories are related to those dealing with social categories and social relationships.

The Audience Component

Individual Differences Perspective. Perhaps one of the most interesting areas of mass communication research is that centering about the audience. It is also an area in which a great deal of progress has been made in terms of theoretical research and development.

The individual difference perspective, which was responsible for the death of the bullet theory, emerged after much experimentation and research in learning theories that had their roots in classical conditioning theory and individual motivation. As it became increasingly apparent that *differences in personality traits and attitudes explained differences in human preferences and actions*, certain fundamental postulates about the individual became widely accepted. These were summarized by DeFleur more or less as follows:[15]

[14] Schramm, W., *Men, Messages and Media.*
[15] See Melvin L. DeFleur, *Theories of Mass Communication* (New York: David McKay Co., 1966), p. 121.

1. Human beings vary greatly in their personal psychological organization.

2. Biological endowment and differential learning contributed to individual differences.

3. The individual's psychological makeup that sets him or her apart from others grows out of a set of attitudes, values, and beliefs acquired from his or her learning environments.

4. Personality variables acquired from the social environment provide for the individual's perception of events, which differs from someone else's.

5. An important product of human learning is the acquiring of stable predispositions concerning one's perception of events.

MORE
HUMAN-
ISTIC

Thus it became clear that some of the earlier theories of mass communication such as stimulus-response, the bullet theory, the hypodermic needle theory, and the power of the press theory were greatly in need of revision. People could not be led around by their collective nose, or be buffeted according to the way the wind happened to be blowing. Typical of this new perspective was the concept of the "obstinate audience," an extraordinarily, active, self-reliant audience that searched for what it *wanted* to find.[16] It was only logical then to take the next step of interposing selective attention and selective perception—formulated as basic propositions with regard to the communication behavior of the ordinary person—as an intervening psychological mechanism between stimulus and response in mass communication theory.

> From a multiplicity of available content, the member of the audience selectively attended to messages particularly if they were related to his interests, consistent with his attitudes, congruent with his beliefs, and supportive of his values. His response to such messages was modified by his psychological make-up. . . . Rather than being *uniform* among the mass audience, the effects of the media could now be seen as *varying* from person to person, because of individual differences in psychological structure.[17]

"The individual difference theory is related to the social categories theory and the social relationships theory, which we shall consider next.

---

[16]See Raymond A. Bauer, "The Obstinate Audience: The Influence Process from the Point of View of Social Communication," *American Psychologist*, **19**, 1964, 319–328.
[17]Ibid., p. 122.

Social Categories and Social Relationships Theories. Based on the premise that people can be grouped into broad collectivities on the basis of shared orientations or characteristics, the social categories theory assumes that people belonging to one of such groups will select roughly identical mass communication content and react to it in a fairly uniform manner. *The thesis is that demographic variables such as age, race, sex, income, education, occupation, and place of residence—singly or in combination—may well determine message saliency for any group.* For example, mass communicators know that a persuasive message to gain support for raising social security taxes will tend to win the favor of the old rather than the young. Advertising messages on sun tan oil have greater appeal for whites than for blacks, hair straighteners for blacks than for whites, "living bras" for women than for men, Mercedes Benzes for the higher income brackets than for the lower, speed reading for the executive than for the assembly line worker, mass transit for the urban dweller than for the farmer, and so on.

In addition to defining the audience in terms of rich/poor, young/old, black/white, and other categories, group relationships were found to account for the salience of a message. Reference groups, both formal and informal, are important determinants of mass communication impact. Occupational, educational, religious, political, fraternal, familial, and informal group relationships become critical factors. The social relationships theory, in addition to its obvious linkages with the individual differences theory and the social catgeories theory, is closely related to the entire area of information diffusion

Cultural Norms Theory. Related to the cultural indicators and agenda-setting hypotheses, as well as to McLuhan's multisensory balance theories, *the cultural norms theory holds that the mass media's power to define cultural norms through the facilitation of opinion change and reinforcement, creation of new values, and modification of present attitudes causes the audience to become "different."* The media establish new shared connections, changing the existing norms.

Ludenic Theory: Play. The basis for William Stephenson's ludenic (meaning "play") theory of mass communication is his personal belief that mass communication, for the first time in history, affords the opportunity for subjective manipulation of the media according to personal interests and preferences.[18] Building on the concepts of Huiz-inga, Szasz, Freud, Schramm, and others, Stephenson stresses the role of the individual as consumer/producer, whose efforts in our postin-dustrial society need not be entirely taken up by working in order to survive. The individual may engage in nonproductive, leisuretime ac-tivities. Stephenson applies his notions of work and play to mass media content, a good deal of which may be described as "work," i.e., information. However, even more may be described as belonging to the realm of entertainment. Aside from the obvious entertainment supplied by standard media fare such as books (fiction), magazines (stories), newspapers (comics), radio (music), and television (drama), to cite only a few examples, also available to the consumer are art mu-seums, theaters, ballet, rock concerts, symphonies, and scores of other cultural carriers.

The major weakness of Stephenson's theory according to some critics is its basic emphasis on play and downgrading of the informa-tion function. Yet his theory is also acclaimed as a brilliant explication of the play-pleasure aspects of communication. This theory is related to some of the uses and gratifications theories as well as to the per-spectives of the "obstinate audience" and the consumer as producer.

Summary The area of audience control of the communication process is a fruitful one for inquiry. The concept of selective exposure places heavy stress on the fact that some messages are much sought after whereas others are actively avoided. The concept of selective percep-tion stresses that the audience attends to the mass media in terms of previous experience and current predispositions, with such factors as individual mood, need, and memory figuring heavily in the percep-tion process. Finally, the concept of selective retention is tied to the notion that messages are deposited in our personal memory banks ac-cording to the salience of the message to our interests and our beliefs.

The Effects Component

Although the greater proportion of communication research has cen-tered about the impact of the media on people, we should point out again, as we have done earlier in this book, that along with many

[18]See William Stephenson, *The Play Theory of Mass Communication* (Chicago: University of Chicago Press, 1967).

other communication theorists we do not consider the "effects" component essential to the communication process. By this we mean that the communication process requires only four components in order to work: a communicator, a message, a channel, and a receiver. Effects, although not an essential component, are obviously important: few wish to communicate unless they could see the results of their effort. For this reason we have included the "effects" category in our inventory and, in fact, devote our next chapter entirely to the subject of communication effects. Therefore, our review of these theories in the present chapter will be brief.

Uses and Gratification Approach. Modern mass communication researchers during the past few years have concentrated heavily on the media gratification and utility school of thought, and this approach may well preoccupy the field for the next decade. What is the uses and gratification approach? Why is it called an "approach" and not a "theory"?

Simply it is an exploration of the way individuals use the mass media of communication to satisfy their needs and achieve their goals. So it is something less than a theory, being rather a way of looking at things—an approach. People select to use the mass media from a variety of alternative resources and activities that are made available to them in their environment; the approach is simply to ask them why they make the choices that they do and to determine whether their needs have been met. According to Lundberg and Hulten, the uses and gratifications approach (they call it a "model") rests on several assumptions: [19]

 1. The audience, being active, seeks out specific types of media content to satisfy its needs.

 2. People select their media fare from a cafeteria of all kinds of offerings, including selecting from competing media as well as from different, more conventional, and more traditional modes of need fulfillment (e.g., visiting friends, engaging in conversation, going for walks, daydreaming, sleeping).

 3. People are sufficiently aware of how the media satisfy their needs and interests and are articulate enough to verbalize this.

4. Audience use of the media should be explored without mak-

[19] Lundberg and O. Hulten, *Individen och Massmedia* (Stockholm: EFI, 1968).

ing value judgments about the cultural significance of their mass media consumption behavior.

In summary, it is no longer fashionable to ask the question "What are the effects of the mass media?" Rather, the question is posed, "What do people do with the mass media?" How do the mass media satisfy our needs and our wants? What part do the mass media play in our education, our political life, our cultural world? How can we better utilize the media to our society's greatest advantage? These are the issues.

Social Learning Theory. In the next chapter when we examine the media's influences on antisocial and prosocial behavior, we will discuss the role played by modeling, imitation, and identification.

Theory of Effects and No-Effects Theory. The theory of effects deals with the interaction of mass communication with other forces; the "no-effects" theory is more difficult to explain. Some theorists maintain that to achieve reinforcement—a common effect of mass communication—is to achieve "no effects." Achieving no effects, according to others, is to achieve an effect.

Theories of Violence

DeFleur and Ball-Rokeach brilliantly show the relationship of the four major theories of televised violence to the three perspectives describing how individuals encounter the media, that is, as filtered through their unique and individual differences, the groups and individuals to whom they relate, and the social categories to which they might be assigned.[20] Although we have charted these theories in Table 4-4, a few additional words of explanation are in order. In the 1960s and early 1970s, there was a good deal of concern in the United States over the potential connection between violence in real life and televised violence. Inasmuch as the nation's youth were the first TV generation as well as obvious participants in real-life violence, it was thought that

[20] Melvin DeFleur and Sandra Ball-Rokeach, *Theories of Mass Communication,* 3rd ed. (New York: David McKay Co., 1975), Chapter 10.

Table 4-4. The Major Theories of Televised Violence as Related to the Individual Differences, Social Categories, and Social Relations Perspectives ¶

Theories of Violence	Major Assumptions	Hypotheses	Related Mass Communication Effects Perspectives
1. Catharsis (Feshbach)	In the course of the day, people build up frustrations and tendencies for aggressive behavior. People relieve their frustrations through vicarious participation in others' aggressions.	1. The TV viewer's exposure to violence on television diminishes the probability of his or her own violent behavior.	1. The *individual differences perspective* leads us to correlate the level of the individual's frustration and hostility prior to exposure to cathartic satisfaction achieved after exposure to violent TV content.
		2. Televised violence serves a greater cathartic function for lower-class than middle-class audiences.	2. The *social categories perspective* posits that group and family relationships affect the perception of media messages, hence the greater catharsis need for the lower-class audience member. People of the same social class, sharing similar values and attitudes, will respond in similar ways to violent TV programming content.

2. Aggressive cues theories (stimulating effects) (Berkowitz)	A person aroused physiologically and emotionally by exposure to aggressive stimuli may behave aggressively.	1. The greater the frustration at the time of exposure to a violent TV program, the greater the likelihood of an aggressive response and increase in the degree of aggressivity of response. 2. The more TV violence is seen as justified, the greater the likelihood of aggressive responses. 3. The greater the similarity of the TV portrayal to real-life anger-provoking circumstances, the greater the likelihood of aggressive response. 4. Similarly, the greater the guilt evoked in the viewer for the pain and suffering of the victim, the lower the probability of an aggressive response (inhibition of aggressive tendencies).	According to the *individual differences perspective*, differences in level of frustration or arousal at the time of exposure affect the probability of aggression after exposure to violent TV programs. The viewer selectively emphasizes the victim's pain and suffering when the camera focuses on painful consequences of aggression, resulting in the viewer's inhibition of aggressive behavior. Also, the extent of prior exposure via TV and personal experience to the pain and gore consequences of violence may affect the degree of inhibition.

Table 4-4. (continued)

Theories of Violence	Major Assumptions	Hypotheses	Related Mass Communication Effects Perspectives
3. Observational learning theory (Bandura and Walters)	Aggressive behavior may be learned through observation of aggression in TV programs, and behavior modeling may occur.	To the extent that TV violence provides opportunities for audiences to learn aggression, to the extent that violent characters are presented as behavior models for viewers, audience aggression will result. People will exhibit learned violent behavior according to their expectation of reward for such behavior.	1. The *individual differences perspective* and the *social relations perspective* hold according to the extent to which viewers encounter real social situations similar to those presented in TV programs. 2. The *social categories perspective* also holds in that females behave less aggressively because female sex roles and subcultural norms against aggressive female behavior reduce the likelihood of girls' displaying learned aggressive behavior.

4. Reinforcement theory (Klapper)

TV violence serves to reinforce the viewer's established patterns of violent behavior that he or she brings to TV viewing.

1. The *individual differences perspective* holds that selective perception accounts for why people with different characteristics are reinforced by the same violent TV program.

2. The *social categories perspective* holds that individuals belonging to the same social categories and sharing similar norms, attitudes, values, and prior experiences will respond very similarly to violent television programs.

3. The *social relations perspective* holds that the role expectations and norms of friends or family will have more effect on the viewer's aggressive behavior than will the behavior of violent television characters, provided that social relationships at work and home are stable.

1. Television violence produces neither increases nor decreases in the probability of audience aggression.

2. To the extent that persons adopt norms and attitudes that support violence as a means to personal and social ends will they perceive the violent actions of TV characters as supporting (reinforcing) their norms and attitudes. For those who have antiviolence norms and attitudes, TV violence will be perceived as supporting nonviolence.

However, for young people and adolescents who lack stable relationships with family, friends, and teachers, violent TV programming may be perceived as filling a void in their lives. The beliefs and actions of violent TV characters may be used as guides for their own behavior.

* Based on Melvin L. DeFleur and Sandra Ball-Rokeach, "Television and Violence," in *Theories of Mass Communication* (New York: David McKay Co., 1975), pp. 218–235.

there might be a cause-and-effect relationship. Research conducted by George Gerbner and his associates in 1969 indicated that 82 per cent of all prime-time television entertainment could be categorized as violent.[21]

The salient aspects of the theories of violence are as follows:

1. The *catharsis theory* posits that people build up frustrations in the normal course of daily life that eventually lead them to engage in aggressive activity. Catharsis is the relief of this frustration; television therefore provides an excellent opportunity for relief through vicarious interaction. It has also been posited that catharsis may be more important for individuals of lower socioeconomic status than for the middle and upper classes, who have the benefits of family unity and socialization. Because catharsis is more effective for those having greater need, both the individual differences and social categories perspectives are central to this theory; however, the theory is not supported by research.

2. The *aggressive cues (stimulating effects) theory* assumes that exposure to violence increases the level of physiological and emotional arousal, thereby increasing the probability of aggressive behavior. The theory further states that such factors as the individual's level of frustration at the time of exposure, the justification for aggression as depicted in the program, and the similarity between an individual's real-life experiences and the televised violence determine the level of aggressive response. The individual differences perspective and selective perception are the basis for this theory; however, the theory is not supported by research.

3. The *observational learning theory* makes the assumption that individuals can learn aggressive behavior through observation of television programs, modeling their behavior on that of the television characters they observe. The theory posits that television programs, by providing opportunities to learn through modeling increase the probability of audience aggression. Such factors as the expectation for reward for the learned violent behavior, the similarity between real and televised situa-

[21] George Gerbner et al., "Dimensions of Violence in Television Drama," in Baker and Ball (eds.), *Violence and the Media* (Washington, D.C.: U.S. Government Printing Office, 1969), pp. 313–327.

tions, and the anticipation of social support by coviewers allegedly determine the program's impact. This theory, which involves both the social categories and social relations perspectives, is supported by research.

4. The *reinforcement theory* states that televised violence reinforces whatever established patterns of violent behavior are possessed by the individual; the theory in itself is said to produce *no significant increases or decreases* in the probability of audience aggression. Such factors as cultural norms, values, social roles, personality characteristics, and family or peer influences are to be considered in terms of reinforcing the viewer's response, although clearly the exceptions to the reinforcement theory apply to those individuals who lack personal and social stability. This theory also has its roots in the individual differences perspective and selective perception; the research findings in the area, however, have been largely discounted.

In conclusion, the theories of the effects of televised violence have been largely based on research conducted in the laboratory, utilizing experimental research designs. Moreover, these theories have been based on short term effects; clearly, long-term field research studies are needed as a basis for comparison with these findings.

Summary

We have considered several theoretical prespectives of the mass communication process as promoted by the field's leading scholars and researchers throughout its brief but remarkable history. We have seen these perspectives evolve from rather elementary definitions of the mass communication process to more sophisticated theories of the interrelationships that impact on the process. We have also looked at theories of televised violence and related them to the ways in which individuals encounter the media and have concluded that there is a need for long-term field studies. The present emphasis in the study of mass communication effects has shifted from short term to long term; that is, it is now believed that the daily media fill in the long run becomes mass media's more permanent and potentially more irreversible deposit in human consciousness.

Chapter 5
Mass Communication
Effects

If you're ever attacked in a hallway, don't yell "Help,"
yell "Fire."
New York City policeman

Throughout the brief history of mass communication, the preoccupation of researchers has largely been the study of effects, resulting in
the accumulation of a large body of literature on this subject. However, only recently has any serious effort been made to systematize
this vast and uneven accumulation, and although the task is difficult
the goal of this chapter is to outline some of the more fruitful insights
of mass communication effects research. Before dealing with effects,
however, it will be helpful to take a brief look at both audience satura-
tion/impact studies and mass communications functions.

Audience Saturation/Impact Studies

We are told that mass communication usage can be broadly predicted
according to demographics or what some communicologists term simply "social categories." This means that mass communication behavior
can be explained according to such variables as the sex, age, education, and interests of the audience. For example, recently a group of 45
undergraduate students at the State University of New York at Buffalo
were asked to keep a record of their communication activities for a
period of 24 hours. It was found that the mean average of their communication activities was close to that of a group of 41 Columbia Uni-

versity students as reported by Davison, Boylan, and Yu.[1] The average achieved by the 45 SUNY/Buffalo students was 15 hours and 35 minutes, distributed as follows:

Television	1 hour 10 minutes
Newspaper	47 minutes
Radio	1 hour 33 minutes
Magazines and journals	25 minutes
Books	2 hours 36 minutes
Recordings	18 minutes
Motion pictures	10 minutes
Billboards, posters, handbills	08 minutes
Personal conversation (less than 5 minutes)	2 hours 02 minutes
Personal conversation (more than 5 minutes)	2 hours 34 minutes
Group discussions (3 or more involved)	1 hour 12 minutes
Lectures	2 hours 30 minutes
Other (reading personal mail, junk mail, other)	10 minutes

The students expressed surprise that their communication activities took up so much time, although many of them pointed out that these activities shifted not only from day to day but also on a weekly basis (on weekends mass media usage was higher and in some instances interpersonal communication behavior patterns were different if not lower) and a yearly basis (vacation times were different quantitatively and qualitatively). Some also noted that their somewhat high TV consumption for the particular 24 hours in question reflected a 2 to 3 hours' sitting to watch *Gone with the Wind*, and others noted that their radio listening included their use of radio programs as background while they read or conversed with their friends. Virtually all of their book reading, they maintained, was done in connection with their school work.

Comparing their mass communication behavior to that of the typical American male between the ages of 35 and 45 years of age, we find that the average college student spends less time with television, radio, and magazines but more time with newspapers and movies. Compared to a school child between 9 and 10 years old, the college student spends less time with television and record playing but more time listening to radio and reading. Compared to a group of Philadel-

[1]See W. Phillips Davison, James Boylan, and Frederick T. C. Yu, *Mass Media Systems and Effects* (New York: Praeger Publishers, 1976), p. 105.

Table 5-1. Average Mass Media Usage by College Students Compared to That of Other Groups

	SUNY/Buffalo* College Group	9–10 Year Olds†	Philadelphia Teenagers	Adult Male 35–45 Years
Television	1 hr 10 min	4 hr	4 hr	3 hr
Radio	1 hr 33 min	1 hr	2 hr	2 hr
Daily newspaper	47 min	Not reported	Some	15–30 min
Magazines	25 min	Not reported	Some	Some
Movies	10 min	Not reported	2 movies/mo	0
Recordings	18 min	30 min	1 hr	0

Reported in Bradley S. Greenberg, "Mass Communication and Social Behavior," in Gerhard J. Hanneman and William J. McEwen, *Communication and Behavior* (Reading, Mass.: Addison-Wesley, 1975), pp. 269–270.
* Based on study at SUNY/Buffalo.
† Does not include time spent in school media-related activities.

phia teenagers, the college student watches less television, listens less to radio, perhaps goes to fewer movies, and listens less to recordings. However, the college student spends more time reading newspapers and magazines than do the Philadelphia teenagers (see Table 5-1).

In summary, we believe it reasonable to state that one effect of mass communications lies in the decisions that users must make about how much time to spend with the various media available.

Functions of Mass Communication

The next step in our attempt to explore mass communication effects is the determination of the role of the mass media in our society. The first attempt to do this was in 1948 when Harold Lasswell, a political scientist, noted that communication specialists carry out three functions: (1) surveillance of the environment, (2) correlation of the parts of society in responding to the environment, and (3) transmission of the social heritage from one generation to the next.[2] To the Lasswell typology, Charles Wright added a fourth function—entertainment—explaining that it probably never occurred to a political scientist to include such a category.[3]

[2] See Harold D. Lasswell, "The Structure and Function of Communication in Society," in Lyman Bryson (ed.), *The Communication of Ideas* (New York: Harper & Row, 1948).
[3] Charles Wright, *Mass Communication: A Sociological Perspective* (New York: Random House, 1975).

In its simplest definition, *surveillance* refers to the watchdog function of the mass media, i.e., the handling of news. *Correlation* refers to the interpretation of news events, i.e., the combining of fact and opinion such as is done by columnists, editorial writers, writers and producers of documentaries, press secretaries, and television news analysts. *Transmission* of the social heritage function is simply the mass media's reinforcing of behavioral norms by holding up a mirror to society, reflecting standards for behavior. The *entertainment* function is perhaps the function of the mass media best appreciated by audiences the world over.

If the mass media are to be credited with carrying out functional roles, they must also be debited for carrying out allegedly dysfunctional roles; for example, the outcome of surveillance—warning society and individuals of natural dangers, war, attack, and so forth—may foster panic, create instability, and promote anxiety or apathy. The socially positive correlation function of aiding mobilization, defining important issues, and promoting efficiency through the assimilation of news also carries dysfunctional threats of increased social conformity, increased passivity, and weakened critical faculties. Although the cultural transmission function increases social cohesion by widening the base for shared norms and experiences, reduces idiosyncratic behavior and anomie, and carries out the continuing education and lifelong functions of society, by the same token the mass media must take the responsibility for fostering the lowest common denominator concept of our society as well as for depersonalizing the acts of socialization. And, finally, although the mass media can take full credit for entertaining millions, they are also accountable for lowering tastes, fostering passivity, and permitting escapism.

Mass Media Accessibility

At this point a comment on accessibility is probably in order. The accessibility of the mass media in the United States makes them potent forces for advertisers and political candidates, to name just two categories. Our most recent statistics claim that 97 per cent of all American households own at least one television set, with more than 30 per cent of these households owning two or three sets, and that there are more radios—300 million—than people in the United States (i.e., three radios for every two people). Television sets are said to outnumber telephones, bathtubs, or toilets in the United States.

As reported by Edwin Diamond:

> The TV set, on the average, flickered more for women than for men, more for people over fifty than for those under fifty, more for blacks, than for whites, more for the poor than for the rich, and more for the grade-school-educated than for the college-educated-but not much more.[4]

Basing his comments on a study by Robert Bower (*Television and the Public*) Diamond concluded that for both the college-educated and the working class "in the 1970s the most frequent human activity after sleep and ahead of working, eating, or making love" was television watching.[5] Not swayed by the power attributed to television as "the great crowd catcher" with the "potential for the control of human beings and nations" greater than the threat "of the atomic bomb or any weapon yet devised," Diamond believes that "It is necessary to look into what brings viewers to the set in the first place, what is happening on the screen, and what the viewers take away from the set."[6] We shall comment on Diamond's statement later in this chapter.

To summarize our thinking at this point, we believe that the student cannot look at "effects" in isolation but must take into account the aspects we have discussed thus far: audience media consumption, mass media functions, and media accessibility. Within this context, we can then begin to ponder the significance of the statement made by Bernard Berelson:

> Now, in the 1940's, a body of empirical research is accumulating which provides some refined knowledge on the effect of communication on public opinion and promises to provide a good deal more in the next years.
>
> But what has such research contributed to the problem? . . . The proper answer to the general question, the answer which constitutes a useful formulation for research purposes, is this: Some kind of *communication* on some kinds of *issues,* brought to the attention of some kinds of *people* under some kinds of *conditions,* have some kinds of *effects.*[7]

In the pages that follow we shall explore some of these propositions.

[4] See Edwin Diamond, *The Tin Kazoo: Television, Politics and the News* (Cambridge, Mass.: MIT Press, 1975), pp. 13–14.

[5] Ibid., p. 14.

[6] Ibid., p. 17.

[7] Bernard Berelson, "Communications and Public Opinions," in Wilbur Schramm (ed.), *Mass Communications* (Urbana: University of Illinois Press, 1949), p. 500.

General Considerations

Now we shall sketch in a bit more of the "theory" with regard to human behavior. Some of the considerations we ask the student to bear in mind are the following:

1. *Laboratory research versus field research.* There will generally be wide discrepancies in the findings of laboratory research versus field research. The more dramatic effects will occur in the laboratory under controlled conditions, where subjects are generally exposed to the communication situation under optimum conditions. The effect, as a consequence, will be dramatic. Field research, however, must contend with the less structured conditions of reality. It is therefore not surprising that the communication effect will be less dramatic.

2. *Selective perception.* We can never underestimate the human need to achieve balance and consistency and to avoid those communications that challenge this condition. Accordingly, people

   choose to expose themselves to information which is in accord with their existing ideas; they selectively give their attention to communications with which they expect to agree; and if they learn something which conflicts with their attitudes or values, they forget it, dismiss it as unimportant, or reinterpret it so as to minimize the dissonance.[8]

3. *Attitude change.* True attitude change is rarely accomplished by the mass media. More often, the media canalize behavior—that is, rather than forming or changing attitudes, the media direct attitudes in one direction or another. An often cited example of this phenomenon is the glut of toothpaste commercials. The advertisers are not trying to persuade people to adopt the attitude that brushing their teeth is good; they already know this and they have already been socialized to do so. The selection of a particular brand of toothpaste is the canalizing of this attitudinal behavior. Thus *any* toothpaste touted by the commercials has a good chance of persuading people to "try it, you'll like it."

4. *Conditions affecting the level of effect.* There are a number of conditions that affect the level and direction of effects.

[8] Davison, Boylan, and Yu, op. cit., p. 138.

a. *Attributes of the source.* Is the source perceived as trustworthy or not trustworthy? Is the source prestigeful? Is the source someone with whom the audience member can identify?

b. *Attributes of the channel.* People of higher socioeconomic standing perceive the print medium as being more credible, whereas those of lower socioeconomic standing lean toward television. A channel is used according to its availability; thus in sparsely populated areas, such as the north of Canada, television may be unavailable, and in areas where the illiteracy rate is high there may be no printed materials. Permanency of the message is an attribute of print. Multiplicative power (its ability to cover extensive geographic areas speedily) and the timeliness and simultaneity of the message are attributes of the channel that affect its effectiveness.

c. *Attributes of the message.* How does the message come across? Is it clear or unclear? Is it plagued by channel or semantic noise? Does it appeal to the emotions or to reason? Which strategy is being used: one side of the argument? two sides? which comes first, pro or con? If the message carries information of threat, is it strong, moderate, or weak?

d. *Attributes of the audience.* How is it that the same message elicits different reactions and interpretations from the audience? What is there about the audience member that explains this? How do personality and educational differences account for the greater persuasiveness of a message for one person than for another? How does the social setting, i.e., interaction with friends and family, account for effects impact? How does attitude strength figure in? What is the relative impact of interpersonal communication versus the mass media in terms of change/effect? And what of the impact of situational factors? A message delivered in peacetime versus wartime? A period of crisis versus noncrisis? Is it the power of the media that accounts for the particular agenda or would the event have happened without the assistance of the media?

Dramatic Effects

Do the mass media have dramatic effects? As simple as this question may seem, it is controversial; it is defensible and it is refutable. We believe it is not that the media are so persuasive but rather that the people who use them (both communicator and consumer) determine the media's impact.

Case History 1. Take, for example, the infamous Orson Welles radio broadcast of *War of the Worlds* on October 30, 1938. The times were tense; the threat of war clouds was hanging over Europe. It was the year that Germany annexed Austria and that France and Great Britain appeased Adolph Hitler with the Munich Pact, allowing Germany to occupy the Sudetenland. The situational context was "right" for the panic brought about by Welles's spoof of an invasion by men from Mars.

The theatrical framework for the play was also right: the background was familiar strains of band music, as on any other ordinary evening in America. But suddenly the music was interrupted by a news bulletin: astronomers had noted a number of baffling explosions on Mars. Back to the music. Another interruption: an expert attempted to explain the cause of the explosions. Back to the music. And so it went: a seesaw of normality and alarm. The audience was being led by its imagination into the center of a growing crisis. The reaction was a mixed response to panic: flight, disbelief, hiding, prayer, thoughts of suicide. The easily persuaded somehow did not hear the carefully worded announcement that it was a dramatization; obviously, they did not bother to check out the discrepancies—phony-sounding names and places, too speedy mobilization of national guardsmen. Of course not! They were not listening! They had selectively blocked out all of the reality checks from their consciousness.

Even more hideously unbelievable is what happened in Ecuador when a translation of the broadcast was aired some 10 years later. Once again history was to repeat itself: the announcements that it was a dramatic program were somehow missed. On realizing that they had been duped, thousands of Ecuadorians spilled into the streets, mobbed the station broadcasting the program, firebombed it, and killed six of its employees. That night the Ecuadorian army dispersed the mob.

Case History 2. In the 1940s, of course, the United States was deeply embroiled in World War II. This time the organizers of a deliberate mass persuasion campaign took advantage of the situational factor of the war, and with an assist from the medium of radio produced a rather startling effect. During the course of a single day, Kate Smith, a popular singer, pleaded with her listeners to purchase war bonds. All day long, Kate Smith sang and talked, talked and sang, in her sacrificial bid to sell war bonds to bring the war to an end. The listeners could hear Kate Smith growing more tired, more hoarse, more weak and faint, but still she carried on! Still she sang, talked, pleaded— good, wholesome, motherly, patriotic Kate Smith! She was doing her part. Why shouldn't her listeners do theirs? Why shouldn't they pledge to buy war bonds? They did! That day 39 million dollars' worth of war bonds were sold, achieving something of a record and making media effects history!

Case History 3. In late 1963, 175 million Americans sat in shock and silence in front of their television sets as the story of the assassination and funeral of President John F. Kennedy began to unfold. Television, so often a scapegoat for all that was wrong in America, had this time "come of age" and with extraordinary dignity and skill. It was agreed that

> During those four fantastic days, television was as integral a part of the nation's life as food or sleep . . . the greatest escapist medium ever devised made escape impossible.[9]

There were those who said that television governed the United States during those sorrowful days. Americans cried and consoled each other at what was perhaps the best-attended wake of all time.

Despite the ability of the media to achieve the dramatic and startling effects described in these three case histories, the media do not always activate such emotional responses. In the remaining pages of this chapter we shall record some of the less spectacular effects of the mass media.

---

[9] "As 175 Million Americans Watched," *Newsweek*, December 9, 1963, p. 52.

Learning Without Involvement

The possibility has often been raised of a connection between the success of advertising and the achievement of more important mass communication effects—such as the changing of attitudes. If commercials are so successful in activating people to purchase products, then why not use these same techniques to motivate people to do more important things? It makes good sense to ask the question; but the answer is not calculated to be helpful in solving the problem. The techniques of Madison Avenue are just not appropriate to attitude and behavioral change campaigns, for the advertising people simply do not get involved with attitudes. Then how do they accomplish so successfully what behavioral scientists have not been able to do? The trick is nonsense and redundancy carried to the point where the response can be learned without any emotional impact on the learner. Moreover, what is learned is will-of-the-wispish; although the beginning phrase or two and the ending phrase or two of the message are remembered, everything in between is quickly forgotten. Attitude adoption requires much more personal investment.

Modeling and Imitation

It has long been held that children learn their behaviors through modeling and imitation. Television and the movies are schools for children, although much of the learning is unintentionally transmitted. One of the strongest criticisms of the mass media, as has been pointed out earlier, is that children learn to behave aggressively as a result of the endless hours they spend watching violence on TV. Laboratory studies have shown the profoundly damaging effects of violence on children, but parental guidance, the influence of school and church, as well as a number of other inhibitors make mass media violence less threatening. However, it has been argued that "learning" does not require the learner to act out the learned behavior immediately: it can be stored for later, more appropriate retrieval. Children do not easily forget a behavior pattern they have learned from the media. They are incredibly talented as mimics and copiers.

Uses and Gratifications Studies

One of the earliest approaches in the study of mass communication effects was that of media uses and gratifications. The focus of this approach in finding out the gratifications people received from the mass media was the survey—i.e., asking them. Herzog, for example, explored the gratifications derived from quiz programs in 1942; Warner and Henry surveyed the audience of the daytime serial (radio) in 1948; Bernard Berelson took advantage of a newspaper strike in New York City to determine the functional role of the daily newspaper in 1949; and in that same year Wolfe and Fishe explored the gratifications children received from reading the comics. Although rich in insights, these studies were methodologically weak. For one thing, they failed to explore the linkages between the gratifications that were determined and the psychological and sociological origins of the needs satisfied. There was little effort to interrelate media functions and media gratifications, resulting in findings that failed to lead to theoretical formulations of functions/gratifications.

But in time the research methodology became more sophisticated, closing the gap between media functions and user needs. All over the world—in the United States, Great Britain, Japan, Israel, Sweden, Finland, Belgium, France, and Germany—gratification and use studies were conducted that concentrated on

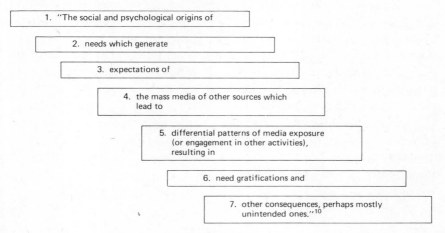

1. "The social and psychological origins of

2. needs which generate

3. expectations of

4. the mass media of other sources which lead to

5. differential patterns of media exposure (or engagement in other activities), resulting in

6. need gratifications and

7. other consequences, perhaps mostly unintended ones."[10]

[10] Elihu Katz, Jay G. Blumer, and Michael Gurevitch, "Uses and Gratifications Research," *Public Opinion Quarterly*, Winter 1973–1974, 510.

Three general approaches have been followed in these studies: (1) specification of needs, followed by determination of the extent to which the media gratify them; (2) observation of gratifications, followed by an attempt to reconstruct the needs that are gratified; and (3) determination of the social origins of audience expectations and gratifications.

However, one attempt that was made to match the four media functions (surveillance, correlation, cultural transmission, and entertainment) to the range of functions revealed by the uses and gratifications studies—diversion (including escape from the humdrum of daily existence, escape from problems, and emotional release), personal relationships (including vicarious companionship and social utility), personal identity, and surveillance—found the match to be less than perfect.

A study that greatly enlightened needs/gratifications research was one done in Israel.[11] Because of the peculiarities of the media in Israel, the findings are not broadly generalizable to media in other countries; nevertheless, the data drawn from this survey can serve for cross-cultural comparisons. The authors based their study on a list of 35 needs statements that they took from the literature and supplemented with their own insights into the functions the media serve in Israel. Among the findings were that newspapers best serve the need of integrating people into the sociopolitical order, books best serve the need of knowing oneself, and television is less helpful as a means of escape than cinema and books. The last we might expect to be different in the United States, where television is the primary medium. But, perhaps, even more important than the findings specifically related to the media was the discovery that alternative modes of satisfying needs—friends/family, holidays, and cultural activities—were often more important than the mass media.

As simple and straightforward as the uses and gratifications approach may seem, the student is cautioned to bear in mind that the motives of the audience member in attending to a particular message importantly determine its influence.

[11] Elihu Katz, Michael Gurevitch, and Hadassah Haas, "On the Use of the Mass Media for Important Things," *American Sociological Review*, **38**, April 1973, 164–181.

Conclusion

Although Joseph Klapper's study on the effects of mass communication is almost 20 years old, it has managed to survive as the most prescriptive of all the studies of effects.[12] Klapper summarizes the findings of hundreds of small studies as five simple laws:

1. Mass Communication *ordinarily* does not serve as a necessary and sufficient cause of audience effects, but rather functions among and through a nexus of mediating factors and influences.
2. The mediating factors . . . typically render mass communication a contributory agent, but not the sole cause, in a process of reinforcing the existing conditions . . . the media are more likely to reinforce than to change.
3. On such occasions as mass communication does function in the service of change . . .
a) the mediating factors will be found to be inoperative and the effect of the media will be found to be direct; or
b) the mediating factors, which normally favor reinforcement, will be found to be themselves impelling toward change.
4. There are certain residual situations in which mass communication seems to produce direct effects . . . to serve certain psycho-physical functions.
5. The efficacy of mass communications . . . is affected by various aspects of the media and communications themselves or of the communication situation.[13]

There is no question that the mass media play an important role in society. Their impact in social change, advertising, cultural taste, instruction, goal achievement, politics, and image and empire building is not to be denied; however, it must not be exaggerated or taken out of the context of the greater social order and the myriad of other important influences. In summary, the media do have effects—some spectacular, but most of them unassuming and quiet. As Schramm has said:

The effects of communication that have most to do with determining what we are and do are the quiet effects of the never-ceasing flow of information to us, through us, from us. Our ways of seeking information and giving it determine a great part of our life patterns and the way we spend our time . . . our picture of our environment and our image of ourselves . . . the many skills we possess and the borders of our knowl-

[12] Joseph Klapper, The Effects of Mass Communication (New York: The Free Press, 1960).
[13] Ibid., p. 8.

edge and understanding. . . . Communication researchers have to face up to the need of studying quiet continuing effects that in perspective, overshadow the more spectacular and more easily measurable ones.[14]

One of the more exciting approaches in mass communication in recent years is DeFleur and Ball-Rokeach's tripartite audience-media-society relationships model, an integrative approach to mass media effects. According to DeFleur and Ball-Rokeach, the media exist in a subsystem of the larger social system to which the audience member relates. All three systems—media, society, and audience—are in dynamic states of dependency and interdependency. They state:

> This general societal system sets important limitations and boundaries on the media system and has considerable impact on its characteristics, information-delivery functions and operating procedures. The societal system also has enormous impact upon persons; it gives rise to mechanisms that inhibit arbitrary media influence, such as individual differences, membership in social categories, and participation in social relations. The societal system also operates to create needs within persons that facilitate media alteration effects, namely the needs to understand, act in, and escape in fantasy from one's world.[15]

Their complex model is also a feedback model in that the effects of mass media messages on the audience about a particular event may themselves trigger another chain of events. Finally, DeFleur and Ball-Rokeach caution that as in any integrative theory the researcher has to go for empirical testing to the specific theories of which it is composed, not to the adduced abstract integrations. Although their theory may seem overwhelming, it nevertheless represents an important first step in the development of the overall theory of mass communication effects that has so far eluded the field.

---

[14] Wilbur Schramm, *Men, Messages and Media: A Look at Human Communication* (New York: Harper & Row, 1973), p. 233.

[15] Melvin DeFleur and Sandra Ball-Rokeach, *Theories of Mass Communication*, 3rd ed. (New York: David McKay Co., 1975), p. 276.

Part Two Readings

Aldrich, Pearl. *The Impact of Mass Media.* New Rochelle, N.J.: Hayden Book Co., 1975.

Blumler, Jay, and Katz, Elihu. *The Uses and Gratifications Approach to Mass Communications Research.* Sage Annual Review of Communication Research, Vol. III. Beverly Hills, Calif.: Sage Publications, 1975.

Boorstin, Daniel J. *The Image: A Guide to Pseudo-events in America.* New York: Harper & Row, 1964.

Browne, Ray B., and Madden, David. *Popular Culture Explosion: Experiencing Mass Media.* Dubuque, Ia.: W. C. Brown Co., 1972.

Ellul, Jacques. *Propaganda: The Formation of Men's Attitudes.* New York: Vintage Books, 1965.

Goldhamer, Herbert, ed. *The Social Effects of Communication Technology.* Santa Monica, Calif.: Rand Corp., 1970.

Innis, Harold A. *The Bias of Communication.* Toronto: University of Toronto Press, 1951.

Katz, Elihu, and Lazarsfeld, Paul F. *Personal Influence: The Part Played by People in the Flow of Mass Communication.* New York: The Free Press, 1969.

Liebert, Robert M., Neale, John M., and Davison, Emily S. *The Early Window: Effects of Television on Children and Youth.* New York: Pergamon Press, 1973.

Lindzey, Gardner, and Aronson, Elliot, eds. *The Handbook of Social Psychology,* 2nd ed. Vol. II: *Research Methods.* Reading, Mass.: Addison-Wesley, 1968.

McQuail, Dennis. *Towards a Sociology of Mass Communications.* London: Collier-Macmillan, 1969.

McLuhan, Marshall. *Understanding Media: The extensions of Man.* New York: McGraw-Hill, 1966.

Schramm, Wilbur, Lyle, Jack, and Pool, Ithiel de Sola. *The People Look at Educational Television.* Stanford, Calif.: Stanford University Press, 1963.

Shannon, Claude E., and Weaver, Warren. *The Mathematical Theory of Communication.* Urbana: University of Illinois Press, 1949.

Steiner, Gary. *The People Look at Television.* New York: Knopf, 1963.

Tunstall, Jeremy, ed. *Media Sociology: A Reader.* Urbana: University of Illinois Press, 1970.

Voelker, Francis, and Voelker, Ludmila. *Mass Media: Forces in Our Society,* 2nd ed. New York: Harcourt Brace Jovanovich, 1975.

Part Three

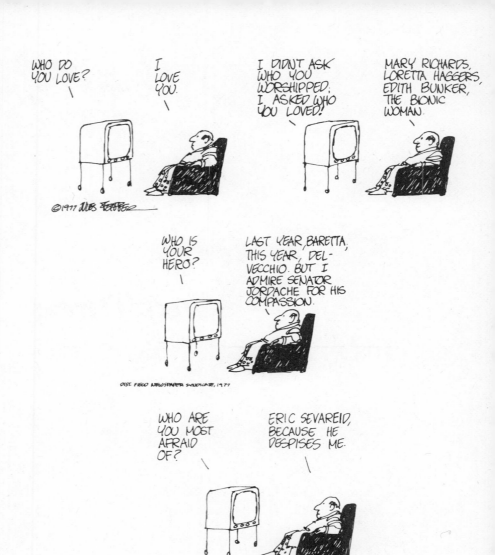

National and International Systems

Chapter 6
Mass Communication: National and International Perspectives

Media of communication . . . are vast social metaphors
that not only transmit information but determine what is
knowledge, that not only orient us to the world but tell us
what kind of world exists, that not only excite and delight
our sense, but by altering the ratio of sensory equipment
which we use actually change our character.
James W. Carey on Marshall McLuhan

International News-Gathering Agencies

There are six major international news-gathering and -disseminating agencies: Agence France-Presse (AFP), Associated Press (AP), Reuters, Telegrafnoie Agenstvo Sovetskavo Soiuza (Soviet Telegraph Agency or TASS), United Press International (UPI), and Hsinhua (New China News Agency). A number of limited agencies exist in various other parts of the world. These include agencies such as Novosti, a Soviet feature service, Prensa Latina, the main Cuban news agency, and Deutsche Presse Agentur (DPA), the West German agency. The six major international news-gathering agencies dominate the dissemination of news items. Minor national agencies supplement the services of the international giants. During the 1976 UNESCO meeting on mass media in Nairobi, Kenya, several Third World delegations expressed interest in forming a Third World news agency that does not have a colonial past. Alfred Opubor of Nigeria and Paul Ansah of Ghana called a meeting in 1977 to discuss formulation of an African agency.

The development of the major news-gathering agencies began in the nineteenth century at a time when British colonial power was at its height. Economics and politics influenced the development of the international news agencies. Among the first attempts to compile news were Bostonian Samuel Gilbert's news books for shippers in 1811. Because much of Boston was interested in shipping news, an assistant, Samuel Topliff, Jr., soon began to sail out to meet the bigger ships to get the news and returned to post it in the news books as general and commerical news. Newspaper owners began to use the compilations of news in American coffeehouses.[1] In order to offset costs, the coffeehouses, following Gilbert and Topliff's Exchange Coffee House, began collecting a small fee from the newspapers that used the services. It is conceivable that similar arrangements occurred in other parts of the world at about the same time or earlier. Boston, however, was the gateway to the New World as a shipping port, and the press was notably hungry for foreign and domestic news.

Perhaps the first real news bureau was organized in Europe by Charles Havas in 1825. Havas's aim was to provide private subscribers with the news faster and more reliably than before. His subscribers were government officials, financiers, industrialists, and merchants. The use of semaphores and carrier pigeons greatly assisted the popularity of Havas's news bureau.[2] Havas's bureau gave birth to the first modern efforts at news gathering. Two employees, Bernard Wolff and Julius Reuter, were so interested in the prospects for news gathering and dissemination that they each opened a separate news agency. Wolff set up a joint relationship between German and Northern European papers, and Reuter opened his office in the London Royal Exchange in 1851, two years after the start of the Wolff News Agency. After considerable difficulty, Reuter succeeded in convincing the London papers to subscribe to his service. Thus in 1858 he became a key news supplier for the London newspapers.[3]

Julius Reuter's early affiliation with British imperial interests helped to lay the groundwork for an extensive international operation. The British Empire was dominant in the world, and the Reuters news service accompanied the Empire to all corners of the globe. It was this symbiotic relationship, in which the Empire profited by the dissemination of news and Reuters benefited by extending its coverage, that led to the suspicion by Third World nations that international news

[1] Victor Rosewater, *History of Cooperative News-Gathering in the United States* (New York: D. Appleton and Company, 1930), p. 5.
[2] UNESCO, *News Agencies: Their Structure and Operation* (Paris: UNESCO, 1953), p. 11.
[3] Ibid., pp. 11–12.

agencies served the political interests of big powers. According to Graham Storey, Reuters was able to make favorable agreements to use the extensive submarine cables laid by the British to connect London with all the colonies and so took an early lead in international news gathering.[4]

The United States did not possess the driving personalities of Reuter, Wolff, and Havas to generate a movement toward an international news agency. The operant element in the United States seems to have been necessity. Individual newspapers were not able to acquire foreign news as rapidly and competently as they wanted to for the price that they could afford. Thus several New York newspapers combined their resources in 1848 to obtain foreign news by using the Boston telegraph. This association was called the Associated Press and was the precursor to the international news organization by the same name.[5] These New York papers had successfully pooled their resources to become competitive with other papers. The New York Associated Press, as it was called, became the first United States news organization with which the European news agencies felt a need to cooperate. At first the three major European agencies, Havas, Wolff, and Reuters, negotiated a news exchange with the New York Associated Press. In 1870 the four agencies agreed to what amounted to a compact of noninterference. Exclusive preserves were established for each agency. The Havas News Agency was granted France, Italy, Spain, Switzerland, Portugal, and Egypt (shared with Reuters), Central America, and South America. Reuters was given the whole of the British Empire, Egypt (shared with Havas), Turkey, and the Far East. The Wolff News Agency was assigned Germany, Austria, Russia, Scandinavia, the Balkans, and the Netherlands. And the New York Associated Press had full rights to gather and distribute news from the United States.[6] Hester's comment about this arrangement summarizes the entire picture: "Newspapers had little choice but to take the news service for their area of the world, whether they liked its methods of operation and quality of news or not."[7] In a period of colonial imperatives the major news agencies had divided the world much like the co-

---

[4] Graham Storey, *Reuter: The Story of a Century of News Gathering* (New York: Crown Publishers, 1951), p. 35.

[5] Edwin Emery, *The Press and America*, 2nd ed. (Englewood Cliffs, N.J.: Prentice-Hall, 1962), pp. 254–255.

[6] UNESCO, op. cit., p. 18.

[7] Al Hester, "International News Agencies," in Alan Wells (ed.), *Mass Communications: A World View* (Palo Alto, Calif.: Mayfield Publishing Company, 1974), p. 213.

lonial powers meeting in Berlin were later to divide Africa among the colonial powers.

The New York Associated Press found the burden of telegraph costs rather heavy and while maintaining its access to the exchange with the European agencies set out to form an American cooperative to help alleviate the cost of telegraph. To this end, numerous United States papers were solicited to join the cooperative. These papers were to share the news service as well as the cost. Three regions were established: the Western Associated Press, the New England Associated Press, and the Southern Associated Press. In 1885 the Western Associated Press withdrew from the cooperative. Dissatisfaction with the New York AP's policies brought about a strained relationship. A series of modifications in the cooperative resulted. It was reorganized in 1892 in Illinois, and the old New York AP ceased to exist.[8] After 8 years as the Associated Press of Illinois and the loss of an antimonopoly suit, the AP was reorganized in New York. This new cooperative is the basis for the present international agency called the AP.[9]

The Associated Press was organized in such a way that only one newspaper could have its services in a given circulation area, a policy that clearly worked against other newspapers established in the area. In effect, those papers were without the services of an international agency.

In 1897 Edward Scripps organized the Scripps-McRae telegraphic services to provide news to his group of newspapers.[10] Scripps was an empire builder. He purchased a rival telegraphic group in 1907 and formed the United Press Association, which was to become AP's chief competition in worldwide news gathering.[11] UPA had some advantages over the AP, among which were its profit-making purpose and its noninvolvement with interagency agreements. AP was a party to agreements with the European agencies that limited its sphere of activity. UPA, with no such agreements, began to set up bureaus in various parts of the world. Largely confined at first to Europe, UPA was to expand into South America and the Far East. The stamina of the Scripps-backed agency produced changes in the news-gathering cartel. AP felt a strong necessity to establish foreign bureaus, and a

[8] Ibid., p. 213.
[9] UNESCO, op. cit., p. 43.
[10] Joe A. Morris, *Deadline Every Minute* (Garden City, N.Y.: Doubleday, 1957), pp. 17–18.
[11] Ibid., p. 19.

breakdown in the interagency agreements on spheres of activity was in the making.

Two years after the founding of UPA, the Hearst chain of newspapers began the International News Service. Thus within 2 years two aggressive world news agencies that were not parties to the international news cartel agreement began challenging the existing order. The AP was pressed into dependence on its own overseas bureaus in order to remain viable. The INS operated until 1958, when it was absorbed by the United Press Association to form the United Press International (UPI).[12]

Change in the European agencies that along with AP formed the international news cartel took place gradually. Yet by the end of World War II the character of the European agencies had changed. In 1933 the Wolff agency based in Germany ceased to exist. Havas, the French agency, was revamped in 1944 to become the Agence France-Presse. Reuters formed a cooperative trust with the British, Australian, and New Zealand media and is no longer a profit-making operation. The change of status in 1941 to a cooperative trust has helped it to retain some of the power it had around the turn of the century.

The six major international agencies may be classified according to whether they are (1) free enterprise profit making, (2) cooperative, or (3) government controlled (see Table 6-1).

Table 6-1. Classification of International News Agencies

Profit	Cooperative	Government
United Press International	Reuters	TASS
	Agence France-Presse	Hsinhua
	Associated Press	

Both government-controlled international news agencies developed as a direct result of political revolutions. In 1918 the Soviet Union established a news agency, ROSTA, which later became TASS. In 1972 the director of TASS was accorded ministerial rank, because the agency participates in disseminating national and international policies. In the Peoples Republic of China, Hsinhua was set up to provide news from worldwide bureaus to Chinese media as well as to disseminate Chinse news information.

[12] Hester, op. cit., p. 214.

Table 6-2. Number of Bureaus

News Agency	Foreign Bureaus
Agence France-Presse	165
Associated Press	53
Reuters	55
TASS	100
United Press International	238
Hsinhua	29

Hester's figures for the size of these international agencies are presented in Table 6-2; he states that these figures are estimates and "should be considered as approximation."[13] The reason for this is that the agencies define bureaus in different ways. The figure for Hsinhua is ours, based on information given by the Peoples Republic of China's mission to the United Nations.

How Does an Agency Function?

A news agency is in the business of gathering and disseminating news. It does not, however, disseminate to a general audience but to the media.

> An agency's job is to gather information anywhere in the world in as timely and accurate a manner as possible and to relay it to the mass media using the agency. The individual mass medium then selects what it wants from the news agency stories and photographs and passes these along to the reader, viewer, or listener. The agency material may be cut, rearranged, or combined to suit the purposes of the individual newspaper, radio, or television station. Sometimes reporters working for the news agencies write stories on the events covered, which are then transmitted to the agencies' mass media clients. At other times, the agencies merely relay or retransmit stories obtained by reporters in the mass media or by other news agencies with which they have exchange agreements.[14]

Most newspapers, and television and radio stations simply do not have the resources to gather information from around the world. It has been estimated that three fourths of all international news items

[13] Ibid., p. 215.
[14] Ibid., p. 208.

are transmitted by agencies. A few major newspapers such as the *London Times*, the *Los Angeles Times,* and the *New York Times* have foreign bureaus of their own. But even the major media institutions receive the largest portion of their international news from the wire service agencies. A media company then selects what it can use in its format from the wire service. Selection of news items from the international agencies' wires ultimately determines what news appears in the newspaper or on the 6 o'clock news. It is impossible for a media institution to use all of the foreign news it receives in one day. A small city daily may subscribe to one agency and receive 20,000 to 40,000 words a day. A story of Thai boxing may be interesting in Thailand but not to newspaper readers in Moultrie, Georgia. The editor for the small Georgia newspaper must select what he or she believes will be of interest to the readers. Therefore, the millions of words and photos that are teletyped and piped into newsrooms around the world supply editors with a pool of news from which to choose the news for their readers.

On a typical day, a news item will be discovered by a stringer, reported to the news agency headquarters, distributed to the media using the agency for news, and broadcast in print, pictures, and sound to the media consumer. Anywhere along the way the news item can be cut, modified, completely rewritten, or ignored. These possibilities explain Hester's findings of what happens to the Latin American reports on the AP trunk wire in the United States (see Table 6-3). One thing that he found was that almost half the news stories retransmitted to United States users of the AP main trunk wire were of crime and criminality.[15]

The international agencies have most of their bureaus and staffs in developed nations. Roving correspondents are used in Asia, South America, and Africa because of the lack of clients. This policy is another reason Third World nations have discussed the need for a news agency that would concentrate on news from their areas.

In several conferences during 1975 and 1976 the nonaligned nations met to discuss an international news pool. In Lima, Peru, in August 1975 delegates from these nations agreed that a cooperative effort would be needed to free them from dependence on the big wire services that monopolize the collection and dissemination of information. The resolution adopted at the Lima conference called for the

[15] Ibid., pp. 221–222.

Table 6-3. AP Latin American News Subjects

Subject Categories	From Latin American Bureaus	On U.S. AP Trunk Wire
Accidents	3.01	2.34
Agriculture	0.86	1.56
Arts, culture	1.16	0.00
Crime, criminality	13.81	47.66
Disasters	3.61	11.72
Domestic government	15.65	14.06
Economics, business	7.58	2.34
Education	1.04	0.00
Foreign relations	19.19	6.25
Human interest features	2.81	5.47
Labor	2.20	0.00
Military, defense	1.16	0.00
Miscellaneous	1.04	0.78
Prominent people	1.47	3.91
Religion	0.79	1.56
Science, medicine	1.34	2.34
Sports	23.23	0.00
Totals (per cent)	99.95	99.99
Number of items	1636	128

Note: Totals do not equal 100% because of rounding.

reorganization of communications channels inherited from colonialists.

During the nonaligned nations summit conference held in Colombo, Sri Lanka, in August 1976 a proposal intended to break the monopoly of Western international news agencies was adopted. The new organization would have a fourteen-member coordinating committee with India as chair. Other initial members would include Egypt, Iraq, Zaire, Peru, Ghana, Indonesia, Mauritius, Cuba, Senegal, Tunisia, Yugoslavia, Vietnam, and Mexico. It is an ambitious step that should produce a high quality of news collection and dissemination. Among the problems to be worked out is the development of national news agencies for those nations without them.

Inasmuch as the intent of the proposal is to secure the best possible coverage of a nation's interests, the delegates have devised a news pool structure so that each nation can select and distribute to the pool any news items it wants to on the basis of common and mutual interest.[16]

As we have seen, international news organizations have become integral parts of the modern media process. Information is gathered and disseminated by news agencies for profit, service, and propaganda purposes. The selection of news for local media by gatekeepers, such as editors, tends to reflect the local organization's perceptions of the needs and interests of the media consumers in its circulation area.

Contrasting Media Systems

Different nations have developed media institutions according to their own particular cultural, social, and political needs. There is little doubt that the use of media for national integration is an essential part of contemporary societies, but how media are to accomplish that goal is debatable. We believe, however, that the achievement of national integration is a function of a society's use of media to enhance the values, customs, and objectives of the people. A few examples of national communication systems will be helpful in trying to analyze media's role in national integration.

United States. The media institutions in the United States constitute the most elaborate network for information in the world. Print, television, radio, and movies exist in greater variety than in any other society. A combination of message carriers, support agencies, manufacturers, libraries and data banks, contributors to content, and data-gathering services add to the complex nature of the United States' media system. In fact, it is perhaps more correct to use the plural and speak of *media systems* with regard to the complexities of information distribution within the United States.

Diversity and particularity of communication services distinguish the United States. Telegraph and telephones are responsible for carrying millions of messages daily. They provide, along with satellites and the postal service, a comprehensive carrier service. Advertis-

[16] Brij Khandelwal, "Third World Presses Ahead on Newspool Plans," *Encore*, October 4, 1976, 16–17.

ing agencies, with their various sales and distribution counterparts, are integral constituents of media institutions. Furthermore, a highly sophisticated electronics manufacturing sector provides creativity and innovation in improving the qualities of communication equipment. A network of libraries, computer services, reproduction centers, and data banks serves as the backbone of the media systems. In addition to these rather formal channels and operations are the alternative (sometimes called fugitive) print systems, usually operating in major metropolitan centers or on university campuses. These alternative presses and their newspapers provide special-interest groups with information that may not be available in the more traditional media. The existence of the alternative press is testimony to the diversity possible within the United States.

Three major commercial television networks and one government-supported corporation broadcast over the airwaves. These four agencies, the American Broadcasting Company, the Columbia Broadcasting System, the National Broadcasting Company, and the Public Broadcasting Corporation, are the only networks with a broad national audience.

The development of communication networks may be divided into two phases: (1) the pretelevision phase and (2) the posttelevision phase. During the pretelevision phase, broadcasting networks were mainly radio businesses engaged in entertainment. According to Lichty and Topping, the early networks were informal and nonbinding associations.[17]

David Sarnoff is an almost mythic character in American communication, the man responsible for suggesting the creation of the first broadcasting network. In a 1922 letter to E. W. Rice, Jr., who at the time was honorary chairman of the board at the General Electric Company, Sarnoff wrote:

> Let us organize a separate and distinct company, to be known as the Public Service Broadcasting Company, or National Radio Broadcasting Company or American Broadcasting Company, or some similar name. This company to be controlled by The Radio Corporation of America, but its board of directors and officers to include members of the General Electric Company and possibly also a few from the outside, prominent in national and civic affairs. The administrative and operating staff of

[17] Lawrence Lichty and Malachi Topping, *A Sourcebook on the History of Radio and Television* (New York: Hastings House, 1975), p. 157.

this company to be composed of those best qualified to do the broadcasting job.[18]

In a real sense Sarnoff was the prophet of networks. He had joined the American Marconi Company (mainly a telegraph company) as an office boy in 1906, and his work there prepared him for the dominant role he was to play in the Radio Corporation of America. Sarnoff foresaw a number of stations connected loosely to each other but joined in their intent to provide America with radio entertainment. His proposal to E. W. Rice, Jr., was that the new company acquire the broadcasting stations operated by Westinghouse and General Electric and those that were planned by The Radio Corporation of America.

It took only 6 months for Sarnoff's letter to Rice to bring results. The World Series was broadcast over radio stations WJZ of Newark, New Jersey, and WGY of Schenectady, New York, which had been connected by telegraph lines. This was the beginning of the close association of various stations. Two years later a dozen stations carried the Republican National Convention over the airwaves. Equal time was afforded the Democratic Convention several weeks later.

New York City was the cultural and economic center of America in the early twentieth century, and WEAF was the vanguard New York station. A 32-station network linked to WEAF during the major part of 1925–26 provided uniformly good entertainment, and radio sales skyrocketed. Other networks followed, one of which, as reported by Lichty and Topping, consisted of six stations dubbed the "Eveready Group" in 1925 (because Eveready Batteries were advertised on them); this group increased to thirteen stations in 1926.[19]

The potential for network broadcasting was readily seen by people in the communication business. In 1926 WEAF was purchased by The Radio Corporation of America, a full 4 years after David Sarnoff's letter to E. W. Rice, Jr. The National Broadcasting Company was announced in 1926 with a 4½-hour radio extravaganza featuring the top entertainers of the day.

The early start and the vision of Sarnoff made NBC the most powerful network in the 1930s. On January 1, 1927, NBC had become two networks in order to accommodate the demand; one chain of stations was named Blue and the other Red by the NBC engineers. This

[18] David Sarnoff, *Looking Ahead* (New York: McGraw-Hill, 1968), pp. 41–44.
[19] Lichty and Topping, op. cit., p. 158.

further increased NBC's ability to gain audiences, advertisers, and performers.

CBS inaugurated its chain on September 18, 1927, and William Paley took control of the company in 1928, exercising a strong personal influence over the company.

NBC and CBS represented the high spirits of the 1930s. However, they were in their infancy as companies when the Depression hit. Although both companies had lots of business, neither made a profit during those years.[20]

As in many creative ventures, NBS and CBS had imitators. In 1929 Quality Network was begun but remained far behind the first two networks. A fourth network, Mutual Broadcasting System, was successful; it is still called the largest radio network. However, it failed to achieve the stature of NBC and CBS because of a lack of powerful affiliated stations. A number of other networks were begun on the regional level but never achieved national success. There were numerous other failures. Companies such as the McClatchy Broadcasting Company, Yankee Network, Inc., Colonial Network, Don Lee Network, Pacific Broadcasting Company, and the Amalgamated Broadcasting System never really competed with the early bird giants NBC and CBS.

The American Broadcasting Company was formed as a result of an investigation of network practices by the Federal Communication Commission. A number of court cases (begun in 1938 and ending in 1943 with a Supreme Court ruling that upheld the FCC ban on one company's operating two networks) resulted in NBC's having to divest itself of NBC Blue. This company was purchased by Edward J. Nobel for approximately $7 million and renamed the American Broadcasting Company.

Each of the major broadcasting companies began a television network in the 1940s, and a fourth network, DuMont, also tried to break into the television network business. In 1955 it had thirteen regular television programs; by 1956 it had none. The intensity of the competition with the "big three" was too great for a small company with neither the prestige nor the resources of its rivals.

The broadcasting giants are huge corporations employing hundreds of people. The American Broadcasting Company has over a hundred officers at the vice-presidential level or above. According to

[20] Lichty and Topping, op. cit., p. 159.

the 1976 edition of the *TV Factbook,* ABC had a sixteen-person board of directors and nine presidents. Each administrative area headed by a president is further divided into smaller units. Thus the ABC television network has divisions of affiliate relations, network sales, and advertising and promotion. These units usually are administered by a vice-president in charge with several vice-presidents and directors reporting to him. CBS has one more member on its present Board of Directors than does ABC but has four fewer presidents. NBC has one fewer board member than ABC but is identical to CBS in its number of presidents.

Among the United States' media giants, budgets and program information are considered trade secrets because of the intense competition for audiences. Although one can tell something about the size of media institutions from the number of officers they employ, the effectiveness of the companies is measured by the number of viewers they can attract. Thus when ABC attracted nearly 80 million viewers in 1977 to its showing of *Roots* other networks were eager to find a similar formula for audience success.

The alternative to commercial television in the United States is public television, which is often referred to as the fourth network. The development and growth of public television in the United States have been singularly unspectacular. Beginning in 1952, when then FCC Commissioner Frieda Hennock set aside a number of television channels and radio frequencies to serve the educational needs of the community, and for more than a decade later, educational radio and television commanded scarcely any notice. Then in the mid-1960s, with educational broadcasting on the verge of bankruptcy, the Carnegie Corporation, responding to urgent calls for help, set up a commission to chart public television's future role. Based on the commission's report (1967), President Johnson and Congress pushed through legislation that established the Corporation for Public Broadcasting. The CPB in turn created the Public Broadcasting System, with the idea that the former would act as a receiving and distribution agency for governmental and private funds and the latter would act as an agency similar to the commercial networks in distributing programs nationally.

What appeared to be a workable plan, however, has fallen victim to territorial bickering and infighting. Both CPB and PBS accuse each other of being overstaffed, wasting funds, and offering duplication of services. Neither one seems to have a clear idea of mission, and PBS, in particular, is claiming that creativity in program development is being stifled by CPB's insistence on approval rights for all programming. Thus the mission to offer an alternative broadcasting network featuring high-quality, noncommercial programming in both the cultural and informational realms is being seriously compromised.

At this moment an interesting addendum is being written that may either save or kill public broadcasting in this country. The reader will encounter more on this subject in Chapter 9 with the discussion of Carnegie II.

The Soviet System. The Union of Soviet Socialist Republics has a comprehensive, centrally directed mass communication system. Its major characteristics appear to be the following:

1. The media are formally structured in both organization and substance. All media are organized to meet the ideological demands of the Communist Party. In this way, the party is able to achieve uniformity of ideology. Such centrally controlled media are easily orchestrated to deal with special national or regional issues.
2. The media are scrutinized by several administrative organizations in order to determine the correctness of the media's transmission. Correctness, of course, consists of being in line with the Party platform. Review and control therefore are essential to the operation of the system.
3. The Soviet media emphasize audience feedback. In fact, as much as half of the staff of newspapers may work in the letter department. Group listening and viewing opportunities are encouraged. People watch news events, see innovative farming techniques, and watch movies projected by mobile units or presented in special reading rooms.
4. The Soviet system appears to concentrate on audiences in a selective rather than a mass manner. Thus a television program may be geared specifically to a given segment of the audience for a particular purpose. Achievement of success is determined by the degree to which the chosen audience understands the message. This differs from the United States' emphasis on mass audiences.

Soviet broadcasting is controlled from Moscow. The system is vast; for example, radio broadcasts are made in nearly ninety languages. These broadcasts are coordinated by the State Committee on

Radio and Television of the Council of Ministers' Union. The State Committee itself has units responsible for national, local, and external broadcasts. Whether the broadcasts are meant for a specific audience or the nation in general, Moscow is the headquarters for all broadcasts. This system is historically tied to the radio diffusion concept. In radio diffusion one receiver is used to relay messages over wires to sets owned by subscribers, which allows central transmission of a message. The reception of messages is thus regulated because the broadcasters know precisely who is and is not wired into the system. Moscow administers the immense system by a tight-knit bureaucracy.

The State Committees depend on Administrations of Central and Local Broadcasting for planning and rebroadcasting. All media are used to further party objectives. The administrations are therefore responsible to the higher authorities for their broadcasts. The organization of the press is equally formal. All newspapers are sponsored either by the government or by workers' groups; private ownership of the press is prohibited. According to Charles Wright:

> Geographically, the levels of the press include: the central all-union press, which circulates throughout the Soviet Union; the provincial press, including the republican, territorial, and regional papers; the local press, including the district, city, and primary press; and single copy typewritten or handwritten "wall" newspapers, tacked on bulletin boards in factories, farm buildings, and the like.[21]

As with the media, each level of the press has its role. Among the Communist Party publications are *Pravda*, the central paper; the *Soviet Ukraine*, a provincial paper; and *Red Star* and *Soviet Fleet*, military organs. Other newspapers include *Izvestiya* of the Supreme Soviets, *Trud*, *Komsomolskaya Pravda*, and 650 others.

The Soviet system places high priority on the transmission of Soviet culture, the selection and presentation of historical events that illustrate the revolutionary processes of socialism, and the political and cultural education of the masses. These emphases are different from those of Western media, although the general means of communication are similar.

Federal Republic of Germany. German media institutions are well developed and are among the more sophisticated in Europe. Newspapers exist in every town of any size. The largest newspaper is a tabloid

[21] Charles Wright, *Mass Communication: A Sociological Perspective* (New York: Random House, 1975), pp. 32–33.

printed in Hamburg and distributed nationally. It has the largest daily circulation (over 3,100,000) of any newspaper on the Continent. Papers in Essen and Frankfurt are also widely read. In 1964 there were at least twenty-five dailies with circulation over 100,000.[22]

The major source of news is the Deutsche Presse Agentur (DPA) with main offices in Hamburg. It transmits news on national affairs in German, English, French, and Spanish. Exchange agreements with over fifty other news agencies give DPA extensive coverage. Other agencies exist such as Nordpress and Vereinigte Wirt Schaftsdienste, but they are primarily complementary to DPA.

Broadcasting services for the domestic population are organized and coordinated by the legislatures of the provinces. Foreign broadcasts are under the control of the federal government. Eleven national broadcasting organizations exist. Nine of them are public corporations and exempt from federal control. Operational expenses are covered by license fees and advertising. The two organizations created by federal law are financed by the federal government budget. The eleven broadcasting corporations are members of the Association of Broadcasting Corporations (ARD), the overall coordinating agency of radio and television in Germany.

Japan. Japanese media are among the most technologically well designed in the world. Japan's television industry is based on the adoption and improvement of Western technology. The Japanese have perfected the television camera and have pioneered in use of the media for educational purposes.

Per capita newspaper readership in Japan is among the highest in the world. Three newspapers have over 5 million circulation. The ratio of radio and television receivers is equal to that of the United States.

The noncommercial public corporation, NHK, has the world's largest television budget. NHK operates two nationwide television and three radio networks. Four commercial networks, owned by newspaper concerns, compete for advertising revenue. Japanese media, highly organized and competitively operated, have contributed greatly to the nation's postwar industrial recovery.

Nigeria. Nigeria is the most populous and the richest country in Africa. Its media institutions are among the best developed in Africa.

[22]*World Communications* (New York: UNESCO, 1964), p. 286.

The major daily newspapers are the *Daily Times* and the *Daily Mirror*. Both papers are published in English, the official language of the country. In 1976 the government of Nigeria made education universal and compulsory, the first African nation to do so. Literacy is expected to increase at a rapid rate. Newspaper subscriptions, as in Western nations, do not indicate the extent of readership, because neswpapers are passed to friends in the community or to relatives.

The Nigerian Broadcasting Corporation began in Lagos at Tugwell House Marina in 1951 under the old Post and Telegraph Department of the Nigerian Broadcasting Service. In 1957 the Nigerian Broadcasting Corporation came into existence to supersede the Nigerian Broadcasting Service. The NBC had the following objectives:

1. To provide efficient broadcasting services to the whole Federation of Nigeria, based on national objectives and aspirations, and to external audiences in accordance with Nigeria's foreign policy.
2. To provide a professional and comprehensive coverage of Nigerian culture through broadcasting, to promote cultural growth through research into indigenous culture, and to disseminate the result of such research.
3. To contribute to the development of Nigerian society and to promote national unity by ensuring a balanced presentation of views from all parts of Nigeria.
4. To ensure the prompt delivery of accurate information to the people.
5. To provide opportunities for the free, enlightened, and responsible discussion of important issues, and to provide a two-day contact between the public and those in authority.
6. To provide special broadcasting services in the field of education and in all other areas where the national policy calls for special action.
7. To promote the orderly and meaningful development of broadcasting in Nigeria through technical improvements, the training of appropriate professional staff, and program and other exchanges with other broadcasting organizations in the country.
8. To promote research into various aspects of the communications media and their effects on Nigerian society. (This will include audience research, the investigation of fresh

methods of production, and the true indigenization of the broadcasting media.)

9. To ensure that the facilities and techniques of broadcasting in Nigeria keep pace with developments in the world of communication (e.g., FM transmission and color television.)

The NBC is controlled by a board of governors composed of forty people. A director-general, appointed by the Federal Supreme Council, chairs the board. In addition to the director-general, four deputies in charge of program services, finance and administration, state services, and technical services are the major policy makers.

Chapter 7
International Satellite Systems

We ought to consider what man needs and society requires.
Ben H. Bagdikian, "How Communications May Shape
Our Future Environment"

Capabilities of Satellites

Communication satellites are now being used for national and international communication. Our world is becoming one of ever closer contact with our neighbors, and the most advanced system for relaying instantaneous messages is the communication satellite. The satellite places us in immediate contact with people in distant places.

What is a communication satellite? How can it be used in contemporary society? *A communication satellite is simply a relay station in space that can be used to provide either intranational or international communication.* Thus a prime minister's or president's speech may be heard simultaneously in the capital city and a town a thousand miles away. Furthermore, the speaker's image can be transmitted. National satellite systems are the most frequently used systems.

Most communication satellites are placed in a circular orbit approximately 35,800 kilometers above the surface of the earth. At that altitude the satellite completes one revolution of its orbit in 24 hours; because the orbital rate is matched to that of the earth, it is called a synchronous satellite. When the orbital path lies entirely within the plane of the terrestrial equator, the orbit is called equatorial. A synchronous satellite in equatorial orbit is referred to as geostationary, because to an observer on the ground it seems to be motionless. Such a satellite at 35,800 kilometers can see almost 42% of the earth's surface. Thus two well-placed satellites can see almost all the inhabitable regions of the earth.

All relay systems are similar. A satellite system has some of the features of a terrestrial radio relay or cable system, but it also has unique capabilities. The four major capabilities of a satellite system are the following:

1. Unlike terrestrial relay stations, a satellite can permit *multiple access* within the coverage area of its antenna. That is, any earth station within the coverage zone can communicate with the satellite and therefore with any other earth station. Thus a large number of earth stations dispersed over a wide area can receive signals or be interconnected with other stations.
2. Satellite systems are distance insensitive. Thus technical performance and operational cost are not affected by the distance between terminal points within the coverage area.
3. Satellites can provide "demand-assigned" circuits. These circuits can be utilized to connect any two earth stations on user demand.
4. Satellites are flexible and can provide television, radio, voice, telex, data, or other wideband communications and can serve stations having high, medium, or low traffic densities.

Because of their flexibility and diversity of applications, satellites are highly effective tools of mass communication. Each satellite usually contains a number of transponders, or repeaters. A typical satellite has twelve, e.g., the domestic satellites of Canada and the United States and Intelsat's international satellites. Usually there is a transponder for each television channel to be distributed. These transponders can be assigned and reassigned from the ground to provide any desired mix of communication services, for a variety of public and private users. This broad range of services makes satellites potent communication instruments.

Uses of Communication Satellites

The effectiveness of international communication satellites has been amply demonstrated since June 1965, when the first commercial communication satellite for Intelsat began service, and satellite systems are also efficient tools for national or regional telecommunications. A national (domestic) satellite system is used wholly within the boundaries of a single country, whereas a regional satellite system is shared by a group of neighboring nations. Intelsat is a regional system.

Multiple access is one of the most valuable attributes of satellites because (1) it allows any terminal to be interconnected to any other terminal within the satellite antenna coverage area and (2) it affords a rapid response capability with high-quality communications. Any place can communicate with any other place by the setting up of earth stations at the desired locations without the need to build intermediate equipment along the path as required for radio relays, coaxial cables, and other transmission systems; a few workers using hand tools can set up a temporary, high-quality communications system in less than a day. Applications include short-term communication at a remote industrial site or backup of terrestrial communication facilities during a natural disaster or other emergency.

Generally, small transportable earth stations or medium-sized stations with 8- to 12-meter-diameter antennas can be flown or trucked to a town and made operational by a trained crew within a few hours. For example, the transportable earth terminals used to transmit newsworthy television events and some voice circuits around the world via Intelsat are flown into a site and readied for operation in only five hours. Thus large cities or isolated towns can be interconnected via satellite to the communication network of a nation in a very short time. This instant communication feature of satellite systems provides an advantage that is difficult to measure in monetary terms, and the satellite system is becoming critically important to industrialized nations.

Characteristics

In addition to the multiple access and instant communication attributes, satellite systems have three other important characteristics:

1. A satellite system permits the interconnection of difficult to reach sites. In numerous instances important towns or communities have inadequate communications because they are

surrounded by difficult terrain such as swamps, forests, deserts, or rugged mountains. In the past, such difficult terrain has inhibited development of terrestrial communications and forced these communities into communication isolation as well as geographic separation from the outside world. Satellite systems sidestep these difficulties as the earth stations can readily be flown or trucked in, or shipped in via river barge or whatever other means of transportation are available.

2. Because satellite transmissions can be received simultaneously by a vast number of earth stations, a communication satellite system is particularly suited to transmit one-way signals, such as television, video, and sound, to a number of remote communities. Earth terminals with 6- to 8-meter-diameter antennas used for television transmission are relatively inexpensive and can be installed in less than a day. In addition, it is economically feasible to provide a few telephone circuits to each remote community. This aspect of satellite systems makes it valuable not only as a means of distributing commercial or national television but also as a means of improving or augmenting education via ETC (educational television).

3. Satellite systems can be implemented to provide two basic types of circuits: (a) permanently assigned and (b) demand assigned.

Permanently assigned circuits provide fixed connections through a satellite from transit center to transit center via earth stations. Satellite circuits operated in this mode can be used in exactly the same manner as cable or microwave circuits. Demand-assigned circuits may also be established between two earth stations, with the component circuit sections being connected together automatically for the duration of the call. The satellite transmission links are then automatically released to a common pool for use in other demand-assigned service, not necessarily between the same two earth stations. Such circuits offer additional flexibility for route planning and circuit routing: direct routing on a "per call" basis. The basic concept of this type of circuit is that the facilities between earth stations are used only when required and are released on termination of the call. Any earth station equipped with demand-assignment terminals can contact any other similarly equipped earth station within the antenna coverage area. Permanently assigned and demand-assigned circuits may be mixed in any network configuration, with the number of each type of circuit dependent on a cost tradeoff.

The use of demand assignment permits substantial increases in traffic-handling capacity. Demand-assigned circuits can be used to provide temporary direct circuits among locations not having sufficient traffic to justify permanent direct circuits. Furthermore, demand-assigned circuits can provide a means of servicing overflow traffic from either permanently assigned satellite or terrestrial direct circuit groups.

The role of demand-assigned circuits, however, is not necessarily to serve as overflow for permanently assigned groups but rather to provide a pool of circuits that can be used flexibly to improve overall network efficiency. For example, demand-assigned circuits in a national system can provide substantial benefits to a terrestrial system by direct interconnection of the farthest terminals, thus relieving congestion at intermediate points. Such peak load use of the satellite system's demand-assignment capability can enhance the performance of the terrestrial radio relay or cable system.

A satellite system is designed to accommodate changing requirements. As traffic requirements for an area increase, the traffic demand will reach a point where economic factors warrant the installation of terrestrial links (if none existed before) or augmentation of the capacity of existing radio relay links to that community. Configuration changes of permanently assigned satellite circuits can be accomplished by rearranging the connection of multiplex and baseband distribution equipment in a manner similar to that required to reallocate terrestrial circuits. Unlike terrestrial circuits, however, the transmission medium does not have to be reallocated. Thus excess circuits on one point-to-point permanently assigned satellite circuit group can be reassigned to an overcongested circuit group between any other two locations that have access to earth stations. Because each demand-assigned circuit gains access to the satellite system through an individual single-channel-per-carrier (SCPC) transmission unit, it is simple to add or remove individual transmission units as traffic levels dictate. This ability to flexibly reassign either type of circuit to any city eases the requirement for accurate traffic forecasts.

Satellite systems can also be used as adjuncts to terrestrial systems, tying into the network at strategic points so that in case of failure, flood, or sabotage the satellite network can back up the terrestrial link.

Educational Television

Present commercial communication satellites operate at C band (6 GHz uplink and 4 Ghz downlink frequency). In 1971, WARC (World Administrative Radio Conference for Space Telecommunication) allocated the frequency band from 2500 to 2690 MHz (downlink frequency) for broadcasting satellite service limited to national and regional systems for community reception. This frequency band is especially useful for educational television (ETV) because relatively inexpensive ground terminals can be employed.

Modern technology allows hybrid configurations that include 2.5-GHz (S band) capability along with the traditional 7- and 4-GHz (C band) capability on medium-sized (national) satellites designed in the United States for launch by Thor Delta class rockets. Such hybrid designs are used to provide varying relative capacity between C and S band transponders. For example, a satellite configuration may have 50 per cent of its power in S band 50 per cent in C band transponders, or 25 per cent in C band and 75 per cent in S band. Also possible are national satellites like the ones built for Canada and the United States where up to four of the transponders (those dedicated for ETV) have more power output than the rest of the transponders. Such flexibility is especially advantageous when national ETV is of high priority.

International Satellite Systems

Substitute Satellites. Some nations place an extra satellite in orbit as backup for a fully utilized satellite. Normally this spare satellite carries the overflow (in case more than twelve transponders are required), and its spare capacity is used in the event of failures on the prime satellite or as a reservoir for growth. Because of satellite reliability, the second satellite is generally considered as a reservoir of utilizable reserve capacity.

Intelsat. The beginning of the Intelsat consortium in 1964 was a new chapter in international communication. The consortium is composed of some eighty-five member nations. It is a jointly owned and operated commercial satellite system. Each member nation has a vote proportionate to its share of Intelsat traffic. When it was first developed, the business end of the consortium was handled by COMSAT, the United States Civilian Satellite Corporation.

The Intelsat consortium has the use of satellites of the third and fourth generations at the present time. In 1965 the satellites averaged 240 circuits with a design lifetime of 1½ years. In 1971 there were 6000 average circuits with a design lifetime of 7 years.[1] Although the cost of initial satellite investment has gone up considerably since the first satellites, the capacity has also increased. This increased capacity has resulted in lower cost per circuit year.

According to Olof Hulten, two aspects of the Intelsat system need to be understood in connection with international mass communication: (1) it is operated in the interest of telecommunications traffic, and (2) its formal jurisdiction and tariffs apply only to the space segment of satellite transmission.[2] Broadcasting accounts for only a small portion of Intelsat traffic. Consequently, tariff policies and utilization patterns reflect the overwhelming telephone and telecommunications usage. Furthermore, the Intelsat system relies on ground stations, land lines, and switching costs. The space segment of satellite-mediated transmission accounts for less of the total cost of international broadcasting than ground stations and other land installations. Nations that participate in the system tend to spend more money for permanent land installations than for the space segment. Other costs are involved with the amount of telecommunication usage.

Nations tend to use Intelsat in direct proportion to their economic and international relationships with other nations. Thus the heaviest utilization occurs in the Atlantic region. Fifty-nine per cent of the total television transmission time in 1969 was used by the Atlantic region.[3] The main flows of Intelsat's traffic are usually between the United States and Puerto Rico and the United States and Europe, and vice versa. Domestic U.S. traffic, U.S. mainland to Hawaii, also consumes a sizable portion of usage time. As we have said, however, the cost of the space segment is borne by the member state corresponding to its usage of the Intelsat system. Thus the United States has paid more than 50 per cent of the cost of Intelsat since its inception. Ground segment costs are borne by the member nations exclusively.

[1] COMSAT, Report to the President and the Congress, 1968.
[2] Olof Hulten, "The Intelsat System: Its Present and Future Use for Broadcasting," Michael C. Emery and Ted Curtis Smythe (eds.), *Readings in Mass Communication* Dubuque, Ia.: W. C. Brown, 1974), pp. 345–346.
[3] Ibid., p. 346.

The present configuration of the fourth generation of Intelsat satellites is as follows: two satellites over the Atlantic Ocean, two over the Pacific Ocean, and one over the Indian Ocean. This configuration allows maximum coverage of the earth's surface. Ground stations are used to relay transmissions from point to point on the earth. Expensive ground stations can reduce the need for more expansive satellites. However, this creates a burden on smaller countries that must invest in expensive ground stations although they use only a small portion of transmission time.

The future of satellites in domestic and international communications is assured by the reliability and efficiency of the current generation of satellites. Permanently assigned and demand-assigned systems will continue to be useful as our world needs for rapid and accurate transmission increase.

Chapter 8
Film:
An International Medium

Since the best way to get to the core of a form is to study its effects in some unfamiliar setting, let us note what President Sukarno of Indonesia announced in 1956 to a large group of Hollywood executives. He said he regarded them as political radicals and revolutionaries who had greatly hastened political change in the East. What the Orient saw in a Hollywood movie was a world in which all the ordinary people had cars and electronic stoves and refrigerators. So the Oriental now regards himself as an ordinary person who has been deprived of the ordinary man's birthright.
Marshall McLuhan, *Understanding Media: The Extensions of Man*, p. 294

Film is a series of images existing with or without sound that can be stored in a flexible celluloid base. Breitrose distingushes *film* from *film recordings*.[1] Film recordings utilize the medium to continuously record an ongoing event from the same point of view. Thus monitoring persons in a department store or bank with a camera would not be considered film. Film attempts to show relationships, angles, and a variety of viewpoints.

The use of film as a communication instrument has become a regular part of contemporary society. Human beings have stored as much information on films in the last 50 years as could be contained in all the books in the world prior to 1850. Furthermore, the detail of information contained in film is more precise than most authors could ever write. Yet film's precision does not make a perfect instrument of com-

[1] Henry Breitrose, "Film as Communication" Ithiel de Sola Pool and Wilbur Schramm (eds.), *Handbook of Communication* (Chiago: Rand McNally, 1973), pp. 559–560.

Table 8-1. Distortion Taxonomy in Film Communication

Distortion Taxonomy	
Process	Distortion
Photography	Temporal Field of view Camera placement Camera direction
Editing	Holistic space Associative space Time relationship

munication because of the possibility of distortion in photography and distortion in editing.

Photography is the key to filmmaking inasmuch as it is the actual recording of a series of images. How those images are recorded is the variable that can cause distortion in the communication process. For example, a *temporal* distortion can occur when the photographer varies either the camera time or the projection time. Most motion pictures are projected at 24 frames per second (usually written "24 fps"). When camera speed is also 24 fps and the film is projected at the same speed, an illusion of real time will occur. What you see on the screen appear to be events occurring as they happened in reality. However, the photographer can decrease the camera speed to 8 fps and project the film at 24 fps, so that the action will be perceived to happen in one third of its real time. Or the camera speed can be increased to 36 fps and projected at 24 fps and the action will seem to take a third longer than it actually did. These processes are commonly referred to as *slow motion* and *fast motion*.

Field of view refers to what one can see with the eye. The field of view for the human eye is normally around 120 degrees. The widest-angle lenses for cameras can give a horizontal angle of about 84 degrees, although the most commonly employed lenses view an angle of about 23 degrees.[2] These lenses are considered "normal" because their distortion resembles the perspective of the human eye. A photographer using the "normal" lenses, which already distort reality, can

[2] Verne Carlson and Sylvia Carlson, *Professional 16/35 mm Cameraman's Handbook* (New York: American Photographic Book Publishing Company, 1970).

use the distortion to achieve other effects. It is also possible to distort the field behind and in front of an object with a telephoto lens.

Where the camera is placed can distort reality. If a photographer places the camera above the object, the object appears smaller. If the camera is below the object, the object appears larger.

Camera distortion can occur if the photographer reverses the film to give the impression that actors, moving objects, and time are moving backward. These distortions of photography suggest that camera and film are not the accurate instruments of communication we tend to assume.

However, it is the editor of the film who holds the most power to make gross or minor distortions. Editorial distortion can occur when the editor manipulates filmic space in a holistic manner. *Filmic space* refers to how far away (in space) an event happened or what the distance is between events communicated in the film. *Holisitc space* relationships are defined by statements about the space in which actions or other events occur. This can be done by one or two shots of the entire area in which the action is to occur, which are called pivotal shots. All subsequent shots take place within the context of the pivotal shots. Thus a film may open with a shot of a city, a house, a street, or a shop. Some editors may show the detail of the actors and events before showing the context; however, in a logically arranged film the editor must establish a context.

Associative space is the second most common way of establishing topography. The editor may show a sailor climbing the steps of a ship without ever showing the full ship. The audience associates a sailor with a ship, and a message has been delivered that may be compared to the figure of speech where a part stands for the whole, a *synechdoche*. So distortion of film communication can occur in the use of both holistic and synecdochic (or associative) space. The audience is able to respond only to the film as edited. The film footage lost in the editing process is not a part of the communicative transaction.

A final way an editor may distort a film is in time conception. The secret of the editor's job is the ability to "abstract from any complex set of actions those actions that are significant to the statement intended."[3]

For example, it is not necessary for a film to show a swimmer swimming the entire length of the English Channel in order to make a

[3] Breitrose, op. cit., p. 563.

statement about how exhausted she is. The editor may choose only to show the swimmer entering the water, a few shots of her struggling in the water, and the end of the swim. The lapsed time can be accounted for using a number of techniques. One such technique is where the film cuts back to action occurring in another place. If it takes 20 hours to swim the channel, then the editor can make us see the time elapse by *matched* action or a *jump cut* to some other scene.[4] Typical ways of indicating that time has passed include showing a physical change in a building, the movement of hands on a clock, or even the changes of age on the characters' faces.

In summary, filmic communication is a major part of our media messages, and it, like other messages, can be distorted, sometimes to serve the purposes of art and sometimes to deceive the audience. Understanding the dimensions of film as a communicative medium, we are now ready to review its history.

Beginnings

Motion pictures have captured the human imagination since the turn of the century. Around 1895 Thomas Edison in the United States, Robert Paul in England, and the Louis and Auguste Lumiere in France began experimenting with cameras and projectors that would show moving images.[5] Cameras and projectors with science fiction names like Cinematographic, Cinephone, Photophone, Klangfilm, and Vitaphone were used to produce films of the movement of ocean waves, running horses, sailboats, trains, fire engines, and parades that attracted audiences who sat for hours watching them.

The present moving picture film is a ribbon of celluloid generally 35 or 16 millimeters wide. Film with sound is usually run at 24 fps, which creates the illusion of continuous action. Technically it was a major breakthrough in still photography that led to the perfection of the moving picture. Joseph Niepce, Louis Daguerre, and George Eastman established these photographic techniques. Knight lists some of the most interesting pre-celluloid animations from photography:

> Perhaps the most popular was the Zoetrope, a slotted revolving drum. As one watched through slits, hand-drawn clowns or acrobats, horses or

---

[4] Karel Reisz, *Technique of Film Editing* (New York: Farrar, Strauss, and Cudahy, 1953).
[5] Arthur Knight, *The Liveliest Art* (New York: New American Library, 1957), p. 13.

dogs seemed to leap through their paces on the strips of paper fitted inside the drum. A simpler device using a similar technique was the stroboscope, with the figures drawn upon a slotted disc. The image was seen by revolving the disc in front of a mirror and again peeping through the slits. More elaborate was the Praxinoscope of Emil Reynaud. In its center was a ring of little mirrors; a band of images was placed opposite them against the shell of the drum. As the drum revolved, the movement almost flowed from one mirror to the next to create a particularly charming effect.[6]

Inventors sprouted all over Europe and America heralding their latest discoveries in photography and projection. The early pictures were hand drawn, but by 1861 Coleman Sellers, a Philadelphian, had invented a kinematoscope in which a series of photographs, posed in such a way as to give the illusion of movement, were rotated before viewers. Numerous other inventions with exotic names appeared. Henry Heyl had a Phantasmatrope, and the Frenchman Jean Louis Meissonier invented a unique contraption called a Zoopraxinoscope. Eadweard Muybridge and John D. Isaacs used a sequential action approach to capture the gait of moving horses.

Thomas Edison's was the first attempt at making a motion picture camera, and his assistant, William Kennedy Laurie Dickson, is credited with developing the sprocket system for moving celluloid film through the camera, a system still used for 35-mm film. In 1891 Edison took out a patent for a battery-driven camera, the Kinetoscope. It was the size of a small upright piano. Later inventors in Europe and the United States experimented with many other kinds of moving picture cameras.

The Rise of the Narrative Film

The narrative film soon followed the technical advances in cameras and projection equipment. George Melies in France and Edwin Porter and D. W. Griffith in the United States made narrative films that were widely popular. Melies's A Trip to the Moon (1902) and Porter's The Great Train Robbery (1903) were among the most popular early narrative films.

D. W. Griffith used film as an art form more than any of his

6 Ibid., p. 15.

predecessors. According to Knight, Griffith "created the art of film, its language, its syntax."[7] Certainly Griffith was a major force in the development of film technique. With the *Birth of a Nation* (1915) he leaped ahead of all competitors as a creative artist. The narrative film had come af age. (For further discussion of the narrative film, see our discussion on the feature industry.)

The Documentary Film

The documentary film, unlike the strictly entertainment film, has as a key objective the presentation of information. In this respect it is similar to the informative speech. The filmmaker selects a subject and films it according to ideas in his or her own head. The intent is usually to provide audiences with information that will enable them to make choices for "the better rather than the worse general policy."[8] The method for providing audiences with choice is the creative presentation of actuality. According to Rotha, Road, and Griffith, "the documentary method may well be described as the birth of creative cinema."[9] As we have seen from the history of the story or narrative film, creative cinema got an early start. The point of this quote, however, may be understood to be that the documentary is more profound than simple story films, or teaching films, or interest films. In many ways documentary combines the creative elements of other film forms.

In 1922 Robert J. Flaherty wrote, directed, and photographed the documentary *Nanook of the North. The film was made in the rugged; icy regions of Canada. Flaherty's creative treatment of the subject brought him fame and brought respectability to the documentary film.* Nanook means bear, and the name is appropriate for the hardy man who is the principal character in the story, a classic portrayal of a family struggling against the elements. Nanook is a Northern nomad traveling with his family from place to place seeking food and shelter. Flaherty shows the solitary and demanding lifestyle of the people of the North so that we can see the poetic simplicity of a family in so many ways like our own families.

---

[7] Ibid., p. 31.

[8] Paul Rotha, Sinclair Road, and Richard Griffith, *Documentary Film* (New York: Hastings House, 1943), p. 49.

[9] Ibid., p. 71.

Although there were questions left unresolved by the presentation of the film, they did not minimize Flaherty's accomplishments. The film communicated. Audiences were compelled by its power. Flaherty's success with *Nanook* caused Paramount (then Famous Players) to dispatch him to the South Pacific to bring back a *Nanook* of the South Seas.[10] What Flaherty brought back was a beautiful picture of idyllic islands. Paramount was disappointed, but Flaherty had done what he wanted to do. *Moana*, as the film was called, demonstrated that there was no real conflict in the Samoan mind between nature and human beings. Flaherty had captured the daily lifestyle of another people.

Vigorously encouraged by innovations in the technical aspects of filmmaking, the documentary film spread rapidly. Dziga-Vertov, John Grierson, and Walther Ruttmann followed Flaherty's lead to make films from naturally existing situations. Five basic classes of documentaries emerged: (1) the naturalist, (2) the realist, (3) the newsreel, (4) the propagandist, and (5) cinema verité.

The Naturalist

Films that used natural surroundings and everyday scenery were in the naturalist tradition. The naturalist filmmakers made symbols of the mountains, rivers, deserts, and forests in order to tap the emotional values in nature. In *The Covered Wagon* (1924), simplicity of theme and natural background had a major role in the film's effect. Its elements of naturalism made it more than a narrative.

Perhaps the most representative films in the naturalist tradition are *Nanook of the North*, *Moana*, and *Man of Aran*.

The Realist

The use of photography to highlight contradictions in urban life produced the realist tradition in documentaries. The filmmaker would show poor and rich, Jew and Gentile, cleanness and dirtiness, and

[10] Knight, op. cit., p. 136.

other points and counterpoints of urban life to make a point. These films were frequently witty but seldom profound. Such films as *Marche des Machines, Menilmontant, Emak Bakia,* and *Rien que les Heures* are typical; were European. Alberto Cavalcanti is one of the most recognized directors in this tradition. His *Rien que les Heures* (1926) broke new ground in that he attempted to show what the passing of time was like in the city of Paris. Rotha, Road, and Griffith see it as the first attempt to express creatively the life of a city on film.[11] Other films in this tradition are Ruttmann's *Berlin, Symphony of a City* (1927) and Joris Ivens's *Rain* (1929).

The Newsreel

A film that presents the events of the day in a straightforward manner with little or no elaboration for effect is in the newsreel tradition. Newsreel makers have no special viewpoint, an approach different from that of most documentary filmmakers who seek to portray events to a special purpose. Whereas newsreel reportage does not take much time and may be accomplished without much thought, the documentary requires contemplation. Montage newsreel films fall within most broad definitions of documentary because their foundations are the same naturally observable phenomena used for documentaries.

The Propagandist

The use of film as a persuasive instrument to produce a particular effect on an audience is the key to the propagandist tradition. Soviet filmmakers were among the first to use film for political propaganda. The rise of the Communist ideology in the Soviet Union coincided with the perfection of the documentary, so it was natural that the young nation used film to promote its special view of the world. S. M. Eisenstein's *October* (1928) and V. I. Pudovkin's *Deserter* (1939) are two notable films that used familiar images and persons to create a unique propagandistic impact. Rotha et al. claim that

[11] Rotha, Road, and Griffith, op. cit., p. 86.

The Soviet approach to the living theme and living scene, inspired by the ideology of a new political and social system, gave rise to new forms of technical construction and to new interpretations of natural material which were to lay a new basis for documentary production.[12]

Whatever the relationship between Soviet politics and propaganda filmmaking, the latter did not remain a Soviet-only phenomenon.

In Britain the ability and energy of John Grierson made publicity films—designed to advertise products and to cultivate markets—a significant part of the Empire Marketing Board. In 1929 Grierson directed the film *Drifters* for the marketing board. It told the story of a herring catch in a way that would appeal to a general audience and give it some understanding of food production.

The propaganda film probably reached a peak during World War II. German filmmakers were eager to activate the masses in support of the Third Reich, and American and British filmmakers told of the heroics of the Allied troops against the German war machine.

Cinema Verité

The rise of cinema verité has been a boon for documentary films. Films such as *Grass* and *Woodstock* have revealed the power of an event or institution to speak for itself. The filmmaker dispenses with the narrator's voice and allows the situation to tell the story.

Frederick Wiseman is perhaps the most effective member of the cinema verité school. Wiseman's fascination is with institutions and his emphasis becomes one of editing and cutting, rather than planning and arranging, in order to document factually without the intrusion of social or political narration. This drama on the doorstep approach, as Grierson called it, captures the impact of discovery.[13] Wiseman allows the camera to rove much as the human eye would naturally do. His *Titicut Follies* (1967), *High School* (1968), *Law and Order* (1969), and *Hospital* (1970) explore every aspect of the functioning of traditional institutions.

What makes *cinema verité* popular today is the portability of camera equipment plus audiences' distaste for "preaching" films. In cin-

[12] Ibid., p. 95.
[13] John Grierson, "The Last Interview," *Film Quarterly*, **26(1)**, Fall 1972, 24–30.

Table 8-2. Representative Documentaries from Several Nations

LA BATAILLE DU RAIL
1944–45 (sound)   French
Production: Cooperative Generale du Cinema Francais
Direction and script: Rene Clement
Dialogue: Colette Audry
Photography: Henri Alekan

THE BATTLE FOR THE UKRAINE
1942–43 (sound)   Soviet
Production: Central Newsreel Studios
Direction: Julia Solntseva, L. Bodik

THE BATTLE OF RUSSIA
1943 (sound)   Soviet
Production: Orientation Branch of the U.S. War Department
Direction: Lt.-Col. Anatole Litvak
Narration: Walter Huston, Capt. Anthony Veiller

B.B.C.: THE VOICE OF BRITAIN
1934–35 (sound)   British
Production: G.P.O. Film Unit for the British Broadcasting Cor-
    poration
Producers: John Grierson, Alberto Cavalcanti
Direction and script: Stuart Legg
Photography: George Noble, J. D. Davidson, W. Shenton

BERLIN
(Symphony of a City)
1927 (silent)   German
Production: Fox-Europa
Direction: Walther Ruttmann
Photography: Reimar Kuntze, Robert Baberski, Laszlo Schaffer

CHILDREN OF THE CITY
1944 (sound)   British
Production: Paul Rotha Productions for the Scottish Office
Producer: Paul Rotha
Direction, script, and editing: Budge Cooper
Photography: Wolfgang Suschitzsky
Narration: Alastair Dunnett

Table 8-2. (continued)

CHILDREN OF THE EARTH (Dharti ke Lal) 1945 (sound) Production: Indian People's Theatre Association Direction and Script: K. A. Abbas	Indian
DRIFTERS 1929 (silent) Production: Empire Marketing Board Film Unit Direction, script, and editing: John Grierson Photography: Basil Emmott	British
THE FACE OF BRITAIN 1934–45 (sound) Production: G. B. Instructional Ltd. Direction, script, and editing: Paul Rotha Photography: George Pocknall, Frank Bundy	British
THE FEELING OF REJECTION 1947 (sound) Production: National Film Board of Canada Direction: R. Anderson Script: Dr. Bruce Ruddick	Canadian
HIGH SCHOOL 1968 (sound) Direction: Frederick Wiseman	American
HOSPITAL 1970 (sound) Direction: Frederick Wiseman	American
THE MAN WITH THE MOVIE-CAMERA 1928–29 (silent) Production: Vufku (Ukraine) Direction: Dziga-Vertov Photography: M. Kauffmann	Soviet
MOANA 1926 (silent) Production: Famous-Players-Lasky (Paramount) Direction, script, and photography: Robert J. Flaherty	American

***Table 8-2.* (continued)**

NANOOK OF THE NORTH

1922 (silent)   American
Production: Reveillon Freres
Direction, script, and photography: Robert J. Flaherty

RIEN QUE LES HEURES

1926–27 (silent)   French
Production: Noefilm
Direction, script, and editing: Cavalcanti
Photography: James E. Rogers

THE SIEGE OF LENINGRAD

1942 (sound)   Soviet
Production: Lenfilm Newsreel Studios
Photography: 22 Soviet cameramen

THE TEN DAYS THAT SHOOK THE WORLD
(October)

1927–28 (silent)   SOVIET
Production: Sovkino
Direction, script, and editing: S. M. Eisenstein, G. V. Alexandrov
Photography: Eduard Tisse

THE TRIUMPH OF THE WILL

1936 (sound)   German
Direction: Leni Riefenstahl

TITICUT FOLLIES

1967 (sound)   American
Direction: Frederick Wiseman

TURKSIB

1928 (silent)   Soviet
Production: Vostok Film
Direction and script: Victor Turin

SALESMAN

1969 (sound)   American
Direction: David Maysles and Albert Maysles

Table 8-2. (continued)

WEALTH OF THE WORLD. NO. L. OIL

1950 (sound)   British
Production: Pathe Documentary Unit (in association with Film
  Centre)
Direction: Grahame Tharp.

For a more extensive listing, see Paul Rotha, Sinclair Road, and Richard Griffith, *Documentary Film* (New York: Communications Arts Books, Hastings House, 1963.

ema verité the filmmaker is able to gather all the evidence needed to communicate a message. The message communicated, of course, is still ultimately the product of the editing room.

Table 8-3 presents a way to look at the various aspects of documentary films.

As the table shows, films are made for audiences who are the respondents to their impact. Approaches to documentaries are represented by the special viewpoints of the filmmakers. In contemporary society the documentary filmmaker continues the tradition of presenting, with a viewpoint, naturally occurring phenomena.

The Entertainment Film

The entertainment film derives its uniqueness from being both an art form and an item of popular culture. In the beginning of the film industry D. W. Griffith succeeded in making his film *The Birth of a Nation* (1915) the vanguard of both art and popular culture. Cinematic construction and technique made the film a great success. It contains historical and mythic elements that give it wide appeal.

**Table 8-3. A Diagram of the
Approaches to Documentary Films**

Approaches	Medium	Respondents
Naturalist	Film	Audiences
Realist	Film	Audiences
Newsreel	Film	Audiences
Propagandist	Film	Audiences
Cinema verité	Film	Audiences

Griffith's film is set in the U.S. South after the Civil War. His portrayal of blacks during Reconstruction has been strongly condemned for leaving the nation with stereotypes of blacks that have been difficult to eradicate. Griffith shows incidents in the war itself, the rise of black state officials, the coming of the northern sympathizers, and the formation of the Ku Klux Klan. But it is his editing that distinguishes him as a craftsman. Cross-cutting between action scenes, integration of long and short shots to build a scene, varying of angle and shot length for rhythm, and dramatic use of the closeup are what give *The Birth of a Nation* a place in feature film history. However, Bohn and Stromgren are correct to state that although the scenes are masterfully executed the underlying sentiment is repugnant to many.[14] As the son of a Confederate colonel, Griffith portrayed the Klan as a benevolent organization of whites trying to protect themselves from blacks:

> This theme, together with the stereotypes that Griffith either consciously or unconsciously produced—the black Mammy and faithful darkies on the one hand and a wide assortment of lust-crazed, arrogant, whiskey-drinking blacks who terrorized the white community on the other—made the film immediately explosive. It was barred from exhibition in a dozen states and where it was shown in the north protests and demonstrations followed.[15]

Riots occurred in several cities after the film was shown, and as late as 1931 it was prohibited in Philadelphia. Controversy over the film may have been heightened by an increase in the number of black lynchings that occurred in the South. So appreciation of Griffith's artistic achievements has been somewhat beclouded. In the spectacular film *Intolerance* (1916), portraying intolerance through the ages, Griffith further demonstrated his artistic abilities and did much to contradict his reputation as a bigot.

In 1915 the Triangle Film Company was formed. D. W. Griffith was in charge of specials and large-budget showcase films, Thomas Ince was responsible for dramas and melodramas, and Mack Sennett worked on comedies. This American company pioneered the consolidation of producing units in American film.[16]

---

[14] Thomas Bohn and Richard Stromgren, *Light and Shadows: A History of Motion Pictures* (Port Washington, N.Y.: Alfred Publishing Co., 1975), p. 56.

[15] Ibid., p. 56.

[16] Ibid., p. 63.

The Stars Are Born

Independent filmmakers such as Carl Laemmle and Adolph Zukor challenged the established motion picture industry by instituting a "star" system for feature films. Under this system actors who appeared to attract followings were featured; audiences came to see the stars. When the independents needed new faces and names, they introduced new stars. The first stars in the movie industry were Mary Pickford and Charlie Chaplin of the silent picture era. Their salaries increased as their names became household words.[17]

Charlie Chaplin	Mary Pickford
1913—$150.00 per week	1913—$1,000 per week
1915—$1250 per week	1915—$2,000 per week
1916—$10,000 per week	1916—$10,000 per week, plus 50% of film profits
1917—$1,075,000 for eight pictures	1918—$15,000–20,000 per week plus 50% of film profits
1919—Has own production company	1919—Has own production company

The interest of the film companies was to establish an image of their stars in the minds of the audience. Thus in 1926 *Photoplay* magazine described male stars in the following manner:

Stars	Images
John Barrymore	Classic simplicity—Greek god in a museum.
Richard Barthelmess	The way every man looks to the woman who loves him.
Ronald Colman	Soldier-man, explorer, adventurer, he draws you against your will.
Reginald Denny	The perfect athlete—the Roman gladiator of our century.
Richard Dix	The typical young American, as storytellers sing of him.
John Gilbert	The fiery Slav—that stirs your pulses with the wanderlust.
Ben Lyon	The way football players should look in their street clothes.

[17]Ibid., p. 111.

Stars	Images
Ramon Navarro	The perfect troubadour, lyric charm and the beauty of a Greek boy.
George O'Brien	The most irresistible thing that walks the globe—a black Irishman.
Lewis Stone	The man of the world, the aristocrat, the diplomat, the seigneur.

Starcasting was practiced with female stars as well. There were the fragile flower, the girl next door, the vamp, the regal aristocratic lady, and the femme fatale. Blacks and other minorities were never cast as stars. Sidney Poitier was to emerge in the 1950s as the first authentic nonwhite movie star. Before Poitier, Hollywood was a harsh place for black actors and actresses.

In the early days of entertainment films a black actor named Frederick Ernest Morrison obtained some popularity as "Sunshine Sammy." Although his screen career had begun around 1913, as had the careers of Chaplin and Pickford, the highest salary he attained was $250.00 per week in the middle 1920s. "Sunshine Sammy" was one of the original *Our Gang* members. Morrison and Noble Johnson, who made 60 films and worked steadily in films for 30 years, were among the very few blacks to make a living from the film industry.[18]

In 1950 Sidney Poitier made his debut as a young intern in the film *No Way Out,* in which, as Dr. Luther Brooks, he has to attend to two white racist holdup men. The men are brothers, and both are injured, one shot in the leg and the other badly beaten. While Dr. Brooks is performing a spinal tap on one of the brothers to relieve pressure on the brain, because he is suspected of having a brain tumor as well, the patient dies. The brother, handcuffed and in the adjoining bed, taunts the doctor with racist remarks. Dr. Brooks demands an autopsy to show that his diagnosis was correct; as the next of kin, the brother refuses to permit it. Brooks with his white mentor, Dr. Wharton, pleads their cause to the widow of the dead man. But she is convinced by the brother that they are lying. As retribution an attack is planned on the black community. Blacks, hearing of the planned action, attack first. To quell the violence, Brooks gives himself up to the police. An autopsy is made that clears him. But the brother is not con-

[18]Daniel J. Leab, *From Sambo to Super Spade: The Black Experience in Motion Pictures* (Boston: Houghton Mifflin, 1975), pp. 54–55.

vinced. He escapes from the prison hospital and corners Brooks in Wharton's house. During the ensuing struggle it appears that Brooks will be killed; however, thanks to the dead man's widow, Brooks gains the upper hand and decides not to shoot the brother. As the thug complains of his pain, Brooks treats his wounds and bruises and says, "Don't cry, white boy, you're going to live."

No Way Out, despite its contrivances, is a historic film that can claim a number of firsts. It shows the life of a black middle-class family; it has antiwhite blacks on the screen; it shows racial violence with blacks holding their own; and it makes a hero of a black man.

Hollywood in Decline

Several factors have contributed to the decline of Hollywood. First, it no longer completely dominates movie production. The rising importance of Japanese and European productions has taken away some of the glory of Hollywood. Italian-made films by Roberto Rossellini, Luigi Zampa, and Federico Fellini; French films by Jean Cocteau, Alain Resnais, and Jean-Luc Godard; British films by Lindsay Anderson, Karel Reisz, and Richard Lester; and Japanese films by Kaneto Shindo, Hiroshi Teshigahara, and Akira Kurosawa attest to the growing power of the foreign entertainment film.

Second, the rise of television as a medium has caused retrenchment in the film industry. With movies being made expressly for television, they have become commonplace and not the important events they once were. Home Box Office, a pay television service that offers first-run movies and other entertainment, will continue the trend toward providing the home audience with a good reason for not going out. Television has a voracious appetite for films; for example, the movie industry sold nearly 9,000 pre-1948 films to television networks between 1955 and 1958.

Third, production budgets have continued to expand even though American audiences have decreased. According to Emery, Ault, and Agee, the following percentages represent the distribution of production costs for a Hollywood movie: [19]

[19] Edwin Emery, Phillip Ault, and Warren Agee, *Introduction to Mass Communications* (New York: Dodd, Mead and Company, 1976), p. 301.

Story costs	5%
Production and direction	5%
Sets and physical properties	35%
Stars and cast	20%
Studio overhead	20%
Income taxes	5%
Net profit after taxes	10%

Such an outlay reflects specialization and unionization in the industry. Thus Hollywood's own financial problems along with increased foreign competition have hastened the decline of the movie capital.

Modern American films in the category of *The Exorcist, Billy Jack, Star Wars, The Godfather, Close Encounters of the Third Kind,* and *Sounder* will continue to attract large audiences. These movies have mass appeal and usually are preceded by considerable advertising. In order for the industry to remain viable, American films must retain their uniqueness as an art form and as items of popular culture.

However, the rise of cinema verité has produced a sophisticated film audience that wishes to see real human tragedy or comedy. Alain Resnais' *Je t'Aime, Je t'Aime* (1968) is a cinema verité film about time. Riddler, the central character, has fallen into the hands of some people who want to make him actually relive a moment of his life. They feed him all kinds of information to help him recall, but he cannot. Resnais gives us an unchronological montage of Riddler's life in search of the actual moment. What Riddler experiences when he is with Olga, the woman he loves, is a kind of anxiety, the anxiety we all feel when we realize that other people's feelings are always an unknown quality.

In a similar vein, Rainer Werner Fassbinder in Germany has sought to examine human emotions: love, prejudice, hostility, and pain. In his award-winning (International Critics Prize, Cannes Film Festival) film *Ali: Fear Eats the Soul* (1974) Fassbinder has a German woman meet an inarticulate Arab mechanic in a seedy bar. They fall in love, enjoy happiness, feel hostility, grow apart, reunite, and experience prejudice. Although the film is a classic tearjerker, it is also a valid examination of society, economics, and love.

Ousmane Sembene, the Senegalese, is Africa's most important filmmaker. His *Black Girl*, which won the prestigious Jean Vigo Prize for 1966, was made to reflect the cruelty of neocolonialism. The heroine, Diouanne, is from the lower-class district of Dakar and aspires to better her position. Finally she succeeds in getting a job with a French couple who take her to Paris with them. Once in France she realizes what it is to be an African. After listening to insults about black people from her employers, she becomes apathetic and can no longer perform her work. Her refusal to work is considered laziness by her employers, who know, of course, that all Africans are lazy. Diouanne commits suicide. When the master returns to Senegal to return Diouanne's belongings to her mother, a young boy in a ceremonial mask follows the man through the crowded streets of Dakar.

Sembene, Fassbinder, and Resnais are finding international audiences for their feature films. Numerous other foreign filmmakers such as Yasujiro Ozu, Jean-Marie Straub, and Robert Bresson have added to growing significance of film centers other than Hollywood. Yet clearly, because Hollywood was first with the best, it will retain its place in the hearts of moviemakers if not in the markets.

Part Three Readings

Aronson, James. *The Press and the Cold War,* Boston: Beacon Press, 1973.

Barnouw, Erik. *Documentary: A History of the Non Fiction Films.* New York: Oxford University Press, 1974.

Barsom, Richard. *Non Fiction: A Critical History.* New York: Dutton, 1973.

Cohen, Bernard C. *The Press and Foreign Policy.* Princeton, N.J.: Princeton University Press, 1963.

Davison, Walter Philips. *Mass Communication and Conflict Resolution: The Role of the Information Media in the Advancement of International Understanding.* New York: Praeger Publishers, 1974.

Edwards, Verne, Jr. *Journalism in a Free Society.* Dubuque, Ia.: Wm. C. Brown Co. Publishers, 1970.

Emery, Walter B. *National and International Systems of Broadcasting: Their History, Operation and Control.* East Lansing: Michigan State University Press, 1963.

Glessings, Robert J. *The Underground Press in America.* Indiana University Press, 1970.

Green, Timothy. *The Universal Eye: World Television in the 1970's.* New York: Stein and Day, 1972.

Grierson, John. *Grierson on Documentary.* Berkeley: University of California Press, 1966.

Harrington, John. *The Rhetoric of Film.* New York: Holt, Rinehart and Winston, 1973.

Heinz-Dietrich, Fisher, and Merrill, John C. *International Communications: Media, Channels, Functions.* New York: Hastings House, 1970.

Hohenberg, John. *The New Media: A Journalist Looks at His Profession.* New York: Holt, Rinehart and Winston, 1968.

Jacobs, Lewis, ed. *The Documentary Tradition from Nanook to Woodstock.* New York: Hopkinson and Blake, 1971.

Kato, Hibetoshi. *Japanese Research on Mass Communications' Selected Abstracts.* Honolulu: University Press of Hawaii, 1974.

Katz, John Stuart, ed. *Perspectives on the Study of Film.* Boston: Little, Brown and Co., 1972.

Kracauer, Siegfried. *From Caigari to Hitler: A Psychological Study of the German Film.* Princeton, N.J.: Princeton University Press, 1947.

Lang, Kurt, and Engel, Gladys. *Politics and Television.* Chicago: Quadrangle Books, 1968.

Lawson, John. *The Creative Process: The Search for an Audio-visual Language and Structure,* 2nd ed. New York: Hill and Wang, Inc., 1967.

Lerner, Daniel, and Schramm, Wilbur, eds. *Communication and Change in the Developing Countries.* Honolulu: East-West Center Press, 1967.

McLuhan, Marshall. *The Gutenberg Galaxy.* Toronto, Canada: University of Toronto Press, 1967.

McLuhan, Marshall. *The Mechanical Bride.* Boston: Beacon Press, 1967.

Schiller, Herbert. *Mass Communication and American Empire.* Clifton, N.J.: Augustus M. Kelley Publishers, 1969.

Schramm, Wilbur. *Mass Media and National Development: The Role of Informa-*

tion in the Developing Countries. Stanford, Calif.: Stanford University Press, 1964.

Schramm, Wilbur, and Lerner, Daniel. *Communication and Change: The Last 10 Years and Next.* Honolulu: East-West Center, University Press of Hawaii, 1976.

Schramm, Wilbur, Lyle, Jack, and Porter, Edwin. *Television in the Lives of Our Children.* Stanford, Calif.: Stanford University Press, 1961.

Surgeon General's Scientific Advisory Committee on Television and Social Behavior. *Television and Growing Up: The Impact of Television Violence.* Washington, D.C.: U.S. Government Printing Office, 1972.

Szalai, Alexander, with Margaret Croke and associates. *The United Nations and the News Media's a Survey of Public Information in the United Nations in the World Press, Radio, and Television.* New York: United Nations Institute for Training and Research, 1972.

UNESCO. *World Communications: A 20th Century Survey of Press, Radio, Television, Film,* 5th ed. Paris: UNESCO, 1975.

Wells, Alan. *Mass Communications: A World View.* Palo Alto, Calif.: National Press Books, 1974.

White, David Manning, and Everson, W. *Sight, Sound and Society.* Boston: Beacon Press, 1968.

Wilcox, Dennis. *Mass Media in Black Africa.* New York: Praeger Publishers, 1975.

Part Four

I DREAMED THEY TOOK CRIME SHOWS OFF TV BECAUSE THEY ENCOURAGED VIOLENCE.

AND PEOPLE MOSTLY WATCHED GAME SHOWS.

AND THEN THEY TOOK GAME SHOWS OFF TV BECAUSE THEY ENCOURAGED GREED.

AND PEOPLE MOSTLY WATCHED SPORTS.

AND THEN THEY TOOK SPORTS OFF TV BECAUSE IT ENCOURAGED AGGRESSION.

©1976 JULES FEIFFER

AND PEOPLE MOSTLY WATCHED TEST PATTERNS.

DIST. FIELD NEWSPAPER SYNDICATE, 1976

WHICH BECAME WILDLY POPULAR BECAUSE PEOPLE COULD READ ANYTHING THEY WANTED INTO THEM.

VIOLENCE.... GREED.... AGGRESSION... SEX.....

It has never been more essential that the media be monitored and corrected and that stories and developments ignored by them be reported.
Nat Hentoff, "Students as Media Critics: A New Course"

What television did in the sixties was to show the American people to the American people. . . . It did show the people, places and things they had not seen before. Some they liked, and some they did not. It was not that television produced or created any of it.
David Brinkley

Mass Communication: Controls and Challenges

Chapter 9

Mass Communication
Regulations and Control

> Oh, Mama, just look at me one minute as though you
> really saw me . . . just for a moment now we're all
> together . . . Let's look at one another.
> Thornton Wilder, *Our Town.*

Regulation

Society has always recognized the enormous potential of mass dissemination of information. The ancient Greeks expressed the view that a
communicator should have a thorough knowledge of the subject and
of the mind of the audience,[1] and people today are still concerned
about the ability of communicators to influence the behavior of their
fellow beings. In order to protect society from malicious media and to
insulate the media from society's undue pressures, regulatory bodies
exist in most modern nations. Media regulation may be classified according to three influences: (1) *legal*, (2) *economic*, and (3) *social*.

Legal

Legal regulatory bodies are set up by governments. They exercise legal
control over the media on either a local or a national level. The types of
legal bodies may differ from nation to nation, but the intent is usually
the same: to regulate what is broadcast over the airwaves or printed in
the newspapers.

---

[1] Plato, *Phaedrus,* 259E, 271D.

Regulatory agencies are by their nature conservative bodies that seek to control and regulate the media's influence on society. In the United States, legal authority to control mass media on a national level rests with Congress, which has traditionally created agencies to regulate various enterprises. The Federal Communications Commission (FCC) was created by Congress with the express purpose of regulating broadcasting, and the FCC has been active in litigation involving media institutions since its inception. A guiding principle for the FCC has been the statutory requirement that broadcasters be fair. It is the chief policy regulation and the controlling influence in the FCC's efforts to carry out its mandate.

The Fairness Doctrine. Broadcasters have been required since 1949 to offer fair opportunity for opposing sides to participate in public discussions of controversial issues. This regulation is known as the fairness doctrine. It is based on the assumptions that the airwaves belong to the nation's public and that licensed broadcasters are obliged to operate in the interest, for the convenience, and at the necessity of the public. Serving the public need and interest is best achieved, according to Congress and the FCC, when broadcasters allow the airing of opposing and diverse points of view.

The fairness doctrine is not universally applauded by broadcasters. Several complaints have been lodged by the electronic media. Among other things, they have argued that the statutory requirement has altered the concept of a free press as traditionally understood to apply to the electronic media industry. Critics further argue that the fairness doctrine permits little discretion. Its terms make difficult any judgments about the quality of a viewpoint being presented, and broadcasters contend that a particular view may be false or may not be held in a local community. However, the FCC's purpose in this requirement is to protect the interest of the opposition by obliging broadcasters to provide access. Otherwise, opponents would be relatively impotent to dispute the views expressed by broadcasters.

The fairness doctrine also provides that an individual who is attacked in an editorial or a program must be sent a tape of it with a reasonable offer of an opportunity to reply (in other words; the broadcasters cannot wait a year to send the tapes and the offer). The intent of this provision is to provide the attacked individual with a format for responding in as nearly as possible the same manner as his or her attacker. However, broadcasters have been rather agitated by this provision, also. If a licensee supports a given political candidate by open editorial endorsement, then a notice has to be given to the opposing candidate within 24 hours. In 1976, Senator James Buckley, running for reelection in the state of New York, was able to secure equal time on the public broadcasting network because his opponent, Daniel P. Moynihan, had been featured; this was one of the few times that public broadcasting has gotten into the debate over the fairness doctrine.

A challenge to the doctrine was instituted by broadcasters; the Supreme Court ruled against them in 1969. The Court held that the rights of the audience, not the rights of the broadcasters, are paramount in the fairness doctrine. Furthermore, the Court contended that the loss of license is a threat consistent with the ends of those constitutional provisions prohibiting the abridgment of press and speech freedom. So this decision (*Red Lion Broadcasting Co.* v. *Federal Communications Commission*) has actually reinterpreted the First Amendment by establishing audience access to the airwaves.

The FCC has been one of the most activist public commissions in American society. The vastness of its territory, the complexities of its issues, and the power of the institutions it seeks to regulate probably demand a fairness doctrine that is upheld vigorously.

The FCC and Its Muscles. In the 1960s the FCC expanded the fairness doctrine to include cigarette advertising; prior to that time the doctrine had been limited to editorials. The controversy over cigarette commercials surfaced when the Surgeon General of the United States declared that cigarette smoking is injurious to human health. Subsequently the FCC ruled that antismoking agencies could advertise against cigarettes. Action by Congress to ban cigarette advertising released the FCC from the growing controversy. It did not, however, keep the FCC from pursuing an aggressive policy of broadcast regulation. In the 1970s the Commission ruled that a single owner could not own more than seven licenses for any group of broadcast media. Thus an owner could have no more than seven AM radio, seven FM radio, or seven television licenses. As the Commission had anticipated, its actions severely reduced acquisitions of smaller stations by powerful economic interests.

Furthermore, the FCC established a clear pattern in the 1970s that militated against an owner's concentrating all of his or her licenses within one market, even under the rule of seven. By employing a tough relicensing process the FCC has been able to control the geographic diversity of companies; applications for relicensing do not assure a licensee that the new license will be granted. Also, the FCC has actively discouraged newspaper owners from acquiring broadcast stations in their own areas. The rule that no single owner can control more than five VHF stations, even if they are in different geographic areas, is another significant factor in the FCC's attempt to minimize the growth of concentrated media power.

The FCC maintains a public interest posture. Regulation of ownership, vigilance in the relicensing process, and intervention in the network's programming practices are all public interest matters. In 1971 the FCC prohibited network affiliate stations from carrying more than 3 hours of network programs (except news programs) during prime time, 7 P.M. to 11:00 P.M. This meant that the local affiliates had to find additional programming for an extra half hour in prime time. The FCC's intent was to provide local viewers with programming of a public or civic nature during prime time, but what happened in many communities amounted to a reduction in the quality of programming. Frederick D. Whitney describes the results of the ruling:

> the ruling has proved a boon to program packagers who put together an assortment of travel, wildlife, quiz, and game shows and sell them individually to local television outlets. The result has been a reduction of prime-time by one hour, a substantial loss of audience, and the extension of daytime television into prime-time hours for no particular public benefit. The networks, at first leery of the ruling, later welcomed it as they were relieved of the enormous costs of one hour's competitive prime-time production.[2]

In a free enterprise system the regulation of media is laden with dangers. On the one hand, there is a clear need to protect the public from the abusive use of the communication media; on the other, free media are basic to the practice of free enterprise. The FCC has tried this balancing act with varying degrees of success. Another problem is that politics finds it difficult to abstain from intruding in a sector where the public can be so readily reached.

FCC Operation. The Federal Communications Commission is presently a six-commissioner board appointed by the President of the United States for 7-year terms. Because the Commission oversees and

[2] Frederick C. Whitney, *Mass Media and Mass Communications in Society* (Dubuque, W. C. Brown Co., 1975), p. 259.

regulates local stations through licensing and regulation of broadcast channels, the Commission pays close attention to community interest. Inasmuch as the regulation of stations is the only regulation of networks, the FCC in effect modifies the policies of networks by these initiatives at the local level.

Every grantee receives a license for 3 years. This, of course, means that each commissioner will normally have three opportunities to review a station's renewal request. A station that has strong community pressure to make programming changes in the interest of the public will usually face a stiff test for renewal, because the FCC's decision to renew licenses must be based on its belief that the license will result in public benefit. Substantial complaints or legal actions by citizens mean that a local station will have a difficult time with renewal. In most cases, however, the station's license is renewed after requirements are met or modifications are promised. Any community group may challenge a station's renewal request.

A station applying for renewal must submit an application with information on programming, performance, and personnel policies. These records are available for public inspection at the local office. Radio and television licenses within a particular state expire simultaneously, so that technically a state may be said to have a period when none of its stations is licensed. If the application to renew shows that a station has not complied with the Commission's policies, the station is ordered to comply by a certain date. The measures that can be taken against a violator are as follows:

1. Revoking an existing license.
2. Assessing fines for violations.
3. Granting a temporary renewal.
4. Denying a request for license renewal.
5. Initiating court actions to force violators to discontinue offensive practices.

Programming Categories. The FCC has identified 14 categories of programming. According to the FCC, every station should develop its programming including these categories:

1. Opportunity for local expression.
2. Development and use of local talent.
3. Programs for children.
4. Religious programs.

5. Educational programs.
6. Public affairs programs.
7. Editorialization by licensees.
8. Political broadcasts.
9. Agricultural programs.
10. News programs.
11. Sports programs.
12. Service to minority groups.
13. Weather and market reports.
14. Entertainment programs.

These categories are not ranked, nor does the FCC demand that a station divide its air time by percentages to each category; the rule of thumb is that each station must meet the interest needs of every major group in its audience. In order to help the stations meet their responsibilities, the FCC requires stations to do contributive planning. Contributive planning involves canvassing the public and consulting with community leaders; these consultations are assumed to reveal the views of substantial groups of listeners and viewers. Broadcasters must report regularly to the FCC on their consultations with community leaders: what issues were discussed, what problems were identified, and what leaders were consulted. A viewer may be able to discover whom the station considers a leader of the community, what groups the station contacted, and what programs are being planned for the community interest by examining the exhibits the station attaches to its application.

Included in a license renewal request are items such as

1. Past program formats.
2. Proposed program formats.
3. Programs designed to respond to the public needs.
4. Past programs broadcast to meet public's needs.
5. News staff and program time for local and regional news.
6. Evaluation of station's role in community program.
7. Number of weekly public service announcements.
8. Network affiliation.
9. Time and percentage of news programming, public affairs programming, and programming other than entertainment and sports.

The FCC and the News. The policies governing a station's responsibility for fairness in news broadcasting are contained in the FCC's fairness doctrine. In order to demonstrate fairness a station has to satisfy two requirements: (1) it must always broadcast issues of great public concern, and (2) it must assure overall fairness in discussion of issues by giving fair coverage to major viewpoints. Normally the FCC examines a station's overall record of compliance rather than a single instance. For example, if a station presents one view on abortion today, it is not obligated to present the opposing view today, also. Reasonable opportunity for presentation of different viewpoints is allowed. In fact, the FCC leaves it up to a station to determine its format, schedule, and technique for complying with fairness. In keeping with its responsibility to be fair, each station is required to maintain impartiality in news coverage. Although this is frequently difficult, impartiality and factual reporting are essential to responsible broadcasting. Deliberate slanting of the news or attempts to stage an event or story are subject to strong action by the FCC. A station is in danger of losing its license if it continues to deliberately distort stories for news value.

Legally qualified political candidates for the same office must be granted time under the same free or payment terms. This part of the FCC's policy has been clarified a number of times. It does not apply to candidates seeking different offices. Additionally there are the provisions that cover personal attack, discussed already. The FCC provisions, however, do not apply to foreign persons or to persons or groups whose beliefs are attacked in news footage. An attack on a Republican by a Democrat or vice versa during a political convention would be exempted from the policy on personal attack.

Marsha O'Brannon Prowitt identifies the three areas of commercial advertising that the FCC has acted on in the public interest: (1) amount and frequency of advertising, (2) false and misleading advertising, and (3) loudness.[3]

There is no required limit on radio or television advertising minutes per hour; most stations average between 15 and 20 minutes. The FCC has no specific standards for commercial advertising. The only possible control that the FCC has is to compare the amount of

[3] Marsha O'Brannan Prowitt, "The Federal Communications Commission," in Joseph Fletcher Littell (ed.), *Coping with Television* (Evanston, Ill.: McDougal; 1973), pp. 35–36.

minutes per hour for one year with those for another to determine if the station is following its proposed amount of time for advertising.

Because the public can hold the broadcaster responsible for false advertisement, it is in the station's interest to investigate the claims of its advertisers before it airs them.

As to loudness of commercials, there are standards for control. The Commission encourages listeners offended by excessively loud advertisements to write the FCC giving the station's call letters, the sponsor of the commercial, the product, date, and time.

The FCC represents one nation's attempt to regulate the broadcast industry by making it responsible to the public needs, and the FCC is constantly modifying its policies to handle various exigencies. Other nations, however, may require different types of control.

The Federal Trade Commission and the Food and Drug Administration. The FCC is by no means the only governmental agency involved in the regulation of the media industry; the Federal Trade Commission and the Food and Drug Administration also have responsibilities related to media broadcasting.

Inasmuch as advertising is the basic source of revenue for media operations, the FTC attempts to prevent deceptive advertisements and to ensure fair methods of competition. Created in 1914 by Congress, the FTC originally concentrated on unfair advertising practices that harmed competitors. Since 1938, when it was amended by the Wheeler-Lea Act, the FTC Act has guarded the industry against any unfair or deceptive practice.[4]

Section 5 of the FTC Act defines a false advertisement as one that is "misleading in a material respect." Thus an advertisement may be considered false if it does not reveal in a material sense the harmful or dangerous side effects of a drug or food. Or an advertisement may be deemed false if it claims to accomplish something that is naturally achieved without the medication, cosmetic, or food.

The FTC regularly monitors radio and television for examples of false advertisement. However, much of the detective work is done by members of the public who file complaints with the Commission regarding objectionable advertising practices, unfair methods of competition, and misleading information in a "material respect" with regard to food, drugs, or cosmetics. Businesses also scan the media for

[4]Wheeler-Lea Act, approved March 21, 1938, 52 Statute III, amending the Federal Trade Commission Act.

what they consider to be unfair practices of their competitors. Because it has regulatory authority over both the trade and media sectors, the FTC has moved into a powerful position in recent years as a monitor of the broadcasting industry.

The Food and Drug Administration enters the media regulation field through its work in monitoring commodities. Whereas the FTC concentrates on false advertising through the media, the FDA concerns itself with false labeling.[5]

A close working relationship exists between the FDA and the FTC in an effort to ensure the integrity and credibility of the trade and media sectors. Their mutual surveillance of the industry is "designed to avoid jurisdictional conflicts and duplication of efforts and to strengthen enforcement procedures."[6]

In addition to the vigorous actions of the FCC, FTC, and FDA in media regulation, there are numerous state and municipal statutes that affect radio and television broadcasters in their roles as corporations. Laws requiring charters, bylaws, and annual reports are a few examples of regulatory efforts by states and municipalities.

The Copyright Law. The United States Constitution provides in Article I, Section 8, that "The Congress shall have power . . . to promote the progress of science and useful arts, by securing for limited times to authors and inventors the exclusive right to their respective writings and discoveries." All copyright regulations stem from that law. In 1870 Congress entrusted the administration of the copyright law to the Library of Congress, and since 1897 the Copyright Office has been a separate branch of the Library of Congress. It has served as a national resource of the highest quality because it contains virtually all records of published materials in the United States.

Several changes in the law have been necessitated by technological advances. The 1909 copyright act allowed an author to control the literary rights to his or her work for 56 years by combining the initial registration of 28 years with a renewal of 28 years. Authors and heirs control unpublished manuscripts forever through common law. In 1976 the Congress passed a new copyright law that, beginning January 1, 1978, provides that copyright extends from the act of creation to 50 years after the death of the creator.

[5]"The Regulation of Advertising," 56 Columbia L. R. 1036–1037 (November 1956).
[6]Walter B. Emery, *Broadcasting and Government: Responsibilities and Regulations* (East Lansing: Michigan State University Press, 1961), p. 66.

The conferral of copyright protection at the moment of creation is new. Under the 1909 law copyright protection began with publication. This revision can be called a proprietor's advantage.

In effect, the law changes the significant date in the creation of a work from the date of publication to the date of the creator's death. Thus if a person publishes a book in 1982 and dies in 1990 the copyright protection extends to 2040.

Creators of a work have far more rights under the 1978 law. The fair use doctrine developed in the 1930s to allow a scholar to make a single reproduction of a work for individual purposes without violating copyright law has been clarified. The law essentially says that anyone can reproduce a copyrighted work for criticism, comment, news reporting, teaching, scholarship, and research without infringing on copyright. However, there are four major considerations that must be clear:

1. Purpose of use (commercial or nonprofit).
2. Nature of the copyrighted work.
3. Amount and substantiality of the portion used.
4. Effect on market potential.

Workbooks, laboratory sheets, and standardized tests are not to be reproduced.

Obtaining a Copyright. The Copyright Office may grant as many as 350,000 copyrights in a single year. The production of communication materials is so varied that the Copyright Office needs 14 classes of application:

Class A*:	Books published and manufactured in the United States.
Class A or B*:	Books manufactured outside the United States or books in the English language manufactured and first published outside the United States and subject to the ad interim provisions. The ad interim provision allows an author up to 6 months to apply for copyright of a book first published abroad in English. Copyright will endure until the expiration of 5 years after the date of first publication abroad.

Class B*:   Periodical manufactured in the United States or contribution to a periodical manufactured in the United States.

Class C*:   Lecture or similar production prepared for oral delivery.

Class D*:   Dramatic or dramatico-musical composition.

Class E*:   Musical composition first published in the United States by an American citizen or domiciliary of the United States. A second category of class E exists for foreign authors of compositions not first published in the United States.

Class F*:   Map.

Class G*:   Model or design for work of art or a work of art.

Class H*:   Reproduction of a work of art.

Class I*:   Drawing of plastic work of a scientific or technical character.

Class J*:   Photograph.

Class K*:   Print of pictorial illustration, or a print or label used for article of merchandise.

Class L or M*:   Motion picture.

Class N*:   There are three forms for class N applications: N for sound recordings, R for renewal of copyright, and U for notice of use of musical compositions on mechanical instruments.

The classes marked with an asterisk are not to be used for unpublished material. However, as already mentioned, unpublished books are protected by common law against unauthorized use prior to publication. In this way the copyright office minimizes the number of items it receives for registration; otherwise, the development of a model for a term paper or the doodling of a lawyer as she or he listened to the monotony of an adversary would be subject to copyright law. Books are generally defined as materials published in book form, pamphlets, leaflets, cards, and single pages containing a test. The Copyright Office has registered fiction, nonfiction, poetry, collections, directories, catalogs, and information in tabular form as books.

Production and publication are not synonymous. Generally in securing a statutory copyright of a book the author must first produce the work in copies by printing or other means of production, although copyright protection extends to the moment of creation. Most copyright notices bear the word "Copyright," the abbreviation "Copr.," or the symbol C, the name of the copyright owner, and the year of publication.

© Kalpana Doe 1968

Once the work is produced with the proper notice, publication is achieved on the earliest date when the first authorized edition is placed on sale, sold, or publicly distributed by the proprietor.

Ascertaining Copyright Status. When a copyright expires 50 years from the date of the creator's death, the work enters the public domain and may be used by anyone without payment or permission.

Three actions may be taken by an individual seeking to find the status of a copyright: (1) examining a copy of the work, (2) searching the Copyright Office catalogs, and (3) having the Copyright Office make the search. In examining a copy of a work published prior to 1977, the most important thing to look for on the copy is the notice of copyright (e.g., "© MARY DOE 1977" or "Copyright by Mary Doe 1977"). If a work fails to have either of these styles for copyright, then it runs the risk of permanently forfeiting copyright protection. The law also provides protection against unauthorized distribution and reproduction of sound recordings first published on or after February 15, 1972, provided that the recording bears a copyright notice with the symbol P, the year of publication, and the name of the owners of the copyright (e.g., "P 1977 Peter Poor, Inc.").

A *Catalog of Copyright Entries,* divided into parts according to the classes of works registered (e.g., "Books," "Music," "Motion Pictures"), is published by the Copyright Office. Each section of the catalog is issued regularly in book form and covers all initial and renewal registrations made during a particular time period.

Most major public and university libraries have copies of the Catalog. This first thing to do with the Catalog is to see if it is up to date with its entries. Several limitations, including time lag, make the Catalog not so useful as it might be. For example:

1. The Catalog does not include entries for one person's assigning rights to another and cannot be used for searches involving the ownership or rights.

2. The Catalog is usually about a year behind on its registrations.
3. The Catalog contains only the bare facts about a registration; it is not a verbatim transcript of the registration record.

Despite the limitations, a person wishing to investigate the copyright status of a work would do well to examine the Catalog. On a visit to the Copyright Office in Arlington, Virginia, a person is free to look through the card catalog, record books, and microfilm records of assignments and related documents.

The Copyright Office will search for copyright status for a statutory fee of five dollars an hour and prepare a typewritten report of the search once it is completed. A person who wants to use the Copyright Office for a search should be certain that all fees are understood ahead of time. Furthermore, as much detailed information as possible should be provided, including the following:

1. Title of the work and any possible variations.
2. Name of the author, including pseudonym.
3. Name of the probable copyright owner, usually the publisher or producer.
4. Approximate date when the work was published or registered.
5. Type of work (book, play, etc.).
6. Title of periodical or collection in which the work may have originally been published, and volume or issue number, if possible.
7. Registration number or any other copyright data.

A complete search may still not ascertain whether or not a work is protected. For example, the work may be unpublished in a technical sense and therefore is protected without the need of registration. Or it is possible that a work is in the public domain in the United States but not in other countries; every nation has its own copyright statutes that apply within its boundaries.

A person attempting to investigate copyright has been given avenues that may bring satisfaction, but there are also numerous detours. The best policy is to follow the traditional avenues first and then examine the possible detours prior to making a judgment regarding a work's protection.

Economic

Part of the desire for programming of good quality by the major networks reflects economic influences. Inability to obtain a sponsor has often meant that a program did not receive air time. Businesses are operated for profit; selling a program to an advertiser means showing its profit possibilities. Among the factors contributing to an advertiser's decision to sponsor a program are audience size and program content, and advertisers are inclined to juggle these two factors for their optimum value.

Withholding of sponsorship is an irregular way of controlling the media. It means that programs of social or educational value may seldom be aired over commercial stations. A sponsor with the audacity to present a documentary on Communism on American stations has not been found. In the same way the Nigerian broadcast stations would find it difficult to show a documentary on the Biafran movement. The famous singer Nat King Cole was the first black American to have a television show of his own. Unwilling to risk a loss of profit, the sponsor abruptly canceled the show after receiving numerous complaints from viewers. Obviously, if the public is to benefit from the advantages of media, regulation of the media industry should not depend solely on economic factors.

The Advertising Factor. Advertising is a huge business. Nearly a half million people work in some field of advertising in the United States. Most of these people are in manufacturing, services, media, retail, and specialty. In addition, there are hundreds of thousands of persons who work as printers, sign painters, and editors without whom the business could not exist. The advertising agencies themselves hire staff directly out of college, but they do not hire as many people as the other areas.[7] J. Walter Thompson, McCann-Erickson, Bates and Company, and Young and Rubicam are large agencies with international offices. These agencies usually seek to hire nationals for their foreign offices.

Advertising is "the dissemination of sales messages through purchased space, time or other media to identify, inform, or persuade," and "television obtains about 80 percent of its income from network

[7]Edwin Emery, Phillip Ault, and Warren Agee, *Introduction to Mass Communications* (New York: Dodd, Mead, 1976), pp. 352–354.

and national spot advertising; the rest comes from local advertising."[8] The mass communication media provide the advertiser with the most effective way to contact the public. A person wishing to sell a cow or a condominium can get wider attention for the sales message if it is presented through the mass communication media than if she or he stands on a street corner speaking to people as they pass by. Purchase of time and space gives the media the money to operate their various programs. With virtually all support coming from advertisers, a television network must be cautious if it does not want to lose clients.

In 1960 Leo Rosten wrote in *Daedulus* that the intellectual has ten principal complaints about the media:[9]

1. The mass media lack originality.
2. The mass media do not use the best brains or the freshest talents.
3. The mass media do not print or broadcast the best material that is submitted to them.
4. The mass media cannot afford to step on anyone's toes.
5. The mass media do not give the public enough or adequate information about the serious problems of our time.
6. The aesthetic level of the mass media is appalling; truth is sacrificed to the happy ending, escapism is exalted, romance, violence, melodrama prevail.
7. The mass media corrupt and debase public taste. They create the kind of audience that enjoys cheap and trivial entertainment.
8. The mass media are what they are because they are operated solely as money-making enterprises.
9. The mass media are dominated—too much influenced—by advertisers.
10. The mass media do not provide an adequate forum for minority views—the dissident and unorthodox.

Rosten rightly understands that the profit motive and the advertisers' influence discourage the expression of dissident views. As money-making enterprises, the media cannot use materials or ideas that are offensive to sponsors and expect to remain economically viable. Thus the economic influence on the media is a double-edged sword; on one hand, advertising pays the costs of high-quality programming; on the other, it serves to control the views expressed in the media.

[8] Ibid., pp. 354, 358.
[9] Leo Rosten, "The Intellectual and the Mass Media: Some Rigorously Random Remarks," *Daedulus* **99(2)**, Spring 1960, 333. Reprinted by permission of the American Academy of Arts and Sciences, Boston, Massachusetts. Spring 1960, *Mass Culture and Mass Media.*

Social

Social influences on the media largely have to do with ethics. Although the legal and economic influences will usually serve to screen out programs, articles, or features that are counter to the public's moral taste, the media institutions themselves exercise considerable discretion in this regard. This does not mean that the media must follow every ethical dictate of the community but rather that they must recognize where their stance differs from that of the community.

This is an axiological issue that helps to direct and guide the ethics of media, and three distinct points must be addressed in examining it: (1) determination of what is good, (2) determination of the basis of publication and broadcasting, and (3) examination of the means-ends controversy.

The Good. A central concern of any source of mass communication must be the welfare of its audience. As government is established to protect the welfare of the society, so mass media may be considered the guardians of the public trust. Abuse of media power is an aberration that cannot be tolerated in organized societies. Power is most often abused when media fail to advance the public welfare. There are numerous ways in which the welfare of the public may be advanced, the most obvious being *presentation of truth, revelation of error,* and *education of the public.*

The Presentation of Truth. Truth is vital in journalism. A writer or director who does not present the truth is not believed for long. Unless it is the stated or implied purpose of communication to be false, then the audience has a right to expect the presentation of truth. In satire or some other form of entertainment that expressly uses false statements, the audience will not normally be offended. An axiology of communication must begin with the presentation of truth.

The Revelation of Error. A counterpart to the presentation of truth is the revelation of error. Respect for media audiences, the public, must be a guiding principle in an axiology of mass communication. To the extent that economic power is derived from audiences, media companies can protect their economic power and goodwill by revealing erroneous stories or facts. There are several ways media can reveal error:

editorials, media-sponsored debates, correspondence read or printed, and immediate correction of any factual inaccuracies. Although most institutions would rather not have any factual errors to correct, those that do correct their mistakes tend to establish credibility with their audiences.

The Education of the Public. Whether anyone admits it or not, the education of the public is one of the media's most powerful functions. As a method for aiding the public welfare, education by the media is essential to political or social progress in contemporary societies, and the enormous reaching capability of media means that the public can seldom act apart from its influence. The 1976 Carter-Ford presidential debates were viewed by a cumulative audience of more than 300 million. The public's need to have social and political information is the rationale for media's role in the educational process; right decisions are based on adequate information. In developing an intelligent audience, however, the media develop a clientele who will demand better programming and writing. By evaluating how well media function in supporting the right of the public to know, in revealing errors, and in presenting truth, a viewer can ascertain what the media's values are.

The Basis of Broadcasting. The basis of all news reporting should be factual information. Terry Ann Knopf has aptly demonstrated how readily journalists can misrepresent fact.[10] She points out that "glaring instances of inaccuracy, exaggeration, distortion, misinterpretation, and bias have continued. . . ."[11]

The wire services are responsible for most of the inaccuracies received by other news gatherers. Inasmuch as nearly 95 per cent of all printed news in the United States is derived from the Associated Press, United Press International, and Reuters, what their reporters send in as news is what we normally receive. Although filing a story later proved to be inaccurate is rarely cause for termination of an employee in the media industry, a policy that ignores the factual accuracy in news reporting contributes to poor media credibility. The control of the means by which bias is produced is at the center of any axiological discussion. What is the objective of the news story? What public inter-

[10]Terry A. Knopf, "Media Myths on Violence," in Alan Wells (ed.), *Mass Media & Society* (Palo Alto, Calif.: Mayfield Publishing Co., 1975), pp. 256–262.
[11]Ibid., p. 257.

est does it serve? How can the story be accurately reported in limited space? These are the major questions in publication or broadcasting.

The Means-Ends Controversy. Few communicationists have attempted to deal with the ethical issues surrounding mass media. However, there are several popular approaches to ethical problems, perhaps the most useful being the means-ends argument. Usually this argument is initiated when a person asks, "Does the ends justify the means?" or "Do the means justify the ends?" The problem is that it is seldom possible to determine with any accuracy the value of an end without intensive examination. A reporter in the field is burdened with making an on-the-spot decision about reporting the facts. Determining whether the facts should or should not be reported is a questionable enterprise, yet it is frequently done. The fact that reporters did not report the militant speeches of blacks after the riots of the 1960s may have had something to do with what was stated in the Kerner Commission Report or may have simply been a sign of television's declining fascination with the drama of black anger. More likely, it was the result of a combination of factors. One certain factor was the individual decisions of news reporters not to report on violent rhetoric. After a while in the 1960s it came to be thought that the reporting of televised militancy had something to do with riots in the streets.

The question remains, however: Should a reporter report what she or he sees or hears, or should the reporter report *discreetly?* To report discreetly means that the reporter must make an individual ethical judgment about what will happen to the facts in deciding whether or not to report them. There are several things that a reporter may do to avoid reporting a given factual event. He or she may (1) *report nothing,* (2) *report an alternative fact,* (3) *report an insignificant fact,* or (4) *distort the central fact* so that it is not understandable or credible.

Ethics enters into everything human beings do. A reporter who decides to report nothing when she has a story is acting on her own decision regarding the ends. If she believes that to report the facts would lead to unacceptable ends and therefore fails to report them, she is guilty of making an individual judgment about society's good. In another instance a reporter who is asked to make a report on a military takeover in a given country may feel obliged to concentrate the report on military rule in a neighboring nation, the history of the

country, previous military leaders, or the origin of the junta leader—
stories that may be of interest and deserving of attention, but nevertheless avoidance of the central fact is another imposition of individual judgment. Or a reporter may decide to report an insignificant fact,
e.g., something regarding the geography or climate of a nation, rather
than anything bordering on the central issue. Finally, a reporter may
choose to so distort the facts that they are rendered ineffective as
information. These techniques for avoiding the reporting of facts must
be considered highly inappropriate for the professional news reporter.
Any attempt to impose censorship, whether individual or corporate,
must be condemned. Reporting inaccurate information means that the
public's decisions and attitudes will be incorrectly shaped, which will
lead to a breakdown in social organization.

A cautionary note should be inserted at this point. Mistakes will
be made in reporting. The best reporters will occasionally fail to catch
the full significance of a news fact. Not until months afterward may
the reporter be able to understand the impact of a single fact. This is
one more reason why a reporter should not seek to determine what is
good for the audience but rather report the facts as they develop.

Free people have the right to assess facts for themselves, however
uneducated or naive their powers of discrimination may be. What one
person hears and understands may not be what an Einstein would
hear and understand, but it is the privilege of every person to make
his or her own judgment about facts. The media's task is to report the
facts as faithfully as possible. When media institutions are operated on
this principle, society benefits.

Investigatory Bodies

National investigatory bodies have occasionally been established by
government or private foundations to assess the responsiveness of the
media to society. These "commissions," as they are most often called
have provided critical insight into how media institutions function,
and in some cases investigatory committees not specifically established to investigate the media have made important statements
regarding the media's role in society. Collectively, the information
contained in the reports of these commissions constitutes a respository
of significant data about press freedom and responsibility and about

the impact, operations, and capacities of media institutions in open societies.

Commission on the Freedom of the Press. Robert M. Hutchins chaired the Commission on the Freedom of the Press in the 1940s and introduced a new term in the lexicon of the press: _social responsibility._ In 1942, through the combined efforts of Time, Inc., and Encyclopaedia Britannica, Inc., the Commission was initiated with a small grant. The final report was made in 1947 and was met with loud objections by members of the press.[12] Among the recommendations were that the press should

1. Provide a truthful, comprehensive account of the day's events in a meaningful context.
2. Regard itself as a forum for the exchange of comment or criticism.
3. Project a representative picture of the constituent groups in society.
4. Present and clarify goals and values of the society.
5. Provide full access to the day's intelligence.

[handwritten marginalia: 5 goals of commission]

The Hutchins Commission was forthright in its guidelines for press responsibility. According to the Commission, society demanded press responsibility from its media. The public interest had to be served in order to justify the public trust of the press. The immediate reaction was reluctance and suspicion, and the Commission was roundly criticized by the press. For one thing, there were no members of the press on the Commission, and this was a sore point with the profession.

In part, the press was reacting to the Commission's conclusion that freedom of the press was in danger for three reasons:

1. Public access to the media had become more limited as the press became a mass instrument.
2. The controllers of the press had not provided what the society needed.
3. The controllers had engaged in practices that society condemned.

[12] Commission on Freedom of the Press, _A Free and Responsible Press_ (Chicago: University of Chicago Press, 1947).

The Hutchins Commission was stepping on sensitive toes in its indictment. If the press did not monitor itself, then control from without was invited. The Commission recommended that

> Some agency which reflects the ambitions of the American people for its press should exist for the purpose of comparing the accomplishments of the press with the aspirations which the people have for it . . . [and] would also educate the people as to the aspirations which they ought to have for the press.[13]

The Commission proposed the agency be independent of the press and government and be granted a 10-year life span before its achievements were assessed. Among the activities of such an independent agency would be the following:[14]

1. Continuing efforts, through conference with practitioners and analysis by its staff, to help the press define workable standards of performance, a task on which the Commission has attempted a beginning.
2. Revelation of the inadequacy of press service in certain areas and the trend toward concentration in others, to the end that local communities and press itself may organize to supply service where it is lacking or to provide alternative service where the drift toward monopoly seems dangerous.
3. Inquiries in areas where minority groups are excluded from reasonable access to the channels of communication.
4. Inquiries abroad regarding the picture of American life presented by the American press and cooperation with agencies in other countries and with international agencies engaged in analysis of communication across national borders.
5. Investigation of instances of press lying, with particular reference to persistent misrepresentation of the data required for judging public issues.
6. Periodic appraisal of the tendencies and characteristics of the various branches of the communications industry.
7. Continuous appraisal of governmental action affecting communications.
8. Encouragement of the establishment of centers of advanced study, research, and criticism in the field of communications at universities.
9. Encouragement of projects that give hope of meeting the needs of special audiences.
10. The widest possible publicity and public discussion on all the foregoing.

[13] Ibid., p. 100.
[14] Ibid., pp. 100–102.

Television had not become a major communication factor in American society at the time of the Hutchins Commission. Nevertheless, the Commission's study of the press had implications for all media.

The initial reaction of the press to the Hutchins Commission was unfortunate, if understandable: that an outside agency would limit rather than guarantee the freedom of journalists. Dealing with the profound issue of press freedom must always be done cautiously; however, the Hutchins Commission was in fact cautious and also highly relevant.

National Advisory Commission on Civil Disorders. During the urban rebellions of the 1960s much attention was focused on the media's role in civil disturbances. President Lyndon B. Johnson appointed a National Advisory Commission on Civil Disorders in 1967. The primary charge of the Commission, chaired by Governor Otto Kerner, was to discover the cause of black riots in the cities. In its report to the President the Commission stated that the media were responsible for at least some of the problem:

> The media report and write from the standpoint of a white man's world. The ills of the ghetto, the difficulties of life there, the Negro's burning sense of grievance, are seldom conveyed. Slights and indignities are part of the Negro's daily life, and many of them come from what he now calls "The white press"—a press that repeatedly, if unconsciously, reflects the biases, the paternalism, the indifference of white America.[15]

The Kerner Commission made pointed references to the inability of the white press to understand the black community. The Commission laid a major part of the blame for black riots on the press, contending that news reports, while attempting balance, were often inflammatory and exaggerative of both event and mood.

Carnegie Commission on Educational Television. In 1965 the Carnegie Commission on Educational Television was established under a grant of $500,000 from the Carnegie Corporation to study the future of educational broadcasting. In 1967 the Commission issued its report. It first of all changed the name "educational television" to "public television" to avoid any pejorative connotations of the word *educational*. Noting that public television was severely underfunded by federal, state, local, and private sources, the Commission stated that a massive

---

[15] National Advisory Commission on Civil Disorders, *Report of the National Advisory Commission on Civil Disorders* (New York: Bantam Books, 1968), p. 360.

transfusion of funds would be required if public television were to fulfill its promise. The Commission envisioned that support funds should principally come from the federal government, to be overseen by a nongovernmental group known as the Corporation for Public Television. The Commission further recommended that the federal government impose an excise tax of 2 to 5 per cent on all new television sets manufactured to provide permanent funding for public television and to insulate it from political interference. A board of 12 members—six to be appointed by the President, with Senate confirmation, and the remaining members to be appointed by the original Commission—would further separate public television from undue governmental influence. Like the commercial networks, the Corporation for Public Television would act as a booking agent to supply programs to all public television stations. National Educational Television (NET) would become one of the major program suppliers, but not the only one, as it had been.

The Carnegie Report was praised for its foresight in recommending governmental funding by many agencies—including the Ford Foundation, which had already pumped several hundred million dollars into educational broadcasting, and by CBS, which immediately pledged $1 million for public television beginning the day the Corporation for Public Television would come into being.

What happened is history, as has been described already in Chapter 6 of this volume. However, it should be pointed out that the Public Broadcasting Act of 1967 deviated from the Carnegie recommendation in three areas: (1) its concern with "public television" became a concern with "public broadcasting," embracing radio as well; (2) the Corporation for Public Television became the Corporation for Public Broadcasting; (3) permanent funding, in the form of an excise tax or otherwise, was not provided.

National Commission on the Causes and Prevention of Violence. In 1969 the National Commission on the Causes and Prevention of Violence released its report, which contained implied criticism of the press. This report came out after the Chicago demonstrations and the violence at the 1968 Democratic Convention, and counseled against the inexpert use of television equipment and cautioned that television lights could attract exhibitionists. Appropriately it recognized the charges that had been made against the press by police and local politicians. Its chief recommendation for the media was the establishment of a center for media study, appointed by the President of the United States and composed of nonpolitical and nonmedia members. In addition, the Commission suggested a media advisory board made up of journalists and scholars.

Surgeon General's Scientific Advisory Committee on Television and Social Behavior. The report of the Surgeon General's Scientific Advisory Committee on Television and Social Behavior was published as *Television and Growing Up: The Impact of Televised Violence* in 1972.[16] A distinguished panel of communication scholars received testimony and discussion from numerous experts on television content, violence, impact, socialization, and programming. The result was a major milestone in the history of a medium. Among other contentions, the report argued that children who view televised episodes of aggression are more willing to engage in aggression against other children. A review of numerous scholarly reports and studies led the Committee to conclude that violence depicted on television can induce mimicking or copying by children. Yet the Committee was careful to caution that research has not shown an adverse effect on the majority of children. So the Committee's indictment of television is rather mild. The report, however, constitutes a solid investigation into television content.

Carnegie Commission on the Future of Public Broadcasting. Ten years after the first Carnegie Commission issued its report on public television, the Carnegie Commission on the Future of Public Broadcasting (referred to as Carnegie II) was formed with a $1 million, 18-month mandate to study every aspect of public broadcasting. President Carter promised to work closely with Carnegie II in its policy development program for the future of public television and public radio. On the new Commission's agenda are such questions as

1. How can public broadcasting maintain control over its own destiny, free from political interference, and still receive adequate federal support?
2. How does one measure "success" in public broadcasting? Should public broadcasting compete for audience numbers?
3. Should public broadcasting concern itself more with national

---

[16]*Television and Growing Up: The Impact of Televised Violence,* Report to the Surgeon General, United States Public Health Service (Washington, D.C.: U.S. Government Printing Office, Behavior, 1972), p. 113.

programming or with programming for minority audiences such as blacks, women, and the aged? What balance should be struck?

4. To what extent should the new communications hardware be regulated?

Carnegie II also faces the troubling question of funding. Some experts have placed this need as high as $1 billion a year. Others are quick to point out that it will be extremely difficult for public broadcasting to steer clear of "accountability" for governmental support, whatever the amount. Therefore, the Commission is being urged to come up with a proposal of a wide range of funding plans to include (1) "directed" or "tied" taxes to be used for public broadcasting, (2) an extra charge on the profits of the commercial broadcasting networks, (3) checkoffs on federal income tax returns, (4) more support from the federally supported endowments for the arts and humanities, and (5) more support from state and local governments.

The entire question of the relationship of public broadcasting to commercial broadcasting will also be explored by Carnegie II. The 1979 target date for Carnegie II's report will soon be here, and the report is eagerly awaited.

Summary. The six investigatory bodies discussed in this section are the major ones that have looked or are looking at media problems and issues. Numerous other state and local commissions have investigated various aspects of the media. In a free society the public must be allowed to examine the operation of mass media institutions, which provide us with so much of our data for making judgments, in order to assure their competence and fairness.

Chapter 10
Minorities:
Coloring the Media

*The news media have not communicated to the majority of
their audience—which is white—a sense of the
degradation, misery, and hopelessness of living in the
ghetto. They have not communicated to whites a feeling
for the difficulties and frustrations of being a negro in the
United States. They have not shown understanding or
appreciation of—and thus have not communicated—a
sense of Negro culture, thought, or history.*
Kerner Commission Report

Minorities

The two largest racial and ethnic minority groups in America are the
Afro-Americans or blacks and the Hispanic-Americans, comprising
Puerto Ricans and Mexican-Americans. Collectively these groups represent about 50 million Americans. The issue of the media's response
to and portrayal of racial and ethnic minorities is of long standing in
the United States. In the nineteenth century Afro-Americans felt the
need to develop their own newspapers in order to present factual accounts of black life in the United States. Samuel Cornish and John
Russwurm began *Freedom's Journal* in 1827 in direct response to racism
in the white press. Similarly for Mexican-Americans in the western
part of the United States the establishment of *El Clamor Publico (The
Public Outcry)* in 1855 was a reaction to the absence of a voice for Mexican-Americans. Its founder, Francisco P. Ramirez, was a champion of
Mexican-American dignity. Thus the advent of minority newspapers
in American society was a precursor of many contemporary racial issues.

The black press has been the most consistent voice of agitation and protest within the Afro-American community. More than 3000 black newspapers have been started. For the last 50 years there have been more than a hundred black newspapers simultaneously in operation. The papers with the largest circulation and most influential editorials have been the *Baltimore Afro-American, Bilalian News* (formerly *Muhammad Speaks*), *The Amsterdam News, The Chicago Defender,* and *The Pittsburgh Courier.* [1] These papers have frequently challenged editorials in the white press, presented alternative solutions to social problems, endorsed progressive political candidates, reported on black social events, and served as an outlet for black poets and short story writers. White dailies have consistently reported sensational black news. Routine news items such as births, deaths, weddings, and business are almost always reported in the black press. The *Chicago Courier* prints no crime news but does print a considerable amount of business news. Unquestionably, the black newspapers represent a major information resource for the black community.

The Black Press Audience

The black press in the United States serves what may be called the twenty-fifth largest nation in the world. When Frederick Douglass started his *North Star,* there were approximately 4 million blacks in the United States. With a current population of over 30 million, blacks in the United States constitute the third largest group of blacks living within the boundaries of a single nation. Nigeria has nearly 80 million people and Brazil has a black population of well over 40 million. Only two of the 54 nations of Africa are larger than black America; only three nations of the 36 in South and North America are larger than black America. The black press has provided information and entertainment to this large black community. Despite the fact that advertising dollars do not find their way to the black press so frequently or so bountifully as to the white press, it is the black press that holds the allegiance of the black community.

[1] L. F. Palmer, Jr., "The Black Press in Transition," in Michael C. Emery and Ted Curtis Smythe (eds.), *Readings in Mass Communication* (Dubuque, Ia.: W. C. Brown Co., 1974), p. 300.

Carlton B. Goodlet estimates that "the ten largest advertising agencies in the United States placed $1.92 billion in national newspaper advertising in 1972, of which the black press, represented by Amalgamated Publishing Company, received less than one-seventh of one per cent, or $2,300,000."[2] Clearly the black press is not affluent. Further evidence of advertisers' general disregard for the black press is the fact that in 1974 the ten largest corporations that advertise the most spent $1.54 billion, but less than $750,000 went to the black press.[3] Although black and minority money is spent with these merchandising firms, they frequently return none of the money to black organizations. In 1972 blacks spent nearly $46 billion, most of it with white-owned businesses. The $900 million generated for public relations and advertising went to the white press and electronic media.[4] Yet the poverty of the black press has not stopped it from becoming the most important nonreligious force in the lives of black Americans. LaBrie says that "the black newspaper and the black church together have formed the two most formidable and aggressive lobbies and change agents throughout the civil rights movement. . . ."[5] Neither the church nor the press can be overlooked as a change agent in the black community.

As the principal source of positive images and community news for blacks, the black press has provided the resources for the white media operations that have employed blacks. More than three fourths of all black employees of white television, radio, and newspaper companies began working for black-owned companies. While this steady stream of black talent has entered the white media agencies, the black media remain viable.

The Johnson Publishing Company of Chicago is the dominant force in black publishing. Its primary media are magazines including the highly popular and widely read *Ebony, Ebony, Jr.,* and *Jet.* An intellectual magazine begun as *Negro Digest* and later called *Black World* was not successful; it ceased publishing in 1976. Other magazines have begun to fill the void created by the demise of *Black World*. *Essence: The Magazine for Today's Black Woman* regularly publishes cre-

---

[2] Carlton B. Goodlet, "The Black Press: A Democratic Society's Catalytic Agent for Building Tomorrow's America," in Henry LaBrie (ed.), *Perspectives of the Black Press, 1974* (*Kennebunkport, Me.: Mercer House Press, 1974*), p. 210.

[3] Ibid., p. 210.

[4] Ibid.

[5] Henry LaBrie, *Perspectives of the Black Press, 1974* (Kennebunkport, Me.: Mercer House Press, 1974), p. iii.

ative writing by new authors. Although Johnson Publishing Company is the largest company, other black publishing firms are providing valuable services to the community. The readers of the black press are from every profession and class, and nearly all blacks have access to some black media. This situation will probably continue for some time inasmuch as the white media have yet to fully recognize their black and other minority audiences.

Black Broadcasting

The rise of radio stations in black communities has meant competition for the press. Some stations are owned by syndicates that control radio stations in several black communities. Typically these stations have concentrated on soul music formats with 5-minute news segments on the hour or half hour. They are usually heavily subscribed to by white businesses that operate in the black communities and by black businesses. Use of the radio as a medium of social or political awareness has been slow in developing, and there has been a reluctance on the part of some owners to decrease the soul music content. However, the nation of Islam, Operation Breadbasket, and a few other social-religious organizations have made use of the airwaves. Thus radio stations are an integral part of the urban black community. Where there are no black-owned stations, white stations usually have a black-oriented disk jockey with a special program for black listeners.

In the 1970s blacks began to consider buying television stations, and the first black-owned television station opened in Detroit in 1975. The development of black radio occurred when there was much more segregation than there is now. Markets were considered to be permanently separate. Television, on the other hand, is a less discriminatory medium, and television stations were never as audience oriented as radio. Specialized programs are possible and are presented, but they are much more difficult than specialized programming on radio.

White-owned and -operated television stations have come under fire from a number of sources for their lack of minority programming because minority viewers are expressing their reactions and desires much more freely in contemporary American society. Images of blacks, Puerto Ricans, native Americans, and Mexican-Americans have frequently been negative. However, progress in this area has occurred with the increase in the sophistication and education of television writers and directors. More sensitivity to cultural differences, lifestyles, value orientations, and customs has resulted from agitation and from the raising of social consciousness. Television now seems to know the difference between Cherokee dress and Apache dress. At one time the writers did not know the difference, or care, and audiences accepted what was presented.

In several communities, notably in the South and West, media institutions owned by whites have concentrated on black and Mexican-American audiences. These stations augment the community-owned stations, if there happen to be any, in the particular location. Their formats also emphasize soul music, community news, and the top forty charts.

Functions

Media institutions in minority communities, as in others, should have five basic functions:

1. Educating the public. The media in minority communities should play a key role in providing the information needed for the people to make informed decisions.
2. Representing political sentiments. The media should speak out on significant issues affecting the community in order to keep the people aware of positions and to enrich the people's ideas.
3. Safeguarding the community's liberties. Responsible media in the minority community must safeguard personal and collective liberties. No person's rights should be trespassed without the media signaling the alarm.
4. Securing a reasonable profit. The media should be able to secure a reasonable profit in the competitive arena of the advertising marketplace. They should, however, never make profit unethically.
5. Providing entertainment. The media should provide wholesome entertainment for the community.

These are fundamental functions of media in any community. However, for minority communities, where information has frequently been distorted, their importance deserves stressing.

In his pioneering book *The Uses of the Media by the Chicano Movement*, Francisco J. Lewels, Jr. studied the problem of Chicano, that is Mexican-American, access to the media and discovered that discrimination against Chicanos is as virulent as it has been against blacks.

In 1970 Chicano groups began to seek national coordination in their media efforts. The Chicano Media Committee was formed

> to enhance the public and private image of Chicanos in the United States by providing appropriate and relevant information, expertise and counsel to national and local news media, including newspapers, magazines, television and radio producers, motion picture producers, advertising agencies and all other media. . . .[6]

The Chicano Media Committee was the first significant attempt on the part of the Chicano community to have a national impact on media institutions. Ruebèn Salazar, a respected *Los Angeles Times* journalist, was one of the leaders of the movement. His articles, critical of the police and the establishment, made him a disliked figure among policemen but a hero to people in the barrios. In 1972, while covering a demonstration in East Los Angeles, Salazar was caught in the midst of violence when he went into a bar to have a beer. Sheriff's deputies had been told that someone in the bar had a gun, and they fired tear gas grenades into the bar. One of these missiles struck Salazar in the skull, killing him immediately.

After Salazar's death the Chicano Media Committee began to fail, although this failure cannot be blamed on any one cause. It attempted to make policy for all media organizations, did not recognize the embryonic stage of Chicano media development, and failed to recognize the unsophisticated nature of most media organizations. Nevertheless, Chicano groups have continued their pressure for employment, media ownership, and minority advisory councils.

Employment of Minorities

The electronic media are overwhelmingly white in the United States. Total employment of blacks is less than 1 per cent, and the employment of Mexican-Americans and Puerto Ricans is less than 0.5 per

[6] Chicano Media Committee, "By-Laws of the National Chicano Media Council" (New York, August 3, 1970), p. 1 (mimeographed).

cent. In effect, America has a white media. On the basis of population figures a portion of minority personnel of about 18 per cent would be more realistic.

Jobs in the media industry change slowly, and the selection process is not predictable. These facts make it difficult for minorities to secure jobs. An editor or a cameraman may hold a job for many years. Unless the company expands, and there is a market limit to expansion, the young potential employee, brown, black, or white, will have to wait or go into some other industry. The unions, on the other hand, are protective of their positions, and minority people have seldom had the necessary apprenticeship training to become full-fledged union members. With the growth of minority television and radio stations, other possibilities will open up. But not even these opportunities will be able to satisfy the demand for employment. There are approximately 200 viable black newspapers, two television stations, and 15 radio stations. The total number of employees is less than 5000. The figures for Spanish surnamed Americans are even more dismal. An indication of the inequalities of American society, the media industry's employment record suggests part of the reason for the stereotypical portrayals of minority people. This situation will improve in proportion to the influence of minority people on programming decisions.

In 1968 CBS reported 365 blacks out of a total work force of 5540, ABC reported 118 out of 2447, and NBC reported 85 of 2901.[7] These figures are several years old, but the situation has probably not changed appreciably. This seems particularly likely in view of the fact that in 1969 there was one black executive for every 40 in the publishing industry and in 1970 there was one for every 65.[8]

The reluctance of the media institutions to open their doors to minorities demonstrates the need for citizens' councils. Using Nicholas Johnson's procedures in *How to Talk Back to Your Television Set*,[9] Chicano and black groups have effectively challenged several stations. Johnson's procedure calls for identifying the factual basis for the grievance and the specific parties involved, naming the appropriate rule, agency decision, or statute that relates to the case, and stating the precise remedy. Any group that believes its rights are being overlooked or trampled on can use these procedures to seek redress.

[7] "Broadcasting and the Minorities," *Broadcasting* (March 18, 1968).
[8] LaBrie, op. cit., p. 94.
[9] Nicholas Johnson, *How to Talk Back to Your Television Set* (New York: Bantam Books), 1970.

The Looking Glass

Television, of all media, reflects our contemporary societal thinking. It portrays for us what we consider humorous, tragic, and touching. It has become a window through which we can get an idea of how we see ourselves. In this respect, it shows that African-Americans, Mexican-Americans, and Oriental-Americans are not yet integrated into our society.

African-Americans tend to be more prominent in television today than they were prior to the civil rights era of the 1960s, although, as already mentioned, not nearly in proportion to their numbers. Furthermore, neither blacks nor any of the other colored minorities in the United States are shown on television in the variety of positions they occupy in the society. Jay Francis, Public Relations Director of Westinghouse Broadcasting Company, has said, "We need to have a total picture presented because what has happened in America is that the white community refuses to socialize with us, refuses to live with us . . . sees us only on television. And television must present the true images of black life—not only for ourselves, but for white people as well."[10]

Our discussion of blacks and Chicanos has not been extensive; it has only shown the difficulty of minority access to mainstream media. Smaller minority groups have similar problems and perhaps face even greater odds against securing redress. Blacks and Hispanics as the largest groups, have started to gain considerable political leverage.

[10] *Buffalo Evening News* (December 30, 1977).

Chapter 11
You've Come a Long Way, Baby . . . from Minnie Mouse to Wonder Woman*

by Mary B. Cassata and Niki Scher

The mass media mold everyone into more passive roles, into roles of more frantic consuming, into human beings with fragmented views of society. But what it does to everyone, it does to women even more. The traditional societal roles for women is already a passive one, already one of a consumer, already one of an emotional nonintellectual who isn't supposed to think or act beyond the confines of her home. The mass media reinforce all these traits.
Alice Embree

Everybody knows about the power of a great idea whose time has come. What often gets overlooked is that the strength of a mediocre idea whose historical moment has arrived can be just as awesome.
Time, November 22, 1976

The television commercial showing a young, sophisticated woman smoking a Virginia Slims cigarette and proclaiming to all that "You've come a long way, baby," may have been construed by some as a positive comment on the remarkable progress made by the American female. But many others—perhaps those members of the television-viewing audience who have become known as "obstinate, self-reliant, and active"—may just as easily have found reason to react to this commercial message with earnest indignation. For the very medium—television—airing this speciously sincere message is the medium that historically has done its best to maintain the status quo.

We suggest that the two emergent points of view may not be

*This essay originally appeared in *The Gospel According to Lilith*, **1(4)**, Spring 1977.

contradictory—for it is well known that one of the functions this most pervasive of all media accomplishes best is the reinforcement of people's most cherished and strongly held opinions, attitudes, and beliefs, accommodating quite handily the most divergent points of view. Also worthy of our respect are a number of other versatile functions. For example, television can enforce cultural norms, can indirectly influence conduct by reinforcing existing patterns of behavior or by creating new shared connections, or can shatter existing norms. In focusing its attention on a particular situation or individual, television confers a special kind of status on that situation or individual. In addition, by emphasizing what elements it chooses to and deemphasizing or entirely ignoring what others it chooses not to recognize (known as gatekeeping), this medium sets the agenda of social issues for our society, defining for one and all that which *it* determines to be important or, by omission, unimportant. It informs, entertains, interprets, and socializes. The end result? Consciousness raising or lack thereof.

In 1968 the Kerner Commission on Civil Disorders stated:

> If what the white American reads in newspapers or sees on television conditions his expectations of what is ordinary and normal in the larger society, he will neither understand nor accept the black American.[1]

It would take but a substitution of a word or two to have this statement apply with equal impact to women and the situation of the mass media's socially irresponsible distortion of their role.

In our culture—which mass-produces symbols in the same way, for instance, that the assemblyline mass-produces any ordinary household item—these symbols take on a kind of shorthand meaning (stereotypes) that is learned as facilely as one learns the ABC's. The shorthand becomes even shorter as the frequency of the symbol-encounter, through day-in and day-out repetition, accelerates. In fact, so instantaneous does this recognition of the symbol become that somewhere inside the minds of audience members a great deal gets lost in translation. Consequently, without giving very much thought at all to the stereotypes that we are encountering in the television medium, we all too easily come to accept lie for fact and myth for reality.

The power of television lies in its construction of pseudopeople acting out their pseudoroles in pseudoenvironments. That television engages with such flair and recklessness in the fabrication of symbols

---

[1] Kerner Commission, *Report of the National Advisory Commission on Civil Disorders* (New York: Bantam, 1968).

and myths bodes ill for all segments of society. For we all become partners in the conspiracy to construct and then to believe what simply isn't so.

Taking, as our example, women, it soon becomes quite obvious how the mass media have maligned this group. And it soon becomes clear, if we think about it, that although womankind may have succeeded in taking a few giant steps forward in the course of many, many years, the mass media have succeeded in shoving her back several decades. The women's movement is being done in—politely and unobtrusively on the face of it—by the mass media, all under the guise of civility and masterful promotion.

Let's examine this in greater depth. To begin with, we know that television viewing somehow becomes calibrated with the life cycle. The young, with a lot of time on their hands, are heavy viewers until they become teenagers, when other interests outside the home, competing for their time and attention, lure them away from the family TV set. But it's back to the small screen again for the young marrieds, who between the ages of 20 and 29 tend to stay home more on evenings and weekends because of family-rearing responsibilities and economics. As their children grow older—and they, too, of course (30 to 49 age group)—television loses out once more to other activities, which they can now afford and move up on their list of priorities. As they reach the age of 50, however, there's a cyclical return to the tube, and once again viewing becomes heavy and assumes an important place in their lives.[2]

However, putting age aside, we know that the amount of television viewing varies with such social categories as the viewer's sex, education, race, and income. Thus women are heavier viewers than men, those with a college education are ligher viewers than those without a college education, blacks watch more television than whites, and lower-income groups watch more than higher-income groups. Although the relative importance of these factors varies according to the unique perceptions of the researcher, perhaps safer predictors of television viewing are time and opportunity, factors that tend to be supported by the observation that all of these different groups spend roughly equal amounts of time with the set on evenings and weekends. Nevertheless, research does support the contention that older

---

[2] Robert T. Bower, *Television and the Public* (New York: Holt, Rinehart and Winston, 1973).

Maude, Rhoda, Alice, Phyllis, Charlie's Angels—is
this finally television's year of the women? Have we
been finally liberated from I Married Joan, I Love
Lucy, *and* Father Knows Best? *It would appear so.*
But let's examine this more closely—Phyllis is a
secretary, Maude a housewife, Alice a waitress, and
Rhoda a very part-time window dresser. Charlie's
three angels are detectives, but they spend an
uncomfortably large percentage of their time in
various stages of undress. The conclusion we must
unhappily draw is that we have not come a long way,
baby. Although the larger number of women's shows
is of significance in terms of the increased visibility
of women as major characters on television, it is by
no means an adequate or satisfying portrayal.

If this be women's liberation, make the most of it.
Beyond the fact that the [Charlie's] Angels do
manage to remain present and feminine while
performing roles until now reserved for men, the
show offers very little to please a woman whose
consciousness has been raised even a degree or
two by the movement. Says Journalist Judith
Coburn, a feminist:

Charlie's Angels *is one of the most misogynist*
shows the networks have produced recently.
Supposedly about "strong" women, it
perpetuates the myth most damaging to women's
struggle to gain professional equality: that women
always use sex to get what they want, even on the
treatment, Charlie's Angels *seems to speak to and*
porn, a mild erotic fantasy that appeals about
equally to men and women. The show has been
launched at a moment when there is a franker
discussion of sexual needs and wishes and when
women in particular, are beginning to reveal their
sexual fantasies. Though hardly a credible
treatment, Charlie's Angels *seems to speak to and*
for them. *

* *Time* (November 22, 1976).

people, women, blacks, and those with less income and education are the heaviest viewers.[3]

At this point it should be noted, however, that a certain anomaly exists between what the researchers are finding in terms of "prime" audiences and what the television monied interests determine should constitute program content. High-sounding theories aside, such as "consumer as producer," we believe that it is the network opinion leaders in concert with the sponsor who decide what programs are appropriate fare for the public. Thus programming is beamed toward the 18 to 49 age groups overall; content, according to these influentials, reflects the tastes and living conditions of the upper middle class. And because many groups lie outside these boundaries, a gap is created between what they see and what they are, making the world of affluence that comes off their screens something to be devoutly wished for—sometimes, unfortunately, accompanied by asocial attempts at implementation.

As interesting as the specific question might be of the viewer and the specific television diet that is available to him or her, more interesting, we believe, are what specific role is ascribed to women in television program content and how this role is perceived by the viewing audience.

The mass media are able "to speak to and for" women by playing on (or preying on) our most strongly held and most potent cultural myths. One of the most popular of American mythologies is centered on the idea of age—or, more accurately, youth. To this end, most of the women portrayed during prime time (and also on commercials) are of an indeterminate age between 20 and 35. Of course, we do see the occasional mother/grandmotherly type—George Jefferson's mother (*The Jeffersons*), Grandma Elizabeth (*The Waltons*), Edith Bunker (*All in the Family*)—but these women are generally found in supporting roles. In a revealing interview on a PBS television program, the creator (a woman) of the ill-fated situation comedy *Fay* confessed that originally *Fay* was intended to be a fiftyish divorcee, a determined woman trying to carve a new life for herself at a rather late stage. The network heads, however, had other plans. (It is important at this point to say a few words about the economic infrastructure of our commercial television industry: programs are not created with the viewer in mind but

[3] W. Phillips Davison, James Boylan, and Frederick T. C. Yu, *Mass Media Systems and Effects* (New York: Praeger Publishers, 1976), p. 113.

for potential sponsors; these sponsors have discovered through careful demographic studies that women between the ages of 20 and 35 compose that majority of American consumers. It logically follows then that sponsors will support the type of program that can guarantee them maximum viewership as measured by Nielsen ratings.) The network heads overseeing the production of *Fay* reasoned that an early-thirtyish divorcee would hold greater appeal for a sponsor than a fiftyish woman. That there is a world of difference between a fiftyish woman starting a new life and a thirtyish woman in the same situation cannot be denied; interestingly enough, when the show was canceled after a very few airings, the network was deluged with letters from viewers (possibly the greatest single response ever received by a network) in favor of retaining *Fay*. The viewers' wishes were ignored, in clear refutation of both the-consumer-as-producer and the-airwaves-belong-to-the-people theories.

Socialization of Children: Sex Role Stereotypes

Let us begin with the very young: What influence does television have on their perceptions of appropriate lifestyles relative to sex? How is the women's movement affecting children's ideas about appropriate sex roles in our culture? Is the larger social picture changing?

One researcher devised a study that included a clever projective technique called "the OK picture game," which graphically depicted ordinary situations as well as others that were "wrong" (e.g., a five-legged cat) and which required children to decide whether any given picture was "OK" or not. Planted among these pictures were three that showed reversed traditional sex role situations: a father feeding a baby, a man serving coffee to a woman, and a female telephone line repairperson. (The study showed that, although not overwhelmingly agreed to, it was OK for the father to feed the baby and to serve coffee to a woman; it was not OK, however, for a woman to become a telephone line repairperson. The implication is that whereas men may invade a woman's traditional territory somewhat, the reverse is not acceptable.)[4]

The overall findings of this study tended to add support to the

[4] Ann Beuf, "Doctor, Lawyer, Household Drudge," *Journal of Communication* **24(2)**, Spring 1974, 142–145.

idea that young children very early in life observe and properly grasp the role structure of our society. Boys aspire to the adventure-type careers of the characters that populate the television screen: cowboy, sports superstar, and policeman; and girls tend to select the appropriate sex role of nurse for themselves. What would they choose if girls could be boys and boys could be girls?

From among the responses emerged two quotes that poignantly underscore how our mass media promote the idea that boys should relate to male-type tasks and careers and girls to female-type tasks and careers: [Girl] "When I grow up I want to fly like a bird. But I'll never do it because I'm not a boy" and [Boy] "A girl? Oh, if I were a girl I'd have to grow up to be nothing."[5]

These two comments—one wistful and one wry—of course highlight the general finding that children's aspirations are controlled and limited by the ideas they gain from the mass media, among other socializing agents. Moreover, the additional finding that moderate television viewers perceive themselves to have a greater range of career choices than do heavier viewers tells us that our children need to be counter-encouraged repeatedly by the real people they know and respect to do and become what they really want to. The women's movement, it was concluded, is not making much of an impact on the depiction of sex roles—at least not at the time of the study.

The accusation leveled at network television, that of sex role stereotyping in the portrayal of women, is not limited to prime time television, but applies to cartoons as well. In a recent article,[6] several conclusions were drawn that emphasize the gross irresponsibility of network children's programmers in the area of sexual socialization. In the Saturday morning cartoons the representation of adult males to adult females is in a ratio of 4 to 1. Sixty-seven per cent of teenage cartoon characters are male, 33 per cent female. Teenage females are more involved with the action than their adult counterparts:

> although the characters are rarely portrayed in occupational roles (while teenage boys frequently have part-time occupations) girls are able to participate in adventures with boys because they have not yet been encumbered by their ultimate and inevitable adult role (at least in cartoons)—mother.[7]

[5] Ibid., p. 143.
[6] Richard M. Levinson, "From Olive Oyl to Sweet Polly Purebread: Sex Role Stereotypes and Televised Cartoons," *Journal of Popular Culture* **9(3)**, Winter 1975, 561–572.
[7] Ibid., p. 565.

This study, as well as many others, bears out the contention that female children viewers are being seriously short-changed in terms of being provided with occupational role models. In the course of a monitoring project, 86 vocational roles filled by men were identified, to the 19 filled by women (one of which was "witch"). This lack of vocational flexibility seriously affects the impact that female cartoon characters can have in any plot—they are generally relegated to supporting roles, and appear as stereotypes—"egghead," "beautiful-but-dumb," "bitchy."

Levinson points to the family series as the most serious offender of sex roles:

> More often, plots raising sex roles issues resemble an episode of *The Barkleys* in which the husband and wife suggest their respective spouses are soft! After an argument, each tries the other's job for a day (bus driving and housewifery) and faces a series of disasters. The episode concludes with a mutual recognition they should remain doing what they "naturally" do best. Their children think so, too! [8]

Advertising and the American Woman

There is perhaps no mass media form that can compare to the television commercial in terms of the hundreds of thousands of symbols spewed forth daily that reinforce the negative stereotyped roles in which women are portrayed in the mass media. One recent study (1974) that was an update of a number of benchmark studies of women in advertising conducted mainly in 1971 supported the finding that the negative stereotyping of women by the media is still alive and well. Among the findings were the following: [9]

1. The sexes are depicted as being concerned with different decision-making spheres. For women these are the home and their personal appearance; for men these are cars, appliances, financial affairs, and the family pet.
2. Males continue to dominate the off-camera voiceover. In the 1971 commercials that were analyzed, 87 per cent of the voiceovers were male. By 1974 there was a slight drop to 84 per cent. (Of the remaining 16 per cent, 10 per cent were "chorus" and only 6 per cent of all voiceovers were made by women.)

[8] Ibid., p. 568.
[9] James D. Culley and Rex Bennett, "Selling Women, Selling Blacks," *Journal of Communication* 26(4), August 1976, 160–173.

3. In 1971 an analysis of the "settings" of commercials tended to place more women than men in a single room in the home and more men than women in business or outdoor settings. The 1974 study revealed a narrowing of this gap, i.e., women's space was being enlarged to include the outdoors.

4. The largest single occupation portrayed for women in both the 1971 and 1974 periods remained housewife/mother. An interesting observation, however, was that whereas the housewife/mother role decreased to 45 per cent for women, only 15 per cent of all male portrayals were husband/father.

5. Another gain for women since 1971 seemed to be in the area of occupational status as depicted in prime time television. A drop of nearly 25 per cent was recorded in the 1974 commercials (from 79 per cent to 55 per cent) that showed women in subservient roles (housewife, cook-domestic, stewardess, secretary). Women also made some gains in the area of white-collar business roles.

6. The range of jobs, however, open to women was significantly narrow in studies of both periods; the range was much wider for men.

7. Older women continued to be less visible than older men in television commercials, but a significant decrease occurred in the use of female characters in the later study who were in the 20–35 age category.

One finding that we are unable to agree with philosophically, however, was the claim that the number of instances of female as sex object/decoration had declined significantly; whatever slight decine may have occurred we interpret as mere tokenism.

An analysis of the commercials of the 1971 period and the 1974 period revealed both consistencies and changes. But perhaps more notable than what can be seen in these commercials is what is unseen. In both periods there was a notable absence of women doctors, lawyers, judges, scientists, and engineers, and, more relevant, the 20 million women who perform the dual role of wife/mother and working woman were almost completely ignored. The conclusion remains that most women are pictured as housewives, to be found in either the kitchen or the bathroom, assisting some male supersalesman (seen or unseen) in selling a household product.

Although another group of researchers based their conclusions on the ads of women found in *Playboy*, *Time*, *Newsweek*, and *Ms* (the majority "put them down" or "keep them in their place"),[10] the consciousness scale for media sexism that they constructed is worth not-

[10] Suzanne Pingree, Robert Parker Hawkins, Matilda Butler, and William Paisley, "A Scale for Sexism," *Journal of Communication* **26(4)**, Autumn 1976, 193–200.

ing and in our opinion has wide application for all media forms. Because we feel that the scale deserves serious study by groups both in and outside of the mass media, our conception of it is presented here as Fig. 11-1.

Women in the Daytime Soaps

Thus far, without even getting into television program content, we believe we have made our case that the mass media project a sexist, stereotyped image of women. It is time to take a look at program content. One researcher asserts that "The woman of the daytime television serial drama is strong, warm, and fallible—a more believable human being than her counterpart in many other forms of television entertainment."[11] She is more adequately represented (there's an equal proportion of women to men in daytime television drama), compared to a disproportionate representation in night time television drama (4 to 1 in favor of men). The general characteristics of the daytime soap opera are as follows: (1) most of the action takes place indoors; (2) time is expanded, i.e., whereas prime time television drama, like the theater, the novel, and film, greatly compresses time, the daytime serial greatly expands it so that events of a few hours' duration may last weeks, thus emphasizing detail rather than broad ideas; (3) the majority of the serial players are white middle-class, at least one-time married Americans, attractive, well dressed, enjoying good health; (4) occupational level is spuriously high, with the "professionals" leading the pack and "full-time housewives" second compared to the real world of work that ranks "clerical workers" first, "operatives" second, and "professional and technical workers" third (of course, male professionals greatly outnumber female professionals); (5) with respect to age, women are younger and men older, with older women falling by the wayside in the employment market but men surviving handsomely.

In a study on advising and ordering in daytime and prime time television drama, it was found that

> Television's dramatic landscape was shaped in such a way that the selection of characters, the assignment of occupations, and the movement of

[11] Mildred Downing, "Heroine of the Daytime Serial," *Journal of Communication* **24(2)**, Spring 1974, 130.

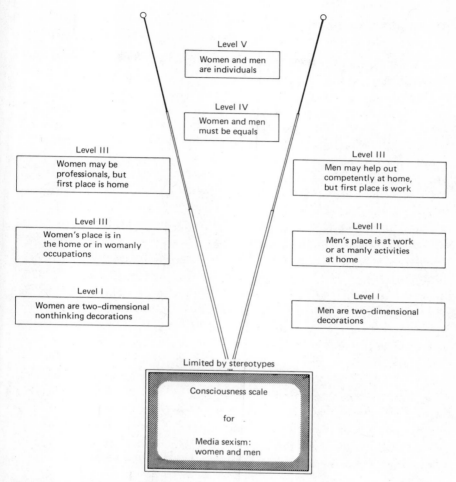

Level V
Women and men
are individuals

Level IV
Women and men
must be equals

Level III
Women may be
professionals, but
first place is home

Level III
Men may help out
competently at home,
but first place is work

Level III
Women's place is in
the home or in womanly
occupations

Level II
Men's place is at work
or at manly activities
at home

Level I
Women are two-dimensional
nonthinking decorations

Level I
Men are two-dimensional
decorations

Limited by stereotypes

Consciousness scale

for .

Media sexism:
women and men

Figure 11-1. Freedom from all stereotypes.

plots operated in concert to minimize the chances of women being given
the opportunity to display superior knowledge with respect to men and
to ensure that the areas in which they were given such opportunities
were compartmentalized along traditional lines. In this manner the fundamental strictures of the culture are not violated while the expectations
and desires of the female audience to see itself portrayed in central roles
are gratified.[12]

[12] Joseph Turow, "Advising and Ordering: Daytime Prime Time," *Journal of Communication* **24(2),** Spring 1974, 141.

Women in Prime Time

And what happens when nighttime descends on America and several millions more gather around the set for the evening's ritual? How do the women come off then? One of the subsets of data gathered for the ongoing Cultural Indicators project at the University of Pennsylvania revealed that the best adjective to describe the women who populate prime-time television programs is *powerless*.[13] This study looked at representation by sex, types of roles portrayed, violence, and personality. The findings on most of these variables paralleled what is already known from other studies; yet new light was cast. For example, although the data reinforced what we already intuitively believe—that on the whole females are less violent than males—still this study found that if television's women were involved in violence they had a greater chance than men of being the victims. Commenting on the overall declines in numbers of victimizers and victims from 1967 to 1969, for example, with the exception that the number of female victims remained stable, the author suggested that "what actually happened was that the symbolic function of violence as a demonstration of social power was strengthened."[14] And when the personality profiles of males and females were constructed, those for the males revealed them to be powerful, smart, rational, tall, and stable, whereas the females were revealed as being more attractive, fair, sociable, warm, happy, peaceful, and youthful. Moreover, females emerged as being less powerful, rational, smart, or stable than males. On another dimension males were depicted as being generally more active, independent, mature, serious, unattached, and likely to be employed than females. The final insight that emerged from this study packs a wallop:

> The focus on different dramatic functions and other dissimilarities based on sex alone makes it difficult for men to view women as equals, for women to view themselves as equal to men, and for both sexes not to view the male role as necessarily the more active, powerful, and independent role.[15]

If anyone should ask, "Does it matter that women come off second best in the media when we know, in our heart of hearts, that they

[13] Nancy S. Tedesco, "Patterns in Prime Times," *Journal of Communication* **24(2)**, Spring 1974, 119–124.
[14] Ibid., p. 119.
[15] Ibid., pp. 122–123.

The Future: Beyond Bionic?

"Sisterhood" is a concept that has been as difficult to cultivate as "equality." Conspicuously lacking from prime time television are programs of women partners. Although we have Sanford and Son, Starsky and Hutch, Chico and the Man, *and* Switch, *the only distaff twosome are* Laverne and Shirley *(roommates and coworkers in a Milwaukee brewery). Nor are there many shows that have all women characters;* Barney Miller, The Rookies, Hawaii Five-O, *and* Baa Baa Black Sheep, *however, seem to flourish. It is only recently that between the hours of 7 and 9 P.M. women have begun to find support in each other, instead of rivalry. (*Rhoda *has her sister, and* One Day at a Time *revolves around the lives of a divorced woman and her two daughters—but then again these ties are all familial.*

Cable television offers the potential to involve women, both singly and in groups, with opportunities not available in commercial television. The public access channel that all cable stations must provide furnishes individual women or women's groups with the chance to work together to express their views in any field to a community audience. A recent expansion of this has been the development of the concept of the "dedicated channel." This is an especially useful tool for a specific interest group and can help build a specialized audience. Women for Cable, *located in Memphis, Tennessee, is programming a channel on the cable system in that city:*

> *While the projected programming service is not to be limited to women's affairs alone, it will be aimed at providing alternative TV fare that expresses women's perceptions of community issues and society in general. It will also be aimed at demonstrating a successful media venture owned and operated by women.* *

New media forms now available to women will provide women with the opportunity to set the record straight, not bionically, but realistically and humanely.

* Richard Adler and Walter S. Baer, *The Electronic Box Office: Aspen Program on Communication and Society* (New York: Praeger Publishers, 1974), p. 115.

are surely the equals of men?" he or she should be reminded of how the media have socialized little children to believe they are or are not made of inferior stuff.

Women Employed in the Industry

Although women constitute over 50 per cent of the population of the United States, the number of women employed by media stations is far less than that percentage. The United Church of Christ published 1975 data obtained from a 40-station sample showing that of the 8176 people employed in those stations only 2358 were women. The data also showed that women were almost nonexistent at the top management levels of the 40 sample stations.[16] Interestingly, the numbers of minorities by sex was more comparable, 944 males and 700 females, than the number of white males, 4874, to white females, 1658. This reflects the fact that minorities of both sexes began to enter media employment at about the same time.

Women are employed by the network-affiliated stations in relatively the same proportion. In no case are there more than 30 per cent of female employees. ABC, CBS, and NBC appear to keep each other in close sight. According to data reported by the United Church of Christ sample of 40 stations, ABC, CBS, and NBC slightly improved the number of women employees between 1971 and 1975: 1699 female employees in 1971, and 2358 in 1975.

Yet few women ever achieve positions that allow them to make broad policy or financial decisions in media stations. There are almost no female presidents or general managers in the industry, although stations have hired women as directors of public relations, personnel, and community affairs. Thus if women have steadily gained entry into the industry they have not yet succeeded in breaking into the decision-making circle. Operations log coordinators, assistant film librarians, film service assistants, and music rights librarians are necessary media positions, but they are not the positions where determining decisions are made. It is still a fact that most women employees in media in the United States are found in clerical positions. As former Federal Communications Commissioner Benjamin Hookes noted, tele-

[16] *Window Dressing on the Set: Women and Minorities in Television* (Report of the United States Commission on Civil Rights, August 1977).

vision's portrayal of women and minorities is "endemic of television institutionally."[17] Beyond that, however, is the fact that the stereotypical images will not change until women assume more top management positions.

---

[17] Benjamin Hookes, in *National Broadcasting Company, Inc.* 58 FCC 2d 419 (1976).

Chapter 12
The Reality of TV Violence:
The Violence of TV Reality

by Mary B. Cassata and Harvey Bondar

So what the hell are we doing you ask? We are dynamiting
brain cells. We are putting people through changes. . . .
We are theatre in the streets: total and committed. We aim
to involve people and use . . . any weapon (prop) we can
find. All is relevant, only "the play's the thing." . . .
The media is the message. Use it! No fund raising, no
full-page ads in The New York Times, *no press releases.*
Just do your thing; the press eats it up. Media is free.
Make news.
Abbie Hoffman

And shall we just carelessly allow our children to hear any
casual tales which may be devised by casual persons and to
receive in their minds for the most part the very opposite of
those we would wish them to have when they are grown up?
Plato, *The Republic*

Although Plato wrote his statement about the effect of "casual tales"
on children more than 2000 years ago, it nevertheless expresses the
concern of modern-day politicians, academicians, and concerned citizens over the potentially harmful influences of the mass media on the
development and behavior of our children. An impressive number of
national commissions, researchers, and scholars from many countries
have independently studied this topic; their findings have revealed a
significant number of divergent opinions as to the effects of the mass
media on social behavior. For example, as a result of the Surgeon General's Inquiry on Television and Social Behavior, Dr. Jesse Steinfeld
concluded that a causative relationship exists between televised violence and subsequent anti social behavior, and he called for the "inter-

vention of responsible authorities, the TV industry, the government, the citizens," to remedy the situation.[1]

On the other hand, there are those who would disagree with the position taken by the Surgeon General, arguing that the propensity to commit acts of violence comes from more than just absorbing violent television content. They believe that the behavior of an individual is a consequence of his or her total life experience, including parental guidance, social group affiliations, institutional influences, and other related factors. Just as vigorous as the Surgeon General's contention that television breeds violence are the passionate disclaimers made by his opponents that the antisocial nature of television is in actuality the reflection of a society presently and historically predisposed toward violent actions. According to psychiatrist Ner Littner, "The sooner we get off the kick of falsely blaming American violence on American television, the sooner we will start grappling with the true causes of our national violence."[2]

It is our view that somewhere between these two perspectives— (1) that there exists a causative relationship between televised violence and aggressive behavior and (2) that televised violence is a symptom of the violence within our society rather than an important determinant—lies a more reasonable focus for looking at this problem. Furthermore, it is our belief that in order to acquire an integrated perspective of the social role of the mass media it becomes necessary to avoid assuming any singular stance toward media functions and effects. Our intention is to use a process orientation in our exploration of the dynamics of television as a medium. For television has become the common carrier of symbolic messages in our culture. It is the universal medium that most effectively creates, offers legitimacy to, and manipulates symbols of its own creation. As symbol-using and -abusing animals we can, and do, unknowingly fall prey to its gospel. According to Harvey Cox, "Mass-Media culture is a religion, and we rarely get out of its temple."[3]

As if in tune with the "rerun-itis" disease of the television medium, the U.S. Congress held still another hearing on the television

[1] U.S. Congress, Senate, Hearings before the Subcommittee on Communications of the Committee on Commerce (March 1972), p. 28.

[2] Ner Littner, M.D., "A Psychiatrist Looks at Television and Violence," in Rod Holgrem and William Norton (eds.), *The Mass Media Book* (Englewood Cliffs, N.J.: Prentice-Hall, 1972), p. 356.

[3] Cited by Benjamin DeMott, "The Viewer's Experience: Notes on TV Criticism and Public Health," Douglas Cater et. al. (eds.), (New York: Praeger Publishers, 1975), p. 50.

violence problem on March 2, 1977. During these hearings George Gerbner, media researcher, presented a summary of his most current "Violence Profile." He revealed that his "Violence index of dramatic TV programming" reached an all-time high on all three networks in 1976. He cited nine out of ten programs sampled in 1976 as exhibiting incidents of violent behavior compared to eight out of ten for the previous year. This upsurge in violent programming is startling in light of the statements made by major network executives.

Statement:

> *Frederick S. Pierce, president of ABC-TV (1975):*
>
> Violence on television continues to be a subject of major concern to all broadcasters. . . . Are there too many police or detective "action" series on television? The answer is probably yes and I look for more comedy, dramatic and variety series in the season ahead.[4]

Facts:

1. Three of the five most violent shows (1976), according to the National Citizens Committee for Broadcasting (NCCB), are aired by ABC.
2. Gerbner's "Violence Profile" shows that the ABC network surpassed the NBC network in incidents of violence during the family viewing hour in 1976.

Statements:

> *Robert T. Howard, president of NBC-TV (1975):*
>
> While television violence may be an inflated issue, it is still something that every broadcaster who believes in social responsibility must take seriously.[5]
>
> People have said they want another direction and that's what we're going to give them.[6]

Facts:

1. Gerbner's "Violence Profile" (1976) shows that NBC has the highest violence index for "Overall Programming;" it has the

---

[4] Robert D. Murphy, *Mass Communication and Human Interaction* (Boston: Houghton-Mifflin, 1977), p. 365.

[5] Ibid., p. 365.

[6] *Newsweek*, "What TV Does to Kids" (February 21, 1977), p. 64.

highest violence index for "Late Evening Programming;" it has the highest violence index for "Weekend Children's Programming;" it ranks second highest to ABC for "Family Viewing Programming."

2. NBC's new midseason (January 1977) entry quickly established Howard's "direction" by moving right into the NCCB's top five most violent programs list.

3. According to *Newsweek*,[7] NBC's Saturday morning programs *Big John*, *Little John* and *Speed Buggy* do nothing more than stereotype parents as "incorrigible clutzes" and give "a weekly lesson in reckless driving."

Although not above reproach, CBS has shown more initiative in reducing the violent content of its programs. This has not been carried out to the point where programs such as *Kojak* and *Barnaby Jones* have been modified or canceled. The CBS violence index for "Late Evening Programming" is significantly higher than its index during the other time periods that Gerbner uses.

The National PTA has recently joined such other organizations as Action for Children's Television (ACT) and the NCCB in condemning the gratuitous display of violence on television. Even the conservative American Medical Association (AMA) has publicly decreed that "TV violence is both a mental-health problem and an environmental issue."[8] The tacit assumption has long been that violence is a necessary ingredient for attracting viewers. In the 1977 congressional hearings on TV violence, Gerbner reported that his research team found no correlation between the popularity of a show (Nielsen rating) and its violence index. He stated that at the time of his report none of the more violent programs was included among the top ten rated shows. Perhaps one of the shrewdest moves to dissuade advertisers from sponsoring certain network programs has been to claim that violence really doesn't sell. According to a survey of adult viewers by J. Walter Thompson, the nation's largest advertising agency, 8 per cent of the buying public "had already boycotted products advertised on such shows, while 10 percent more were considering doing so."[9]

[7] Ibid.
[8] Ibid.
[9] Ibid., p. 70.

TV News and Violence

What is news? is a question deceptively simple in the asking but surprisingly complex in the answering. One definition that seems to come close to being an all-purpose answer describes news as that which stands out from "the vast, flat and presumably irrelevant plain of mundane events . . . [that which] deviates from the ordinary and the normal."[10]

More than any other medium, television selectively presents news items that have spectacular visual presence. "This emphasis on spectacle is revealed in the television news organization's preoccupation with film, and especially 'good' film—i.e., film that clearly depicts action, conflict, ritual, or color."[11]

Televised War and Social Values

The atrocities of the Vietnam War were served up daily for us to watch in the comfort of our homes. The TV news coverage of the war, often referred to the "livingroom war," blurred the gap between the grim realities of the world and the theatrics of a dramatic presentation. The daily broadcasts of napalm bomb attacks, destroyed villages, mortally wounded civilians and soldiers, and whimpering, orphaned children seemed to evoke one of two distinct responses from its audience: (1) some grew increasingly callous and desensitized and (2) some were motivated to try to end the war.

Research by American broadcast news consultants ascertained the existence of a hierarchy of news values shared by audiences. In *ascending* order of viewer interest, the hierarchy ranks news values in the following order: [12]

8. African/Asian/Latin American news.
7. European and British news.

[10] Marty Glass, "What's News?" in Robert J. Glessing and William P. White (eds.), *Mass Media: The Invisible Environment Revisited* (Chicago: Science Research Associates, 1976), p. 119.

[11] Paul H. Weaver, "Newspaper News and Television News," in Douglas Cater et al. (eds.), *Television as a Social Force: New Approaches to TV Criticism* (New York: Praeger Publishers, 1975), p. 91.

[12] Edwin Diamond, the Tin Kazoo: Television, Politics, and the News (Cambridge, Mass.: MIT Press, 1975).

6. Washington political news and national news.
5. National disasters on a large scale.
4. Local disasters.
3. Local sports.
2. Local weather.
1. Local personal news, emphasizing sex and violence.

This appears to us to be a uniquely American phenomenon, which leads us to suspect that the news media have functioned as "agenda setters" in this hierarchy of values.

A study that supports our hypothesis of the uniqueness of the American value structure was conducted by Benjamin D. Singer. Comparing the content of the American network *CBS Evening News* program with that of Canada's *CBC National News* program, he found that the American news program reported twice as much violence as its Canadian counterpart:

> The American television news show exceeds the Canadian program in aggression items for every one of the 21 consecutive days monitored. CBS-TV has carried as much as 78 percent aggression items . . . compared to 38 percent for CBC-TV.[13]

Television as a Major Societal Force

A radical change in the social order of the Western world was dictated by the industrial revolution. It prompted a transition from a *Gemeinschaft* (small, collective, and homogeneous) society to a *Gesellschaft* (large, individualized, and heterogeneous) society. The communicative needs of the members of this new social structure were upset by its transient and isolatory nature. The potential for strong and reliable interpersonal bonds was usurped by a technocratic culture whose populace changed residency on the average of five times in a 20-year period. Sociologists suggest that the mass media played a significant role in preventing societal self-destruction by providing a ready substitute for personal interaction. Whereas television is most often perceived as a source of entertainment, "It has become the prin-

[13] Benjamin D. Singer, "Violence, Protest, and War in Television News: The U.S. and Canada Compared," *The Public Opinion Quarterly* **34**, Winter 1970–1971.

cipal means by which Americans maintain contact with the daily flow of life." [14]

Tony Schwartz, an educator and practitioner in the communication field, reinforces this idea:

> Kitty Genovese may have been the first startling, terrifying example of just how isolated the street has become. When an apartment dweller leaves his house he loses touch with his *world*. He is alone, even on a crowded street. [15]

Television has become the most pervasive, and often most persuasive, means of information diffusion in our society. It can disseminate information with lightning speed and impact, as well as infuse viewers with imagery and values in a subtle, perhaps almost imperceptible manner. Indications from recent research suggest that for certain subgroups of the television-viewing public the inability to separate factual TV content from dramatic TV fare has had a significant impact on their own personal reality structure. TV drama for them has become at times as real as TV news and personal experience.

Study after study has stated that people learn from television. Pollster after pollster has reported that the most prevalent response to the question "Where do you get most of your information about the world?" is "Television." But what do people really learn from television? It has been demonstrated in the research literature that, at best, learning from television is incidental and that, at worse (and often), it is erroneous. A few years back, *The National Enquirer* constructed a test to determine how accurate a picture TV gave of the world as demonstrated by the scores of heavy viewers versus light viewers. The assumption was made that the more television an individual watched, the less accurate was his or her conception of reality. On the other hand, those who were lighter viewers were posited to have a more accurate picture of the world. The test was administered to two classes of mass communication students at the State University of New York at Buffalo; the results in both classes supported *The National Enquirer's* hypothesis.

Besides a biased picture of the world, what other "bonuses" does television offer the public? In their often quoted *Psychology Today* article, George Gerbner and Larry Gross maintain that

---

[14] Richard Adler, "Understanding Television: An Overview of the Literature of the Medium as a Social and Cultural Force," in Cater et al., op. cit., p. 25.

[15] Tony Schwartz, *The Responsive Chord*, Garden City, New York: Anchor Press/Doubleday, 1973, p. 146.

We have found that people who watch a lot of TV see the real world as more dangerous and frightening than those who watch very little. Heavy viewers are less trustful of their fellow citizens, and more fearful of the real world.[16]

Most research studies on the effects of violent TV content have focused on the impact of televised violence on children. Dr. Jesse Steinfeld estimates that by age 12 the average American child has spent 13,500 hours in front of the television set, exceeding by a factor of 2 the amount of time spent in school.[17] Content analysis studies show that during this period a child will have witnessed over 100,000 violent episodes, including well over 13,000 deaths.

It seems reasonable that young, impressionable children should be shielded from excessive exposure to violent TV content. Yet we find that the content of shows designed specifically for children exhibits the highest number of aggressive acts. Cartoons have as many as 30 aggressive acts per half hour segment compared to an average of seven aggressive acts per half hour of prime time programming.[18]

Although we cannot be sure of the specific effects of TV violence on children, an overwhelming number of research studies support the notion that some kinds of violent TV content have some kinds of effects on some kinds of children some of the time.

Whereas TV serves as a major competitor to the classroom for our children, it serves as the classroom for another subset of the population—the imprisoned. In a survey conducted by Grant H. Hendrick, a prisoner at Marquette Prison, Michigan's maximum-security penal institution, nine out of ten respondents told their fellow prisoner-researcher

> that they have actually learned new tricks and improved their criminal expertise by watching crime programs. Four out of 10 said that they have attempted specific crimes they saw on television crime dramas. . . .[19]

Hendrick relates a number of specific incidents of crimes that were portrayed on TV. Stating that it would be much more difficult to

---

[16] George Gerbner and Larry Gross, "The Scary World of TV's Heavy Viewer," *Psychology Today* (April 1976), p. 41.

[17] Jesse L. Steinfeld, M.D., "TV Violence Is Harmful," in Alan Wells (ed.), *Mass Media and Society* (Palo Alto, Calif., Mayfield Publishing Co., 1975), p. 263.

[18] Alan D. Haas, "How Violent Is Junior's TV Fare?" *Buffalo Courier Express Magazine* (November 14, 1976), p. 16.

[19] Grant H. Hendrick, "When Television Is a School for Criminals," *TV Guide* (January 29, 1977), p. 5.

do time in Marquette without access to TV—"It's a window on the world for us . . . and some of us take great pains to keep tuned into the crime shows"—when he queried a fellow prisoner as to the potential benefits of watching TV crime shows in prison, the response was "Hey, I sit and take notes—do my homework, you know? No way would I sit in my cell and waste my time watching comedies for five hours—no way!"

The portrayal of dramatized violence has become a mainstay of television. In the case of children, researchers fear a "stalagmite" effect, that the constant daily exposure to televised violence slowly develops its potential as an effective socializing agent. According to this theory, if indeed there is a causative relationship between TV violence and antisocial behavior its development is so gradual and so imperceptible that a long time is required for the effect to become visible. As we have already pointed out, members of the criminal subgroup may well seek information from TV crime shows, and it may well be that those who remain outside of penal institutions use these dramatizations as models for subsequent behavior.

The major problem of substantiating the claims of social scientists about the consequences of televised violence is that this area of study lends itself to multivariate analysis so complex as to be beyond the methodological and predictive range of current empirical techniques. The state of research methodology notwithstanding, there is enough evidence about the relationship between televised violence and antisocial behavior for already existing as well as new public interest groups to take a unified and concerted stand against televised violence. We have already reported on the activities of such public interest groups, federal legislative bodies, and the television industry itself with regard to the continuing debate on this subject. Especially over the past few years, status has been conferred on this issue through its extensive treatment in the mass media. As the issue has become popularized, the findings of the numerous scientific studies on this topic have more regularly found their way into newspapers and large general interest magazines. The agenda has been set; violence in our society is an issue of major significance. The recently televised 3-hour documentary on violence in our society received extraordinarily high ratings for a major news telecast. The question remains, however: was this the result of the attractiveness of its violent fare or the result of concern by an attentive public about the issues at hand?

Out of the concerns of the legislative and public interest groups have come certain proposed solutions to this problem. The body that took the first remedial steps was the National Association of Broadcasters. Its Television Code suggests that

> Violence, physical or psychological, may only be projected in reasonably handled contexts, not used exploitatively. Programs involving violence for its own sake and the detailed dwelling upon brutality or physical agony, by sight or by sound, are not permissible.[20]

Although the code is admirable in intent, the broadcasters have neither vigorously adhered to their own stated policy nor considered its real consequences. Timothy P. Meyer believes that in avoiding the depiction of the agony and suffering that surround real-world violence we are doing more harm than good.[21] Further, it is reported in the scientific literature that the presentation of violence in a justified context leads "to greater amounts of aggression by the viewer than the viewing of unjustified or gratuitous violence."[22] It is our view that violence, if presented, should be shown in a manner that does not disguise the agony and pain that go along with it and that the most careful consideration should be given before any violence at all is presented, especially to a younger audience who lacks the ability to discriminate between different situational contexts. Inasmuch as self-regulation has failed to solve the problem, we might ask whether government control becomes the next alternative.

Conclusion

There is little disagreement among students of mass communication and responsible citizens that television violence is a major force to be dealt with in our society. It has been demonstrated that a relationship does exist between violence in society and violence on the tube. However, although the nature of that relationship remains unclear and the debate seems to be over the *kind* and the *degree* of that relationship,

[20] See Paragraph IV of the Program Standards of the Television Code, National Association of Broadcasters, 18 ed. (June 1975).

[21] Timothy P. Meyer, "Some Observations on the Differences Between Current Film and Television Violence," *Journal of the University Film Association* **24**, 1972, 112–115.

[22] Stanley J. Baran and Lucy L. Henke, "The Regulation of Televised Violence," *Communication Quarterly* **24(4)**, Fall 1976, 30.

there is substantial recognition that the amount of televised violence is excessive and perhaps has gotten out of hand. Moreover, there is agreement that children learn from television and resort to television to satisfy their needs, both fancied and real. We know also that adult subgroups of our population use TV fare for specific gratifications, as in the case of criminals—both imprisoned and at large—who use television crime shows as material for their continuing education.

We have already reviewed the concern of various governmental agencies and investigatory bodies on the subject of TV violence, and we have noted the emergence of various pressure groups such as Action for Children's Television and the National Association for Better Broadcasting; the outrage of such establishment forces as the American Medical Association and the Parent-Teacher Association; and the emphatic action of the J. Walter Thompson and other advertising agencies in refusing to sponsor violent programs.

Even as television continues unabated over the protestations of various organized groups, the print media, too, have taken up the cause, commenting on and analyzing the subject of television violence.

As a result of pressure applied on the FCC by the House and Senate Appropriations Committee, the National Association of Broadcasters consented to accept the notion of Family Viewing Time for its Code members. This notion has proved to be a dismal failure, for although TV violence was banished from the first hour of prime time and the hour immediately preceding it, little consideration was given to either the versatility or the persistence of children in finding other violent programming time slots. In general, it was found that the Family Viewing Time concept merely rearranged the violent fare; there was no diminution of violent content.

On the other side of the coin are the concept of government regulation and the notions of exercised prior restraint and modification of the First Amendment. However, these desperate notions are rarely considered seriously. That course is considered far too dangerous to follow.

There is an inherent contradiction in the fact that the FCC applies different standards in the regulation of offensive or sex-related materials. In a number of cases the FCC has censored broadcasters for the dissemination of what have been considered obscene or antisocial messages. Both the FCC's declaratory order against station WBAI's broadcast of George Carlin's "filthy words" monologue and its order in 1973 regarding the broadcast of drug-oriented music continued refutations of the claims that it was infringing on First Amendment rights, citing these messages' potentially harmful effects on society as being of greater importance. In the WBAI case, one of the government's major contentions was that "These words were broadcast at a time when children were undoubtedly in the audience (i.e., in the early afternoon)."[23] The government has obviously taken steps to control exposure to what it considers to be profane or obscene material; its failure to go beyond the investigation of TV violence, on the other hand, demonstrates what some critics consider to be a double standard. It is our opinion that the government must not infringe on First Amendment rights but that some means is necessary to offset the overwhelming antisocial or violent programming balance and ensure a diversified, prosocial spectrum. Rather than continuing to take broadcasters to task for presenting such large amounts of antisocial programming, the FCC might take more constructive action by establishing a commission to investigate prosocial programming alternatives.

Convinced that "Any steady diet of television, regardless of its content, can exert a powerful influence on children," three American researchers devised a code of seven prosocial behavior categories that are presently being tested and refined with network programs. They describe their effort as being "two-pronged, involving both the identification of existing commercial programs which have positive effects and—more importantly—the creation of new programs which teach a variety of such lessons."[24] These researchers, who have already expended a considerable amount of energy synthesizing the sizable literature on the subject of TV violence in addition to conducting studies of their own, are experimenting with prosocial formats that will attract the high ratings required for a program to survive on commercial television.[25] Our feeling is that their efforts can be greatly enhanced by positive support from the FCC in terms of a mandate for all broadcasters. In the absence of such a mandate the chances of any one of the networks experimenting with this approach appear to be slim, given the competition.

[23] Ibid., p. 29.

[24] Robert M. Liebert, Emily S. Davidson, and John M. Neale, "Aggression in Childhood: The Impact of Television," in Victor B. Cline, (ed.), *Where Do You Draw the Line?* (Provo, Utah: Brigham Young University Press, 1974), pp. 124–126.

[25] Robert M. Liebert, John M. Neale, and Emily S. Davidson, *The Early Window: Effects of Television on Children and Youths* (New York: Pergamon Press, 1973).

From the evidence at hand it appears that change is both necessary and long overdue. The question that remains is who will initiate this change. It seems clear to us that the industry itself is not going to do it, which leaves the government and the community as the sole potential activating agents.

Chapter 13
Canada/United States: The Limits of Media

by Mary B. Cassata and Emanuel J. Levy

Angie to Marty: Well, we're back to that, huh? I say to
you: "What do you feel like doing tonight?" And you say
to me: "I don't know, what do you feel like doing?"
Paddy Chayefsky, *Marty*

The Canadian Struggle for National Identity

Canada and the United States share the same continent and generally
use the same language; our two nations are each other's best customer; we share a familiarity with the same products, equipment,
food, religions, recreation, dress, climate, and mass media; we cooperate in the defense of North America; and we have comparable standards of living and life-styles. Every year we visit each other's country, pleased with the friendly reception we encounter. Intermarriage
between people of our two nations is frequent; close personal and
family ties bind us together. Such similarities are not frequently encountered by two foreign nations; yet the very characteristics that
make us alike now are threatening to drive our two countries apart.
Part of the problem is that "Americans" (a term that realistically
should include Canadians, but in this chapter will refer to citizens of
the United States) do not recognize the differences—that Canada has a
different kind of government, a different history, a different perspective; that indeed Canada is an independent national power.

Much has been said about the lack of awareness on the part of
the people of the United States for their Canadian neighbors. Writing
in his column for the *Washington Post* (October 24, 1965), Art Buchwald counseled Canada on how to get noticed in the United States:

Burn the Stars and Stripes at Niagara Falls; demand that the U.S. give back the St. Lawrence Seaway; or build a Berlin-type wall along the boundary.

Canada scarcely needs to cause an international incident to be noticed. It is the second largest country in the world based on measures of land mass (larger than the United States), has a population approaching 25 million (placing it among the top one fifth of all countries in population), has the seventh highest per capita gross national product in the world and the ninth highest life expectancy rate; as an original member of the United Nations, Canada has always been active in international programs of peace keeping, education, technology, and culture. In the last few years in particular, Canada has had a high profile in international interest, having hosted a first-class international exhibition, Expo '67, and the 1976 Summer Olympic Games. By whatever measure one cares to use, Canada has firmly established itself as a progressive, successful, and significant nation.

But in the process of establishing itself as a major force in the world Canada has had to overcome many factors that tended to inhibit its growth. The struggle to unify the various regions of the country and to forge an accurate self-image has now taken well over two centuries. For a long time Canadians have labored with an unjustly self-inflicted lack of national purpose, at times almost seeming to approach an inferiority complex of sorts. Constantly being compared to its powerful neighbor, the United States, because of similarity of size, geographic region, and colonial heritage, Canada has been hard put to match statistical analyses, figure for figure, fact for fact, in comparisons. A multicultural country, Canada has been traditionally quick to classify diversity as weakness and devisiveness rather than a source of strength arising from differences contributing unique perspectives. Population density was often mistakenly promoted at the cost of quality-of-life considerations. Finally, Canada was made to feel inferior because of the ability of sources in the United States to dominate Canadian thought through its mass media and virtual monopoly of information flow on the continent.

The struggle for full national independence has been a long, drawn-out, step-by-step process for Canada. The difficulties of its experience in establishing itself as a unique, independent entity were great. In contrast, the American colonies, more prosperous from the start, found their rebellion against British control to be a rallying point for their countrymen. Those who disagreed promptly found themselves separated from their property and surroundings. Those who remained were predominantly of English Protestant heritage, resulting in a homogeneity that kept divisiveness to a minimum. Immigrants to the United States quickly recognized that the only way to succeed in their new environment was to emulate the ideals and the life-style of the majority. Thus was born the idea of the American melting pot where all could become one, sharing in the success of the country by joining together to eliminate differences that might act as barriers to prosocial behavior. Secure in its borders, militarily strong, and rich in the national resources necessary for growth, "Fortress America" set out to forge "one nation under God."

However, at the time of the start of the American quest for independence, although Canada found itself with the same sort of frontiers to conquer in forming a nation out of the North American wilderness, it soon became apparent that historical and geographic conditions would make the task of establishing a unified nation much more difficult. In the late eighteenth century most Canadians were French-speaking residents of Quebec who only a few years before had been conquered by the British, who turned what was New France into a British colony. Never fully trusting the British, but always suspicious of American motives, the French chose to remain under British rule on the promise that they would be allowed to maintain their heritage and traditions. Constant threats and suspicions of American attempts to "liberate" Quebec only served to reinforce Quebec's reliance on the British Crown. Canada developed slowly at first because of its harsh climate where the amount of effort needed for survival was great, but Canada's population in 1840 approximated that of the United States in 1776, mainly as a result of British migration into the interior.

In 1840 the first attempts were made to forge an alliance between French- and English-speaking segments of Canada, when a weak union was established between Lower and Upper Canada (Quebec and Ontario). Dissension made the union impractical, and in 1867, with the approval of Queen Victoria, the Confederation was proclaimed. Provinces Quebec, Ontario, New Brunswick, and Nova Scotia were joined to form a federal government for the administration of Canadian affairs, but Confederation was not complete until the tenth province, Newfoundland, entered the union in 1949. That union was still under the direct authority of the British monarchy, Canada having been granted only the right of internal self-government. Not until 1927 was Canada first allowed to establish diplomatic relations with foreign nations and not until 1947 were "citizens" of Canada anything other than citizens of Great Britain. That year, for the first time, one was able to obtain a Canadian passport. Even today Canadians born prior to 1947 may still be eligible for British passports.

Another barrier to the struggle of making a "Canada" composed of "Canadians" has been the focal matter of Canadian public thought and life. Canadian society is multicultural. Whereas the Americans were quick to accept the notion of a "melting pot," Canadians were willing to accept nothing less than the notion of a "mosaic," which posits that each member of a society is capable of maintaining his or her heritage. In other words, one would not need to forsake cultural or spiritual origins to fit into Canadian life; instead, there could be a pattern of people, all with their differences, fitting together to make something that could be more than just the sum of its parts. But this cultural diversity is not without its costs: school systems are segregated, communities are segregated, and mass communication systems are segregated. Moreover, less than one eighth of the population is able to speak both national languages equally well (most of these people live in predominantly French-speaking Quebec), and two thirds of the population is capable of speaking only English, one fifth only French, and one fiftieth neither language.[1]

And, as already mentioned, Canada's sprawling geography has hindered its development into a unified nation. But what the land, the people, their cultural differences, and the history of Canada could not do to retard the growth of national unity, the nature of information flow in North America accomplished. From the earliest times, the busiest commercial ports in North America were the first to receive news from Europe. Most of these ports were situated in the United States. The larger and more centralized populations of the United States were able to attract more printers, writers, and journalists than Canada. Trade routes were more easily established in the United States along its canals, lakes, rivers, and oceans; they became natural information routes as well. On every front, the United States' development was more spectacular: railroads, telegraph lines, giant daily newspapers, and great publishing houses seemed to fill the country overnight. And the United States' land grant universities provided much of the teaching and research conducted in North America. It was inevitable that

[1] Canada, Statistics Canada, *Canada Yearbook, 1966* (Ottawa: Information Canada, 1966).

the great mass of English language communication on the continent, for Canadians and for Americans, was originating in the United States.

Still, before the coming of broadcasting it was easier for Canada to attempt to establish a separate national identity. The impact of living next to the United States was relatively muted. The school, the church, the store, and working facilities were the mainstays of one's public activity. Involvement meant involvement in the community; when one came into contact with other human beings, they would almost have to be fellow Canadians. It is not impossible to argue that Canada probably had a better chance of achieving a unique national identity within the first 60 or so years of its existence (before 1927) than it has had since.

The Role of Broadcasting

Broadcasting has played a contradictory role in Canada's drive to establish its national identity. On the positive side, broadcasting has used "many voices" to talk to Canadians; it is almost another mosaic—the mosaic of networks and independent broadcasters representing many differing viewpoints that brings entertainment and information to all of Canada. In radio three networks serve the nation: two are English language and one is French language. All are operated by a government agency but rely mainly on independent broadcasters to carry their programs. Most urbanized areas and many rural areas have other stations not affiliated with the networks that provide additional service. The same government agency (the Canadian Broadcasting Corporation) that operates the radio networks operates one French and one English national television network that reach all but a few in each language group. More recently a network of previously independent television stations has pooled resources to form a competing network (CTV), whereas still others provide additional services in the large metropolitan areas.

Founded in the 1930s, the CBC has traditionally been a strong supporter of Canadian idealism and independent development. From its beginning the CBC has been partially funded by the government and has carried only a limited number of advertisements, freeing it from the need to have the largest possible audience in order to survive. The CBC is able to devote a substantial portion of its energies to producing programs intended to be of vital value to relatively small segments of the population and other programs partially intended to do more than provide sheer escapist entertainment. In addition, it has carried some of the best popular programs produced in Canada, Britain, France, and the United States. As a tribute to the quality of its programming (particularly radio programming), U.S. networks have rebroadcast many CBC programs.

In short, the existing system of broadcasting is one of the best and most competitive in the world. Through its formal and informal structure, the broadcasters of Canada have done much, often at great expense, to serve their people. They have been in the position to have a potent impact on the development of Canadian values and have taken that responsibility seriously.

The other side of the role that broadcasting has played in the development of Canada's national identity has gone far to undo the positive aspects of the CBC, CTV, and independent broadcasters' involvement. The combined effects of having the United States so close by and the few problems that Canada itself has had in developing its broadcasting system have seriously hindered the fullest use of Canadian mass media by its citizens.

The most serious problem has been the direct competition for broadcast audiences. The population of Canada is largely strung out along the border with the United States, and radio waves recognize no political borders. If the signal is strong enough, any AM radio station broadcasting from the United States can be received in some part of Canada. In the earliest days of broadcasting the impact of this was overwhelming. Because of the regulatory policies of the Canadian government, only one station could be on the air at any one time in any one city in Canada and then only at very low strength. At the same time, lax government restrictions on stations in the United States permitted stations to populate the full length of the AM dial, broadcasting at any hour, using as much power as the station could generate—in short, largely without restrictions of any nature. At about the same time, U.S. stations began to organize networks that permitted a number of outlets to pool their resources and buy the very best talent on the continent to entertain and inform their audiences. The aggressiveness of the networks and their dedication to providing popular entertainment were rewarded with enormous audiences, both American and Canadian. Largely because of the government policies, often the only radio service that Canadians could get was from a nearby American station. Where there might be a choice between stations of either nation, American stations were runaway winners, so much so that when Canadian policies were relaxed in order to allow stations largely the same rights as U.S. stations, the first move that some of these competing Canadian outlets made was to join the U.S. networks. The popularity of the American stations and the lack of competition from the CBC had a marked influence on Canadian listening habits. After listening to American programs for so long, Canadians were reluctant to settle for any other type.

The same situation existed with the coming of television. American networks experimented with programs in the late 1930s and began fullscale operations in the late 1940s. By the early 1950s three networks were competing for audiences and winning over Canadian viewers, who were buying sets long before the first Canadian station took to the air. The CBC started its network late in 1952 and one by one slowly added cities to the chain; independent stations were allowed to go on the air beginning in 1961, but, again, by that time American broadcasters had already won over the hearts of many Canadian viewers. Some sources, for example, point out that about half of the viewers in Toronto could usually be found watching programs coming from Buffalo, less than 100 miles away.

There are a number of possible explanations for the popularity of American shows in Canada. The first, which is perhaps the hardest for Canada to deal with, is the difference in "production values" in the shows of the two countries. "Production values" cover a great many areas that add up to a generalized view of the quality of a program, most of which is dictated by the money available for production. Because of the larger audiences in the United States, generating larger advertising revenues, more money is available for investment in programming. Despite government subsidies to the CBC, Canadian-produced shows are rarely budgeted at more than one-eighth the amount of similar U.S. shows. With obvious differences mandated by lack of funds, Canadians often consider their own shows to be of poor quality. Many of these shows are "public affairs" type shows that are easy and relatively inexpensive to produce but offer little of the titillation or cathartic release of action shows and traditionally get fewer viewers.

In addition, much of the broadcast day on Canadian television is made up of American imports. American producers who have been paid for their shows to run on TV there are free to sell their shows to other nations. Because producers have already been paid once, foreign prices tend to be a bargain. As American programming is popular, Canadian stations and networks are quick to buy rights to them, often at prices far lower than those of the inferior programs they could produce themselves. This process accelerates the undermining of Canadian programming in many important areas: Canadian stations are sending valuable production money out of the country, enriching the already well-developed American producers at the expense of Canadian producers, thus further reducing Canada's ability to produce its own shows; American talent is being utilized at the expense of possible jobs for Canadian creative artists, often forcing Canadians to go to the United States for employment. Canadians come to assume the American values and sensibilities embodied in the shows. An example is when Canadians falsely assume that after arrest they must be read their rights just like on television, but this is only an American requirement. Canadian display of American shows further reinforces the habits of watching U.S. television. As more Canadians watch American TV, more Canadian advertisers will spend their money on American stations to reach Canadian audiences, which in turn leaves less money to be spent in Canada on Canadian problems. Thus a strong system of Canadian broadcasting has been wracked by several serious problems that have caused many Canadians to question its ultimate mobility and usefulness to the nation. Is the system living up to its capability? Is the system serving the cause of Canadian nationalism? The answer is too often no. Something must be done if Canada is to be able to establish and maintain a separate national identity. Part of the answer is to lessen the gross dependence for television material on the United States that has been allowed to develop. A nationalist response must be made to meet national needs.

Looking Through the Looking Glass—Darkly?

The consequences of one nation's looking at the world through the eyes of another are revealed in the assimilated attitudes and viewpoints of the people of these two nations, which are American biased. To test the extent of the Canadian proclivity for the American viewpoint, Earle Beattie, a professor at the University of Western Ontario, conducted a survey among more than 650 Canadian freshman students from 11 universities across Canada.[2] The survey concentrated specifically on the attention Canadian students paid to U.S. and Canadian affairs. The results of Beattie's study support the notion that Canadian students score higher in their knowledge of American political figures and issues than on similar Canadian concerns, that CBS newscaster Walter Cronkite is more familiar to them than CBC's popular newscaster Earl Cameron, and that through their absorption with American mass media, particularly television, Canadian students tend to substitute American terminology for Canadian, thus giving some small indication of their Americanization through the mass media.

Canada's alarm over the American cultural invasion of the Canadian mind prompted the Canadian Radio and Television Commission (CRTC) to dictate that by 1972 all Canadian stations were to carry 60 per cent Canadian programming and of the 40 per cent remaining no more than 30 per cent was to come from one foreign country.

The CRTC's "content" regulation, although reasonable from the Canadian government's point of view, provoked a storm of protest. The Canadian cable companies were able, as a result, to do a land office business because of their ability to deliver the preferred American programming for a large, eager Canadian audience by legally side-stepping the CRTC regulation. Counteraction by the Canadian government, however, has resulted in what many observers have termed "the TV border war." This counteraction, which polarized influentials in the TV industry on both sides of the border, consisted of the Canadian government's encouraging the cable companies to delete commercials from U.S./originated programming relayed to Canadian audiences and further to substitute Canadian commercials or public service announcements for the deleted commercials.

For months the border war has continued with little visible progress being made to reach a resolution of the problem. Some of the pros and cons of the dispute are listed as follows:

The Canadian Viewpoint: [3]

1. The Canadian broadcaster has a commitment to protect and promote the Canadian culture and information industry. Sixty per cent of all programming must be indigenous to Canada.

[2] Earle Beattie, "In Canada's Centennial Year, U.S. Mass Media Influence Probed," *Journalism Quarterly* **44,** 1967, 667–672.

[3] Moses Znaimer, "The Television 'Border War'—Canada's View: Profits Not Only Issue," *Buffalo Courier-Express* (February 29, 1976), p. 8.

2. The Canadian broadcaster must spend a great deal of money to produce material expressive of the community in which he lives.
3. The Canadian broadcaster regards the American broadcaster whose signal happens to spill over the border as an encroacher. The American broadcaster is not licensed to serve that Canadian community; he prepares no programs expressly for that community; he spends not one penny for Canadian content.
4. Because his programs spill over into Canada, the American broadcaster increases his audience, which in turn generates new advertising revenue as a bonus windfall.
5. The border war is an economic war, not a moral war or a legalistic war as claimed. The Americans earn at least $20 million along the border, coast to coast. This money deprives Canadians of jobs, corporate profits, additional or improved Canadian programs, and a strong Canadian identity and posture.
6. Canadian bill C-58, an income tax amendment disallowing the cost of advertisements, should be introduced.
7. If the income tax disallowance does not work, then commercial deletion should be tried.

The American Viewpoint: [4]

1. The Canadian cable industry has been successful largely because it has been able to supply U.S. television signals to Canadian viewers. Canadian viewers prefer American television to their own.
2. It is erroneously assumed that the Canadian income tax amendment would discourage Canadian business from advertising in American sources and that the advertising revenues would go to the smaller Canadian stations. In reality, advertising dollars follow audience saturation.
3. The matter of commercial deletion is a double-edged sword used by the CRTC to keep American programs, cost free, on Canadian cable, while at the same time blocking the Americans from earning any compensation for their programs.
4. The protest from Canadians over their forced deprivation of American programs and the deliberate attempts of the Canadian government to cripple the Canadian cable industry are not viable alternatives for the Canadian government.
5. The American stations pay extra fees for their penetration of the Canadian market; they do not have a free ride in Canada as charged.
6. If American commercials continue to be deleted, the American broadcasters will deny service to Canada through signal jamming without impairing service to U.S. viewers.

[4] Philip R. Beuth, "Canada Stance Is Called 'Discriminatory,' " *Buffalo Courier-Express* (February 29, 1976), p. 9.

Up to this point, although many threats for commercial deletion and jamming have been made, each country appears to have called a moratorium on further counterproductive acts. Beuth probably expressed the situation as well as anyone personally and closely involved in the situation might:

> We hope that reasonable people can find reasonable solutions so that television signals from our countries can continue to cross the border in both directions, carrying entertainment, information and advertising to viewers in both countries.[5]

At least for the present, a "cease fire" appears to have been called.

[5]Ibid., p. 9.

Chapter 14
Mass Communication:
Prospects and Directions

If Booth Tarkington were to write Seventeen *today, he
would have to call it* 8½.
Tony Schwartz, *The Responsive Chord*

And tomorrow? Would he have to call it 4¼?
Mary B. Cassata and Molefi K. Asante

Technology

In our discussion of the roots of mass communication in the second
chapter of this book, we promised our readers a look into the future of
mass communication. It would be appropriately McLuhanesque to
declare at this point that what we are really doing is looking into our
rearview mirrors, for the future has been upon us for some time.

What is happening in our mass media today is what some authors like to call a "demassification" of the media—a specialization,
fragmentation, or individualization, if you will. Our large newspapers, for example, have become fewer, but our small newspapers—underground papers, the radical press, and community news-
sheets—have become more prominent. Many of our mass circulation
national magazines have disappeared from the newsstands, whereas
once again the special interest magazines with their more predictable
readerships have appeared by the hundreds. Books are being published on all kinds of specialized topics, in hard covers and in paper-
back as well as in "nonprint" formats—i.e., microcards, microfilm,
and microfiche. At this moment, through the wonders of technology,
any one of us could carry the equivalent of a good-sized college library
collection in a back pocket—a small portable, lightweight reader and a

pack of ultramicrofiche cards on which are printed thousands of words of thousands of books.

For as little as $200 or as much as $5000—the difference between a well-equipped ten-speed bicycle and a four-cylinder gas-saving automobile—you can purchase a minicomputer. For $200 you can buy one that will play chess with you, or for $5000 you can purchase one that will perform a wide range of business and educational functions from managing all of your banking and business transactions to retrieving information from data banks. The heart of the minicomputer is the integrated circuits or tiny silicon chips (which are also found in digital watches, calculators, and electronic cameras), with each chip performing the work of 10,000 transistor-based components!

In the electronic media we now have the videocassette, which possesses one of the more individualized advantages of print—i.e., use on demand. We already have seen the introduction of media centers into our homes and of holography, "sense-around" movie screens, and wall-size or pocket-size television.

The technological advances in television will outstrip anything we have experienced. As Ben Bagdikian has said, changes are inexorable and will be in the capability and flexibility of our technology.[1] A limit of seven UHF television channels is not sacred. There may be as many as a hundred television channels in a community. It may be possible for viewers to tune in to foreign TV stations much as listeners use the shortwave radio.

Community cohesion may be facilitated by cable television. A concept of television *by* the people and not television *for* the people is the key to understanding how community cohesion can be maintained. Viewers utilizing the facilities of cable television may air specific issues of interest to them and their community. In addition, community-derived and -based entertainment may be programmed for the local audience. Technological changes, inexorable as they may be, are not necessarily positive or necessarily negative. What we choose to do in response to the new technology and how we choose to interpret its use are the critical questions. We believe that the future of mass communication is filled with creative potential. The development of communication cohesion, domestic and international, will be made more certain by the revolutionary changes in media during the next few years.

[1] Ben H. Bagdikian, "How Communications May Shape Our Future Environment," *AAUW Journal* **62(3)**, March 1969, 123–126.

Pope Gregory I regarded images of saints and holy people as useful for the illiterates who could read on the walls of church buildings what they could not read in books. Mass media images may be regarded not only as useful for contemporary society but also as a record for posterity. Images of our world, our values, interests, customs, and behaviors are preserved in celluloid for future audiences. Those who may not want to spend time reading essays and novels will have pictures with which to get a glimpse of our society.

Yet the revolutionary changes we anticipate in media for the next few years will be more in format and presentation than in technology. This is not to say, as we shall see, that we will not continue to make enormous strides in the sophistication of mechanical and electronic parts of media systems, but we do believe that the greatest advances will be in the coming to be of new configurations, new patterns, and more meaningful directions in the dissemination of news and entertainment.

The News

Indications exist that the media have universally failed to meet the challenges of an educated public. The growth of the underground press, citizens band radio, and shortwave radio and the numerous attempts to challenge radio and television stations are all signs of the problem; people do not believe that the broadcast news programs are giving them all of the news. In the future we are sure to see clearer reporting of the news and less simultaneous analysis; there will be a particular segment of each news program allotted for analysis. This format will encourage the reading of news from various parts of the world, which will obviate the problem of too much selection on the part of the news managers and not enough coverage of all the news. For example, news of art and culture and of education and construction in Africa will be of interest to larger numbers of people. Such a development will forestall the rise of check-and-balance demands from citizens' groups who believe that a handful of people select news and pass it to the commentators who then pass it to audiences.

There could also be changes in the concept of news reporting. For example, in the Communist nations disasters and natural catastrophes are seldom reported as news. A different conception of news leads the

Western press to place a premium on action footage. This means fires, automobile chases, earthquakes, aircraft crashes, and other disasters.

Thus the question to be asked in the future is, what is newsworthy? The answer will be found largely in the psychological and philosophical changes we experience in the next few years. At present, our news is generally divided into three broad segments of (1) general news, (2) sports, and (3) weather, and the way the general news is presented is an indication of the media's judgment of value. A news program that always begins with a fire or some other disaster suggests an emphasis on the dramatic, although this is not necessarily valuable in securing audience understanding of the news.

Entertainment

News may become more a form of entertainment than in the past; news reporters and broadcast announcers will be competing for attention with stars of mystery movies and soap operas. The electronic media demand uniqueness from those who use it, and a news reporter on the electronic media who lacks uniqueness is indistinguishable from others. Media seek to gain and hold audiences. Thus all messages are designed to attract viewers whose attention will be held for advertisers selling their products. The entertainment aspect of the electronic media, particularly television, extends to the playing of music during weather reports and station pauses. The idea is never to leave the viewer alone. Of all of the news, the weather appears the segment most susceptible to a humorous approach. Furthermore, because the weather segment of the news seldom has moving pictures, the reporter must improvise for action. When a tornado or blizzard strikes, footage is most likely to appear on the general news segment before being reported on the weather segment. Thus the weather reporter is left to his or her imagination.

The news as entertainment will continue to be part of the structure of American television. To keep viewers interested in a program, television reporters will experiment with new techniques in studio atmosphere, style, and organization of the news.

Consumer Awareness Training

We have already seen some progress being made in the area of consumer awareness, especially in the case of television. There are movements under way to enable the television viewer to become a more educated, and therefore more critical, user of programming. For example, a national organization that calls itself Prime Time School Television (PTST) encourages parents and teachers to use evening television to educate students to become more critical and more conscious of what they view. "Discrimination and selection," according to the *New York Times*, "are the crucial keys of future control of the TV monster." PTST supplements evening television fare by producing and distributing study materials both on TV specials and documentaries and on series programs on the commercial and public TV networks. With the help of PTST's study guides, provocative and lively discussions have taken place on such subjects as death and dying, violence, drugs, morality, human relationships, the women's liberation movement, politics, religion, and culture.

Another effort along the same lines as PTST is Television Awareness Training (TAT). TAT is based on the concept that the average viewer needs to have certain areas of "consumer awareness" heightened. Therefore, would-be trainers or leaders in television awareness are put through a rigorous training program that educates them to see through some of the "show biz" tactics of television. These areas include television advertising, the role of women in television, the impact of television on children, the presentation of violence, and the stereotyping of minorities and other groups. Once the trainers have earned their certification as "aware" leaders, they organize various community groups in an effort to share with them what they themselves have learned, thereby adding to the numbers of criticial consumers.

It is our prediction that in the future such efforts as PTST and TAT will result in the achievement of what heretofore has been an elusive goal: an improvement in the quality of television programming.

Research Instruments

Students of mass communication will begin more and more to utilize the traditional research methods of the social and behavioral sciences. Already evident in the research of contemporary communicationists such as Wilbur Schramm, Melvin DeFleur, Harold Mendelsohn, and Samuel Becker are the paradigms of social science. The Yale psychologists, the Princeton political scientists, and the Michigan State developmental communicationists have provided an orientation that influences mass communication research. Understanding the basic methods of the field is one way to gain an insight into the nature of original mass communication research. A clear prospect for the future is more basic research into the nature of communication's impact on our society. Facts are the essential ingredients for sound research.

The best way to discover the facts in any case is to take a situational attitude. Of course, this is not always possible. However, other techniques exist for arriving at an understanding of mass media problems, and various topics related to the media may be examined by different methods.

This section introduces some of the research tools helpful to the social scientist interested in studying the concepts of feedback, development, application, and diffusion as they relate to the media. Just as the artist must have an approach to her or his art, the social scientist must begin with an approach. What is provided in the following pages is not an exhaustive account of all research methods that may be applicable to the media but rather a listing of those most common in the exploration of media communication.

Content Analysis. Content analysis in communication studies, particularly as discussed by Ole Holsti, is suited to the examination of mass media messages. Content analysis is a method for coding and categorizing messages. It can be used in a variety of ways: a person may use content analysis to arrive at an understanding of what messages are being sent by the media to a given audience, or it may be used as a feedback mechanism to analyze what messages the audiences are sending to the media sources. For example, a recent doctoral dissertation used content analysis to investigate the reaction of several newspapers toward the Arab-Israeli conflict.[2] Media messages, whether from television, newspapers, or films, may be analyzed according to their description, potency, or critical content. Supposedly, once we understand the nature of the messages we can modify them or modify our behavior. What audiences are exposed to and what media sources send, however, do not necessar-

---

[2] Alan Zaremba, "An Exploratory Analysis of National Perceptions of the Arab-Israeli Conflict as Represented Through World Newspapers: An International Communication Study," unpublished dissertation, State University of New York at Buffalo, 1977.

ily result in audiences' believing or accepting a presentation or in media sources' being effective. An assessment of a medium's goals and messages can provide information on the correspondence between what an organization says its goals are and what it actually does with its messages.

Likert Scale. The Likert scale is an attitude measurement instrument that allows the assignment of symbols by rule. A set of items considered approximately equal in attitude loading is presented to the subjects, and the subjects respond with varying degrees of intensity on a scale ranging between extremes such as like–dislike. When the scale is completed, the scores are totaled or averaged to arrive at a subject's attitude on a set of items. A typical Likert scale would be one constructed to elicit audience responses to future programming plans or past news articles. Generally, a Likert-type scale has five or seven positions. The following example is of a five-position scale:

1. Television has too much violence	SA A U D SD*
2. Newspapers should have more good news	SA A U D SD

* *Strongly Agree–Agree–Undecided–Disagree–Strongly Disagree.*

Depth Interview. Depth interviews are what the name implies. The researcher using this technique seeks to get at the underlying attitudes of audiences. Typically the questions are not prepared ahead of time; rather, an interview guide is prepared by the researcher who allows the interviewee to speak freely and fully about an issue. This is a qualitative methodology, and it demands a keen analyst as interviewer in order to make sense out of the answers given by the interviewee. For example, if a media organization wanted to know the attitudes behind opinions of business executives that a certain product is useless, the researcher would have to be capable of drawing out of the interviewee the reasons for negative attitudes toward the product. This requires both skill and intelligence.

Questionnaires. Although the questionnaire is simple and relatively inexpensive in terms of time and money for the researcher who seeks to find out what people feel about a phenomenon, concept, or person, there are several technical drawbacks in using it as a research instrument. First, the questionnaire must often be sent out in a shotgun fashion. Second, the questionnaire must be developed with expert attention to assure that it will be successful. Third, the rate of return is often dismal. Fourth, a researcher using a questionnaire does not have the flexibility of the interviewer to ask a follow-up question for more information or clarification. Despite these drawbacks, the questionnaire is perhaps the most frequently used methodology in media organizations. Questionnaires have a tendency to be valuable when there is a sharp cleavage between groups. For example, if a researcher surveyed broadcasters on the subject of the Family Hour on television, he or she would probably be pleased with the results, because the questionnaire is useful in revealing praise or blame. Thus, used with caution, and with the provision of space for respondents' additional comments, the questionnaire can be helpful.

Case Methods. Case method research in mass communication is used to examine the history, present status, and interactions of a media institution. An intensive study of the public broadcasting station in a large urban community is an example of the use of case methodology. Most case studies are exhaustive investigations that yield a comprehensive view of the institution under study. The purposes of researchers in developing a case method approach to mass communication can be many. For example, if the purpose is to determine the particular characteristics of a newspaper's growth over the last 10 years, the scope of the study may include the examination of every aspect of the newspaper's production and dissemination. On the other hand, if the purpose is to establish the management policies that have influenced a decline in subscriptions, the scope of the study may be limited to specific factors or to a selected segment of the company.

The person employing case methodology should follow five guidelines for effective research:

1. Give your objectives. State what units of study, characteristics, and relationships will direct your study.
2. Design your study. How will the units be selected? What sources will be tapped for data? What collection procedures will be followed? What protections for data sources, if necessary, will be granted?
3. Collect your data. Organize the data into coherent information about your unit of study.

4. Analyze your data. What are their significance? What do they show about your unit?
5. Report your findings and discuss their implications.

Semantic Differential. The semantic differential is a method for measuring the meaning of words. There are two recognizable applications of the semantic differential in mass communication research. One application is the objective measurement of the semantic properties of concepts. A second, perhaps more popular, use is as an attitude scale to measure the affective domain of subjects' responses.

The researcher employing this instrument in mass communication studies must first decide what objective is important to the study; selection of the concept to be rated is made subsequently. All concepts used in the scale should be relevant to the research purpose. The next step is to select polar adjective pairs that will anchor the scale. For example,

Weak	7	6	5	4	3	2	1	Strong
Good	7	6	5	4	3	2	1	Bad

The polar adjectives are arranged so that the favorable, active, or potent end is randomly placed in a right or left position to avoid the effect of consistencies in subjects' response habits. Most studies use several concepts. Let us imagine how the scale might look if we wanted the newspaper subscribers to rate the concept "*Daily Times* editorial page":

Daily Times Editorial Page

Weak	7	6	5	4	3	2	1	Strong
Good	7	6	5	4	3	2	1	Bad
Active	7	6	5	4	3	2	1	Passive
Dull	7	6	5	4	3	2	1	Bright
Rugged	7	6	5	4	3	2	1	Delicate
Large	7	6	5	4	3	2	1	Small

Used in this way, the semantic differential is an attitude scale. Analysis of the data derived from the scale can demonstrate difference between subjects, scales, and concepts.

Other Tools. Additional research tools are available to the person seeking to investigate mass communication. The researcher may have to develop his or her own instrument if the problem demands it. In any case, the empiricist, using the best available methodological tools, seeks to discover the facts in a given situation. Because the ultimate intent in any empirical research situation is the prediction of outcomes, the future of research in mass communication will be realized through constant change in methodology to enhance the ability of researchers to determine human and media behavior with a high degree of probability.

Our attention in the future will also be drawn to the international communication problems that have to do with the survival of humanity. Questions of poverty, war, urbanization, depletion of resources, and population control will have to be addressed in mass communication terms. How do we succeed in getting the world to realize that in 75 years we will have depleted the available energy resources in the world? What strategy can we use to explain the extent of world poverty to affluent people? These are the meaningful issues that must be addressed by research if our future is to be secure.

UNESCO Communication Activities

The United Nations through one of its divisions, UNESCO, has been active in international communication activities since the early 1960s. It is this agency that must keep the world's future secure. In 1962 the General Assembly of the United Nations confirmed the role of the United Nations Educational, Scientific, and Cultural Organization as a source for helping media development in less industrialized nations.

Robert P. Knight has said that UNESCO's role was comprehensive:

> In its first years, UNESCO's mass media efforts concentrated on building up media and professionalism in war-devastated nations, while breaking down barriers to the free flow of ideas; in the 1960's, the organization's communications emphasis centered on developing nations and on education; in the early 1970's UNESCO's thrust apparently will be toward the use made of communications satellites, toward book production and toward getting maximum benefit from exchange of persons among nations.[3]

[3] Robert P. Knight, "UNESCO's International Communication Activities," in Heinz-Dietrich Fischer and John Calhoun Merrill (eds.), *International Communication* (New York: Hastings House, 1970), p. 219.

Indeed, the United Nations has recognized the impact communication technology can make on both the developing and the developed nations. In a series of international conferences designed to highlight world communications and the uses of various technologies, UNESCO has demonstrated its interest in solving problems of literacy, adult education, and information diffusion.

The United Nations encourages electronic hotlines between nations. The Moscow to Washington hotline telephone may well be the forerunner of numerous other lines between world capitals, such as a Cairo to Tel Aviv line or an Ankara to Athens line. Such communication contact provides immediate discussion and debate. World cohesion should result from improved access to national allies as well as traditional rivals.

UNESCO's activities have been confined to initiating conferences, organizing communications technology resource pools, and providing technical support to nations that do not have the electronic and computer-assisted technologies of communication. However, UNESCO's future orientation appears to be in developing regional frameworks for cooperative uses of communication technology. Such a development augurs well for international relations as well as for mass information systems; the miracles already wrought by international satellites are minor in comparison with the potential. UNESCO's future course in the international production and distribution of knowledge seems assured by its efforts to organize a news-gathering agency that will concentrate on the less developed industrial countries.

The business of the United Nations is world peace, and the best way to achieve peace is surely through communication. All nations will have to apply themselves more intently toward cooperation as more rapid mobility puts us in contact with diverse peoples in ways never dreamed of by our forefathers. UNESCO as an organization dedicated to expanding cultural, educational, and scientific knowledge should enter the future boldly and with faith in the effectiveness of world communication.

Part Four Readings

Agee, Warren. *Mass Media in a Free Society*. Wichita: University of Kansas Press, 1969.

Asante, Molefi K. "Television and Black Consciousness." *Journal of Communication*, Fall 1976.

Barron, Jerome A. *Freeedom of the Press: For Whom the Rise of Access to Media*. Bloomington: Indiana University Press, 1973.

Boulding, Kenneth. *The Image: Knowledge in Life and Society*. Ann Arbor: University of Michigan Press, 1956.

Cater, Douglas. *The Fourth Branch of Government*. Boston: Houghton-Mifflin, 1959.

Chafee, Zechariah. *Government and Mass Communications*. Chicago: University of Chicago Press, 1947.

Clark, David, and Hutchinson, Earl R. (eds.). *Mass Media and the Law: Freedom and Restraint*. New York: David McKay Co., 1970.

Davison, W. Phillips, and Yu, Frederick T. C. (eds.). *Mass Communications Research: Major Issues and Future Directions*. New York: Praeger Publishers, 1974.

Dennis, Everette E., and Rivers, William L. *Other Voices: The New Journalism in America*. San Francisco: Canfield Press, 1974.

Deutsch, Karl. *The Nerves of Government, Models of Political Communication and Conflict*. London: Free Press, 1963.

Diamond, Edwin. *The Tin Kazoo: Television, Politics and the News*. Cambridge, Mass.: MIT Press, 1975.

Dickson, David. *Alternative Technology: The Politics of Technical Change*. Glasgow: Williams Collins Sons and Co., Ltd., 1974.

Edgar, Patricia, and McPhee, Hilary. *Media She*. Melbourne: Heinemann, 1974.

Gerald, J. Edward. *The Social Responsibility of the Press*. Minneapolis: University of Minnesota Press, 1963.

Gerbner, George, and Gross, Larry. "Living with Television: The Violence Profile." *Journal of Communication*, Spring 1976.

Gerbner, George, et al. (eds.). *The Analysis of Communication Content: Developments in Scientific Theories and Computer Techniques*. New York: Wiley, 1969.

Gerbner, George, Gross, Larry P., and Melody, William H. *Communications Technology and Social Policy: Understanding the New "Cultural Revolution."* New York: Interscience, 1973.

Geylin, Philip L., and Cater, Douglass. *American Media: Adequate or Not?* Washington, D.C.: American Enterprise Institute for Public Policy Research, 1970.

Gillmor, Donald M., and Barron, Jerome A. *Mass Communication Law: Cases and Comment*, 2nd ed. St. Paul, Minn.: West Publishing Co., 1974.

Gordon, Donald R. *The New Literacy*. Toronto: University of Toronto Press, 1971.

Haskell, Molly. *From Reverence to Rape: The Treatment of Women in the Movies*. New York: Holt, Rinehart, and Winston, 1974.

Hatchen, William H. *The Supreme Court on the Freedom of the Press: Decisions and Dissent*. Ames: Iowa State University Press, 1968.

Hollowell, Mary Louise (ed.). *Cable Handbook 1975–1976.* Washington, D.C. Communications Press, 1975.

Howitt, Dennis, and Cumberbatch, Guy. *Mass Media, Violence and Society.* New York: Wiley, 1975.

Hughes, Frank. *Prejudice and the Press.* New York: Devin-Adair, 1950.

Hutchinson, Earl R. *Tropic of Cancer on Trial: A Case History of Censorship.* New York: Grove Press, 1968.

Kline, Gerald F., and Tichener, Philip J. (eds.). *Current Perspectives in Mass Communication Research.* Sage Annual Review of Communication Research, Vol. I. Beverly Hills, Calif.: Sage Publications, 1972.

Larsen, Otto N. (ed.). *Violence and the Mass Media.* New York: Harper & Row, 1968.

Levy, Leonard W. (ed.). *Freedom of the Press from Zenger to Jefferson.* Indianapolis: Bobbs-Merrill, 1967.

Lowels, Francisco J. *The Uses of the Media by the Chicano Movement: A Study in Minority Access.* New York: Praeger Publishers, 1974.

Macy, John W., Jr. *To Irrigate a Wasteland: The Struggle to Shape a Public Television System in the United States.* Berkeley: University of California Press, 1974.

Mapp, Edward. *Blacks in American Films: Today and Yesterday.* Metuchen, N.J.: Scarecrow Press, 1972.

Mendelsohn, Harold. *Mass Entertainment.* New Haven, Conn.: College and University Press, 1966.

Merton, Robert K., Fisk, Marjorie, and Artis, Alberta. *Mass Persuasion: The Social Psychology of a War Bond Drive.* New York: Harper & Row, 1946.

Nelson, Harold L. (ed.). *Freedom of the Press from Hamilton to the Warren Court.* Indianapolis: Bobbs-Merrill, 1967.

Nelson, Harold L., and Teeter, Dwight C. *Law of Mass Communications: Freedom and Control of Print and Broadcast Media,* 2nd ed. New York: Foundation Press, 1973.

Nimmo, Dan D. *Newsgathering in Washington.* New York: Atherton Press, 1969.

Pines, Jim. *Blacks in Films: A Survey of Racial Themes and Images in the American Film.* London: Studio Vista, 1975.

Pool, Ithiel de Sola. *Talking Back: Citizen Feedback and Cable Technology,* Cambridge, Mass.: MIT Press, 1973.

Powers, Anne. *Blacks in American Movies: A Selected Bibliography.* Metuchen, N.J.: Scarecrow Press, 1974.

Prize, Monroe, and Wicklein, John. *Cable Television: A Guide for Citizen Action.* Philadelphia: A Pilgrim Press Book, 1972.

Reston, James. *The Artillery of the Press.* New York: Harper & Row, 1967.

Rivers, William L., and Schramm, Wilbur. *Responsibility in Mass Communication,* 2nd ed. New York: Harper & Row, 1969.

Rourke, Francis E. *Secrecy & Publicity.* Baltimore: Johns Hopkins Press, 1961.

Seiden, Martin H. *Who Controls the Mass Media? Popular Myths and Economic Realities.* New York: Basic Books, 1974.

Strainchamps, Ethel. *Rooms with No View: A Women's Guide to the Man's World of the Media.* New York: Harper & Row, 1974.

Sullivan, Marjorie, and Goodell, John S. *Media Use in the Study of Minorities.* Emporia State Research Studies, Vol. 24, No. 2, 1975.

Valenzuela, Nicholas, Williams, Frederick, and Knight, Pamela. *Media Habits and Attitudes of Mexican-Americans.* Washington, D.C.: U.S. Department of Health, Education, and Welfare, National Institute of Education, 1973.

Wiener, Norbert. *Cybernetics,* 2nd ed., Cambridge, Mass.: MIT Press, 1969.

Wilson, Bryan Key. *Media Sexploitation.* Englewood Cliffs, N.J.: Prentice-Hall, 1976.

Appendix A
The Codes

Codes of Ethics

Professional organizations usually have codes of ethics. These codes represent the professions' attempt to regulate themselves. Believing that self-control is preferable to external control and regulation, they propose rules of conduct and business to provide an ethical statement. In this regard, the mass communication institutions are no different from other professions. In fact, the proliferation of codes of ethics among media professionals probably indicates a strong sense of public commitment on their part. None of the codes and standards that follow can be considered immutable. Indeed, several of them have gone through numerous revisions. The ability to monitor the changes in society and to reflect those changes judiciously in a code of ethics is one basis for professional maturity. Perhaps the Canons of Journalism stand alone in longevity. In the electronic media fields, revisions have been more frequent as the professions try to discover a satisfactory statement of ethics.

Journalism Codes

The Canons of Journalism were the first set of codes for media professionals. Thirty-two years later, in 1975, the Canons were supplanted by the American Society of Newspaper Editors' "A Statement of Principles."

Canons of Journalism *
Code of Ethics or Canons of Journalism
The American Society of Newspaper Editors

The PRIMARY function of newspapers is to communicate to the human race what its members do, feel and think. Journalism, therefore, demands of its practitioners the widest range of intelligence, or knowledge, and of experience, as well as natural and trained powers of observation and reasoning. To its opportunities as a chronicle are indissolubly linked its obligations as teacher and interpreter.

To the end of finding some means of codifying sound practice and just aspirations of American journalism, these canons are set forth:

I. RESPONSIBILITY

The right of a newspaper to attract and hold readers is restricted by nothing but considerations of public welfare. The use a newspaper makes of the share of public attention it gains serves to determine its sense of responsibility, which it shares with every member of its staff. A journalist who uses his power for any selfish or otherwise unworthy purpose is faithless to a high trust.

II. FREEDOM OF THE PRESS

Freedom of the press is to be guarded as a vital right of mankind. It is the unquestionable right to discuss whatever it is not explicitly forbidden by law, including the wisdom of any restrictive statute.

III. INDEPENDENCE

Freedom from all obligations except that of fidelity to the public interest is vital.

1. Promotion of any private interest contrary to the general welfare, for whatever reason, is not compatible with honest journalism. So-called news communications from private sources should not be published without public notice of their source or else substantiation of their claims to value as news, both in form and substance.

2. Partisanship, in editorial comment which knowingly departs from the truth, does violence to the best spirit of American journalism; in the news columns it is subversive of a fundamental principle of the profession.

IV. SINCERITY, TRUTHFULNESS, ACCURACY

Good faith with the reader is the foundation of all journalism worthy of the name.

---

* Reprinted by permission of the American Society of Newspaper Editors. Adopted in 1923.

1. By every consideration of good faith a newspaper is constrained to be truthful. It is not to be excused for lack of thoroughness or accuracy within its control, or failure to obtain command of these essential qualities.

2. Headlines should be fully warranted by the contents of the articles which they surmount.

V. IMPARTIALITY

Sound practice makes clear distinction between news reports and expressions of opinion. News reports should be free from opinion or bias of any kind.

1. This rules does not apply to so-called special articles unmistakably devoted to advocacy or characterized by a signature authorizing the writer's own conclusions and interpretation.

VI. FAIR PLAY

A newspaper should not publish unofficial charges affecting reputation or moral character without opportunity given to the accused to be heard; right practice demands the giving of such opportunity in all cases of serious accusation outside judicial proceedings.

1. A newspaper should not invade private rights or feelings without sure warrant of public right as distinguished from public curiosity.

2. It is the privilege, as it is the duty, of a newspaper to make prompt and complete correction of its own serious mistakes of fact or opinion, whatever their origin.

DECENCY

A newspaper cannot escape conviction of insincerity if while professing high moral purpose it supplies incentives to base conduct, such as are to be found in details of crime and vice, publication of which is not demonstrable for the general good. Lacking authority to enforce its canons the journalism here presented can but express the hope that deliberate pandering to vicious instincts will encounter effective public disapproval or yield to the influence of a preponderant professional condemnation.

A Statement of Principles*
American Society of Newspaper Editors

PREAMBLE

The First Amendment, protecting freedom of expression from abridgment by any law, guarantees to the people through their press a constitutional right, and thereby places on newspaper people a particular responsibility.

* Reprinted by permission of the American Society of Newspaper Editors.
Adopted by the ASNE board of directors, October 23, 1975.

Thus journalism demands of its practitioners not only industry and knowledge but also the pursuit of a standard of integrity proportionate to the journalist's singular obligation.

To this end the American Society of Newspaper Editors sets forth this Statement of Principles as a standard encouraging the highest ethical and professional performance.

ARTICLE I—RESPONSIBILITY

The primary purpose of gathering and distributing news and opinion is to serve the general welfare by informing the people and enabling them to make judgments on the issues of the time. Newspapermen and women who abuse the power of their professional role for selfish motives or unworthy purposes are faithless to that public trust.

The American press was made free not just to inform or just to serve as a forum for debate but also to bring an independent scrutiny to bear on the forces of power in the society, including the conduct of official power at all levels of government.

ARTICLE II—FREEDOM OF THE PRESS

Freedom of the press belongs to the people. It must be defended against encroachment or assault from any quarter, public or private.

Journalists must be constantly alert to see that the public's business is conducted in public. They must be vigilant against all who would exploit the press for selfish purposes.

ARTICLE III—INDEPENDENCE

Journalists must avoid impropriety and the appearance of impropriety as well as any conflict of interest or the appearance of conflict. They should neither accept anything nor pursue any activity that might compromise or seem to compromise their integrity.

ARTICLE IV—TRUTH AND ACCURACY

Good faith with the reader is the foundation of good journalism. Every effort must be made to assure that the news content is accurate, free from bias and in context, and that all sides are presented fairly. Editorials, analytical articles and commentary should be held to the same standards of accuracy with respect to facts as news reports.

Significant errors of fact, as well as errors of omission, should be corrected promptly and prominently.

ARTICLE V—IMPARTIALITY

To be impartial does not require the press to be unquestioning or to refrain from editorial expression. Sound practice, however, demands a clear distinction for the reader between news reports and opinion. Articles that contain opinion or personal interpretation should be clearly identified.

ARTICLE VI—FAIR PLAY

Journalists should respect the rights of people involved in the news, observe the common standards of decency and stand accountable to the public for the fairness and accuracy of their news reports.

Persons publicly accused should be given the earliest opportunity to respond.

Pledges of confidentiality to news sources must be honored at all costs, and therefore should not be given lightly. Unless there is clear and pressing need to maintain confidences, sources of information should be identified.

These principles are intended to preserve, protect and strengthen the bond of trust and respect between American journalists and the American people, a bond that is essential to sustain the grant of freedom entrusted to both by the nation's founders.

Code of Ethics *
The Society of Professional Journalists, Sigma Delta Chi

The Society of Professional Journalists, Sigma Delta Chi, believes the duty of journalists is to serve the truth.

We believe the agencies of mass communication are carriers of public discussion and information, acting on their Constitutional mandate and freedom to learn and report the facts.

We believe in public enlightenment as the forerunner of justice, and in our Constitutional role to seek the truth as part of the public's right to know the truth.

We believe those responsibilities carry obligations that require journalists to perform with intelligence, objectivity, accuracy, and fairness.

To these ends, we declare acceptance of the standards of practice here set forth:

RESPONSIBILITY

The public's right to know of events of public importance and interest is the overriding mission of the mass media. The purpose of distributing news and enlightened opinion is to serve the general welfare. Journalists who use their professional status as representatives of the public for selfish or other unworthy motives violate a high trust.

* Reprinted with the permission of The Society of Professional Journalists, Sigma Delta Chi.

FREEDOM OF THE PRESS

Freedom of the press is to be guarded as an inalienable right of people in a free society. It carried with it the freedom and the responsibility to discuss, question, and challenge actions and utterances of our government and of our public and private institutions. Journalists uphold the right to speak unpopular opinions and the privilege to agree with the majority.

ETHICS

Journalists must be free of obligation to any interest other than the public's right to know the truth.

1. Gifts, favors, free travel, special treatment or privileges can compromise the integrity of journalists and their employers. Nothing of value should be accepted.

2. Secondary employment, political involvement, holding public office, and service in community organizations should be avoided if it compromises the integrity of journalists and their employers. Journalists and their employers should conduct their personal lives in a manner which protects them from conflict of interest, real or apparent. Their responsibilities to the public are paramount. That is the nature of their profession.

3. So-called news communications from private sources should not be published or broadcast without substantiation of their claims to news value.

4. Journalists will seek news that serves the public interest, despite the obstacles. They will make constant efforts to assure that the public's business is conducted in public and that public records are open to public inspection.

5. Journalists acknowledge the newsman's ethic of protecting confidential sources of information.

ACCURACY AND OBJECTIVITY

Good faith with the public is the foundation of all worthy journalism.

1. Truth is our ultimate goal.

2. Objectivity in reporting the news is another goal, which serves as the mark of an experienced professional. It is a standard of performance toward which we strive. We honor those who achieve it.

3. There is no excuse for inaccuracies or lack of thoroughness.

4. Newspaper headlines should be fully warranted by the contents of the articles they accompany. Photographs and telecasts should give an accurate picture of an event and not highlight a minor incident out of context.

5. Sound practice makes clear distinction between news reports and expressions of opinion. News reports should be free of opinion or bias and represent all sides of an issue.

6. Partisanship in editorial comment which knowingly departs from the truth violates the spirit of American journalism.

7. Journalists recognize their responsibility for offering informed analysis, comment, and editorial opinion on public events and issues. They accept

the obligation to present such material by individuals whose competence, experience, and judgment qualify them for it.

8. Special articles or presentations devoted to advocacy or the writer's own conclusions and interpretations should be labeled as such.

FAIR PLAY

Journalists at all times will show respect for the dignity, privacy, rights, and well-being of people encountered in the course of gathering and presenting the news.

1. The news media should not communicate unofficial charges affecting reputation or moral character without giving the accused a chance to reply.

2. The news media must guard against invading a person's right to privacy.

3. The media should not pander to morbid curiosity about details of vice and crime.

4. It is the duty of news media to make prompt and complete correction of their errors.

5. Journalists should be accountable to the public for their reports and the public should be encouraged to voice its grievances against the media. Open dialogue with our readers, viewers, and listeners should be fostered.

PLEDGE

Journalists should actively censure and try to prevent violations of these standards, and they should encourage their observance by all newspeople. Adherence to this code of ethics is intended to preserve the bond of mutual trust and respect between American journalists and the American people.

Motion Picture Codes

For historical and comparative purposes, we are reprinting The Motion Picture Production Code, which was adopted on March 30, 1930; The Motion Picture Code of Self-Regulation, which was adopted on September 20, 1966; and finally Jack Valenti's statement on the existing system of self-regulation—the voluntary rating system—which supersedes the two previous codes and was adopted on November 1, 1968. The Motion Picture Production Code was a constant source of irritation and controversy. Written primarily by a Catholic layman and a Jesuit, Martin Quigley and Father Daniel Lord, the Code was more restrictive than the standards of any government censors. The 1966 Code was an attempt to bring some maturity and sophistication to the industry in dealing with the presentation of sexual themes, but naturally sensitivity and restraint were urged "in presentations dealing with sexual aberrations." Although theater managers advertised their intentions to uphold the Code, what they neglected to advertise was their intention also to present films that did not carry the Code seal. The 1968 Code requires members of the Motion Picture Association of America to submit their films prior to commercial release to the Association's Code and Rating Administration for rating.

The Motion Picture Production Code *

PREAMBLE

Motion picture producers recognize the high trust and confidence which have been placed in them by the people of the world and which have made motion pictures a universal form of entertainment.

They recognize their responsibility to the public because of this trust and because entertainment and art are important influences in the life of a nation.

Hence, though regarding motion pictures primarily as entertainment without any explicit purpose of teaching or propaganda, they know that the motion picture within its own field of entertainment may be directly responsible for spiritual or moral progress, for higher types of social life, and for much correct thinking.

During the rapid transition from silent to talking pictures they realized the necessity and the opportunity of subscribing to a Code to govern the production of talking pictures and of reacknowledging this responsibility.

On their part, they ask from the public and from public leaders a sympathetic understanding of their purposes and problems and a spirit of cooperation that will allow them the freedom and opportunity necessary to bring the motion picture to a still higher level of wholesome entertainment for all the people.

GENERAL PRINCIPLES

1. No picture shall be produced which will lower the moral standards of those who see it. Hence the sympathy of the audience shall never be thrown to the side of crime, wrong-doing, evil or sin.
2. Correct standards of life, subject only to the requirements of drama and entertainment, shall be presented.
3. Law, natural or human, shall not be ridiculed, nor shall sympathy be created for its violation.

* Reprinted with permission of the Motion Picture Association of America, Inc.

PARTICULAR APPLICATIONS

I. Crimes Against the Law

These shall never be presented in such a way as to throw sympathy with the crime as against law and justice or to inspire others with a desire for imitation.

1. Murder
    a) The technique of murder must be presented in a way that will not inspire imitation.
    b) Brutal killings are not to be presented in detail.
    c) Revenge in modern times shall not be justified.
2. Methods of crime should not be explicitly presented.
    a) Theft, robbery, safe-cracking, and dynamiting of trains, mines, buildings, etc., should not be detailed in method.
    b) Arson must be subject to the same safeguards.
    c) The use of firearms should be restricted to essentials.
    d) Methods of smuggling should not be presented.
3. The illegal drug traffic must not be portrayed in such a way as to stimulate curiosity concerning the use of, or traffic in, such drugs; nor shall scenes be approved which show the use of illegal drugs, or their effects, in detail (as amended September 11, 1946).
4. The use of liquor in American life, when not required by the plot or for proper characterization, will not be shown.

II. Sex

The sanctity of the institution of marriage and the home shall be upheld. Pictures shall not infer that low forms of sex relationship are the accepted or common thing.

1. Adultery and illicit sex, sometimes necessary plot material, must not be explicitly treated or justified, or presented attractively.
2. Scenes of passion
    a) These should not be introduced except where they are definitely essential to the plot.
    b) Excessive and lustful kissing, lustful embraces, suggestive postures, and gestures are not to be shown.
    c) In general, passion should be treated in such manner as not to stimulate the lower and baser emotions.
3. Seduction or rape
    a) These should never be more than suggested, and then only when essential for the plot. They must never be shown by explicit method.
    b) They are never the proper subject for comedy.
4. Sex perversion or any inference to it is forbidden.
5. White slavery shall not be treated.
6. Miscegenation (sex relationship between the white and black races) is forbidden.
7. Sex hygiene and venereal diseases are not proper subjects for theatrical motion pictures.

8. Scenes of actual childbirth, in fact or in silhouette, are never to be presented.

9. Children's sex organs are never to be exposed.

III. *Vulgarity*

The treatment of low, disgusting, unpleasant, though not necessarily evil subjects should be guided always by the dictates of good taste and a proper regard for the sensibilities of the audience.

IV. *Obscenity*

Obscenity in word, gesture, reference, song, joke, or by suggestion (even when likely to be understood only by part of the audience) is forbidden.

V. *Profanity*

Pointed profanity and every other profane or vulgar expression, however used, is forbidden.

No approval by the Production Code Administration shall be given to the use of words and phrases in motion pictures including, but not limited to, the following:

> Alley cat (applied to a woman); bat (applied to a woman); broad (applied to a woman); Bronx cheer (the sound); chippie; cocotte; God, Lord, Jesus, Christ (unless used reverently); cripes; fanny; fairy (in a vulgar sense); finger (the); fire, cries of; Gawd; goose (in a vulgar sense); "hold your hat" or "hats"; hot (applied to a woman); "in your hat"; louse; lousy; Madam (relating to prostitution); nance; nerts; nuts (except when meaning crazy); pansy; razzberry (the sound); slut (applied to a woman); S.O.B.; son-of-a; tart; toilet gags; tom cat (applied to a man); traveling salesman and farmer's daughter jokes; whore; damn, hell (excepting when the use of said last two words shall be essential and required for portrayal, in proper historical context, of any scene or dialogue based upon historical fact or folklore, or for the presentation in proper literary context of a Biblical, or other religious quotation or a quotation from a literary work provided that no such use shall be permitted which is intrinsically objectionable or offends good taste.

In the administration of Section V of the Production Code, the Production Code Administration may take cognizance of the fact that the following words and phrases are obviously offensive to the patrons of motion pictures in the United States and more particularly to the patrons of motion pictures in foreign countries:

> Chink, Dago, Frog, Greaser, Hunkie, Kike, Nigger, Spig, Wop, Yid

VI. *Costume*

1. Complete nudity is never permitted. This includes nudity in fact or in silhouette, or any licentious notice thereof by other characters in the pictures.

2. Undressing scenes should be avoided, and never used save where essential to the plot.
3. Indecent or undue exposure is forbidden.
4. Dancing costumes intended to permit undue exposure or indecent movements in the dance are forbidden.

VII. Dances

1. Dances suggesting or representing sexual actions or indecent passion are forbidden.
2. Dances which emphasize indecent movements are to be regarded as obscene.

VIII. Religion

1. No film or episode may throw ridicule on any religious faith.
2. Ministers of religion in their character as ministers of religion should not be used as comic characters or as villains.
3. Ceremonies of any definite religion should be carefully and respectfully handled.

IX. Locations

The treatment of bedrooms must be governed by good taste and delicacy.

X. National Feelings

1. The use of the flag shall be consistently respectful.
2. The history, institutions, prominent people and citizenry of all nations shall be represented fairly.

XI. Titles

Salacious, indecent, or obscene titles shall not be used.

XII. Repellent Subjects

The following subjects must be treated within the careful limits of good taste:
1. Actual hangings or electrocutions as legal punishments for crime.
2. Third-degree methods.
3. Brutality and possible gruesomeness.
4. Branding of people or animals.
5. Apparent cruelty to children or animals.
6. The sale of women, or a woman selling her virtue.
7. Surgical operations.

SPECIAL REGULATIONS ON CRIME IN MOTION PICTURES

Resolved, That the Board of Directors of the Motion Picture Producers and Distributors of America, Incorporated, hereby ratifies, approves, and confirms the interpretations of the Production Code, the practices thereunder, and the resolutions indicating and confirming such interpretations heretofore adopted by the Association of Motion Picture Producers, Incorporated, all effectuating regulations relative to the treatment of crime in motion pictures, as follows:

1. Details of crime must never be shown and care should be exercised at all times in discussing such details.
2. Action suggestive of wholesale slaughter of human beings, either by criminals, in conflict with police, or as between warring factions of criminals, or in public disorder of any kind, will not be allowed.
3. There must be no suggestion, at any time, of excessive brutality.
4. Because of the increase in the number of films in which murder is frequently committed, action showing the taking of human life, even in the mystery stories, is to be cut to the minimum. These frequent presentations of murder tend to lessen regard for the sacredness of life.
5. Suicide, as a solution of problems occurring in the development of screen drama, is to be discouraged as morally questionable and as bad theatre—unless absolutely necessary for the development of the plot.
6. There must be no display, at any time, of machine guns, sub-machine guns or other weapons generally classified as illegal weapons in the hands of gangsters, or other criminals, and there are to be no off-stage sounds of the repercussions of these guns.
7. There must be no new, unique or trick methods shown for concealing guns.
8. The flaunting of weapons by gangsters, or other criminals, will not be allowed.
9. All discussions and dialogue on the part of gangsters regarding guns should be cut to the minimum.
10. There must be no scenes, at any time, showing law-enforcing officers dying at the hands of criminals. This includes private detectives and guards for banks, motor trucks, etc.
11. With special reference to the crime of kidnapping—or illegal abduction—such stories are acceptable under the Code only when the kidnapping or abduction is (a) not the main theme of the story; (b) the person kidnapped is not a child; (c) there are no details of the crime of kidnapping; (d) no profit accrues to the abductors or kidnappers; and (e) where the kidnappers are punished.

    It is understood, and agreed, that the word kidnapping, as used in paragraph 11 of these Regulations, is intended to mean abduction, or illegal detention, in modern times, by criminals for ransom.
12. Pictures dealing with criminal activities, in which minors participate, or to which minors are related, shall not be approved if they incite demoralizing imitation on the part of youth.

SPECIAL RESOLUTION ON COSTUMES

On October 25, 1939, the Board of Directors of the Motion Picture Producers and Distributors of America, Inc., adopted the following resolution:

Resolved, That the provisions of Paragraphs 1, 3, and 4 of sub-division VI of the Production Code, in their application to costumes, nudity, indecent or undue exposure and dancing costumes, shall not be interpreted to exclude authentically photographed scenes photographed in a foreign land, of natives of such foreign land, showing native life, if such scenes are a necessary and integral part of a motion picture depicting exclusively such land and native life, provided that no such scenes shall be intrinsically objectionable nor made a part of any motion picture produced in any studio; and provided further that no emphasis shall be made in any scenes of the customs of garb of such natives or in the exploitation thereof.

SPECIAL REGULATIONS ON CRUELTY TO ANIMALS

On December 27, 1940, the Board of Directors of the Motion Picture Producers and Distributors of America, Inc., approved a resolution adopted by the Association of Motion Picture Producers, Inc., reaffirming previous resolutions of the California Association concerning brutality and possible gruesomeness, branding of people and animals, and apparent cruelty to children and animals:

Resolved, by the Board of Directors of the Association of Motion Picture Producers, Inc., That

(1) Hereafter, in the production of motion pictures, there shall be no use by the members of the Association of the contrivance or apparatus in connection with animals, which is known as the "running W," nor shall any picture submitted to the Production Code Administration be approved if reasonable grounds exist for believing that use of any similar device by the producer of such picture resulted in apparent cruelty to animals; and

(2) Hereafter, in the production of motion pictures, by the members of the Association, such members shall, as to any picture involving the use of animals, invite on the lot during such shooting and consult with the authorized representative of the American Humane Association; and

(3) Steps shall be taken immediately by the members of the Association and by the Production Code Administration to require compliance with these resolutions, which shall bear the same relationship to the sections of the Production Code quoted herein as the Association's special regulations re: Crime in Motion Pictures bear to the sections of the Production Code dealing therewith; and it is

Further resolved, That the resolutions of February 19, 1925 and all other resolutions of this Board establishing its policy to prevent all cruelty to animals in the production of motion pictures and reflecting its determination to prevent any such cruelty, be and the same hereby are in all respects reaffirmed.

REASONS SUPPORTING PREAMBLE OF CODE

1. Theatrical motion pictures, that is, pictures for the theatre as distinct from pictures intended for churches, schools, lecture halls, educational movements, social reform movements, etc., are primarily to be regarded as Entertainment.

    Mankind has always recognized the importance of entertainment and its value in rebuilding the bodies and souls of human beings.

    But it has always recognized that entertainment can be of a character either HELP-FUL or HARMFUL to the human race, and in consequence has clearly distinguished between:

    a) Entertainment which tends to improve the race, or at least to re-create and rebuild human beings exhausted with the realities of life; and

    b) Entertainment which tends to degrade human beings, or to lower their standards of life and living.

    Hence the MORAL IMPORTANCE of entertainment is something which has been universally recognized. It enters intimately into the lives of men and women and affects them closely; it occupies their minds and affections during leisure hours; and ultimately touches the whole of their lives. A man may be judged by his standard of entertainment as easily as by the standard of his work. So correct entertainment raises the whole standard of a nation. Wrong entertainment lowers the whole living conditions and moral ideals of a race.

    Note: for example, the healthy reactions to healthful sports, like baseball, golf; the unhealthy reactions to sports like cockfighting, bullfighting, bear baiting, etc.

    Note: too, the effect on ancient nations of gladitorial combats, the obscene plays of Roman times, etc.

    Motion pictures are very important as ART.

    Though a new art, possibly a combination art, it has the same object as the other arts, the presentation of human thought, emotion, and experience, in terms of an appeal to the soul through the senses.

    Here, as in entertainment,

    Art enters intimately into the lives of human beings.

    Art can be morally good, lifting men to higher levels. This has been done through good music, great painting, authentic fiction, poetry, drama.

    Art can be morally evil in its effects. This is the case clearly enough with unclean art, indecent books, suggestive drama. The effect on the lives of men and women is obvious.

    Note: It has often been argued that art in itself is unmoral, neither good nor bad. This is perhaps true of the THING which is music, painting, poetry, etc. But the thing is the PRODUCT of some person's mind, and the intention of that mind was either good or bad morally when it produced the thing. Besides, the thing has its EFFECT upon those who come into contact with it. In both these ways, that is, as a product of a mind and as the cause of definite effects, it has a deep moral significance and an unmistakable moral quality. Hence: The motion pictures, which are the most popular of modern arts for the masses, have their moral quality from the intention of the minds which produce them and from their effects on the moral lives and reactions of their audiences. This gives them a most important morality.

    1. They reproduce the morality of the men who use the pictures as a medium for the expression of their ideas and ideals.

2. They affect the moral standards of those who, through the screen, take in these ideas and ideals.

In the case of the motion pictures, this effect may be particularly emphasized because no art has so quick and so widespread an appeal to the masses. It has become in an incredibly short period the art of the multitudes.

3. The motion picture, because of its importance as entertainment and because of the trust placed in it by the peoples of the world, has special MORAL OBLIGATIONS:

A. Most arts appeal to the mature. This art appeals at once to every class, mature, immature, developed, undeveloped, law abiding, criminal. Music has its grades for different classes; so has literature and drama. This art of the motion picture, combining as it does the two fundamental appeals of looking at a picture and listening to a story, at once reaches every class of society.

B. By reason of the mobility of a film and the ease of picture distribution, and because of the possibility of duplicating positives in large quantities, this art reaches places unpenetrated by other forms of art.

C. Because of these two facts, it is difficult to produce films intended for only certain classes of people. The exhibitor's theatres are built for the masses, for the cultivated and the rude, the mature and the immature, the self-respecting and the criminal. Films, unlike books and music, can with difficulty be confined to certain selected groups.

D. The latitude given to film material cannot, in consequence, be as wide as the latitude given to book material. In addition:
   a) A book describes; a film vividly presents. One presents on a cold page; the other by apparently living people.
   b) A book reaches the mind through words merely; a film reaches the eyes and ears through the reproduction of actual events.
   c) The reaction of a reader to a book depends largely on the keenness of the reader's imagination; the reaction to a film depends on the vividness of presentation.
   Hence many things which might be described or suggested in a book could not possibly be presented in a film.

E. This is also true when comparing the film with the newspaper.
   a) Newspapers present by description, films by actual presentation.
   b) Newspapers are after the fact and present things as having taken place; the film gives the events in the process of enactment and with apparent reality of life.

F. Everything possible in a play is not possible in a film:
   a) Because of the larger audience of the film, and its consequential mixed character. Psychologically, the larger the audience, the lower the moral mass resistance to suggestion.
   b) Because through light, enlargement of character, presentation, scenic emphasis, etc., the screen story is brought closer to the audience than the play.
   c) The enthusiasm for and interest in the film actors and actresses, developed beyond anything of the sort in history, makes the audience largely sympathetic toward the characters they portray and the stories in which they fig-

ure. Hence the audience is more ready to confuse actor and actress and the characters they portray, and it is most receptive of the emotions and ideals presented by their favorite stars.

G. Small communities, remote from sophistication and from the hardening process which often takes place in the ethical and moral standards of groups in larger cities, are easily and readily reached by any sort of film.

H. The grandeur of mass settings, large action, spectacular features, etc., affects and arouses more intensely the emotional side of the audience.

In general, the mobility, popularity, accessibility, emotional appeal, vividness, straightforward presentation of fact in the film make for more intimate contact with a larger audience and for greater emotional appeal.

Hence the larger moral responsibilities of the motion pictures.

REASONS UNDERLYING THE GENERAL PRINCIPLES

1. No picture shall be produced which will lower the moral standards of those who see it. Hence the sympathy of the audience should never be thrown to the side of crime, wrong-doing, evil or sin.

   This is done:
   1. When evil is made to appear attractive or alluring, and good is made to appear unattractive.
   2. When the sympathy of the audience is thrown on the side of crime, wrong-doing, evil, sin. The same thing is true of a film that would throw sympathy against goodness, honor, innocence, purity or honesty.

   Note: Sympathy with a person who sins is not the same as sympathy with the sin or crime of which he is guilty. We may feel sorry for the plight of the murderer or even understand the circumstances which led him to his crime. We may not feel sympathy with the wrong which he had done.

   The presentation of evil is often essential for art or fiction or drama. This in itself is not wrong provided:
   a) That evil is not presented alluringly. Even if later in the film the evil is condemned or punished, it must not be allowed to appear so attractive that the audience's emotions are drawn to desire or approve so strongly that later the condemnation is forgotten and only the apparent joy of the sin remembered.
   b) That throughout, the audience feels sure that evil is wrong and good is right.

2. Correct standards of life shall, as far as possible, be presented. A wide knowledge of life and of living is made possible through the film. When right standards are consistently presented, the motion picture exercises the most powerful influences. It builds character, develops right ideals, inculcates correct principles, and all this in attractive story form.

If motion pictures consistently hold up for admiration high types of characters and present stories that will affect lives for the better, they can become the most powerful natural force for the improvement of mankind.

3. Law, natural or human, shall not be ridiculed, nor shall sympathy be created for its violation.

   By natural law is understood the law which is written in the hearts of all mankind, the great underlying principles of right and justice dictated by conscience.

By human law is understood the law written by civilized nations.

1. The presentation of crimes against the law is often necessary for the carrying out of the plot. But the presentation must not throw sympathy with the crime as against the law nor with the criminal as against those who punish him.

2. The courts of the land should not be presented as unjust. This does not mean that a single court may not be represented as unjust, much less that a single court official must not be presented this way. But the court system of the country must not suffer as a result of this presentation.

REASONS UNDERLYING PARTICULAR APPLICATIONS

1. Sin and evil enter into the story of human beings and hence in themselves are valid dramatic material.

2. In the use of this material, it must be distinguished between sin which repels by its very nature, and sins which often attract.

   a) In the first class come murder, most theft, many legal crimes, lying, hypocrisy, cruelty, etc.

   b) In the second class come sex sins, sins and crimes of apparent heroism, such as banditry, daring thefts, leadership in evil, organized crime, revenge, etc.

   The first class needs less care in treatment, as sins and crimes of this class are naturally unattractive. The audience instinctively condemns all such and is repelled.

   Hence the important objective must be to avoid the hardening of the audience especially of those who are young and impressionable, to the thought and deed of crime. People can become accustomed even to murder, cruelty, brutality, and repellent crimes, if these are too frequently repeated. The second class needs great care in handling, as the response of human nature to their appeal is obvious. This is treated more fully below.

   A careful distinction can be made between films intended for general distribution, and films intended for use in theatres restricted to a limited audience. Themes and plots quite appropriate for the latter would be altogether out of place and dangerous in the former.

   Note: The practice of using a general theatre and limiting its patronage during the showing of a certain film to "Adults Only" is not completely satisfactory and is only partially effective.

   However, maturer minds may easily understand and accept without harm subject matter in plots which do younger people positive harm.

   Hence: If there should be created a special type of theatre, catering exclusively to an adult audience, for plays, of this character (plays with problem themes, difficult discussions and maturer treatment) it would seem to afford an outlet, which does not now exist, for pictures unsuitable for general distribution but permissible for exhibitions to a restricted audience.

I. Crimes Against the Law

The treatment of crimes against the law must not:

1. Teach methods of crime.
2. Inspire potential criminals with a desire for imitation.
3. Make criminals seem heroic and justified.

Revenge in modern times shall not be justified. In lands and ages of less developed civilization and moral principles, revenge may sometimes be presented. This would be the case especially in places where no law exists to cover the crime because of which revenge is committed.

Because of its evil consequences, the drug traffic should not be presented in any form. The existence of the trade should not be brought to the attention of audiences.

The use of liquor should never be excessively presented. In scenes from American life, the necessities of plot and proper characterization alone justify its use. And in this case, it should be shown with moderation.

II. Sex

Out of regard for the sanctity of marriage and the home, the triangle, that is, the love of a third party for one already married, needs careful handling. The treatment should not throw sympathy against marriage as an institution.

Scenes of passion must be treated with an honest acknowledgement of human nature and its normal reactions. Many scenes cannot be presented without arousing dangerous emotions on the part of the immature, the young or the criminal classes.

Even within the limits of pure love, certain facts have been universally regarded by lawmakers as outside the limits of safe presentation.

In the case of impure love, the love which society has always regarded as wrong and which has been banned by divine law, the following are important:

1. Impure love must not be presented as attractive and beautiful.
2. It must not be the subject of comedy or farce, or treated as material for laughter.
3. It must not be presented in such a way as to arouse passion or morbid curiosity on the part of the audience.
4. It must not be made to seem right and permissible.
5. In general, it must not be detailed in method and manner.

III. Vulgarity; IV. Obscenity; V. Profanity

Hardly need further explanation than is contained in the Code.

VI. Costume

General principles:
1. The effect of nudity or semi-nudity upon the normal man or woman, and much more upon the young and upon immature persons, has been honestly recognized by all lawmakers and moralists.
2. Hence the fact that the nude or semi-nude body may be beautiful does not make its use in the films moral. For, in addition to its beauty, the effect of the nude or semi-nude body on the normal individual must be taken into consideration.
3. Nudity or semi-nudity used simply to put a "punch" into a picture

comes under the head of immoral actions. It is immoral in its effect on the average audience.

4. Nudity can never be permitted as being necessary for the plot. Semi-nudity must not result in undue or indecent exposures.

5. Transparent or translucent materials and silhouette are frequently more suggestive than actual exposure.

VII. Dances

Dancing in general is recognized as an art and as a beautiful form of expressing human emotions.

But dances which suggest or represent sexual actions, whether performed solo or with two or more; dances intended to excite the emotional reaction of an audience; dances with movement of the breasts, excessive body movements while the feet are stationary, violate decency and are wrong.

VIII. Religion

The reason why ministers of religion may not be comic characters or villains is simply because the attitude taken toward them may easily become the attitude taken toward religion in general. Religion is lowered in the minds of the audience because of the lowering of the audience's respect for a minister.

IX. Locations

Certain places are so closely and thoroughly associated with sexual life or with sexual sin that their use must be carefully limited.

X. National feelings

The just rights, history, and feelings of any nation are entitled to most careful consideration and respectful treatment.

XI. Titles

As the title of a picture is the brand on that particular type of goods, it must conform to the ethical practices of all such honest business.

XII. Repellent Subjects

Such subjects are occasionally necessary for the plot. Their treatment must never offend good taste nor injure the sensibilities of an audience.

The Code was a failure. Under two administrators the Code floundered. Studios did not want to be restricted. Catholic clergy saw no change in motion pictures. They formed the National Legion of Decency (NLOD), which was renamed National Catholic Office for Motion Pictures in 1965. It exercised strong influence on movie production for a score of years.

Code of Self-Regulation

—Motion Picture Association of America *

The Code of Self-Regulation of the Motion Picture Association of America shall apply to production, to advertising, and to titles of motion pictures.

The Code shall be administered by an Office of Code Administration, headed by an Administrator.

There shall also be a Director of the Code for Advertising, and a Director of the Code for Titles.

Nonmembers are invited to submit pictures to the Code Administrator on the same basis as members of the Association.

DECLARATION OF PRINCIPLES OF THE CODE OF SELF-REGULATION OF THE MOTION PICTURE ASSOCIATION

This revised Code is designed to keep in closer harmony with the mores, the culture, the moral sense and the expectations of our society.

The revised Code can more completely fulfill its objectives, which are:

1. To encourage artistic expression by expanding creative freedom and

2. To assure that the freedom which encourages the artist remains responsible and sensitive to the standards of the larger society.

Censorship is an odious enterprise. We oppose censorship and classification-by-law (or whatever name or guise these restrictions go under) because they are alien to the American tradition of freedom.

Much of this nation's strength and purpose is drawn from the premise that the humblest of citizens has the freedom of his own choice. Censorship destroys this freedom of choice.

It is within this framework that the Motion Picture Association continues to recognize its obligation to the society of which it is an integral part.

In our society the parents are the arbiters of family conduct.

Parents have the primary responsibility to guide their children in the kind of lives they lead, the character they build, the books they read, and the movies and other entertainment to which they are exposed.

The creators of motion pictures undertake a responsibility to make available pertinent information about their pictures which will enable parents to fulfill their function.

An important addition is now being made to the information already provided to the public in order to enable parents better to choose which motion pictures their children should see.

As part of the revised Code, there is a provision that producers in cooperation with the Code Administration, will identify certain pictures as suggested for mature audiences.

Such information will be conveyed by advertising, by displays at the theatre and by other means.

* Reprinted by permission of the Motion Picture Association of America, Inc.

Thus parents will be alerted and informed so that they may decide for themselves whether a particular picture because of theme, content or treatment, will be one which their children should or should not see, or may not understand or enjoy.

We believe self-restraint, self-regulation, to be in the tradition of the American purpose. It is the American society meeting its responsibility to the general welfare. The results of self-discipline are always imperfect because that is the nature of all things mortal. But this Code, and its administration, will make clear that freedom of expression does not mean toleration of license.

The test of self-restraint . . . the rule of reason . . . lies in the treatment of a subject for the screen. The SEAL of the Motion Picture Association on a film means that the picture has met the test of self-regulation.

All members of the Motion Picture Association, as well as many independent producers, cooperate in this self-regulation. Not all motion pictures, however, are submitted to the Production Code Administration of the MPA, and the presence of the Seal is the only way the public can know which pictures have come under the Code.

We believe in and pledge our support to these deep and fundamental values in a democratic society:

Freedom of choice . . .

The right of creative man to achieve artistic excellence . . .

The role of the parent as the arbiter of the family's conduct.

The men and women who make motion pictures under this Code value their social responsibility as they value their creative skills. The Code, and all that is written and implied in it, aims to strengthen both those values.

STANDARDS FOR PRODUCTION

In furtherance of the objectives of the Code to accord with the mores, the culture, and the moral sense of our society, the principles stated above and the following standards shall govern the Administrator in his consideration of motion pictures submitted for Code approval:

The basic dignity and value of human life shall be respected and upheld. Restraint shall be exercised in portraying the taking of life.

Evil, sin, crime and wrong-doing shall not be justified.

Special restraint shall be exercised in portraying criminal or antisocial activities in which minors participate or are involved.

Detailed and protracted acts of brutality, cruelty, physical violence, torture and abuse, shall not be presented.

Indecent or undue exposure of the human body shall not be presented.

Illicit sex relationships shall not be justified. Intimate sex scenes violating common standards of decency shall not be portrayed. Restraint and care shall be exercised in presentations dealing with sex aberrations.

Obscene speech, gestures or movements shall not be presented. Undue profanity shall not be permitted.

Religion shall not be demeaned.

Words or symbols contemptuous of racial, religious or national groups, shall not be used so as to incite bigotry or hatred.

Excessive cruelty to animals shall not be portrayed and animals shall not be treated inhumanely.

STANDARDS FOR ADVERTISING

The principles of the Code cover advertising and publicity as well as production. There are times when their specific application to advertising may be different. A motion picture is viewed as a whole and may be judged that way. It is the nature of advertising, however, that it must select and emphasize only isolated portions and aspects of a film. It thus follows that what may be appropriate in a motion picture may not be equally appropriate in advertising. This must be taken into account in applying the Code standards to advertising. Furthermore, in application to advertising, the principles and standards of the Code are supplemented by the following standards for advertising:

Illustrations and text shall not misrepresent the character of a motion picture.

Illustrations shall not depict any indecent or undue exposure of the human body.

Advertising demeaning religion, race, or national origin shall not be used.

Cumulative overemphasis on sex, crime, violence and brutality shall not be permitted.

Salacious postures and embraces shall not be shown.

Censorship disputes shall not be exploited or capitalized upon.

STANDARDS FOR TITLES

A salacious, obscene, or profane title shall not be used on motion pictures.

PRODUCTION CODE REGULATIONS

I. Operations

A. Prior to commencement of production of a motion picture, the producer shall submit a shooting, or other, script to the Office of Code Administration. The Administrator of the Code shall inform the producer in confidence whether a motion picture based upon the script appears to conform to the Code. The final judgment of the Administrator shall be made only upon reviewing of the completed picture.

B. The completed picture shall be submitted to the Code Office and if it is approved by the Administrator, the producer or distributor shall upon public release of the picture place upon an introductory frame of every print distributed for exhibition in the United States the official Seal of the Association with the word "Approved" above the Seal, and below, the words "Certificate

Number," followed by the number of the Certificate of Approval. All prints bearing the Code Seal shall be identical.

C. The Administrator, in issuing a Certificate of Approval, shall condition the issuance of the Certificate upon agreement by the producer or distributor that all advertising and publicity to be used for the picture shall be submitted to and approved by the Director of the Code for Advertising.

D. The Administrator, in approving a picture under the Code, may recommend that advertising for the picture carry the informational line Suggested for Mature Audiences. If the Administrator so determines, the distributing company shall carry the line Suggested for Mature Audiences in its advertising. The Administrator shall notify the Director of the Code for Advertising of all such pictures.

E. The title of an approved motion picture shall not be changed without prior approval of the Director of the Code for Titles.

F. Nonmembers of the Association may avail themselves of the services of the Office of Code Administration in the same manner and under the same conditions as members of the Association.

G. The producer or distributor, upon receiving a Certificate of Approval for a picture, shall pay to the Office of Code Administration a fee in accordance with the uniform schedule of fees approved by the Board of Directors of the Association.

II. Motion Picture Code Board

A. A Motion Picture Code Board is established with these two principal functions:

To hear appeals from decisions of the Code Administrator.

To act as an advisory body on Code matters.

1. The Code Board shall be composed of the following:

(a) The President of the Motion Picture Association of America, and nine other directors of the Association appointed by the President;

(b) Six exhibitors appointed by the President upon nomination by the National Association of Theatre Owners; and

(c) Four producers appointed by the President upon nomination by the Screen Producers Guild.

2. The President of the Motion Picture Association of America shall be Chairman of the Code Board, and the Association shall provide the secretariat.

3. The President may designate not more than two pro tempore members for each category as substitutes for members unable to attend a particular Board meeting or a hearing.

4. The presence of ten members shall constitute a quorum of the Board for meetings and hearings.

5. The members of the Board required to travel to attend a meeting shall be reimbursed for transportation and subsistence expenses, which shall be paid to them from funds of the Office of Code Administration.

B. Advisory

The procedures governing meetings of the Board in its advisory function shall be as follows:

1. The Board shall meet upon call of the Chairman at a time and place he may designate.

2. Members may submit suggestions for an agenda, which shall be prepared and circulated by the Chairman in advance of meetings. Upon majority vote, additional items may be submitted and brought up for discussion at meetings.

3. The Board through the Chairman may request the presence of the Code Administrator at meetings; may request oral and written reports from its distributor, exhibitor and producer members on the status of the Code; may call for advice and reports upon others in a position to contribute to a better understanding and more efficacious operation of the system of self-regulation; and may perform such other functions of an advisory nature as may redound to the benefit of the Code.

C. Appeals

1. Any producer or distributor whose picture has not been approved by the Code Administrator may appeal the decision to the Motion Picture Code Board by filing a notice of appeal to the Chairman of the Board.

2. The procedures governing appeals before the Code Board shall be as follows:

(a) The Board, upon being called into meeting by the Chairman, shall view an identical print of the picture denied a Certificate of Approval by the Code Administrator.

(b) The producer or the distributor and the Code Administrator, or their representatives, may present oral or written statements to the Board.

(c) The Board shall decide the appeal by majority vote of the members present and its decision shall be final.

(d) No member of the Board shall participate in an appeal involving a picture in which the member has a financial interest.

3. The jurisdiction of the Board is limited to hearing the appeal and it is without power to change or amend the Code.

4. The Code Board, if it authorizes the issuance of a Certificate of Approval, may do so upon such terms and conditions as it may prescribe.

ADVERTISING CODE REGULATIONS

1. These regulations are applicable to all members of the Motion Picture Association of America, and to all producers and distributors of motion pictures with respect to each picture for which the Association has granted its Certificate of Approval.

2. The term "advertising" as used herein shall be deemed to mean all forms of motion picture advertising and exploitation, and ideas therefor, including the following: pressbooks; still photographs; newspaper, magazine and trade paper advertising; publicity copy and art intended for use in pressbooks or otherwise intended for general distribution in printed form or for theatre use; trailers; posters, lobby displays, and other outdoor displays; advertising accessories, including heralds and throwaways; novelties; copy for exploitation tieups; and all radio and television copy and spots.

3. All advertising shall be submitted to the Director of the Code for Advertising for approval before use, and shall not be used in any way until so submitted in duplicate with the exception of pressbooks, which shall be submitted in triplicate.

4. The Director of the Code for Advertising shall proceed as promptly as feasible to approve or disapprove the advertising submitted.

The Director of the Code for Advertising shall stamp "Approved" on one copy of all advertising approved by him and return the stamped copy to the Company which submitted it. If the Director of the Code for Advertising disapproves of any advertising, the Director shall stamp the word "Disapproved" on one copy and return it to the Company which submitted it, together with the reasons for such disapproval; or, if the Director so desires, he may return the copy with suggestions for such changes or corrections as will cause it to be approved.

5. All pressbooks approved by the Director of the Code for Advertising shall bear in a prominent place the official seal of the Motion Picture Association of America. The word "Approved" shall be printed under the seal. Pressbooks shall also carry the following notice:

"All advertising in this pressbook, as well as all other advertising and publicity materials referred to therein, has been approved under the Standards for Advertising of the Code of Self-Regulation of the Motion Picture Association of America. All inquiries on this procedure may be addressed to: Director of Code for Advertising, Motion Picture Association of America, 522 Fifth Avenue, New York, New York 10036.

6. When the Code Administrator determines that any picture shall carry the informational line "Suggested for mature audiences," the Director of the Code for Advertising shall require this line to appear in such advertising for that picture as the Director may specify. When the advertisement is limited in size, the Director may authorize the initials SMA to stand for "Suggested for mature audiences."

7. Appeals. Any Company whose advertising has been disapproved may appeal from the decision of the Director of the Code for Advertising, as follows:

It shall serve notice of such appeal on the Director of the Code for Advertising and on the President of the Association. The President, or in his absence a Vice President designated by him, shall thereupon promptly and within a week hold a hearing to pass upon the appeal. Oral and written evidence may be introduced by the Company and by the Director of the Code for Advertising, or their representatives. The appeal shall be decided as expeditiously as possible and the decision shall be final.

8. Any Company which uses advertising without prior approval may be brought up on charges before the Board of Directors by the President of the Association. Within a reasonable time, the Board may hold a hearing, at which time the Company and the Director of the Code for Advertising, or their representatives, may present oral or written statements. The Board, by a majority vote of those present, shall decide the matter as expeditiously as possible.

If the Board of Directors finds that the Company has used advertising without prior approval, the Board may direct the Administrator of the Code to void and revoke the Certificate of Approval granted for the picture and require the removal of the Association's seal from all prints of the picture.

9. Each Company shall be responsible for compliance by its employees and agents with these regulations.

The Movie Rating System *
by Jack Valenti

HOW IT ALL BEGAN

By the summer of 1966, it had become clear to knowledgeable observers that the U.S. film industry was in radical change. Where the change specifically started, and why, are obscured in a mix of social and economic upheaval.

But change there was.

Perhaps it started in the early 1950s when the Department of Justice, following a U.S. Supreme Court decision, brought about the divorcement of studio-and-theater ownership. When the big studios relinquished their theaters, the power that existed in my predecessors, Will H. Hays and Eric Johnston, and the Hollywood establishment was forever broken. From that collapse of authority came, slowly, the onward thrust of the filmmaker to garner a larger share in the creative command decisions.

When I became president of the Motion Picture Association of America (MPAA)†, and the Association of Motion Picture and Television Producers (AMPTP)‡, in May 1966, the slippage of Hollywood studio authority over the content of films collided with an avalanching revision of American mores and customs.

The national scene was marked by insurrection on the campus, riots in the streets, rise in women's liberation, protest of the young, questioning of church, doubts about the institution of marriage, abandonment of old guiding slogans, and the crumbling of social traditions. It would have been foolish to believe that movies, that most creative of art-forms, could have remained unaffected by the change and torment in our society.

A NEW KIND OF AMERICAN MOVIE

The result of all this was the emergence of a "new kind" of American movie—frank and open, and made by filmmakers subject to very few self-imposed restraints.

---

*Reprinted by permission of the Motion Picture Association of America, Inc.

†Member Companies of MPAA: Allied Artists, Avco-Embassy, Columbia Pictures, MGM, 20th Century-Fox, Paramount Pictures, United Artists, MCA-Universal, Warner Bros.

‡Member Companies include: 72 organizations producing theatrical motion pictures and television material.

Almost within weeks in my new duties I was confronted with controversy neither amiable nor fixable. The first issue was the film "Who's Afraid of Virginia Woolf?" in which for the first time on the screen the word "screw" and the phrase "hump the hostess" were heard. In company with the MPAA's general counsel, Louis Nizer, I met with Jack Warner, the legendary chieftain of Warner Bros. and his top aide, Ben Kalmenson. We talked for three hours, and the result was deletion of "screw" and retention of "hump the hostess," but I was uneasy over the meeting.

It seemed wrong that grown men should be sitting around discussing such matters. More, I was uncomfortable with the thought that this was just the beginning of an unsettling new era in film, in which we would lurch from crisis to crisis, without any suitable solutions in sight.

The second issue surfaced only a few months later. This time it was Metro-Goldwyn-Mayer and the Antonioni film "Blow-Up." I met with the company head, Bob O'Brien, for this movie also represented a first—the first time a major distributor was marketing a film with nudity in it. The Production Code Administration in California had denied the seal. I backed the decision whereupon MGM distributed the film through a subsidiary company, thereby flouting the voluntary agreement of MPAA member companies that none would distribute a film without a Code seal.

Finally, in April 1968, the U.S. Supreme Court upheld the constitutional power of states and cities to prevent the exposure of children to books and films which could not be denied to adults.

It was plain that the old system, begun with the formulation of MPAA in 1922, had broken down. What few threads holding together the structure created by Will H. Hays had now snapped.

I knew that the mix of new social currents, the irresistible force of creators determined to make "their" films (full of wild candor, groused some social critics), and the possible intrusion of government into the movie arena demanded my immediate action.

Within weeks, discussions of my plan for a movie rating system began with the president of the National Association of Theater Owners (NATO), and with the governing committee of the International Film Importers & Distributors of America (IFIDA), an assembly of independent producers and distributors.

Over the next five months, I held more than 100 hours of meetings with these two organizations, as well as with guilds of actors, writers, directors and producers, with craft unions, with critics, with religious organizations, and with the heads of MPAA member companies.

THE BIRTH OF THE RATINGS

By early fall, the plan was designed and approved. On November 1, 1968, the voluntary film rating system of the motion picture industry became a fact, with three organizations, NATO, IFIDA, and MPAA, as partners in the enterprise.

That initial plan was, in essence, the same as the program now in effect.

Few changes of substance have occurred. There were four rating categories: G for general audiences—all ages admitted; M* for mature audiences—parental guidance suggested; R for Restricted—under 16s† must be accompanied by parent or guardian; X no one under 16† admitted.

My original intent had been to use only three rating categories, ending in R. It was my view that a parent ought to have the right to accompany children to any movie the parent chose, without the movie industry or the government denying that right. But the exhibitor organization (NATO) urged the creation of the X category, fearful of possible legal redress under local or state law. I acquiesced in NATO's reasoning and the four-category system was installed.

The rating system meant the dismantling of the Production Code Administration with its rigid restrictions, which had been in effect since the 1930s. Our rating concept was a totally new approach.

We would no longer "approve or disapprove" the content of a film, but rather would rate movies for parents who could then make an informed decision on whether their children should attend. This turnabout was not easy to achieve. My predecessors, Will Hays, and Eric Johnston, had been opposed to changing the stern Seal of Approval test to a system of rating for children.

But it was a turn in philosophy and action that social change demanded we make, and in the light of a new social environment we made the turn.

DUAL RESPONSIBILITIES

From the very beginning of my tenure at the Association, I had sought a way to assure freedom of the screen, to underbrace the right of the filmmaker to say what he chose in the way and form he determined without anyone forcing him to cut one millimeter of film or threatening to refuse him exhibition.

Yet, at the same time, there had to be some framework of self-discipline, some manner of restraint, in order to fulfill a public obligation. Parents needed to know *in advance* what kind of movie was being exhibited at the local theater. It was because of this juxtaposition of ideals and goals that the voluntary film rating system seemed to be the sanest and most practical design to achieve both objectives, despite obvious frailties and inevitable public disagreements over specific ratings.

Under the rating program, the filmmaker became free to tell his story in his way without anyone thwarting him. The price he would pay for that freedom would be the possible restriction on viewing by children. I held the view that freedom of the screen was not defined by whether children must see everything a filmmaker conceived.

I would hope it is fair to say that today the screen has never been more free from the standpoint of the filmmaker's right to create any story he wants to tell. And, at the same time, the public is better advised in advance by the ratings about the content of films than ever before, and parents can be con-

---

*Because this label was misunderstood by the public, it was finally changed to "PG—parental guidance suggested—some material may not be suitable for pre-teenagers."
†Later raised to under 17 years of age.

fident their children are restricted in viewing certain films. No other entertainment communications medium turns away business at the boxoffice to fulfill its pledge to the public.

THE PURPOSE OF THE RATING SYSTEM

From the outset the purpose of the rating system was to provide *advance information to enable parents* to make judgments on movies they wanted their children to see or not to see. Basic to the program was and is the *responsibility of the parent to make the decision.*

The Rating Board does not rate for quality or the lack of it. That role is left to the movie critic and the audience. We would have destroyed the rating program in its infancy if we had become arbiters of how "good" or how "bad" creatively a movie was.

The only objective of the ratings is to advise the parent in advance so he may determine the possible suitability or unsuitability of viewing so he may determine the possible suitability or unsuitability of viewing by his children. But, to repeat, the rating would not even make a final judgment on that; except for the X-rating, the parent's decision remained the key to children's attendance.

Inherent in the rating system is the fact that to those 17 and over, and/or married without children, the ratings have little if any meaning.

The Rating Board's criteria are four: theme, language, nudity and sex, and violence, and part of the rating comes from the assessment of how each of these elements is treated in each individual film.

There is no special emphasis on any of the elements. All are considered and all are examined before a rating is given.

Contrary to popular but uninformed notions, violence has from the outset been a key factor in ratings. (Many violent films have been given X ratings, but most of the directors have chosen, on their own, to revise the extremely violent sequences in order to receive an R rating.)

HOW THE RATINGS ARE ARRIVED AT

The ratings are decided by a Rating Board located in Hollywood. It is a full-time Board, composed of seven persons, headed by a chairman. There are no special qualifications for Board membership, except one must love movies, must possess an intelligent maturity of judgment, and have the capacity to put himself or herself in the role of most parents and view a film as most parents might—parents trying to decide whether their younger children ought to see a specific film.

In my role as MPAA president, I do not take part in rating discussions, do not interfere in rating decisions, and do not overrule or dissuade the Board or its chairman from any decisions they make.

In the near-decade of the rating system's existence, its critics have been vocal about many things, but no one has yet accused the Board of deliberately fudging a decision or bowing to pressure or doing anything that would be inconsistent with its integrity. And that is no insubstantial asset.

No one is forced to submit a film to the Board for rating, but I would judge some 99% of the producers creating entertaining, seriously intended, responsible films (*not* hard core pornography) do in fact submit their films for rating. Most makers of pornographic movies do not submit their films but instead, within the rules of the rating system, self-apply an X rating and go to market. The other symbols, G, PG, and R, are registered with the U.S. Patent and Trademark Office as Certification marks of the MPAA and cannot be used in advertising by any company which has not officially submitted its film for rating. They may *not* be self-applied.

NATO estimates that about 85% of the exhibitors in the nation participate in the rating program and enforce its admission restrictions.

THE BOARD VOTES ON RATINGS

The Board views each film and after group discussion votes on the rating. Each Board member completes a rating form spelling out his or her reason for the rating in each of the four categories of theme, violence, language, and nudity and sex, and then gives the film an overall rating based on the category assessments.

The rating is decided by majority vote.

The producer of a film has a right under the rules to inquire as to the "why" of the rating. The producer also has the right, based on the reasons for his rating, to edit his film if he chooses to try for a less severe rating. The re-edited film is brought back to the Rating Board, and the process of rating goes forward again.

ADVERTISING AND TRAILER POLICY

Film advertising is also part of the rating mechanism.

Print and broadcast material of films which seek a rating are examined by the Advertising Code office. That part of any ads deemed not to be in conformity are requested to be deleted. Conflicts between the advertising office and the producer are brought to the president of the MPAA for final resolution.

Trailers are an important aspect of this monitoring. In order to assure parents that children attending a G- or PG-rated movie will not be seeing unedited trailers of R- and X-rated films, a simple plan has been devised to prevent this problem. For any trailer of an R- or X-rated movie to be exhibited with a film rated G or PG, the trailer must be edited to conform with the rating of the film being exhibited at the theater. A trailer rated G may be shown with all feature films. One rated R may be shown only with features rated R or X. The trailer's rating appears at the beginning, and another at the end indicates the rating of the picture being advertised.

APPEAL OF RATINGS

Should the producer for any reason be displeased with the rating he can appeal the decision to the Rating Appeals Board, which sits as the final arbiter of ratings.

The Appeals Board comprises 22 members, men and women from MPAA, NATO, and IFIDA.

They gather as a quasi-judicial body to view the film and hear the appeal. After the screening, the producer whose film is being appealed explains why he believes the rating was wrongly decided. The chairman of the Rating Board states the reason for the film's rating. The producer has an opportunity for rebuttal. In addition, the producer, if he desires, may submit a written presentation to the Board prior to the oral hearing.

After Appeals Board members question the two opposing representatives they are excused from the room. The Board discusses the appeal and then takes a secret ballot. It requires a two-thirds vote of those present to overturn a Rating Board decision.

By this method of appeal, controversial decisions of the Rating Board can be examined and any rating deemed a mistake set right.

From November 1, 1968 through March 8, 1977, the Appeals Board heard 84 appeals. The Board upheld 56 ratings, changed 25, and three cases were not decided.

The decision of the Appeals Board is final and cannot be appealed, although the Appeals Board has the authority to grant a rehearing on the request of the producer.

WHAT THE RATINGS MEAN

Essentially the ratings mean the following:

G: *"General Audiences*—All ages admitted."

This is a film which contains nothing in theme, language, nudity and sex, or violence which would, in the view of the Rating Board, be offensive to parents whose younger children view the film. The G rating is *not* a "certificate of approval,"' nor does it signify a children's film. Some profoundly significant films are rated G (for example, "A Man For All Seasons").

Some snippets of language may go beyond polite conversation but they are common everyday expressions. No words with sexual connotations are present in G-rated films. The violence is at a minimum. Nudity and sex scenes are not present.

PG: "Parental Guidance Suggested; some material may not be suitable for children." This is a film which clearly needs to be examined or inquired about by parents before they let their younger children attend. The label PG plainly states that parents *may* consider some material unsuitable for their children, but the parent must make this decision.

Parents are warned against sending their children, unseen without inquiry, to PG-rated movies.

There may be profanity in these films, but the harsher sexually derived word will vault a PG rating into the R category. There may be violence but it is not deemed so strong that everyone under 17 need be restricted unless accompanied by a parent. Nor is there cumulative horror or violence that may take a film into the R category.

There is no explicit sex on the screen, although there may be some indication of sensuality. Brief nudity may appear in PG-rated films, but anything beyond that puts the film into R.

The PG rating, suggesting parental guidance, is thus an alert for special examination of a film by parents before deciding on its viewing by their children.

Obviously the line is difficult to draw and the PG-rated film is the category most susceptible to criticism. In our plural society it is not easy to make subjective judgments for more than 215 million persons without some disagreement. So long as the parent knows he must exercise his parental responsibility, the PG rating serves as a meaningful guide and as a warning.

R: "Restricted, under 17s require accompanying parent or guardian."

This is an adult film in some of its aspects and treatment so far as language, violence, or nudity, sexuality or other content is concerned. The parent is advised in advance the film contains adult material and he takes his children with him with this advisory clearly in mind.

The language may be rough, the violence may be hard, and while explicit sex is not to be found in R-rated films, nudity and lovemaking may be involved.

Therefore, the R rating is strong in its advance advisory to parents as to the adult content of the film.

X: "No one under 17 admitted." This is patently an adult film and no children are allowed to attend. It should be noted, however, that X does *not* necessarily mean obscene or pornographic in terms of sex or violence. Serious films by lauded and skilled filmmakers may be rated X. The Rating Board does not attempt to mark films as obscene or pornographic; that is for the courts to decide legally. The reason for not admitting children to X-rated films can relate to the accumulation of brutal or sexually connected language, or of explicit sex or excessive and sadistic violence.

APPRAISAL

In any appraisal what is "too much" becomes a controversial issue. How much is too much violence? Are classic war-type films too violent; marines storming the beaches of Iwo Jima killing and wounding the enemy, is that too much? Is the dirt-street duel between the cattle rustler and the sheriff too violent, or does it require the spilling of blood to draw a more severe rating? How does one handle a fist fight on the screen, where is the dividing line between "all right" and "too much" for a particular classification?

The same vexing doubts occur in sex scenes or those where language rises on the Richter scale. The result is controversy, inevitable, inexorable, and that is what the rating system has to endure.

The raters try to estimate what most American parents think about the appropriateness of film content so that parents at the very least are cautioned to think seriously about what films they may wish their children to see.

HOW THE CRITERIA ARE CONSTRUCTED

To oversee the Rating Board, the film industry has set up a Policy Review Committee consisting of officials of MPAA, NATO, and IFIDA. These men and women gather quarterly to monitor past ratings, to set guidelines for the Rating Board to follow, and to make certain that the Rating Board carries them out reasonably and appropriately.

Because the rating program is a self-regulatory apparatus of the film industry, it is important that no single element of the industry take on the authority of a "czar" beyond any discipline or self-restraint.

THE PUBLIC REACTION

We count it crucial to take public soundings annually to find out how the public reacts to the rating program, and to measure the public's approval or disapproval of what we are doing.

Each year the Opinion Research Corporation of Princeton, New Jersey, conducts a scientifically sampled nationwide survey of 2,600 persons.

A basic question is asked:

"How useful do you think the motion picture industry's rating system—with the symbols G, PG, R and X—is in helping parents decide what movies their children should see—very useful, fairly useful, not very useful, or have you not heard of the rating system"?

In 1976, the results were:

—57% of adults with children thought the rating system was very useful or fairly useful.

—27% of adults with children thought it was not useful.

—16% had no opinion.

—79% of the important population segment, those between the ages of 18 and 29, are frequent or occasional moviegoers, and many of them are parents of young children.

This group gave higher marks to the rating program.

—63% judged it very useful or fairly useful.

—28% thought it not useful.

—9% had no opinion.

Within this group of young adults, reliance on the rating system has been steadfast, the approval mark of 6 out of 10 holding with little change:

1972—59%
1973—62%
1974—63%
1975—63%
1976—63%

Research analysts call results impressive in approval of the classification program. They show the public seems to appreciate the rating system as a source of information worthy and useful to parents in making decisions on their children's viewing habits.

Broadcasting Codes

Code of Broadcast News Ethics *

The Code of Broadcast News Ethics was initially adopted on January 2, 1966, and amended on October 13, 1973. The members of the Radio Television News Directors Association agree that their prime responsibility as journalists—and that of the broadcasting industry as the collective sponsor of news broadcasting—is to provide to the public they serve a news service as accurate, full and prompt as human integrity and devotion can devise. To that end, they declare their acceptance of the standards of practice here set forth, and their solemn intent to honor them to the limits of their ability.

ARTICLE ONE

The primary purpose of broadcast journalists—to inform the public of events of importance and appropriate interest in a manner that is accurate and comprehensive—shall override all other purposes.

ARTICLE TWO

Broadcast news presentations shall be designed not only to offer timely and accurate information, but also to present it in the light of relevant circumstances that give it meaning and perspective.

> This standard means that news reports, when clarity demands it, will be laid against pertinent factual background; that factors such as race, creed, nationality or prior status will be reported only when they are relevant; that comment or subjective content will be properly identified; and that errors in fact will be promptly acknowledged and corrected.

ARTICLE THREE

Broadcast journalists shall seek to select material for newscast solely on their evaluation of its merits as news.

> This standard means that news will be selected on the criteria of significance, community and regional relevance, appropriate human interest, service to defined audiences. It excludes sensationalism or mis-

* Reprinted by permission of Radio Television News Directors Association.

leading emphasis in any form; subservience to external or "interested" efforts to influence news selection and presentation, whether from within the broadcasting industry or from without. It requires that such terms as "bulletin" and "flash" be used only when the character of the news justifies them; that bombastic or misleading descriptions of newsroom facilities and personnel be rejected, along with undue use of sound and visual effects; and that promotional or publicity material be sharply scrutinized before use and identified by source or otherwise when broadcast.

ARTICLE FOUR

Broadcast journalists shall at all times display humane respect for the dignity, privacy and the well-being of persons with whom the news deals.

ARTICLE FIVE

Broadcast journalists shall govern their personal lives and such nonprofessional associations as may impinge on their professional activities in a manner that will protect them from conflict of interest, real or apparent.

ARTICLE SIX

Broadcast journalists shall seek actively to present all news the knowledge of which will serve the public interest, no matter what selfish, uninformed or corrupt efforts attempt to color it, withhold it or prevent its presentation. They shall make constant effort to open doors closed to the reporting of public proceedings with tools appropriate to broadcasting (including cameras and recorders), consistent with the public interest. They acknowledge the journalist's ethic of protection of confidential information and sources, and urge unswerving observation of it except in instances in which it would clearly and unmistakably defy the public interest.

ARTICLE SEVEN

Broadcast journalists recognize the responsibility borne by broadcasting for informed analysis, comment and editorial opinion on public events and issues. They accept the obligation of broadcasters, for the presentation of such matters by individuals whose competence, experience and judgment qualify them for it.

ARTICLE EIGHT

In court, broadcast journalists shall conduct themselves with dignity, whether the court is in or out of session. They shall keep broadcast equipment as unobtrusive and silent as possible. Where court facilities are inadequate, pool broadcasts should be arranged.

ARTICLE NINE

In reporting matters that are or may be litigated, the journalists shall avoid practices which would tend to interfere with the right of an individual to a fair trial.

ARTICLE TEN

Broadcast journalists shall not misrepresent the source of any broadcast news material.

ARTICLE ELEVEN

Broadcast journalists shall actively censure and seek to prevent violations of these standards, and shall actively encourage their observance by all journalists, whether of the Radio Television News Directors Association or not.

The two major broadcasting codes—the Radio Code and the Television Code—have undergone several revisions. The Radio Code in its twentieth edition (June 1976) and the Television Code in its nineteenth edition (June 1976) cover similar ground: Program Standards, Advertising Standards, and Regulations and Procedures. Published by the Code Authority of the National Association of Broadcasters, they are here reprinted by permission in their entirety.

The Radio Code*

PREAMBLE

In 1937 a major segment of U.S. commercial radio broadcasters first adopted industry-wide standards of practice. The purpose of such standards then, as now, is to establish guideposts and professional tenets for performance in the areas of programming and advertising content.

Admittedly, such standards for broadcasting can never be final or complete, because broadcasting is a creative art, always seeking new ways to achieve maximum appeal and service. Therefore, its standards are subject to periodic revision to reasonably reflect changing attitudes in our society.

In 1945 after two years devoted to reviewing and revising the 1937 document, new standards were promulgated. Further revisions were made in subsequent years when deemed necessary. The objectives behind them have been to assure that advertising messages be presented in an honest, responsible and tasteful manner and that broadcasters, in their programming, tailor their content to meet the needs and expectations of that particular audience to which their programming is directed.

*The Radio Code, published by The Code Authority of the National Association of Broadcasters, Twentieth Edition, June 1976.

The growth of broadcasting as a medium of entertainment, education and information has been made possible by its commercial underpinning. This aspect of commercial broadcasting as it has developed in the United States has enabled the industry to grow as a free medium in the tradition of American enterprise. The extent of this freedom is underscored by those laws which prohibit censorship of broadcast material. Rather, those who own the nation's radio broadcasting stations operate them—pursuant to this self-adopted Radio Code—in recognition of the needs of the American people and the reasonable self-interests of broadcasters and broadcast advertisers.

We Believe:

That Broadcasting in the United States of America is a living symbol of democracy; a significant and necessary instrument for maintaining freedom of expression, as established by the First Amendment to the Constitution of the United States;

That its contributions to the arts, to science, to education, to commerce, and therefore to the public welfare have the potential of influencing the common good achievements of our society as a whole;

That it is our obligation to serve the people in such a manner as to reflect credit upon our profession and to encourage aspiration toward a better estate for our audiences. This entails making available to them through all phases of the broadcasting art such programming as will convey the traditional strivings of the U.S. towards goals beneficial to the populace;

That we should make full and ingenious use of the many sources of knowledge, talents and skills and exercise critical and discerning judgment concerning all broadcasting operations to the end that we may, intelligently and sympathetically:

Observe both existing principles and developing concepts affecting our society;

Respect and advance the rights and the dignity of all people;

Enrich the daily life of the people through the factual reporting and analysis of news, and through programming of education, entertainment, and information;

Provide for the fair discussion of matters of public concern; engage in works directed toward the common good; and volunteer our aid and comfort in times of stress and emergency;

Contribute to the economic welfare of all by expanding the channels of trade, by encouraging the development and conservation of natural resources, and by bringing together the buyer and seller through the broadcasting of information pertaining to goods and services.

Toward the achievement of these purposes we agree to observe the following:

I. PROGRAM STANDARDS

A. News

Radio is unique in its capacity to reach the largest number of people first with reports on current events. This competitive advantage bespeaks caution—being first is not as important as being accurate. The Radio Code standards relating to the treatment of news and public events are, because of constitutional considerations, intended to be exhortatory. The standards set forth hereunder encourage high standards of professionalism in broadcast journalism. They are not to be interpreted as turning over to others the broadcaster's responsibility as to judgments necessary in news and public events programming.

1. *News Sources.* Those responsible for news on radio should exercise constant professional care in the selection of sources—on the premise that the integrity of the news and the consequent good reputation of radio as a dominant well-balanced news medium depend largely upon the reliability of such sources.

2. *News Reporting.* News reporting should be factual, fair and without bias. Good taste should prevail in the selection and handling of news. Morbid, sensational, or alarming details not essential to factual reporting should be avoided. News should be broadcast in such a manner as to avoid creation of panic and unnecessary alarm. Broadcasters should be diligent in their supervision of content, format, and presentation of news broadcasts. Equal diligence should be exercised in selection of editors and reporters who direct news gathering and dissemination, since the station's performance in this vital informational field depends largely upon them.

3. *Commentaries and Analyses.* Special obligations devolve upon those who analyse and/or comment upon news developments, and management should be satisfied completely that the task is to be performed in the best interest of the listening public. Programs of news analysis and commentary should be clearly identified as such, distinguishing them from straight news reporting.

4. *Editorializing.* Broadcasts in which stations express their own opinions about issues of general public interest should be clearly identified as editorials.

5. *Coverage of News and Public Events.* In the coverage of news and public events broadcasters should exercise their judgments consonant with the accepted standards of ethical journalism and should provide accurate, informed and adequate coverage.

6. *Placement of Advertising.* Broadcasters should exercise particular discrimination in the acceptance, placement and presentation of advertising in news programs so that such advertising is clearly distinguishable from the news content.

B. *Controversial Public Issues*

1. Radio provides a valuable forum for the expression of responsible views on public issues of a controversial nature. Controversial public issues of importance to fellow citizens should give fair representation to opposing sides of issues.

2. Requests by individuals, groups or organizations for time to discuss their views on controversial public issues should be considered on the basis of their individual merits, and in the light of the contributions which the use requested would make to the public interest.

3. Discussion of controversial public issues should not be presented in a manner which would create the impression that the program is other than one dealing with a public issue.

C. *Community Responsibility*

1. Broadcasters and their staffs occupy a position of responsibility in the community and should conscientiously endeavor to be acquainted with its needs and characteristics to best serve the welfare of its citizens.

2. Requests for time for the placement of public service announcements or programs should be carefully reviewed with respect to the character and reputation of the group, campaign or organization involved, the public interest content of the message, and the manner of its presentation.

D. *Political Broadcasts*

1. Political broadcasts, or the dramatization of political issues designed to influence voters, shall be properly identified as such.

2. Political broadcasts should not be presented in a manner which would mislead listeners to believe that they are of any other character.
(Reference: Communications Act of 1934, as amended, Secs. 315 and 317, and FCC Rules and Regulations, Sec. 3.654, 3.657, 3.663, as discussed in NAB's "Political Broadcast Catechism & The Fairness Doctrine.")

3. Because of the unique character of political broadcasts and the necessity to retain broad freedoms of policy void of restrictive interference, it is incumbent upon all political candidates and all political parties to observe the canons of good taste and political ethics, keeping in mind the intimacy of broadcasting in the American home.

E. *Advancement of Education and Culture*

1. Because radio is an integral part of American life, there is inherent in radio broadcasting a continuing opportunity to enrich the experience of living through the advancement of education and culture.

2. Radio broadcasters, in augmenting the educational and cultural influences of the home, schools, religious institutions and institutions of higher education and other entities should:

    (a) be thoroughly conversant with the educational and cultural needs and aspirations of the community served;

    (b) develop programming consonant with the stations particular target audience.

F. *Religion and Religious Programming*

1. Religious programming shall be presented by responsible individuals, groups or organizations.

2. Radio broadcasting reaches audiences of all creeds simultaneously. Therefore, both the advocates of broad or ecumenical religious precepts, and the exponents of specific doctrines, are urged to present their positions in a manner conducive to listener enlightenment on the role of religion in society.

G. Responsibility Toward Children

Broadcasters have a special responsibility to children. Programming which might reasonably be expected to hold the attention of children should be presented with due regard for its effect on children.

1. Programming should be based upon sound social concepts and should include positive sets of values which will allow children to become responsible adults, capable of coping with the challenges of maturity.

2. Programming should convey a reasonable range of the realities which exist in the world to help children make the transition to adulthood.

3. Programming should contribute to the healthy development of personality and character.

4. Programming should afford opportunities for cultural growth as well as for wholesome entertainment.

5. Programming should be consistent with integrity of realistic production, but should avoid material of extreme nature which might create undesirable emotional reaction in children.

6. Programming should avoid appeals urging children to purchase the product specifically for the purpose of keeping the program on the air or which, for any reason, encourage children to enter inappropriate places.

7. Programming should present such subjects as violence and sex without undue emphasis and only as required by plot development or character delineation.

Violence, physical or psychological, should only be projected in responsibly handled contexts, not used to excess or exploitatively. Programs involving violence should present the consequences of it to its victims and perpetrators.

The depiction of conflict, and of material reflective of sexual considerations, when presented in programs designed primarily for children, should be handled with sensitivity.

8. The treatment of criminal activities should always convey their social and human effects.

H. Dramatic Programming

1. In the design of dramatic programs it is in the interest of radio as a vital medium to encourage those that are innovative, reflect a high degree of creative skill, deal with significant moral and social issues and present challenging concepts and other subject matter that relate to the world in which the listener lives.

2. Radio programming should not only reflect the influence of the established institutions that shape our values and culture, but also expose the dynamics of social change which bear upon our lives.

3. To achieve these goals, radio broadcasters should be conversant with the general and specific needs, interests and aspirations of all the segments of the communities they serve.

4. Radio should reflect realistically the experience of living, in both its pleasant and tragic aspects, if it is to serve the listener honestly. Nevertheless,

it holds a concurrent obligation to provide programming which will encourage positive adjustments to life.

In selecting program subjects and themes, great care must be exercised to be sure that treatment and presentation are made in good faith and not for the purpose of sensationalism or to shock or exploit the audience or appeal to prurient interests or morbid curiosity.

5. In determining the acceptability of any dramatic program, especially those containing elements of crime, mystery, or horror, consideration should be given to the possible effect on all members of the listening audience.

In addition, without sacrificing integrity of presentation, dramatic programs on radio shall avoid:

(a) the presentation of techniques of crime in such detail as to be instructional or invite imitation;

(b) presentation of the details of violence involving the excessive, the gratuitous and the instructional;

(c) sound effects calculated to mislead, shock, or unduly alarm the listener;

(d) portrayals of law enforcement in a manner which does not contribute to its proper role in our society.

I. General

1. The intimacy and confidence placed in radio demand of the broadcaster, the networks and other program sources that they be vigilant in protecting the audience from deceptive broadcast practices.

2. Sound effects and expressions characteristically associated with news broadcasts (such as "bulletin," "flash," "we interrupt this program to bring you," etc.) shall be reserved for announcement of news, and the use of any deceptive techniques in connection with fictional events and non-news programming shall not be employed.

3. The broadcasters shall be constantly alert to prevent inclusion of elements within programming dictated by factors other than the requirements of the programming itself. The acceptance of cash payments or other considerations in return for including the choice and identification of prizes, the selection of music and other creative programming elements and inclusion of any identification of commercial products or services, trade names or advertising slogans within the programming are prohibited unless consideration for such inclusion is revealed to the listeners in accordance with Sections 317 and 508 of the Communications Act.

4. Special precautions should be taken to avoid demeaning or ridiculing members of the audience who suffer from physical or mental afflictions or deformities.

5. The broadcast of gambling sequences deemed necessary to the development of plot or as appropriate background is acceptable only when presented with discretion and in moderation, and in a manner which would not excite interest in, or foster, betting nor be instructional in nature.

6. Quiz and similar programming that is presented as a contest of knowledge, information, skill or luck must, in fact, be a genuine contest and

the results must not be controlled by collusion with or between contestants, or by any other action which will favor one contestant against any other.

7. Contests may not constitute a lottery.

8. Listener contests should not mislead as to the nature of value of prizes, likelihood of winning, nor encourage thoughtless or unsafe acts.

9. No programming shall be presented in a manner which through artifice or simulation would mislead the audience as to any material fact. Each broadcaster must exercise reasonable judgment to determine whether a particular method of presentation would constitute a material deception, or would be accepted by the audience as normal theatrical illusion.

10. Legal, medical and other professional advice will be permitted only in conformity with law and recognized ethical and prefessional standards.

11. Narcotic addiction shall not be presented except as a destructive habit. The use of illegal drugs or the abuse of legal drugs shall not be encouraged or be presented as desirable or socially acceptable.

12. Material pertaining to fortune-telling, occultism, astrology, phrenology, palmreading, numerology, mind-reading, character-reading, or subjects of a like nature, is unacceptable if it encourages people to regard such fields as providing commonly accepted appraisals of life.

13. Representations of liquor and smoking shall be de-emphasized. When represented, they should be consistent with plot and character development.

14. Obscene, indecent or profane matter, as proscribed by law, is unacceptable.

15. Special sensitivity is necessary in the use of material relating to sex, race, color, age, creed, religious functionaries or rites, or national or ethnic derivation.

16. The presentation of marriage, the family and similarly important human relationships, and material with sexual connotations, should not be treated exploitatively or irresponsibly, but with sensitivity.

17. Broadcasts of actual sporting events at which on-the-scene betting is permitted by law should be presented in a manner in keeping with federal, state and local laws, and should concentrate on the subject as a public sporting event.

18. Detailed exposition of hypnosis or material capable of having an hypnotic effect on listeners is forbidden.

19. Any technique whereby an attempt is made to convey information to the listener by transmitting messages below the threshold of normal awareness is not permitted.

20. The commonly accepted standards of humane animal treatment should be adhered to as applicable in programming.

21. Broadcasters are responsible for making good faith determinations on the acceptability of lyrics under applicable Radio Code standards.

22. Guests on discussion/interview programs and members of the public who participate in phone-in programs shall be treated with due respect by the program host/hostess.

Interview/discussion programs, including telephone participation programs, should be governed by accepted standards of ethical journalism. Any agreement substantively limiting areas of discussion/questions should be announced at the outset of the program.

23. The standards of this Code covering programming content are also understood to include, wherever applicable, the standards contained in the advertising section of the Code.

24. To assure that broadcasters have the freedom to program fully and responsibly, none of the provisions of this Code should be construed as preventing or impeding broadcasts of the broad range of material necessary to help broadcasters fulfill their obligations to operate in the public interest.

II. ADVERTISING STANDARDS

Advertising is the principal source of revenue of the free, competitive American system of radio broadcasting. It makes possible the presentation to all American people of the finest programs of entertainment, education, and information.

Since the great strength of American radio broadcasting derives from the public respect for and the public approval of its programs, it must be the purpose of each broadcaster to establish and maintain high standards of performance, not only in the selection and production of all programs, but also in the presentation of advertising.

This Code establishes basic standards for all radio broadcasting. The principles of acceptability and good taste within the Program Standards section govern the presentation of advertising where applicable. In addition, the Code establishes in this section special standards which apply to radio advertising.

A. General Advertising Standards

1. Commerical radio broadcasters make their facilities available for the advertising of products and services and accept commerical presentations for such advertising. However, they shall, in recognition of their responsibility to the public, refuse the facilities of their stations to an advertiser where they have good reason to doubt the integrity of the advertiser, the truth of the advertising representations, or the compliance of the advertiser with the spirit and purpose of all applicable legal requirements.

2. In consideration of the customs and attitudes of the communities served, each radio broadcaster should refuse his/her facilities to the advertisement of products and services, or the use of advertising scripts, which the station has good reason to believe would be objectionable to a substantial and responsible segment of the community. These standards should be applied with judgment and flexibility, taking into consideration the characteristics of the medium, its home and family audience, and the form and content of the particular presentation.

B. Presentation of Advertising

1. The advancing techniques of the broadcast art have shown that the quality and proper integration of advertising copy are just as important as

measurement in time. The measure of a station's service to its audience is determined by its overall performance.

2. The final measurement of any commercial broadcast service is quality. To this, every broadcaster shall dedicate his/her best effort.

3. Great care shall be exercised by the broadcaster to prevent the presentation of false, misleading or deceptive advertising. While it is entirely appropriate to present a product in a favorable light and atmosphere, the presentation must not, by copy or demonstration, involve a material deception as to the characteristics or performance of a product.

4. The broadcaster and the advertiser should exercise special caution with the content and presentation of commercials placed in or near programs designed for children. Exploitation of children should be avoided. Commercials directed to children should in no way mislead as to the product's performance and usefulness. Appeals involving matters of health which should be determined by physicians should be avoided.

5. Reference to the results of research, surveys or tests relating to the product to be advertised shall not be presented in a manner so as to create an impression of fact beyond that established by the study. Surveys, tests or other research results upon which claims are based must be conducted under recognized research techniques and standards.

C. Acceptability of Advertisers and Products

In general, because radio broadcasting is designed for the home and the entire family, the following principles shall govern the business classifications:

1. The advertising of hard liquor shall not be accepted.

2. The advertising of beer and wines is acceptable when presented in the best of good taste and discretion.

3. The advertising of fortune-telling, occultism, astrology, phrenology, palm-reading, numerology, mind-reading, character-reading, or subjects of a like nature, is not acceptable.

4. Because the advertising of all products and services of a personal nature raises special problems, such advertising, when accepted, should be treated with emphasis on ethics and the canons of good taste, and presented in a restrained and inoffensive manner.

5. The advertising of tip sheets and other publications seeking to advertise for the purpose of giving odds or promoting betting is unacceptable.

The lawful advertising of government organizations which conduct legalized lotteries is acceptable provided such advertising does not unduly exhort the public to bet.

The advertising of private or governmental organizations which conduct legalized betting on sporting contests is acceptable provided such advertising is limited to institutional type announcements which do not exhort the public to bet.

6. An advertiser who markets more than one product shall not be permitted to use advertising copy devoted to an acceptable product for purposes of publicizing the brand name or other identification of a product which is not acceptable.

7. Care should be taken to avoid presentation of "bait-switch" advertising whereby goods or services which the advertiser has no intention of selling are offered merely to lure the customer into purchasing higher-priced substitutes.

8. Advertising should offer a product or service on its positive merits and refrain from discrediting, disparaging or unfairly attacking competitors, competing products, other industries, professions or institutions.

Any identification or comparison of a competitive product or service, by name, or other means, should be confined to specific facts rather than generalized statements or conclusions, unless such statements or conclusions are not derogatory in nature.

9. Advertising testimonials should be genuine, and reflect an honest appraisal of personal experience.

10. Advertising by institutions or enterprises offering instruction with exaggerated claims for opportunities awaiting those who enroll, is unacceptable.

11. The advertising of firearms/ammunition is acceptable provided it promotes the product only as sporting equipment and conforms to recognized standards of safety as well as all applicable laws and regulations. Advertisements of firearms/ammunition by mail order are unacceptable.

D. Advertising of Medical Products

Because advertising for over-the-counter products involving health considerations is of intimate and far-reaching importance to the consumer, the following principles should apply to such advertising:

1. When dramatized advertising material involves statements by doctors, dentists, nurses or other professional people, the material should be presented by members of such profession reciting actual experience, or it should be made apparent from the presentation itself that the portrayal is dramatized.

2. Because of the personal nature of the advertising of medical products, the indiscriminate use of such words as "safe," "without risk," "harmless," or other terms of similar meaning, either direct or implied, should not be expressed in the advertising of medical products.

3. Advertising material which offensively describes or dramatizes distress or morbid situations involving ailments is not acceptable.

E. Time Standards for Advertising Copy

1. The amount of time to be used for advertising should not exceed 18 minutes within any clock hour. The Code Authority, however, for good cause may approve advertising exceeding the above standard for special circumstances.

2. Any reference to another's products or services under any trade name, or language sufficiently descriptive to identify it, shall, except for normal guest identification, be considered as advertising copy.

3. For the purpose of determining advertising limitations, such program types as "classified," "swap shop," "shopping guides," and "farm auction"

programs, etc., shall be regarded as containing one and one-half minutes of advertising for each five-minute segment.

F. Contests

1. Contests shall be conducted with fairness to all entrants, and shall comply with all pertinent laws and regulations.

2. All contest details, including rules, eligibility requirements, opening and termination dates, should be clearly and completely announced or easily accessible to the listening public; and the winners' names should be released as soon as possible after the close of the contest.

3. When advertising is accepted which requests contestants to submit items of product identification or other evidence of purchase of products, reasonable facsimiles thereof should be made acceptable. However, when the award is based upon skill and not upon chance, evidence of purchase may be required.

4. All copy pertaining to any contest (except that which is required by law) associated with the exploitation or sale of the sponsor's product or service, and all references to prizes or gifts offered in such connection should be considered a part of and included in the total time limitations heretofore provided. (*See Time Standards for Advertising Copy.*)

G. Premiums and Offers

1. The broadcaster should require that full details of proposed offers be submitted for investigation and approval before the first announcement of the offer is made to the public.

2. A final date for the termination of an offer should be announced as far in advance as possible.

3. If a consideration is required, the advertiser should agree to honor complaints indicating dissatisfaction with the premium by returning the consideration.

4. There should be no misleading descriptions or comparisons of any premiums or gifts which will distort or enlarge their value in the minds of the listeners.

REGULATIONS AND PROCEDURES

The following Regulations and Procedures shall obtain as an integral part of the Radio Code of the National Association of Broadcasters:

I. Name

The name of this Code shall be the Radio Code of the National Association of Broadcasters, hereinafter referred to as the Radio Code.*

---

* The Radio Board of the NAB shall have power: "to enact, amend and promulgate Radio Standards of Practice or Codes, and to establish such methods to secure observance theoreof as it may deem advisable;—." By-Laws of the National Association of Broadcasters, Article VI, Section 8, B. Radio Board.

Definitions:

Wherever reference is made to programs it shall be construed to include all program material including commercials.

II. *Purpose of the Code*

The purpose of this Code is cooperatively to establish and maintain a level of radio programming which gives full consideration to the educational, informational, cultural, economic, moral and entertainment needs of the American public to the end that more and more people will be better served.

III. *The Radio Code Board*

Section 1. *Composition*

There shall be a continuing Committee entitled the Radio Code Board.* The Code Board shall be composed of 11 members. Members of the Radio Board shall not be eligible to serve on the above specified Board. The Chairperson and members of the Code Board shall be appointed by the President of the NAB, subject to confirmation by the Radio Board, and may include no more than two members as representatives of subscribing nationwide radio networks. Due consideration shall be given, in making such appointments, to factors of diversification, such as market size, geographical location, network affiliation, class of broadcast service, etc. The Board shall be fully representative of the radio industry. All Code Board members shall be selected from subscribers to the Radio Code. In every odd-numbered year, four members shall be appointed for two-year terms; in every even-numbered year, five members shall be appointed for two-year terms provided, however, that network representatives be rotated on an annual basis. Appointments become effective at the conclusion of the annual NAB convention of the year in which appointments are made.

A. *Limitation of Service:*

A person shall not serve consecutively as a member of the Board for more than two two-year terms or for more than four years consecutively provided, however, that appointment to fill an unexpired term shall not count toward the limitation of service as previously stated.

Network representatives on the Radio Code Board shall be limited to non-consecutive two-year terms; provided, in the first year of such representation one network member may be appointed for a one-year term and one for a two-year term. Thereafter, all network members may be appointed for two-year terms. Any one network representative may be reappointed following an interim two-year period.

A majority of the membership of the Radio Code Board shall constitute a quorum for all purposes unless herein otherwise provided.

Section 2. Authorities and Responsibilities

The Radio Code Board is authorized and directed:

(1) To recommend to the Radio Board amendments to the Radio Code; (2) to consider in its discretion, any appeal from any decision made by the Code Authority Director with respect to any matter which has arisen under the Code, and to suspend, reverse, or modify any such decision; (3) to prefer formal charges, looking toward the suspension or revocation of the subcription and/or the authority to use the Radio Code Audio and Visual Symbols, to the Radio Board concerning violations and breaches of the Radio Code by a subscriber; (4) to be available to the Code Authority Director for consultation on any and all matters affecting the Radio Code.

A. Meetings:

The Radio Code Board shall meet regularly semi-annually on a date to be determined by the Chairperson. The Chairperson of the Board may, at any time, on at least five days' written notice, call a special meeting of the Board.

IV. Code Authority Director

Section 1. Director

There shall be a position designated as the Code Authority Director. This position shall be filled by appointment of the President of NAB, subject to the approval of the Board of Directors.

Section 2. Authority and Responsibilities

The Code Authority Director is responsible for the administration, interpretation and enforcement of the Radio Code. In furtherance of this responsibility he/she is authorized and directed:

(1) To maintain a continuing review of all programming and advertising material presented over radio, especially that of subscribers to the Radio Code of NAB; (2) to receive, screen and clear complaints concerning radio programming; (3) to define and interpret words and phrases in the Radio Code; (4) to develop and maintain appropriate liaison with governmental agencies and with responsible and accountable organizations and institutions; (5) to inform, expeditiously and properly, a subscriber to the Radio Code of complaints or commendations, as well as to advise all subscribers concerning the attitudes and desires program-wise of accountable organizations and institutions, and of the American public in general; (6) to receive and monitor, if necessary, any certain series of programs, daily programming, or any other program presentations of a subscriber, as well as to request recorded material, or script and copy, with regard to any certain program presented by a subscriber; (7) to reach conclusions and make recommendations or prefer charges to the Radio Code Board concerning violations and breaches of the Radio Code by a subscriber; (8) to recommend to the Code Board amendments to the Radio Code; (9) to take such action as may be necessary to enforce the Code, including revocation of subscription as hereinafter provided in Chapter V, Section 4.

A. Delegation of Powers and Responsibilities:

The Code Authority Director shall appoint such executive staff as is needed, consistent with resources, to carry out the above described functions, and may delegate to this staff such responsibilities as he/she may deem necessary.

V. Subscribers

Section 1. Eligibility

A. Any individual, firm or corporation which is engaged in the operation of a radio broadcast station or radio network; or which holds a construction permit for a radio broadcast station within the United States or its dependencies, shall, subject to the approval of the Radio Board, as hereinafter provided, be eligible to subscribe to the Radio Code of the NAB to the extent of one subscription for each such station or network, or each station which holds a construction permit; provided, that a non-radio member of NAB shall not become eligible via Code subscription to receive any of the member services or to exercise any of the voting privileges of a member.

B. The Radio Code Board may recommend categories of affiliate subscribers as may be desired, together with applicable fees for such affiliate subscriptions.

Section 2. Certification of Subscription

Upon subscribing to the Code there shall be granted forthwith to each such subscribing station authority to use such copyrighted and registered audio and visual symbols as will be provided. The symbols and their significance shall be appropriately publicized by the NAB.

Section 3. Duration of Subscription

Subscription shall continue in full force and effect until there has been received a written notice of resignation or until subscription is revoked by action of the Code Authority, the Radio Code Board or the Radio Board of Directors.

Section 4. Revocation of Subscription

Any subscription and/or the authority to utilize the above-noted symbols, may be voided, revoked or temporarily suspended for radio programming, including commercial copy, which, by theme, treatment or incident, in the judgment of the Code Authority constitutes a continuing, willful or gross violation of any of the provisions of the Radio Code: provided, however, that the following conditions and procedures shall govern:

A. Conditions Precedent:

Prior to Revocation of Subscription, the Code Authority (1) Shall appropriately inform the subscriber of any and all complaints and information it possesses relating to the programming of said subscriber, (2) Shall have reported to, and advised, said subscriber by analysis, interpretation, recommendation or otherwise, of the possibility of a violation or breach of the Radio Code, and (3) Shall have served upon the subscriber by registered mail a Notice of Intent to Revoke Subscription; such Notice shall contain a statement of the grounds and reasons for the proposed revocation, including appropriate references to the Radio Code and shall give the subscriber 30 days to take such action as will satisfy the Code Authority. During this interim period the Code Authority may, within its sole discretion, reconsider its proposed action based upon such written reply as the subscriber may care to make, or upon such action as the subscriber may care to take program-wise, in conformance with the analysis, interpretation or recommendation of the Code Authority. If upon termination of the 30 day period, no such action has been taken or the subscriber has not requested a hearing, as hereinafter provided, his/her subscription to the Code shall be considered revoked.

B. Time:

In the event that the nature of the program in question is such that the Code Authority deems time to be of the essence, the Code Authority may limit the time in which compliance must be made, provided that a time certain in which subscriber may reply is included in the Notice of Intent, and provided further that the Code Authority's reasons therefor are specified in its Notice of Intent to Revoke Subscription.

C. Hearing:

The subscriber shall have the right to a hearing before the Code Board by requesting same and by filing an answer within 20 days of the date of receipt of the Notice of Intent. Said answer and request for hearing shall be directed to the Chairperson of the Code Board with a copy to the Code Authority.

D. Waiver:

Failure to request a hearing shall be deemed a waiver of the subscriber's right thereto. If a hearing is requested, action of the Code Authority is suspended pending decision of the Code Board.

E. Designation:

If hearing is requested by the subscriber, it shall be designated as promptly as possible and at such time and place as the Code Board may specify.

F. Confidential Status:

Hearings shall be closed; and all correspondence between a subscriber and the Code Authority and/or the Code Board concerning specific programming shall be confidential; provided, however, that the confidential status of these procedures may be waived by a subscriber.

G. Presentation; Representation:

A subscriber who has exercised his/her right to a hearing, shall be entitled to effect presentation of his/her case personally, by agent, by attorney, or by deposition and interrogatory.

H. Intervention:

Upon request by the subscriber-respondent or the Code Authority, the Code Board, in its discretion, may permit the intervention of one or more subscribers as parties-in-interest.

I. Transcript:

A stenographic transcript record may be taken if requested by respondent and shall be certified by the Chairperson of the Code Board to the Office of the Secretary of the National Association of Broadcasters, where it shall be maintained. The transcript shall not be open to inspection unless otherwise provided by the party respondent in the proceeding.

J. Code Authority; Counsel:

The Code Authority may, at its discretion, utilize the services of an attorney from the staff of the NAB for the purpose of effecting its presentation in a hearing matter.

K. Order of Procedure:

At hearings, the Code Authority shall open and close.

L. Cross-Examination:

The right of cross-examination shall specifically obtain. Where procedure has been by deposition or interrogatory, the use of cross-interrogatories shall satisfy this right.

M. Presentation:

Oral and written evidence may be introduced by the subscriber and by the Code Authority. Oral argument may be had at the hearing and written memoranda or briefs may be submitted by the subscriber and by the Code Authority. The Code Board may admit such evidence as it deems relevant, material and competent, and may determine the nature and length of the oral argument and the written argument or briefs.

N. Transcriptions, etc.:

Records, transcriptions, or other mechanical reproductions of radio programs, properly identified, shall be accepted into evidence when relevant.

O. Authority of Presiding Officer of Code Board:

The Presiding Officer shall rule upon all interlocutory matters, such as, but not limited to, the admissibility of evidence, the qualifications of witnesses, etc. On all other matters, authority to act shall be vested in a majority of the Code Board unless otherwise provided.

P. Continuances and Extensions:

Continuance and extension of any proceeding or for the time of filing or performing any act required or allowed to be done within a specific time may be granted upon request, for a good cause shown. The Code Board or the Presiding Officer may recess or adjourn a hearing for such time as may be deemed necessary, and may change the place thereof.

Q. Findings and Conclusions:

The Code Board shall decide the case as expeditiously as possible and shall notify the subscriber. Code Authority, and the Radio Board in writing, of the decision. The decision of the Code Board shall contain findings of fact with conclusions, as well as the reasons or bases therefor. Findings of fact shall set out in detail and with particularity all basic evidentiary facts developed on the record (with appropriate citations to the transcript of record or exhibit relied on for each evidentiary fact) supporting the conclusion reached.

R. Disqualification:

Any member of the Code Board may disqualify himself/herself, or upon good cause shown by any interested party, may be disqualified by a majority vote of the Code Board.

S. Review:

A request for review of the Code Board's decision may be filed by the subscriber with the Radio Board. Such petition for review must be served upon the Chairperson of the Radio Board within 10 days after receipt by the subscriber of the Code Board's decision.

T. Penalty, Suspension of:

At the discretion of the Code Board, application of any penalty provided for in the decision may be suspended until the Radio Board makes final disposition of the Petition for Review. The entire record in the proceedings before the Code Board shall be certified to the Radio Board. The review will be limited to written statements and no provision is made for further oral argument.

U. Final Decision:

The Radio Board shall have the discretion upon review to uphold, reverse, or amend with direction the decision of the Code Board. The decision of the Radio Board is final.

Section 5. Additional Procedures

When necessary to the proper administration of the Code, additional rules of procedure will be established from time to time as authorized by the By-Laws of the NAB; in keeping therewith, special consideration shall be given to the procedures for receipts and processing of complaints and to necessary rules to be adopted from time to time, taking into account the source and nature of such complaints; such rules to include precautionary measures such as the posting of bonds to cover costs and expenses of processing same;

and further provided that special consideration will be given to procedures insuring the confidential status of proceedings relating to Code observance.

Section 6. Amendment and Review

The Radio Code may be amended from time to time by the Radio Board
which shall specify the effective date of each amendment; provided, that said
Board is specifically charged with review and reconsideration of the entire
Code, its appendices and procedures, at least once each year.

Section 7. Termination of Contracts

All subscribers on the air shall be in compliance at the time of subscription to the Code.

VI. Rates

Each subscriber shall pay fees in accordance with such schedule, at such
time, and under such conditions as may be determined from time to time by
the Radio Board (*See Article VI, Section 8, B. Radio Board By-Laws of the NAB*).

The Television Code*
National Association of Broadcasters
Nineteenth Edition, June 1976

PREAMBLE

Television is seen and heard in nearly every American home. These
homes include children and adults of all ages, embrace all races and all varieties of philosophic or religious conviction and reach those of every educational
background. Television broadcasters must take this pluralistic audience into
account in programming their stations. They are obligated to bring their positive responsibility for professionalism and reasoned judgment to bear upon all
those involved in the development, production and selection of programs.

The free, competitive American system of broadcasting which offers
programs of entertainment, news, general information, education and culture
is supported and made possible by revenues from advertising. While television broadcasters are responsible for the programming and advertising on
their stations, the advertisers who use television to convey their commercial
messages also have a responsibility to the viewing audience. Their advertising
messages should be presented in an honest, responsible and tasteful manner.
Advertisers should also support the endeavors of broadcasters to offer a diversity of programs that meet the needs and expectations of the total viewing audience.

The viewer also has a responsibility to help broadcasters serve the public. All viewers should make their criticisms and positive suggestions about

*The Television Code, published by The Code Authority of the National Association of Broadcasters,
Nineteenth Edition, June 1976.

programming and advertising known to the brodcast licensee. Parents particularly should oversee the viewing habits of their children, encouraging them to watch programs that will enrich their experience and broaden their intellectual horizons.

PROGRAM STANDARDS

I. Principles Governing Program Content

It is in the interest of television as a vital medium to encourage programs that are innovative, reflect a high degree of creative skill, deal with significant moral and social issues and present challenging concepts and other subject matter that relate to the world in which the viewer lives.

Television programs should not only reflect the influence of the established institutions that shape our values and culture, but also expose the dynamics of social change which bear upon our lives.

To achieve these goals, television broadcasters should be conversant with the general and specific needs, interests and aspirations of all the segments of the communities they serve. They should affirmatively seek out responsible representatives of all parts of their communities so that they may structure a broad range of programs that will inform, enlighten, and entertain the total audience.

Broadcasters should also develop programs directed toward advancing the cultural and educational aspects of their communities.

To assure that broadcasters have the freedom to program fully and responsibly, none of the provisions of this Code should be construed as preventing or impeding broadcast of the broad range of material necessary to help broadcasters fulfill their obligations to operate in the public interest.

The challenge to the broadcaster is to determine how suitably to present the complexities of human behavior. For television, this requires exceptional awareness of considerations peculiar to the medium.

Accordingly, in selecting program subjects and themes, great care must be exercised to be sure that treatment and presentation are made in good faith and not for the purpose of sensationalism or to shock or exploit the audience or appeal to prurient interests or morbid curiosity.

Additionally, entertainment programming inappropriate for viewing by a general family audience should not be broadcast during the first hour of network entertainment programming in prime time and in the immediately preceding hour. In the occasional case when an entertainment program in this time period is deemed to be inappropriate for such an audience, advisories should be used to alert viewers. Advisories should also be used when programs in later prime time periods contain material that might be disturbing to significant segments of the audience.

These advisories should be presented in audio and video form at the beginning of the program and when deemed appropriate at a later point in the program. Advisories should also be used responsibly in promotional material in advance of the program. When using an advisory, the broadcaster should attempt to notify publishers of television program listings.

Special care should be taken with respect to the content and treatment of audience advisories so that they do not disserve their intended purpose by containing material that is promotional, sensational or exploitative. Promotional announcements for programs that include advisories should be scheduled on a basis consistent with the purpose of the advisory. (*See Television Code Interpretation No. 5*)

II. Responsibility Toward Children

Broadcasters have a special responsibility to children. Programs designed primarily for children should take into account the range of interests and needs of children from instructional and cultural material to a wide variety of entertainment material. In their totality, programs should contribute to the sound, balanced development of children to help them achieve a sense of the world at large and informed adjustments to their society.

In the course of a child's development, numerous social factors and forces, including television, affect the ability of the child to make the transition to adult society.

The child's training and experience during the formative years should include positive sets of values which will allow the child to become a responsible adult, capable of coping with the challenges of maturity.

Children should also be exposed, at the appropriate times, to a reasonable range of the realities which exist in the world sufficient to help them make the transition to adulthood. Because children are allowed to watch programs designed primarily for adults, broadcasters should take this practice into account in the presentation of material in such programs when children may constitute a substantial segment of the audience.

All the standards set forth in this section apply to both program and commercial material designed and intended for viewing by children.

III. Community Responsibility

1. Television broadcasters and their staffs occupy positions of unique responsibility in their communities and should conscientiously endeavor to be acquainted fully with the community's needs and characteristics in order better to serve the welfare of its citizens.

2. Requests for time for the placement of public service announcements or programs should be carefully reviewed with respect to the character and reputation of the group, campaign or organization involved, the public interest content of the message, and the manner of its presentation.

IV. Special Program Standards

1. Violence, physical or psychological, may only be projected in responsibly handled contexts, not used exploitatively. Programs involving violence should present the consequences of it to its victims and perpetrators.

Presentation of the details of violence should avoid the excessive, the gratuitous and the instructional.

The use of violence for its own sake and the detailed dwelling upon brutality or physical agony, by sight or by sound, are not permissible.

The depiction of conflict, when presented in programs designed primarily for children, should be handled with sensitivity.

2. The treatment of criminal activities should always convey their social and human effects.

The presentation of techniques of crime in such detail as to be instructional or invite imitation shall be avoided.

3. Narcotic addiction shall not be presented except as a destructive habit. The use of illegal drugs or the abuse of legal drugs shall not be encouraged or shown as socially acceptable.

4. The use of gambling devices or scenes necessary to the development of plot or as appropriate background is acceptable only when presented with discretion and in moderation, and in a manner which would not excite interest in, or foster, betting nor be instructional in nature.

5. Telecasts of actual sports programs at which on-the-scene betting is permitted by law shall be presented in a manner in keeping with federal, state and local laws, and should concentrate on the subject as a public sporting event.

6. Special precautions must be taken to avoid demeaning or ridiculing members of the audience who suffer from physical or mental afflictions or deformities.

7. Special sensitivity is necessary in the use of material relating to sex, race, color, age, creed, religious functionaries or rites, or national or ethnic derivation.

8. Obscene, indecent or profane matter, as proscribed by law, is unacceptable.

9. The presentation of marriage, the family and similarly important human relationships, and material with sexual connotations, shall not be treated exploitatively or irresponsibly, but with sensitivity. Costuming and movements of all performers shall be handled in a similar fashion.

10. The use of liquor and the depiction of smoking in program content shall be deemphasized. When shown, they should be consistent with plot and character development.

11. The creation of a state of hypnosis by act or detailed demonstration on camera is prohibited, and hypnosis as a form of "parlor game" antics to create humorous situations within a comedy setting is forbidden.

12. Program material pertaining to fortune-telling, occultism, astrology, phrenology, palm-reading, numerology, mind-reading, character-reading, and the like is unacceptable if it encourages people to regard such fields as providing commonly accepted appraisals of life.

13. Professional advice, diagnosis and treatment will be presented in conformity with law and recognized professional standards.

14. Any technique whereby an attempt is made to convey information to the viewer by transmitting messages below the threshold of normal awareness is not permitted.

15. The use of animals, consistent with plot and character delineation, shall be in conformity with accepted standards of humane treatment.

16. Quiz and similar programs that are presented as contests of knowl-

edge, information, skill or luck must, in fact, be genuine contests; and the results must not be controlled by collusion with or between contestants, or by any other action which will favor one contestant against any other.

17. The broadcaster shall be constantly alert to prevent inclusion of elements within a program dictated by factors other than the requirements of the program itself. The acceptance of cash payments or other considerations in return for including scenic properties, the choice and identification of prizes, the selection of music and other creative program elements and inclusion of any identification of commercial products or services, their trade names or advertising slogan within the program are prohibited except in accordance with Sections 317 and 508 of the Communications Act.

18. Contests may not constitute a lottery.

19. No program shall be presented in a manner which through artifice or simulation would mislead the audience as to any material fact. Each broadcaster must exercise reasonable judgment to determine whether a particular method of presentation would constitute a material deception, or would be accepted by the audience as normal theatrical illusion.

20. A television broadcaster should not present fictional events or other non-news material as authentic news telecasts or announcements, nor permit dramatizations in any program which would give the false impression that the dramatized material constitutes news.

21. The standards of this Code covering program content are also understood to include, wherever applicable, the standards contained in the advertising section of the Code.

V. Treatment of News and Public Events

General

Television Code standards relating to the treatment of news and public events are, because of constitutional considerations, intended to be exhortatory. The standards set forth hereunder encourage high standards of professionalism in broadcast journalism. They are not to be interpreted as turning over to others the broadcaster's responsibility as to judgments necessary in news and public events programming.

News

1. A television station's news schedule should be adequate and well-balanced.

2. News reporting should be factual, fair and without bias.

3. A television broadcaster should exercise particular discrimination in the acceptance, placement and presentation of advertising in news programs so that such advertising should be clearly distinguishable from the news content.

4. At all times, pictorial and verbal material for both news and comment should conform to other sections of these standards, wherever such sections are reasonably applicable.

5. Good taste should prevail in the selection and handling of news:

Morbid, sensational or alarming details not essential to the factual report, especially in connection with stories of crime or sex, should be avoided. News should be telecast in such a manner as to avoid panic and unnecessary alarm.

6. Commentary and analysis should be clearly identified as such.

7. Pictorial material should be chosen with care and not presented in a misleading manner.

8. All news interview programs should be governed by accepted standards of ethical journalism, under which the interviewer selects the questions to be asked. Where there is advance agreement materially restricting an important or newsworthy area of questioning, the interviewer will state on the program that such limitation has been agreed upon. Such disclosure should be made if the person being interviewed requires that questions be submitted in advance or participates in editing a recording of the interview prior to its use on the air.

9. A television broadcaster should exercise due care in the supervision of content, format, and presentation of newscasts originated by his/her station, and in the selection of newscasters, commentators, and analysts.

Public Events

1. A television broadcaster has an affirmative responsibility at all times to be informed of public events, and to provide coverage consonant with the ends of an informed and enlightened citizenry.

2. The treatment of such events by a television broadcaster should provide adequate and informed coverage.

VI. Controversial Public Issues

1. Television provides a valuable forum for the expression of responsible views on public issues of a controversial nature. The television broadcaster should seek out and develop with accountable individuals, groups and organizations, programs relating to controversial public issues of import to his/her fellow citizens; and to give fair representation to opposing sides of issues which materially affect the life or welfare of a substantial segment of the public.

2. Requests by individuals, groups or organizations for time to discuss their views on controversial public issues should be considered on the basis of their individual merits, and in the light of the contribution which the use requested would make to the public interest, and to a well-balanced program structure.

3. Programs devoted to the discussion of controversial public issues should be identified as such. They should not be presented in a manner which would mislead listeners or viewers to believe that the program is purely of an entertainment, news, or other character.

4. Broadcasts in which stations express their own opinions about issues of general public interest should be clearly identified as editorials. They should be unmistakably identified as statements of station opinion and should be appropriately distinguished from news and other program material.

VII. Political Telecasts

1. Political telecasts should be clearly identified as such. They should not be presented by a television broadcaster in a manner which would mislead listeners or viewers to believe that the program is of any other character. (Ref.: Communications Act of 1934, as amended, Secs. 315 and 317, and FCC Rules and Regulations, Secs. 3.654, 3.657, 3.663, as discussed in NAB's "Political Broadcast Catechism & The Fairness Doctrine.")

VIII. Religious Programs

1. It is the responsibility of a television broadcaster to make available to the community appropriate opportunity for religious presentations.

2. Programs reach audiences of all creeds simultaneously. Therefore, both the advocates of broad or ecumenical religious precepts, and the exponents of specific doctrines, are urged to present their positions in a manner conducive to viewer enlightenment on the role of religion in society.

3. In the allocation of time for telecasts of religious programs the television station should use its best efforts to apportion such time fairly among responsible individuals, groups and organizations.

ADVERTISING STANDARDS

IX. General Advertising Standards

1. This Code establishes basic standards for all television broadcasting. The principles of acceptability and good taste within the Program Standards section govern the presentation of advertising where applicable. In addition, the Code establishes in this section special standards which apply to television advertising.

2. Commercial television broadcasters make their facilities available for the advertising of products and services and accept commercial presentations for such advertising. However, television broadcasters should, in recognition of their responsibility to the public, refuse the facilities of their stations to an advertiser where they have good reason to doubt the integrity of the advertiser, the truth of the advertising representations, or the compliance of the advertiser with the spirit and purpose of all applicable legal requirements.

3. Identification of sponsorship must be made in all sponsored programs in accordance with the requirements of the Communications Act of 1934, as amended, and the Rules and Regulations of the Federal Communications Commission.

4. Representations which disregard normal safety precautions shall be avoided.

Children shall not be represented, except under proper adult supervision, as being in contact with or demonstrating a product recognized as potentially dangerous to them.

5. In consideration of the customs and attitudes of the communities served, each television broadcaster should refuse his/her facilities to the advertisement of products and services, or the use of advertising scripts, which the

station has good reason to believe would be objectionable to a substantial and responsible segment of the community. These standards should be applied with judgment and flexibility, taking into consideration the characteristics of the medium, its home and family audience, and the form and content of the particular presentation.

6. The advertising of hard liquor (distilled spirits) is not acceptable.

7. The advertising of beer and wines is acceptable only when presented in the best of good taste and discretion, and is acceptable only subject to federal and local laws. (*See Television Code Interpretation No. 4*)

8. Advertising by institutions or enterprises which in their offers of instruction imply promises of employment or make exaggerated claims for the opportunities awaiting those who enroll for courses is generally unacceptable.

9. The advertising of firearms/ammunition is acceptable provided it promotes the product only as sporting equipment and conforms to recognized standards of safety as well as all applicable laws and regulations. Advertisements of firearms/ammunition by mail order are unacceptable. The advertising of fireworks is unacceptable.

10. The advertising of fortune-telling, occultism, astrology, phrenology, palm-reading, numerology, mind-reading, character-reading or subjects of a like nature is not permitted.

11. Because all products of a personal nature create special problems, acceptability of such products should be determined with especial emphasis on ethics and the canons of good taste. Such advertising of personal products as is accepted must be presented in a restrained and obviously inoffensive manner.

12. The advertising of tip sheets and other publications seeking to advertise for the purpose of giving odds or promoting betting is unacceptable.

The lawful advertising of government organizations which conduct legalized lotteries is acceptable provided such advertising does not unduly exhort the public to bet.

The advertising of private or governmental organizations which conduct legalized betting on sporting contests is acceptable provided such advertising is limited to institutional type announcements which do not exhort the public to bet.

13. An advertiser who markets more than one product should not be permitted to use advertising copy devoted to an acceptable product for purposes of publicizing the brand name or other identification of a product which is not acceptable.

14. "Bait-switch" advertising, whereby goods or services which the advertiser has no intention of selling are offered merely to lure the customer into purchasing higher-priced substitutes, is not acceptable.

15. Personal endorsements (testimonials) shall be genuine and reflect personal experience. They shall contain no statement that cannot be supported if presented in the advertiser's own words.

X. Presentation of Advertising

1. Advertising messages should be presented with courtesy and good taste; disturbing or annoying material should be avoided; every effort should be made to keep the advertising message in harmony with the content and general tone of the program in which it appears.

2. The role and capability of television to market sponsors' products are well recognized. In turn, this fact dictates that great care be exercised by the broadcaster to prevent the presentation of false, misleading or deceptive advertising. While it is entirely appropriate to present a product in a favorable light and atmosphere, the presentation must not, by copy or demonstration, involve a material deception as to the characteristics, performance or appearance of the product.

Broadcast advertisers are responsible for making available, at the request of the Code Authority, documentation adequate to support the validity and truthfulness of claims, demonstrations and testimonials contained in their commercial messages.

3. The broadcaster and the advertiser should exercise special caution with the content and presentation of television commercials placed in or near programs designed for children. Exploitation of children should be avoided. Commercials directed to children should in no way mislead as to the product's performance and usefulness.

Commercials, whether live, film or tape, within programs initially designed primarily for children under 12 years of age shall be clearly separated from program material by an appropriate device.

Trade name identification or other merchandising practices involving the gratuitous naming of products is discouraged in programs designed primarily for children.

Appeals involving matters of health which should be determined by physicians should not be directed primarily to children.

4. No children's program personality or cartoon character shall be utilized to deliver commercial messages within or adjacent to the programs in which such a personality or cartoon character regularly appears. This provision shall also apply to lead-ins to commercials when such lead-ins contain sell copy or imply endorsement of the product by program personalities or cartoon characters.

5. Appeals to help fictitious characters in television programs by purchasing the advertiser's product or service or sending for a premium should not be permitted, and such fictitious characters should not be introduced into the advertising message for such purposes.

6. Commercials for services or over-the-counter products involving health considerations are of intimate and far-reaching importance to the consumer. The following principles should apply to such advertising:

　　a. Physicians, dentists or nurses or actors representing physicians, dentists or nurses, shall not be employed directly or by implication. These restrictions also apply to persons professionally engaged in medical services (e.g., physical therapists, pharmacists, dental assistants, nurses' aides).

b. Visual representations of laboratory settings may be employed, provided they bear a direct relationship to bona fide research which has been conducted for the product or service. (*See Television Code, X, 11*) In such cases, laboratory technicians shall be identified as such and shall not be employed as spokespersons or in any other way speak on behalf of the product.

c. Institutional announcements not intended to sell a specific product or service to the consumer and public service announcements by non-profit organizations may be presented by accredited physicians, dentists or nurses, subject to approval by the broadcaster. An accredited professional is one who has met required qualifications and has been licensed in his/her resident state.

7. Advertising should offer a product or service on its positive merits and refrain from discrediting, disparaging or unfairly attacking competitors, competing products, other industries, professions or institutions.

8. A sponsor's advertising messages should be confined within the framework of the sponsor's program structure. A television broadcaster should avoid the use of commercial announcements which are divorced from the program either by preceding the introduction of the program (as in the case of so-called "cow-catcher" announcements) or by following the apparent sign-off of the program (as in the case of so-called trailer or "hitch-hike" announcements). To this end, the program itself should be announced and clearly identified, both audio and video, before the sponsor's advertising material is first used, and should be signed off, both audio and video, after the sponsor's advertising material is last used.

9. Since advertising by televison is a dynamic technique, a television broadcaster should keep under surveillance new advertising devices so that the spirit and purpose of these standards are fulfilled.

10. A charge for television time to churches and religious bodies is not recommended.

11. Reference to the results of bona fide research, surveys or tests relating to the product to be advertised shall not be presented in a manner so as to create an impression of fact beyond that established by the work that has been conducted.

XI. *Advertising of Medical Products*

1. The advertising of medical products presents considerations of intimate and far-reaching importance to consumers because of the direct bearing on their health.

2. Because of the personal nature of the advertising of medical products, claims that a product will effect a cure and the indiscriminate use of such words as "safe," "without risk," "harmless," or terms of similar meaning should not be accepted in the advertising of medical products on television stations.

3. A television broadcaster should not accept advertising material which in his/her opinion offensively describes or dramatizes distress or morbid situations involving ailments, by spoken word, sound or visual effects.

XII. Contests

1. Contests shall be conducted with fairness to all entrants, and shall comply with all pertinent laws and regulations. Care should be taken to avoid the concurrent use of the three elements which together constitute a lottery—prize, chance and consideration.

2. All contest details, including rules, eligibility requirements, opening and termination dates should be clearly and completely announced and/or shown, or easily accessible to the viewing public, and the winners' names should be released and prizes awarded as soon as possible after the close of the contest.

3. When advertising is accepted which requests contestants to submit items of product identification or other evidence of purchase of products, reasonable facsimiles thereof should be made acceptable unless the award is based upon skill and not upon chance.

4. All copy pertaining to any contest (except that which is required by law) associated with the exploitation or sale of the sponsor's product or service, and all references to prizes or gifts offered in such connection should be considered a part of and included in the total time allowances as herein provided. (See Television Code, XIV)

XIII. Premiums and Offers

1. Full details of proposed offers should be required by the television broadcaster for investigation and approved before the first announcement of the offer is made to the public.

2. A final date for the termination of an offer should be announced as far in advance as possible.

3. Before accepting for telecast offers involving a monetary consideration, a television broadcaster should be satisfied as to the integrity of the advertiser and the advertiser's willingness to honor complaints indicating dissatisfaction with the premium by returning the monetary consideration.

4. There should be no misleading descriptions or visual representations of any premiums or gifts which would distort or enlarge their value in the minds of the viewers.

5. Assurances should be obtained from the advertiser that premiums offered are not harmful to person or property.

6. Premiums should not be approved which appeal to superstition on the basis of "luck-bearing" powers or otherwise.

XIV. Time Standards for Non-Program Material*

In order that the time for non-program material and its placement shall best serve the viewer, the following standards are set forth in accordance with sound television practice:

1. Non-Program Material Definition:

Non-program material, in both prime time and all other time, includes billboards, commercials, promotional announcements and all credits in excess

*See Time Standards for Independent Stations, p. 20.

of 30 seconds per program, except in feature films. In no event should credits exceed 40 seconds per program. The 40-second limitation on credits shall not apply, however, in any situation governed by a contract entered into before October 1, 1971. Public service announcements and promotional announcements for the same program are excluded from this definition.

2. Allowable Time for Non-Program Material:

a. In prime time on network affiliated stations, non-program material shall not exceed nine minutes 30 seconds in any 60-minute period.

Prime time is a continuous period of not less than three consecutive hours per broadcast day as designated by the station between the hours of 6:00 PM and midnight.

b. In all other time, non-program material shall not exceed 16 minutes in any 60-minute period.

c. Children's Programming Time—Defined as those hours other than prime time in which programs initially designed primarily for children under 12 years of age are scheduled.

Within this time period on Saturday and Sunday, non-program material shall not exceed nine minutes 30 seconds in any 60-minute period.

Within this time period on Monday through Friday, non-program material shall not exceed 12 minutes in any 60-minute period.

3. Program Interruptions:

a. Definition: A program interruption is any occurrence of non-program material within the main body of the program.

b. In prime time, the number of program interruptions shall not exceed two within any 30-minute program, or four within any 60-minute program.

Programs longer than 60 minutes shall be prorated at two interruptions per half-hour.

The number of interruptions in 60-minute variety shows shall not exceed five.

c. In all other time, the number of interruptions shall not exceed four within any 30-minute program period.

d. In children's weekend programming time, as above defined in 2c, the number of program interruptions shall not exceed two within any 30-minute program or four within any 60-minute program.

e. In both prime time and all other time, the following interruption standard shall apply within programs of 15 minutes or less in length:

5-minute program—1 interruption;
10-minute program—2 interruptions;
15-minute program—2 interruptions.

f. News, weather, sports and special events programs are exempt from the interruption standard because of the nature of such programs.

4. No more than four non-program material announcements shall be scheduled consecutively within programs, and no more than three non-program material announcements shall be scheduled consecutively during station breaks. The consecutive non-program material limitation shall not apply to a single sponsor who wishes to further reduce the number of interruptions in the program.

5. A multiple product announcement is one in which two or more products or services are presented within the framework of a single announcement. A multiple product announcement shall not be scheduled in a unit of time less than 60 seconds, except where integrated so as to appear to the viewer as a single message. A multiple product announcement shall be considered integrated and counted as a single announcement if:

    a. the products or services are related and interwoven within the framework of the announcement (related products or services shall be defined as those having a common character, purpose and use); and

    b. the voice(s), setting, background and continuity are used consistently throughout so as to appear to the viewer as a single message.

Multiple product announcements of 60 seconds in length or longer not meeting this definition of integration shall be counted as two or more announcements under this section of the Code. This provision shall not apply to retail or service establishments.

6. The use of billboards, in prime time and all other time, shall be confined to programs sponsored by a single or alternate week advertiser and shall be limited to the products advertised in the program.

7. Reasonable and limited identification of prizes and donors' names where the presentation of contest awards or prizes is a necessary part of program content shall not be included as non-program material as defined above.

8. Programs presenting women's/men's service features, shopping guides, fashion shows, demonstrations and similar material provide a special service to the public in which certain material normally classified as nonprogram is an informative and necessary part of the program content. Because of this, the time standards may be waived by the Code Authority to a reasonable extent on a case-by-case basis.

9. Gratuitous references in a program to a non-sponsor's product or service should be avoided except for normal guest identification.

10. Stationary backdrops or properties in television presentations showing the sponsor's name or product, the name of the sponsor's product, trademark or slogan should be used only incidentally and should not obtrude on program interest or entertainment.

Time Standards for Independent Stations

1. Non-program elements shall be considered as all-inclusive, with the exception of required credits, legally required station identifications, and "bumpers." Promotion spots and public service announcements, as well as commercials, are to be considered non-program elements.

2. The allowed time for non-program elements, as defined above, shall not exceed seven minutes in a 30-minute period or multiples thereof in prime time (prime time is defined as any three contigous hours between 6:00 PM and midnight, local time), or eight minutes in a 30-minute period or multiples thereof during all other times.

3. Where a station does not carry a commercial in a station break between programs, the number of program interruptions shall not exceed four within any 30-minute program, or seven within any 60-minute program, or 10 within any 90-minute program, or 13 in any 120-minute program. Stations

which do carry commercials in station breaks between programs shall limit the number of program interruptions to three within any 30-minute program, or six within any 60-minute program, or nine within any 90-minute program. News, weather, sports, and special events are exempted because of format.

4. Not more than four non-program material announcements as defined above shall be scheduled consecutively. An exception may be made only in the case of a program 60 minutes or more in length, when no more than seven non-program elements may be scheduled consecutively by stations who wish to reduce the number of program interruptions.

5. The conditions of paragraphs three and four shall not apply to live sports programs where the program format dictates and limits the number of program interruptions.

INTERPRETATIONS

Interpretation No. 1

June 7, 1956, Revised June 9, 1958
"Pitch" Programs
The "pitchman" technique of advertising on television is inconsistent with good broadcast practice and generally damages the reputation of the industry and the advertising profession.

Sponsored program-length segments consisting substantially of continuous demonstrations or sales presentation, violate not only the time standards established in the Code but the broad philosophy of improvement implicit in the voluntary Code operation and are not acceptable.

Interpretation No. 2

June 7, 1956
Hollywood Film Promotion
The presentation of commentary or film excerpts from current theatrical releases in some instances may constitute commercial material under the Time Standards for Non-Program Material. Specifically, for example, when such presentation, directly or by inference, urges viewers to attend, it shall be counted against the commercial allowance for the program of which it is a part.

Interpretation No. 3

January 23, 1959
Prize Identification
Aural and/or visual prize identification of up to 10 seconds duration may be deemed "reasonable and limited" under the language of Paragraph 7 of the Time Standards for Non-Program Material. Where such identification is longer than 10 seconds, the entire announcement or visual presentation will be charged against the total commercial time for the program period.

Interpretation No. 4

March 4, 1965
Drinking on Camera
    Paragraph 7, Section IX, General Advertising Standards, states that the "advertising of beer and wine is acceptable only when presented in the best of good taste and discretion." This requires that commercials involving beer and wine avoid any representation of on-camera drinking.

Interpretation No. 5

April 8, 1975
    The scheduling provisions of Section I (Principles Governing Program Content) shall not apply to programs under contract to a station as of April 8, 1975, all episodes of which were then in existence, if such station is unable, despite reasonable good faith efforts, to edit such programs to make them appropriate for family viewing or to reschedule them so as not to occupy family viewing periods. This exception shall in no event apply after September 1, 1977. Any such programs excepted from scheduling provisions shall, of course, bear the required advisory notices.

REGULATIONS AND PROCEDURES

    The following Regulations and Procedures shall obtain as an integral part of the Television Code of the National Association of Broadcasters:

I. Name

    The name of this Code shall be *The Television Code of the National Association of Broadcasters.**

II. Purpose of the Code

    The purpose of this Code is cooperatively to maintain a level of television programming which gives full consideration to the educational, informational, cultural, economic, moral and entertainment needs of the American public to the end that more and more people will be better served.

III. Subscribers

Section 1. Eligibility

    Any individual, firm or corporation which is engaged in the operation of a television broadcast station or network, or which holds a construction permit for a television broadcast station within the United States or its dependencies, shall, subject to the approval of the Television Board of Directors as hereinafter provided, be eligible to subscribe to the Television Code of the NAB to the extent of one subscription for each such station and/or network

---

* By-Laws of the National Association of Broadcasters, Article VI. Section 8, C: "Television Board. The Television Board is hereby authorized—(4) to enact, amend and promulgate standards of practice or codes for its Television members, and to establish such methods to secure observance thereof as it may deem advisible:—."

which it operates or for which it holds a construction permit; provided, that a nontelevision member of NAB shall not become eligible via Code subscription to receive any of the member services or to exercise any of the voting privileges of a member.

Section 2. Certification of Subscription

Upon subscribing to the Code, subject to the approval of the Television Board of Directors, there shall be granted forthwith to each such subscribing station authority to use the "NAB Television Seal of Good Practice," a copyrighted and registered seal to be provided in the form of a certificate, a slide and/or a film, signifying that the recipient thereof is a subscriber in good standing to the Television Code of the NAB. The seal and its significance shall be appropriately publicized by the NAB.

Section 3. Duration of Subscription

Subscription shall continue in full force and effect until 30 days after the first of the month following receipt of notice of written resignation. Subscription to the Code shall be effective from the date of application subject to the approval of the Television Board of Directors; provided, that the subscription of a television station going on the air for the first time shall, for the first six months of such subscription, be probationary, during which time its subscription can be summarily revoked by an affirmative two-thirds vote of the Television Board of Directors without the usual processes specified below.

Section 4. Suspension of Subscription

Any subscription, and/or the authority to utilize and show the above-noted seal, may be voided, revoked or temporarily suspended for television programming, including commercial copy, which, by theme, treatment or incident, in the judgment of the Television Board constitutes a continuing, willful or gross violation of any of the provisions of the Television Code, by an affirmative two-thirds vote of the Television Board of Directors at a regular or special meeting; provided, however, that the following conditions and procedures shall apply:

A. Preferring of Charges—Conditions Precedent:

Prior to the preferring of charges to the Television Board of Directors concerning violation of the Code by a subscriber, the Television Code Review Board (hereinafter provided for) (1) Shall have appropriately, and in good time, informed and advised such subscriber of any and all complaints and information coming to the attention of the Television Code Review Board and relating to the programming of said subscriber, (2) Shall have reported to, and advised, said subscriber by analysis, interpretation, recommendation or otherwise, of the possibility of a violation or breach of the Television Code by the subscriber, and (3) Shall have served upon the subscriber, by Registered Mail a Notice of Intent to prefer charges, at least 20 days prior to the filing of any such charges with the Television Board of Directors. During this period the Television Code Review Board may, within its sole discretion, reconsider its proposed action based upon such written reply as the subscriber may care to make, or upon such action as the subscriber may care to take program-wise, in conformance with the analysis, interpretation, or recommendation of the Television Code Review Board.

(i) Notice of Intent

The Notice of Intent shall include a statement of the grounds and reasons for the proposed charges, including appropriate references to the Television Code.

(ii) Time

In the event that the nature of the program in question is such that time is of the essence, the Television Code Review Board may prefer charges within less than the 20 days above specified, provided that a time certain in which reply may be made is included in its Notice of Intent, and provided that its reasons therefor must be specified in its statement of charges preferred.

B. *The Charges:*

The subscriber shall be advised in writing by Registered Mail of the charges preferred. The charges preferred by the Television Code Review Board to the Television Board of Directors shall include the grounds and reasons therefor, together with specific references to the Television Code. The charges shall contain a statement that the conditions precedent, herein before described, have been met.

C. *Hearing:*

The subscriber shall have the right to a hearing and may exercise same by filing an answer within 10 days of the date of such notification.

D. *Waiver:*

Failure to request a hearing shall be deemed a waiver of the subscriber's right thereto.

E. *Designation:*

If a hearing is requested by the subscriber, it shall be designated as promptly as possible and at such time and place as the Television Board may specify.

F. *Confidential Status:*

Hearings shall be closed; and all correspondence between a subscriber and the Television Code Review Board and/or the Television Board of Directors concerning specific programming shall be confidential; provided, however, that the confidential status of these procedures may be waived by a subscriber.

G. *Presentation; Representation:*

A subscriber against whom charges have been preferred, and who has exercised his/her right to a hearing, shall be entitled to effect presentation of his/her case personally, by agent, by attorney, or by deposition and interrogatory.

H. Intervention:

Upon request by the subscriber-respondent or the Television Code Review Board, the Television Board of Directors, in its discretion, may permit the intervention of one or more other subscribers as parties-in-interest.

I. Transcript:

A stenographic transcript record shall be taken and shall be certified by the Chairperson of the Television Board of Directors to the office of the Secretary of the National Association of Broadcasters, where it shall be maintained. The transcript shall not be open to inspection unless otherwise provided by the party respondent in the proceeding.

J. Television Code Review Board; Counsel:

The Television Code Review Board may, at its discretion, utilize the services of an attorney from the staff of the NAB for the purpose of effecting its presentation in a hearing matter.

K. Order of Procedure:

At hearings the Television Code Review Board shall open and close.

L. Cross-Examination:

The right of cross-examination shall specifically obtain. Where procedure has been by deposition or interrogatory, the use of cross-interrogatories shall satisfy this right.

M. Presentation:

Oral and written evidence may be introduced by the subscriber and by the Television Code Review Board. Oral argument may be had at the hearing and written memoranda or briefs may be submitted by the subscriber and by the Television Code Review Board. The Television Board of Directors may admit such evidence as it deems relevant, material and competent, and may determine the nature and length of the oral argument and the written argument of briefs.

N. Authority of Presiding Officer; of Television Board of Directors:

The Presiding Officer shall rule upon all interlocutory matters, such as, but not limited to, the admissibility of evidence, the qualifications of witnesses, etc. On all other matters, authority to act shall be vested in a majority of the Television Board unless otherwise provided.

O. Films, Transcriptions, etc.:

Films, kinescopes, records, transcriptions, or other mechanical reproductions of television programs, properly identified, shall be accepted into evidence when relevant.

P. Continuances and Extensions:

Continuance and extension of any proceeding or for the time of filing or performing any act required or allowed to be done within a specific time may be granted upon request, for a good cause shown. The Board or the Presiding Officer may recess or adjourn a hearing for such time as may be deemed necessary, and may change the place thereof.

Q. Findings and Conclusions:

The Television Board of Directors shall decide the case as expeditiously as possible and shall notify the subscriber and the Television Code Review Board, in writing, of the decision. The decision of the Television Board of Directors shall contain findings of fact with conclusions, as well as the reasons or bases therefor. Findings of fact shall set out in detail and with particularlity all basic evidentiary facts developed on the record (with appropriate citations to the transcript of record or exhibit relied on for each evidentiary fact) supporting the conclusion reached.

R. Reconsideration or Rehearing:

A request for reconsideration or rehearing may be filed by parties to the hearing. Requests for reconsideration or rehearing shall state with particularity in what respect the decision or any matter determined therein is claimed to be unjust, unwarranted, or erroneous, and with respect to any finding of fact shall specify the pages of record relied on. If the existence of any newly discovered evidence is claimed, the request shall be accompanied by a verified statement of the facts together with the facts relied on to show that the party, with due diligence, could not have known or discovered such facts at the time of the hearing.

The request for rehearing may seek:
a. Reconsideration
b. Additional oral argument
c. Reopening of the proceedings
d. Amendment of any findings, or
e. Other relief.

S. Time for Filing:

Requests for reconsideration or rehearing shall be filed within 10 days after receipt by the respondent of the decision. Opposition thereto may be filed within five days after the filing of the request.

T. Penalty, Suspension of:

At the discretion of the Television Board, application of any penalty provided for in the decision may be suspended until the Board makes final disposition of the requests for reconsideration or rehearing.

U. Disqualification:

Any member of the Television Board may disqualify himself/herself, or upon good cause shown by any interested party, may be disqualified by a majority vote of the Television Board.

Section 5. Additional Procedures

When necessary to the proper administration of the Code, additional rules of procedure will be established from time to time as authorized by the By-Laws of the NAB; in keeping therewith, special consideration shall be given to the procedures for receipt and processing of complaints and to necessary rules to be adopted from time to time, taking into account the source and nature of such complaints; such rules to include precautionary measures such as the posting of bonds to cover costs and expenses of processing same; and further provided that special consideration will be given to procedures insuring the confidential status of proceedings relating to Code observance.

Section 6. Amendment and Review

Because of the new and dynamic aspects inherent in television broadcast, the Television Code, as a living, flexible and continuing document, may be amended from time to time by the Television Board of Directors; provided that said Board is specifically charged with review and reconsideration of the entire Code, its appendices and procedures, at least once each year.

Section 7. Termination of Contracts

All subscribers on the air at the time of subscription to the Code shall be permitted that period prior to and including the earliest legal cancellation date to terminate any contracts, then outstanding, calling for program presentations which would not be in conformity with the Television Code, provided, however, that in no event shall such period be longer than 52 weeks.

IV. Affiliate Subscribers

Section 1. Eligibility

Any individual, firm or corporation, which is engaged in the production or distribution, lease, or sale of recorded programs for television presentation, subject to the approval of the Television Code Review Board as hereinafter provided, shall be eligible to become an affiliate subscriber to the Television Code of the NAB.

Section 2. Certification of Subscription

Upon becoming an affiliate subscriber to the Code, subject to the approval of the Television Code Review Board, there shall be granted forthwith to each such affiliate subscriber authority to use a copyrighted and registered seal and declaration, in a manner approved by the Television Code Review Board, identifying the individual firm or corporation as an affiliate subscriber to the Television Code of the NAB. Such authority shall not constitute formal clearance or approval by the Television Code Review Board of specific film programs or other recorded material.

Section 3. Duration of Affiliate Subscription

The affiliate subscription shall continue in full force and effect until 30 days after the first of the month following receipt of a written notice of resignation. The affiliate subscription of the Code shall be effective from the date of application subject to the approval of the Television Code Review Board.

Section 4. Suspension of Affiliate Subscription

Any affiliate subscription and the authority to utilize and show the above-noted seal may be voided, revoked, or temporarily suspended for the sale or distribution for television presentation of any film or other recorded material which by theme, treatment, or incident, in the judgment of the Television Code Review Board, constitutes a continuing, willful or gross violation of any of the provisions of the Television Code, by a majority vote of the Television Code Review Board at any regular or special meeting. The conditions and procedures applicable to subscribers shall not apply to affiliate subscribers.

Section 5. Representation of Affiliate Subscribers

Any affiliate subscriber or group of affiliate subscribers may authorize an individual or association to act for them in connection with their relations with the Television Code Review Board by filing a written notice of such representation with the Board. Such representation, however, in no way will limit the right of the Television Code Review Board to suspend individual affiliate subscribers in accordance with the provisions of Section 4.

V. Rates

Each subscriber and affiliate subscriber shall pay "adminstrative" rates in accordance with such schedule, at such time, and under such conditions as may be determined from time to time by the Television Board (*See Article VI, Section 8, C. Television Board (3) and (4), By-Laws of the NAB*); provided, that appropriate credit shall be afforded to a television member of the NAB against the regular dues paid to NAB.

VI. The Television Code Review Board

Section I. Composition

There shall be a continuing committee entitled the Television Code Review Board to be composed of not more than nine members, all of whom shall be from subscribers to the Television Code. They shall be appointed by the President of NAB, subject to confirmation by the Television Board, and may include one member from each of the subscribing nationwide television networks. Members of the Television Board shall not be eligible to serve on the Review Board. Due consideration shall be given, in making the appointments, to factors of diversification of geographical location, market size, company representation and network affiliation.

No person shall continue as a member of the Television Code Review Board if the station or entity he/she represents ceases to subscribe to the Television Code. In such case a vacancy occurs in the office immediately, and a successor may be appointed to serve out the unexpired term.

All terms shall be for two years, commencing at the close of the annual meeting of the membership following appointment.

A. Limitation of Service:

No person shall serve for more than two terms of two years each, consecutively, as a member of the Television Code Review Board; provided, however, this limitation shall not apply to network representatives.

Serving out the unexpired term of a former member shall not constitute a term within the meaning of this section.

B. Meetings:

The Television Code Review Board shall meet at least twice in each calendar year on a date to be determined by the Chairperson. The Chairperson, or the Code Authority Director, may, at any time, on at least five days written notice, call a special meeting of the Board.

C. Quorum:

For all purposes, a majority of the members of the Television Code Review Board shall constitute a quorum.

Section 2. Authority and Responsibilities

The Television Code Review Board is authorized and directed:

(1) To recommend to the Television Board of Directors amendments to the Television Code; (2) to consider, in its discretion, any appeal from any decision made by the Code Authority Director with respect to any matter which has arisen under the Code, and to suspend, reverse, or modify any such decision; (3) to prefer formal charges, looking toward the suspension or revocation of the authority to show the Code seal, to the Television Board of Directors concerning violations and breaches of the Television Code by a subscriber; (4) to be available to the Code Authority Director for consultation on any and all matters affecting the Television Code.

VII. Code Authority Director

Section 1. Director

There shall be a position designated as the Code Authority Director. This position shall be filled by appointment of the President of NAB, subject to the approval of the Board of Directors.

Section 2. Authority and Responsibilities

The Code Authority Director is authorized and directed: 1) To maintain a continuing review of all programming and advertising material presented over television, especially that of subscribers to the Television Code of NAB: (2) to receive, screen and clear complaints concerning television programming; (3) to define and interpret words and phrases in the Television Code; (4) to develop and maintain appropriate liaison with governmental agencies and with responsible and accountable organizations and institutions; (5) to inform, expeditiously and properly, a subscriber to the Television Code of complaints or commendations, as well as to advise all subscribers concerning the attitudes and desires program-wise of accountable organizations and institutions, and of the American public in general; (6) to review and monitor, if necessary, any certain series of programs, daily programming, or any other program presentations of a subscriber, as well as to request recorded material, or script and copy, with regard to any certain program presented by a subscriber; (7) to reach conclusions and make recommendations or prefer charges to the Television Code Review Board concerning violations and breaches of the Television Code by a subscriber; (8) to recommend to the Code Review Board amendments to the Television Code.

A. Delegation of Powers and Responsibilities:

The Code Authority Director shall appoint such executive staff as is needed, consistent with resources, to carry out the above described functions, and may delegate to this staff such responsibilities as he/she may deem necessary.

Code of the Comics Magazine Association of America, Inc. *

CODE FOR EDITORIAL MATTER

General Standards—Part A
1. Crimes shall never be presented in such a way as to promote distrust of the forces of law and justice, or to inspire others with a desire to imitate criminals.
2. No comics shall explicitly present the unique details and methods of a crime, with the exception of those crimes that are so farfetched or pseudoscientific that no would-be lawbreaker could reasonably duplicate.
3. Policemen, judges, government officials and respected institutions shall not be presented in such a way as to create disrespect for established authority. If any of these is depicted committing an illegal act, it must be declared as an exceptional case and that the culprit pay the legal price.
4. If crime is depicted it shall be as a sordid and unpleasant activity.
5. Criminals shall not be presented in glamorous circumstances, unless an unhappy end results from their ill-gotten gains, and creates no desire for emulation.
6. In every instance good shall triumph over evil and the criminal punished for his misdeeds.

* Reprinted by permission of the Comics Magazine Association of America, Inc.

7. Scenes of excessive violence shall be prohibited. Scenes of brutal torture, excessive and unnecessary knife and gun play, physical agony, gory and gruesome crime shall be eliminated.
8. No unique or unusual methods of concealing weapons shall be shown, except where such concealment could not reasonably be duplicated.
9. Instances of law enforcement officers dying as a result of a criminal's activities should be discouraged, except when the guilty, because of their crime, live a sordid existence and are brought to justice because of the particular crime.
10. The crime of kidnapping shall never be portrayed in any detail, nor shall any profit accrue to the abductor or kidnapper. The criminal or the kidnapper must be punished in every case.
11. The letters of the word "crime" on a comics magazine cover shall never be appreciably greater in dimension than the other words contained in the title. The word "crime" shall never appear alone on a cover.
12. Restraint in the use of the word "crime" in titles or subtitles shall be exercised.

General Standards—Part B

1. No comic magazine shall use the word horror or terror in its title. These words may be used judiciously in the body of the magazine.*
2. All scenes of horror, excessive bloodshed, gory or gruesome crimes, depravity, lust, sadism, masochism shall not be permitted.
3. All lurid, unsavory, gruesome illustrations shall be eliminated.
·4. Inclusion of stories dealing with evil shall be used or shall be published only where the intent is to illustrate a moral issue and in no case shall evil be presented alluringly nor so as to injure the sensibilities of the reader.
5. Scenes dealing with, or instruments associated with walking dead, or torture shall not be used. Vampires, ghouls and werewolves shall be permitted to be used when handled in the classic tradition such as Frankenstein, Dracula and other high calibre literary works written by Edgar Allen Poe, Saki (H. H. Munro), Conan Doyle and other respected authors whose works are read in schools throughout the world.
6. Narcotics or Drug addiction shall not be presented except as a vicious habit.
   Narcotics or Drug addiction or the illicit traffic in addiction-producing narcotics or drugs shall not be shown or described if the presentation:
   (a) Tends in any manner to encourage, stimulate or justify the use of such narcotics or drugs; or
   (b) Stresses, visually, by text or dialogue, their temporarily attractive effects; or
   (c) Suggests that the narcotics or drug habit may be quickly or easily broken; or
   (d) Shows or describes details of narcotics or drug procurement, or

---

*The Board of Directors has ruled that a judicious use does not include the words "Horror" or "Terror" in story titles within the magazine.

the implements or devices used in taking narcotics or drugs, or of the taking of narcotics or drugs in any manner; or

(e) Emphasizes the profits of the narcotics or drug traffic; or

(f) Involves children who are shown knowingly to use or traffic in narcotics or drugs; or

(g) Shows or implies a casual attitude towards the taking of narcotics or drugs; or

(h) Emphasizes the taking of narcotics or drugs throughout, or in a major part, of the story, and leaves the denouement to the final panels.

General Standards — Part C

All elements or techniques not specifically mentioned herein, but which are contrary to the spirit and intent of the Code, and are considered violations of good taste or decency, shall be prohibited.

DIALOGUE

1. Profanity, obscenity, smut, vulgarity, or words or symbols which have acquired undesirable meanings—judged and interpreted in terms of contemporary standards—are forbidden.
2. Special precautions to avoid disparaging references to physical afflictions or deformities shall be taken.
3. Although slang and colloquialisms are acceptable, excessive use should be discouraged and wherever possible good grammar shall be employed.

RELIGION

1. Ridicule or attack on any religious or racial group is never permissible.

COSTUME

1. Nudity in any form is prohibited. Suggestive and salacious illustration is unacceptable.
2. Females shall be drawn realistically without undue emphasis on any physical quality.

MARRIAGE AND SEX

1. Divorce shall not be treated humorously nor represented as desirable.
2. Illicit sex relations are not to be portrayed and sexual abnormalities are unacceptable.
3. All situations dealing with the family unit should have as their ultimate goal the protection of the children and family life. In no way shall the breaking of the moral code be depicted as rewarding.
4. Rape shall never be shown or suggested. Seduction may not be shown.
5. Sex perversion or any inference to same is strictly forbidden.

CODE FOR ADVERTISING MATTER

These regulations are applicable to all magazines published by members of the Comics Magazine Association of America, Inc. Good taste shall be the guiding principle in the acceptance of advertising.

1. Liquor and tobacco advertising is not acceptable.
2. Advertisement of sex or sex instruction books are unacceptable.
3. The sale of picture postcards, "pin-ups," "art studies," or any other reproduction of nude or semi-nude figures is prohibited.
4. Advertising for the sale of knives, concealable weapons, or realistic gun facsimiles is prohibited.
5. Advertising for the sale of fireworks is prohibited.
6. Advertising dealing with the sale of gambling equipment or printed matter dealing with gambling shall not be accepted.
7. Nudity with meretricious purpose and salacious postures shall not be permitted in the advertising of any product; clothed figures shall never be presented in such a way as to be offensive or contrary to good taste or morals.
8. To the best of his ability, each publisher shall ascertain that all statements made in advertisements to conform to fact and avoid misrepresentation.
9. Advertisement of medical, health, or toiletry products of questionable nature are to be rejected. Advertisements for medical, health or toiletry products endorsed by the American Medical Association, or the American Dental Association, shall be deemed acceptable if they conform with all other conditions of the Advertising Code.

THE COMICS CODE AUTHORITY

The Code Authority of the Comics Magazine Association of America, Inc. was established at the same time the Code was adopted, to ascertain compliance with the terms of the Code. It is headed by a Code Administrator, who has no connection with any publisher, and who exercises independent judgment to determine whether the material intended for publication meets Code standards.

Publisher-members of the CMAA are required to submit their original text and art-work to the Code Authority, *in advance of publication*. The staff carefully checks each panel of art and every line of text, ordering such changes or deletions as in the judgment of the Administrator violates any tenet or the over-all principle of the Code. Being an industry self-regulation program, the publisher may appeal the decision of the Administrator to the CMAA's Board of Directors, but in nearly two decades of operation, this privilege has been rarely used. In almost every instance, the decision of the Administrator has prevailed.

Finally, each individual page must receive the stamp of approval of the Code Authority, or authorization from the Board of Directors, before the publisher may place the official Seal of Approval on the upper right-hand portion of the comics magazine's cover.

Public Relations Society of America Code of Professional Standards for the Practice of Public Relations *

(This Code, adopted by the PRSA Assembly, replaces a similar Code of Professional Standards for the Practice of Public Relations previously in force since 1954 and strengthened by revisions in 1959)

DECLARATION OF PRINCIPLES

Members of the Public Relations Society of America base their professional principles on the fundamental value and dignity of the individual, holding that the free exercise of human rights, especially freedom of speech, freedom of assembly and freedom of the press, is essential to the practice of public relations.

In serving the interests of clients and employers, we dedicate ourselves to the goals of better communication, understanding and cooperation among the diverse individuals, groups and institutions of society.

We pledge:

To conduct ourselves professionally, with truth, accuracy, fairness and responsibility to the public;

To improve our individual competence and advance the knowledge and proficiency of the profession through continuing research and education;

And to adhere to the articles of the Code of Professional Standards for the Practice of Public Relations as adopted by the governing Assembly of the Society.

ARTICLES OF THE CODE

These articles have been adopted by the Public Relations Society of America to promote and maintain high standards of public service and ethical conduct among its members.

1. A member shall deal fairly with clients or employers, past and present, with fellow practitioners and the general public.

2. A member shall conduct his or her professional life in accord with the public interest.

3. A member shall adhere to truth and accuracy and to generally accepted standards of good taste.

4. A member shall not represent conflicting or competing interests without the express consent of those involved, given after a full disclosure of the facts; nor place himself or herself in a position where the member's interest is or may be in conflict with a duty to a client, or others, without a full disclosure of such interests to all involved.

5. A member shall safeguard the confidences of both present and former clients or employers and shall not accept retainers or employment which may

---

* Reprinted by permission of the Public Relations Society of America.
Adopted and effective April 29, 1977.

involve the disclosure or use of these confidences to the disadvantage or prejudice of such clients or employers.

6. A member shall not engage in any practice which tends to corrupt the integrity of channels of communication or the processes of government.

7. A member shall not intentionally communicate false or misleading information and is obligated to use care to avoid communication of false or misleading information.

8. A member shall be prepared to identify publicly the name of the client or employer on whose behalf any public communication is made.

9. A member shall not make use of any individual or organization purporting to serve or represent an announced case, or purporting to be independent or unbiased, but actually serving an undisclosed special or private interest of a member, client or employer.

A member shall not intentially injure the professional reputation or practice of another practitioner.

However, if a member has evidence that another member has been guilty of unethical, illegal or unfair practices, including those in violation of this Code, the member shall present the information promptly to the proper authorities of the Society for action in accordance with the procedure set forth in Article XIII of the Bylaws.

11. A member called as a witness in a proceeding for the enforcement of this Code shall be bound to appear, unless excused for sufficient reason by the Judicial Panel.

12. A member, in performing services for a client or employer, shall not accept fees, commissions or any other valuable consideration from anyone other than the client or employer in connection with those services without the express consent of the client or employer, given after a full disclosure of the facts.

13. A member shall not guarantee the achievement of specified results beyond the member's direct control.

14. A member shall, as soon as possible, sever relations with any organization or individual if such relationship requires conduct contrary to the articles of this Code.

Appendix B
Glossary of Mass Communication Concepts

Agenda Setting refers to the ability of the media to channel or focus attention on one issue over another. The amount of attention the media give to a topic determines its importance in the minds of the public.

Aggressive Cues Theory assumes that exposure to aggressive stimuli on television will increase a person's level of physiological and emotional arousal, which in turn will increase the probability of his or her aggressive behavior.

Authoritarian is a philosophy based on the idea that control should be in the hands of the wise; hence the authority of the state over the individual. The government assumes caretaking powers, whereas the rights of the individual become restricted for the greater good of the state. Thus the government may exercise open or more subtle control of its media.

Canalization refers to the ability of the mass media to influence public attitudes and behavior. The mass media can be effective in maintaining, creating, or changing particular values, attitudes, and behaviors through confirming something we already believe, clarifying something we already know, or extending our knowledge of what we have already accepted. An example would be a toothpaste commercial that reinforces the idea that brushing our teeth is good for us and that trying the new brand of toothpaste may prove to be a pleasant and rewarding experience.

Catharsis is the relief of normal frustrations acquired in daily life, which eventually might lead individuals to engage in aggression, through vicarious participation in others' aggressions as depicted, for example, on television.

Channel is the medium through which messages are transmitted from source to receiver.

Channel Noise refers to any distraction or disturbance in the reception of a mass-communicated message caused by such factors as radio static, fuzziness on a TV screen, torn pages in a book, or blurred newsprint.

Communication Satellite is a relay station in space that can be used to provide either intranational or international communications.

Communications Revolution refers to the period beginning with the advent of printing and extending to contemporary communication technology—a period embracing a mere 500 years compared to the million years or so that intervened between the development of speaking and the development of writing. The Communications Revolution is marked by the mass production of symbols.

Cultural Indicators is the name given by George Gerbner to describe his analytical approach to television programming according to carefully constructed measures. According to Gerbner, over a long-term period, researchers might be able to better assess the impact of television on society through a scientific study of the content of television.

Cultural Norms Perspectives refers to the power of the mass media to define cultural norms through the facilitation of opinion change and reinforcement, the creation of new values, and the modification of present values, hence "changing" the audience.

Entropy represents the measure of uncertainty or freedom of choice within a system.

Equifinality means that the same final state may be reached by initial conditions in various ways.

Fairness Doctrine is based on the twin concepts that the airwaves belong to the public and that broadcasters are licensed to operate in the public interest, need, and necessity and states that broadcasters must offer fair opportunity for opposing sides to answer controversial public discussions.

Feedback monitors back a communicator's activity and allows for self-regulation.

Feedfront is the process of pretesting ideas, concepts, and programs on a group of experts or on a select audience by producers and programmers.

Gatekeeper, in a formal mass communication network, may be a communicator such as a reporter, editor, or publisher who is instrumental in the transmission of information and decision making with regard to mass media content. In an informal communication situation a gatekeeper is anyone who has access to information and who is instrumental in the relay and transmission of that information from one individual to another.

Individual Differences is a theoretical concept that points out that the differences in mass communications behavior are the products of differences in the individual's personality traits, attitudes, values, and beliefs.

Libertarian applies to privately owned media that advocate the "open marketplace of ideas" and whose mission is to keep a check on the government so that the individual can discriminate between right and wrong.

Ludenic (Play) Theory of Mass Communication simply states that the individual uses the mass media for his or her enjoyment, hence play versus work. Stephenson, the author of this theory, makes the distinction between communication-pleasure and communication-pain and neither debits communication-pleasure nor credits communication-pain. He feels that mass communication play behavior is useful and that more emphasis should be placed on the play and pleasure elements of mass communication and not on information theory of mass communication.

Mass Communication is the process by which the same message is simultaneously and publicly transmitted via a mass medium to large numbers of people, who are heterogeneous, spatially separated, and unknown to each other and to the communicator.

Mass Communications are the mass media.

Medio Communication is a hybrid form of communication that has the elements of both interpersonal and mass communication. As in mass communication a technical instrument is used to transmit messages to reach a heterogeneous audience at different times and places, but as in interpersonal communication the senders and receivers are small in number. Medio communication may include communication via telephone, audio tapes, home movies, or closed-circuit television.

N-Step Flow refers to the process by which mass media messages reach audience members—often indirectly through those who attend to the mass media and then pass the messages along, in their roles as influentials or opinion leaders, to their less active associates.

Narcotization results from the individual's substituting awareness as a result of his or her exposure to the mass media's reporting of public issues for social action.

"No-Effects Theory" (Reinforcement) refers to the reinforcement effect of the mass media; hence an effect.

Observational Learning Theory assumes that aggressive behavior results from the observation of aggression on TV programs and under certain conditions, from the modeling of behavior after aggressive TV characters.

Opinion Leaders are those individuals who attend more to the mass media than do those whom they influence. They pass on information gained from the mass media along with their own interpretations of the media content.

Privatization refers to the dysfunctional behavior of the individual who retreats to matters of private concern as a result of communication overload from the news media.

Reinforcement Theory of Violence states that televised violence reinforces whatever established patterns of violent behavior are possessed by the individual; *no significant increases or decreases* in the probability of audience aggression are implied.

Selective Exposure refers to the individual's exposure to those communications that are in accord with his or her interests and opinions and the avoidance of those communications that are not in accord with his or her interests and opinions.

Selective Perception refers to the individual's ability to misperceive and misinterpret communications that do not agree with his or her predispositions in the direction favorable to those predispositions.

Selective Retention refers to the tendency of the individual to learn material with which he or she agrees more readily and to forget more readily material with which he or she disagrees.

Semantic Noise in mass communication can occur when the communicator speaks in a different language, has cultural differences, or otherwise communicates in a manner not understood by the audience.

Social Categories Perspectives assumes that individuals can be grouped into broad collectivities on the basis of shared orientations or characteristics such as age, education, sex, income, and occupation, which in turn will cause them to select roughly identical mass communication content and react to it in a fairly uniform manner.

Social Relationships Perspectives refers to the individual's reference group relationships as determinants of the influence of mass media messages on his or her behavior.

Social Responsibility Philosophy is an extension of the libertarian philosophy in that the media recognize their responsibility to resolve conflict through discussion and to promote public opinion, consumer action, private rights, and important social interests.

Soviet-Communist Philosophy is an extension of the authoritarian philosophy whose purpose is to utilize its media to promote the objectives of the Soviet Socialist Party.

Status Conferral is the ability of the mass media to confer status, legitimize, or single out a person, organization, social issue, or social movement by focusing attention on it.

System represents a portion of the universe that is perceived as an entity capable of maintaining its identity in spite of internal changes.

Uses and Gratifications Approach Contends that the audience goes to the media for specific gratifications, using the mass media rather than being used by the mass media.

Appendix C
Referenced Bibliography

Adler, Richard. "Understanding Television: An Overview of the Literature of the Medium as a Social and Cultural Force." In Douglass Cater et al. (eds.), *Television as a Social Force: New Approaches to TV Criticism*. New York: Praeger Publishers, 1975, pp. 23–47.

Adler, Richard, and Baer, Walter S. *The Electronic Box Office*. New York: Praeger Publishers, 1974.

Aldrich, Paul. *The Impact of Mass Media*. New Rochelle, N.J.: Hayden Book Company, 1975.

"As 175 Million Americans Watched." *Newsweek* **62**, December 9, 1963, 88–90.

Bagdikian, Ben H. "How Communications May Shape Our Future Environment." *AAUW Journal* **62(3)**, March 1969, 123–126.

Baran, Paul. "On The Impact of the New Communications Media upon Social Values." In Alan Casty (ed.), *Mass Media and Mass Man*. New York: Holt, Rinehart and Winston, 1973.

Baran, Stanley J., and Henke, Lucy L. "The Regulation of Televised Violence." *Communication Quarterly* **24(4)**, Fall 1976, 24–30.

Barker, Larry L., and Kibler, Robert J. *Speech Communication Behavior: Perspectives and Principles*. Englewood Cliffs, N.J.: Prentice-Hall, 1971.

Bauer, Raymond. "The Obstinate Audience: The Influence Process from the Point of View of Social Communication." *American Psychologist* **19**, 1964, 319–328.

Beattie, Earle. "In Canada's Centennial Year, U.S. Mass Media Influence Probed." *Journalism Quarterly* **44**, 1967, 667–672.

Berelson, Bernard. "Communications and Public Opinion." In Wilbur Schramm (ed.), *Mass Communications*. Urbana: University of Illinois Press, 1949.

Berlo, David K. *The Process of Communication*. New York: Holt, Rinehart and Winston, 1960.

Beuf, Ann. "Doctor, Lawyer, Household Drudge." *Journal of Communication* **24(2)**, Spring 1974, 142–145.

Beuth, Philip R. "Canada Stance Is Called 'Discriminatory.' " *Buffalo Courier-Express*, February 29, 1976, 9.

Bohn, Thomas, and Shomgren, Richard. *Light and Shadows: A History of Motion Pictures.* Port Washington, N.Y.: Alfred Publishing Co., 1975.

Bower, Robert T. *Television and the Public.* New York: Holt, Rinehart and Winston, 1973.

Breitrose, Henry S. "Film as Communication." In Ithiel de Sola Pool and Wilbur Schramm (eds.), *Handbook of Communication.* Chicago: Rand McNally, 1973, pp. 559–576.

"Broadcasting and the Minorities." *Broadcasting* **74,** March 18, 1968, 50, 52.

Brown, Lee. *The Reluctant Reformation.* New York: David McKay Co., 1974.

Canada. Statistics Canada. *Canada Yearbook, 1966.* Ottawa: Information Canada, 1966.

Carey, James W. "The Communications Revolution and the Professional Communicator." In Paul Halmos (ed.), *The Sociology of Mass-Media Communicators. The Sociological Review*, Monograph 13, January 1969, 23–38.

Carey, James W. "Harold Adam Innes and Marshall McLuhan." *Antioch Review* **27,** 1967, 5–39.

Carlson, Verne, and Carlson, Sylvia. *Professional 16/35 mm Cameraman's Handbook.* New York: American Photographic Book Publishing Company, 1970.

Carpenter, Edmund, and Heyman, Ken. *They Became What They Beheld.* New York: Dutton, 1970.

Cassata, Mary B., and Palmer, Roger Cain. *Reader in Library Communication.* Englewood, Colo.: Information Handling Services, 1976.

Chayefsky, Paddy. "Marty." In *Television Plays.* New York: Simon and Schuster, 1955, pp. 135–172.

Chicano Media Committee. "By-Laws of the National Chicano Media Council." New York, August 3, 1970.

Cohen, Bernard C. *The Press and Foreign Policy.* Princeton, N.J.: Princeton University Press, 1963.

Commission on Freedom of the Press. *A Free and Responsible Press.* Chicago: University of Chicago Press, 1947.

COMSAT. Report to the President and the Congress, 1968.

Culley, James D., and Bennett, Rex. "Selling Women, Selling Blacks." *Journal of Communication* **26(4),** August 1976, 160–173.

Davison, W. Phillips, Boylan, James, and Yu, Frederick T. C. *Mass Media Systems and Effects.* New York: Praeger Publishers, 1976.

DeFleur, Melvin L. *Theories of Mass Communication.* New York: David McKay Co., 1966.

DeFleur, Melvin L., and Ball-Rokeach, Sandra. *Theories of Mass Communication*, 3rd ed. New York: David McKay Co., 1975.

DeMott, Benjamin. "The Viewer's Experience: Notes on TV Criticism and Public Health." in Douglas Cater et al. (eds.), *Television as a Social Force: New Approaches to TV Criticism.* New York: Praeger Publishers, 1975, pp. 49–60.

Diamond, Edwin. *The Tin Kazoo: Television, Politics, and the News.* Cambridge, Mass.: MIT Press, 1975.

Downing, Mildred. "Heroine of the Daytime Serial." *Journal of Communication* **24(2)**, Spring 1974, 130–137.

Emery, Edwin. *The Press and America*, 2nd ed. Englewood Cliffs, N.J.: Prentice-Hall, 1962.

Emery, Edwin, Ault, Phillip, and Agee, Warren. *Introduction to Mass Communications*. New York: Dodd, Mead and Company, 1976.

Gerbner, George. "Communication and Social Environment." *Scientific American*, September 1972, 153–162.

Gerbner, George. "Towards a General Model of Communication." *Audio-Visual Communication Review* **4(3)**, 1956, 171–199.

Gerbner, George, and Gross, Larry. "Living with Television: The Violence Profile." *Journal of Communication* **26(2)**, Spring 1976, 173–199.

Gerbner, George, and Gross, Larry. "The Scary World of TV's Heavy Viewer." *Psychology Today*, April 1976, 41–45, 89.

Glass, Marty. "What's News?" In Robert J. Glessing and William P. White (eds.), *Mass Media: The Invisible Environment Revisited*. Chicago: Science Research Associates, 1976, pp. 115–116.

Goodlet, Carlton B. "The Black Press: A Democratic Society's Catalytic Agent for Building Tomorrow's America." In Henry La Brie (ed.), *Perspectives of the Black Press, 1974*. Kennebunkport, Me.: Mercer House Press, 1974.

Grierson, John. "The Last Interview." *Film Quarterly* **26(1)**, Fall 1972, 24–30.

Haas, Alan D. "How Violent Is Junior's TV Fare?" *Buffalo Courier Express Magazine*, November 14, 1976.

Hanneman, Gerhard J., and McEwen, William J. *Communication and Behavior*. Reading, Mass.: Addison-Wesley, 1975.

Hendrick, Grant H. "When Television Is a School for Criminals," *TV Guide* (January 29, 1977).

Hentoff, Nat. "Students as Media Critics: A New Course." In Robert J. Glessing and William P. White (eds.), *Mass Media: The Invisible Environment*. Chicago: Science Research Associates, 1973, pp. 288–291.

Hester, Al. "International News Agencies." In Alan Wells (ed.) *Mass Communications: A World View*. Palo Alto, Calif.: Mayfield Publishing Co., 1974.

Hiebert, Ray Eldon, Ungurait, Donald F., and Bohn, Thomas W. *Mass Media: An Introduction to Modern Communication*. New York: David McKay Co., 1974.

Hulten, Olof. "The Intelsat System: Its Present and Future Use for Broadcasting." In Michael C. Emery and Ted Curtis Smythe (eds.), *Readings in Mass Communication*. Dubuque, Ia.: W. C. Brown Co., 1974, pp. 343–352.

Johnson, Nicholas. *How to Talk Back to Your Television Set*. New York: Bantam Books, 1970.

Katz, Elihu, Blumler, Jay G., and Gurevitch, Michael. "Uses and Gratifications Research." *Public Opinion Quarterly*, Winter 1973–1974.

Katz, Elihu, Gurevitch, Michael, and Haas, Hadassah. "On the Use of the Mass Media for Important Things." *American Sociological Review* **38**, April 1973, 164–181.

Khandelwal, Brij. "Third World Presses Ahead on Newspool Plans." *Encore*, October 4, 1976, 16–17.

Klapper, Joseph. *The Effects of Mass Communication.* New York: Free Press, 1960.

Knight, Arthur. *The Liveliest Art.* New York: New American Library, 1957.

Knight, Robert P. "UNESCO's International Communication Activities." In Heinz-Dietrich Fischer and John Calhoun Merrill (eds.), *International Communication.* (New York: Hastings House, 1970.

Knoff, Terry A. "Media Myths on Violence." In Alan Wells (ed.), *Mass Media and Society.* Palo Alto, Calif.: Mayfield Publishing Co., 1975, pp. 256–262.

LaBrie, Henry. *Perspectives of the Black Press, 1974.* Kennebunkport, Me.: Mercer House Press, 1974.

Lasswell, Harold D. "The Structure and Function of Communication in Society." In Lyman Bryson (ed.), *The Communication of Ideas.* New York: Harper & Bros., 1948.

Lazarsfled, Paul F., Berelson, Bernard, and Gaudet, Hazel. *The People's Choice.* New York: Columbia University Press, 1948.

Leab, Daniel J. *From Sambo to Super Spade: The Black Experience in Motion Pictures.* Boston: Houghton-Mifflin, 1975.

Levinson, Richard M. "From Olive Oyl to Sweet Polly Purebread: Sex Role Stereotypes and Televised Cartoons." *Journal of Popular Culture* **9(3)**, Winter 1975, 561–572.

Lichty, Lawrence, and Topping, Malachi. *A Sourcebook on the History of Radio and Television.* New York: Hastings House, 1975.

Liebert, Robert M., Davidson, Emily S., and Neale, John M. "Aggression in Childhood: The Impact of Television." In Victor B. Cline (ed.), *Where Do You Draw the Line?* Provo, Utah: Brigham Young University Press, 1974, pp. 113–128.

Liebert, Robert M., Neale, John M., and Davidson, Emily S. *The Early Window: Effects of Television on Children and Youths.* New York: Pergamon Press, 1973.

Lippmann, Walter. *Public Opinion.* New York: Free Press, 1965.

Littner, Ner. "A Psychiatrist Looks at Television and Violence." In Rod Halgrem and William Norton (eds.), *The Mass Media Book.* Englewood Cliffs, N.J.: Prentice-Hall, 1972, pp. 343–356.

Lundberg, D., and Hulten, Olof. *Individen Och Massmedia.* Stockholm: EFI, 1968.

Machlup, Fritz. *The Production and Distribution of Knowledge.* Princeton, N.J.: Princeton University Press, 1962.

McGarry, K. L. *Communication, Knowledge, and the Librarian.* Hamden, Conn.: Shoe String Press, 1975.

McLuhan, Marshall. *Understanding Media: The Extensions of Man.* New York: McGraw-Hill, 1964.

Merrill, John C., and Lowenstein, Ralph L. *Media, Messages and Men: New Perspectives in Communication.* New York: David McKay Co., 1971.

Meyer, Timothy P. "Some Observations on Differences Between Current Film and Television Violence." *Journal of the University Film Association* **24,** 1972, 112–115.

Morris, Joe A. *Deadline Every Minute.* Garden City, N.Y.: Doubleday, 1957.

Murphy, Robert D. *Mass Communication and Human Interaction.* Boston: Houghton-Mifflin, 1977.

National Association of Broadcasters. "The Television Code," 18 ed. June 1975.

Palmer, L. F., Jr. "The Black Press in Transition." In Michael C. Emery and Ted Curtis Smythe (eds.), *Readings in Mass Communication.* Dubuque, Ia.: W. C. Brown Co., 1974, pp. 297–305.

Pingree, Suzanne et al. "A Scale for Sexism." *Journal of Communication* **26(4),** Autumn 1976, 193–200.

Plato. *Phaedrus.* New York: Liberal Arts Press, 1956.

Plato. *The Republic.* New York: Basic Books, 1968.

Prowitt, Marsha O'Bannon. "The Federal Communications Commission." In Joseph Fletcher Littell (ed.), *Coping with Television.* Evanston, Ill.: McDougal, Littell & Company, 1973, pp. 31–36.

Reisz, Karel. *Technique of Film Editing.* New York: Farrar, Straus, and Cudahy, 1953.

Rosewater, Victor. *History of Cooperative News—Gathering in the United States.* New York: D. Appleton and Company, 1930.

Rosten, Leo. "The Intellectual and the Mass Media: Some Rigorously Random Remarks." *Daedalus* **89(2),** Spring 1960, 333–346.

Rotha, Paul, Road, Sinclair, and Griffith, Richard. *Documentary Film.* New York: Hastings House, 1943.

Salisbury, Harrison Evans. *Russia.* New York: Atheneum, 1965.

Sarnoff, David. *Looking Ahead.* New York: McGraw-Hill, 1968.

Schramm, Wilbur. "Information Theory and Mass Communication." *Journalism Quarterly* **32,** Spring 1955, 131–146.

Schramm, Wilbur. *Men, Messages, and Media: A Look at Human Communication.* New York: Harper & Row, 1973.

Schramm, Wilbur. "The Nature of Communications Between Humans." In Wilbur Schramm and Donald F. Roberts (eds.), *The Process and Effects of Mass Communication,* rev. ed. Urbana: University of Illinois Press, 1971, pp. 3–53.

Schwartz, Tony. *The Responsive Chord.* Garden City, N.Y.: Anchor Press/Doubleday, 1973.

Sears, David O. "Selective Exposure of Information: A Critical Review." In Thomas Beisecker and Donn Parson (eds.), *The Process of Social Influence.* Englewood Cliffs, N.J.: Prentice-Hall, 1972.

Sereno, Kenneth K., and Mortensen, C. David. *Foundations of Communication Theory.* New York: Harper & Row, 1970.

Siebert, Fred S., Peterson, Theodore, and Schramm, Wilbur. *Four Theories of the Press.* Urbana: University of Illinois Press, 1956.

Singer, Benjamin D. "Violence, Protest, and War in Television News: The

U.S. and Canada Compared." *The Public Opinion Quarterly* **34**, Winter 1970–1971, 234–241.

Smith, Arthur L. *Transracial Communication*. Englewood Cliffs, N.J.: Prentice-Hall, 1973.

Steinfeld, Jesse L., M.D. "TV Violence Is Harmful." In Alan Wells (ed.), *Mass Media and Society*. Palo Alto, Calif.: Mayfield Publishing Co., 1975, pp. 263–265.

Stephenson, William. *The Play Theory of Mass Communication*. Chicago: University of Chicago Press, 1967.

Storey, Graham. *Reuter: The Story of a Century of News Gathering*. New York: Crown Publishers, 1951.

Tedesco, Nancy S. "Patterns in Prime Time." *Journal of Communication* **24(2)**, Spring 1974, 119–124.

Television and Growing Up: The Impact of Televised Violence. Surgeon General's Scientific Advisory Committee on Television and Social Behavior, 1972.

Turow, Joseph. "Advising and Ordering: Daytime Prime Time." *Journal of Communication* **24(2)**, Spring 1974, 138–141.

UNESCO. *News Agencies: Their Structure and Operation*. Paris: UNESCO, 1953.

UNESCO. *World Communications*. New York: UNESCO, 1964.

U.S. National Advisory Commission on Civil Disorders. New York: Bantam Books, 1968.

Vora, Erika Wenzel. "The Development of Concept Diffusion Models and Their Application to the Diffusion of the Social Concept of Race." Ph.D. dissertation, State University of New York at Buffalo, 1978.

Weaver, Paul H. "Newspaper News and Television News." In Douglass Cater et al. (eds.), *Television as a Social Force: New Approaches to TV Criticism*. New York: Praeger Publishers, 1975, 81–94.

Webber, Andred Lloyd. *Jesus Christ Superstar: The Original Motion Picture Album*. MCA Records MCA2 11000 (1973) 4s. 12 in. 33⅓ rpm, stereophonic.

Wells, Herbert George. *The War of the Worlds*. New York: Harper, 1926.

Westley, Bruce H., and Mac Lean, Malcolm S., Jr. "A Conceptual Model for Communications Research." *Journalism Quarterly* **34**, 1957, 31–38.

"What TV Does to Kids." *Newsweek*, February 21, 1977, 62–70.

Whitney, Frederick C. *Mass Media and Mass Communications in Society*. Dubuque, Ia.: W. C. Brown Co., 1975.

Wiio, Osmo A. "Contingency Views of Human Communication." A paper presented at the International Communication Association Conference, Chicago, April 1975.

Wilcox, Dennis. *Mass Media in Black Africa*. New York: Praeger Publishers, 1975.

Wilder, Thornton. *Our Town, a Play in Three Acts*. New York: Coward McCann, Inc., 1938.

Wright, Charles. *Mass Communication: A Sociological Perspective*. New York: Random House, 1975.

Zaremba, Alan. "An Exploratory Analysis of National Perceptions of the Arab-Israeli Conflict as Represented Through World Newspapers: An International Communication Study." Unpublished dissertation, State University of New York at Buffalo, 1977.

Znaimer, Moses. "The Television 'Border War'—Canada's View: Profits Not Only Issue." *Buffalo Courier Express*, February 29, 1976, 8.

Index of Names

Adler, Richard, 215, 225
Agee, William, 159
Aldrich, Pearl, 52
Anderson, Lindsay, 159
Ansah, Paul, 117
Asante, Molefi, 245
Ault, Phillip, 159

Baer, Walter S., 215
Bagdikian, Ben H., 135, 246
Ball-Rokeach, Sandra, 89, 110
Baran, Paul, 45
Baran, Stanley J., 228
Barker, Larry L., 66, 68
Bauer, Raymond A., 85
Beattie, Earle, 240, 241
Becker, Samuel, 250
Beisecker, Thomas, 50
Bennett, Rex, 210
Berelson, Bernard, 15, 50, 83, 107
Berlo, David K., 6-7, 14, 50-51, 64, 65, 66
Beuf, Ann, 208
Beuth, Philip R., 242, 243
Blake, Reed H., 10
Blumer, Jay G., 107
Bohn, Thomas, 65, 71, 156
Bondar, Harvey, 219
Bower, Robert T., 101, 205
Boylan, James, 98, 102, 207
Breitrose, Henry, 143
Bresson, Robert, 161
Brinkley, David, 167
Bryson, Lyman, 99
Buchwald, Art, 233

Buckley, James, 171
Butler, Matilda, 211

Cavalcanti, Alberto, 150
Cameron, Earl, 241
Carey, James W., 19-20, 117
Carlin, George, 229
Carlson, Sylvia, 144
Carlson, Verne, 144
Carpenter, Edmund, 43
Cassata, Mary B., 73, 77, 203, 245
Casty, Alan, 45
Cater, Douglas, 220, 223
Chaplin, Charles, 157, 158
Cline, Victor B., 230
Cocteau, Jean, 159
Cohen, Bernard C., 81
Cole, Nat King, 182
Cornish, Samuel, 195
Cox, Harvey, 220
Cronkite, Walter, 241
Culley, James D., 210

Daguerre, Louis, 146
Davidson, Emily S., 230
Davison, W. Phillips, 98, 102, 207
DeFleur, Melvin, 65, 69, 71, 84, 89, 110, 250
DeMott, Benjamin, 220
Diamond, Edwin, 101, 223
Dickson, William Kennedy Laurie, 147
Douglass, Frederick, 196
Downing, Mildred, 212
Dziga-Vertov, 149

Eastman, George, 146
Edison, Thomas, 146, 147
Eisenstein, S. M., 150
Embree, Alice, 203
Emery, Edwin, 119, 159
Emery, Michael C., 141, 196
Emery, Walter B., 177
Erskine, John, 77

Fassbinder, Rainer Werner, 160, 161
Feiffer, Jules, 2, 60, 114, 166
Fellini, Federico, 159
Fischer, Heinz-Dietrich, 254
Flaherty, Robert J., 148, 149
Francis, Jay, 202

Gaudet, Helen, 15, 50, 83
Genovese, Kitty, 225
Gerbner, George, 1, 64, 65, 66, 67, 68, 69, 80, 81, 221, 222, 225, 226
Gilbert, Samuel, 118
Glass, Marty, 223
Glessing, Robert J., 223
Godard, Jean-Luc, 159
Goodlet, Carlton B., 197
Greenberg, Bradley S., 99
Grierson, John, 149, 151
Griffith, D. W., 147, 148, 155, 156
Griffith, Richard, 148, 150
Gross, Larry, 80, 81, 225, 226
Gurevitch, Michael, 107, 108
Gutenberg, Johann, 5

Haas, Alan D., 226
Haas, Hadassah, 108
Halmos, Paul, 19
Hanneman, Gerhard J., 64, 72, 99
Haroldsen, Edwin O., 10
Havas, Charles, 118, 119
Hawkins, Robert Parker, 211
Hendrick, Grant H., 226
Henke, Lucy L., 228
Hennock, Frieda, 129
Henry, William E., 107
Hentoff, Nat, 167
Heraclitus, 7
Herzog, Herta, 107
Hester, Al, 119, 122
Heyl, Henry, 147

Hicks, Ronald, 5
Hiebert, Ray Eldon, 65, 71
Hitler, Adolph, 104
Hoffman, Abbie, 219
Holgrem, Rod, 220
Holsti, Ole, 250
Hookes, Benjamin, 216, 217
Howard, Robert T., 221
Hulten, Olof, 88, 141
Hutchins, Robert M., 188

Isaacs, John D., 147
Ivens, Joris, 150

Jefferson, Thomas, 77
Johnson, Lyndon B., 190
Johnson, Nicholas, 201
Johnson, Noble, 158

Katz, Elihu, 15, 107, 108
Kennedy, John F., 105
Kerner, Otto, 190
Khandelwal, Brij, 125
Kibler, Robert J., 66, 68
Klapper, Joseph T., 50, 81, 109
Knight, Arthur, 146, 148
Knight, Robert P., 254
Knopf, Terry Ann, 185
Kojak, 222
Kurosawa, Akira, 159

LaBrie, Henry, 197
Laemmle, Carl, 157
Lasswell, Harold, 64, 65, 66, 99
Lazarsfeld, Paul F., 15, 50, 83
Leob, Daniel J., 158
Lester, Richard, 159
Levinson, Richard M., 209, 210
Levy, Emanuel J., 233
Lewels, Francisco J., Jr., 200
Lewin, Kurt, 69
Lichty, Lawrence, 126, 127
Liebert, Robert M., 230
Littell, Joseph Fletcher, 175
Littner, Ner, 220
Lowenstein, Ralph L., 49, 53, 54
Lumiere, Auguste, 146

Lumiere, Louis, 146
Lundberg, D., 88

Machlup, Fritz, 43
MacLean, Malcolm S., 65, 68, 69
McEwen, William J., 64, 72, 99
McGarry, K. L., 67
McLuhan, Marshall, 80, 82-83, 117, 143
Meissonier, Jean Louis, 147
Melies, George, 147
Mendelsohn, Harold, 250
Merrill, John Calhoun, 49, 53, 54, 254
Meyer, Timothy P., 228
Mill, John Stuart, 77
Milton, John, 77
Morris, Joe A., 120
Morrison, Frederick Ernest, 158
Mortensen, C. David, 64
Moynihan, Daniel P., 171
Murphy, Robert D., 221
Muybridge, Eadweard, 147

Neale, John M., 230
Newcomb, T. M., 69
Niepce, Joseph, 146
Noble, Edward J., 128
Norton, William, 220

Opubor, Alfred, 117
Ozu, Yasujiro, 161

Paine, Thomas, 77
Paisley, William, 211
Paley, William, 128
Palmer, Roger Cain, 73, 77
Parson, Donn, 50
Paul, Robert, 146
Peterson, Theodore, 78
Pickford, Mary, 157
Pierce, Frederick S., 221
Pingree, Suzanne, 211
Plato, 219
Poitier, Sidney, 158
Pool de Sola, Ithiel, 143
Pope Gregory I, 247
Porter, Edwin, 147
Prowitt, Marsha O'Brannon, 175
Pudovkin, V. I., 150

Ramirez, Francisco P., 195
Reisz, Karel, 146, 159
Resnais, Alain, 159, 160, 161
Reuter, Julius, 118, 119
Rice, E. W., Jr., 126
Road, Sinclair, 148, 150
Roberts, Donald F., 79
Roosevelt, Franklin D., 46
Rosewater, Victor, 118
Rossellini, Roberto, 159
Rosten, Leo, 183
Rotha, Paul, 148, 150
Russwurm, John, 195
Ruttmann, Walther, 149, 150

Salazar, Rueben, 200
Sarnoff, David, 126, 127
Scher, Niki, 203
Schramm, Wilbur, 9, 10, 71, 72, 78, 79, 84, 101, 109, 110, 143, 250
Schwartz, Tony, 63, 225
Scripps, Edward, 120
Sears, David O., 50
Sellers, Coleman, 147
Sembene, Ousmane, 160, 161
Sennett, Mack, 156
Sereno, Kenneth K., 64
Shannon, Claude E., 14, 15, 65, 71, 72
Shindo, Kaneto, 159
Siebert, Fred S., 78
Singer, Benjamin D., 224
Smith, Arthur L., 13
Smith, Kate, 105
Smythe, Ted Curtis, 141, 196
Stein, Gertrude, 19
Steinfeld, Dr. Jesse, 219, 226
Stephenson, William, 86, 87
Storey, Graham, 119
Straub, Jean-Marie, 161
Stromgren, Richard, 156

Tedesco, Nancy S., 214
Teshigahara, Hiroshi, 159
Topliff, Samuel, 118
Topping, Malachi, 126, 127
Turow, Joseph, 213

Ungurait, Donald F., 65, 71

Valenti, Jack, 284
Vora, Erika Wenzel, 65, 70, 71

Warner, W. Lloyd, 107
Weaver, Warren, 14, 15, 65, 71, 72, 223
Welles, Orson, 104
Wells, Alan, 119, 185, 226
Westley, Bruce H., 65, 68, 69
White, William P., 223
Whitefield, George, 9
Whitney, Frederick C., 9, 172
Wiio, Osmo, 14, 16, 17

Wilcox, Dennis, 54
Wilder, Thornton, 169
Wiseman, Frederick, 151
Wolff, Bernard, 118, 119

Yu, Frederick T. C., 98, 102, 207

Zampa, Luigi, 159
Zaremba, Alan, 250
Znaimer, Moses, 241
Zukor, Adolph, 157

Index of Subjects

Action for Children's Television (ACT), 222, 229
Advertising, 51-56, 182-86, 207, 210-12
Aeropagitica, 77
Africa, 54
Afro-Americans, 194-202
Agence France-Presse (AFP), 117, 121-22
see also News Services
Agenda Setting, 74, 81
see also Press, theories of
Aggressive cues, 91, 94
see also Violence theories
All in the Family, 50, 207
Amalgamated Broadcasting System, 128
American Broadcasting Company, 126, 128-29, 201, 216, 221-22
American Marconi Company, 127
American Medical Association, 229
Apollo-Soyuz, 9
Ashanti, 44
Associated Press (AP), 117, 120-23, 185
see also News services
Attitude change, 102
Audiences, 10-14, 64, 75, 84-86, 97-99, 103, 130, 196-97, 205-207, 238
Audience, theories of, 75, 84-86
Authoritarian theory, 73-74
see also Press, theories of

Bell Laboratories, 14
Birth of a Nation, The, 148, 155-56
Bit, 14
Black broadcasting, 198-99
Black press, 195-98

Black World, 197
Blue network, 127-28
Brazil, 196
Broadcasting systems, 125-34
Germany, 132
Japan, 133
United States, 125-30
USSR, 130-31
Bullet theory, 74, 79
see also Press, theories of

CTV, Canada, 237-38
Cable television, 215, 241, 246
Canada, 233-43
Americanization of, 238-40
Broadcasting, 237-43
Canadian Broadcasting Corporation (CBC), 237-39, 241
Canadian Radio and Television Commission (CRTC), 241
Canons of journalism, 260-61
Capacity, see Channel
Carnegie Commission on Educational Television, 190-91
Carnegie Commission on the Future of Public Broadcasting, 192-93
Carnegie Corporation, 129, 190
Catharsis theory, 90, 94
see also Violence theories
Channel, 14, 64, 72, 103
Channel, theories of, 74-75
Chicano Media Committee, 200
Chronology, 21-41
Code of Broadcast News Ethics, 292-94
Code of the Comics Magazine Association of America, Inc., 333-36

Code of ethics, 263-65
Code of self-regulation, 278-84
Coffeehouses, 118
   see also News services
Colonial network, 128
Columbia Broadcasting System, 126, 128-29, 216, 222
Columbia University, 98
Commission on the Freedom of the Press, 188-90
Communication and Behavior, 64
Communication, constituents of, 6-7, 9-10, 44, 46, 54, 103
   see also Communication process
Communication models
   analog, 65
   basic, 9
   constituents, 6-7, 9
   critical school, 17
   definition, 64-65
   diagrammatic, 65
   iconic, 65
   mathematical, 65
   mental, 64
   Shannon and Weaver, 15
   SMCR, 6-7, 64, 66
   taxonomy of, 64
   two-step flow, 15
   verbal, 64-67
   see also Mass communication models
Communication, process, 6-13, 74-76
Communication revolution, 5-6, 19, 40
Communication satellites, see Satellites
Communication, sensory, 12
Communication, theory, 14, 16, 102
   see also Mass communication theory
Communicator, theories of, 73-74, 77-80, 103
COMSAT, 141
Consumer awareness training, 249
Copyright, 177-82
Corporation for Public Broadcasting, 129-130, 191
Corporation for Public Television, 191
Critical school, 17
Cultural acceptability, 47
Cultural indicators, 74, 80-81, 214
Cultural norms theory, 74, 86

Demassification, 245
Deutsche Presse Agentur (DPA), 117
   see also News services
Don Lee network, 128
DuMont, 128
Dyadic communication, 7

Ebony, 197
Ebony, Jr., 197
Educational television, 140
Effects, theories of, 76, 87-89
El Clamor Publico, 195
Entrophy, 14, 72
Essence: The Magazine for Today's Black Woman, 197
Everready group, 127

Fairness doctrine, 170-72
Family viewing time, 229
Federal Communications Commission, 170-76, 229-30
Federal Republic of Germany, 131-32
Federal Trade Commission, 176-77
Feedback, 12-13, 14, 16, 49-51, 110, 130
Feedfront, 13
Film, as communication, 145-46
   cinema verite, 151
   definitions, 143
   documentary, 148-49
   entertainment, 155
   narrative, 147-48
   newsreel, 150
   propagandist, 150-51
   realist, 149-50
Filthy words, 229-30
Food and Drug Administration, 176-77
Freedom's Journal, 195

Gatekeeping, 74, 79-80
Germany: Association of Broadcasting Corporations (ARD), 132
Gone With the Wind, 98
Great Train Robbery, The, 147

Havas News Service, 119
   see also News services
Hollywood, decline of, 159

Home Box Office, 159
"Hot" and "cool" media, 75, 82-83
    see also McLuhan, theories
Hsinhua (New China News Agency),
    117, 121-22
    see also News services
Hypodermic needle theory, 74, 79
    see also Press, theories of

Individual differences theory, 75, 84,
    90-93
Industrial revolution, 19, 40
Information control theory, 74
    see also Gatekeeping; Press, theories
    of
International News Service, 121
    see also News services
Interpersonal communication, 9-11
    see also Communication process
Israel, 106
Izvestiya, 131

Japan, 132
Jet, 197
Johnson Publishing Company, 197-98

Knowledge industry, 43
Komsomolskaya Pravda, 131

Lagos, 6
Learning without involvement, 106
Libertarian theory, 74, 77
    see also Press, theories of
Lima, Peru, 123
Lundenic theory, see also Play theory

McClatchy Broadcasting Company,
    128
McGuffey Readers, 46
McLuhan, theories, 74-75, 82-83
Mass communication, 9-11, 44-56
    see also Communication process
Mass Communication, constituents of
    circulation, 46-49
    feedback, 49-51
    ownership, 54-56

reproduction, 44-46
support, 51-54
Mass communication effects, 76,
    87-89, 96-111
Mass communication functions, 99-
    100, 108
Mass communication models
    Berlo, 64-67
    DeFleur, 64, 69, 71
    Gerbner, 64, 66-69
    Hiebert, Ungurait, and Bohn, 65-66,
        69, 71
    Lasswell, 64-65, 69
    Shannon and Weaver, 71-72
    Vora, 66, 69, 71
    Westley-MacLean, 65, 67-68
Mass communication regulations and
    control, 169-76
Mass communication research, 249-54
    case methods, 252-53
    content analysis, 250-51
    depth interview, 251
    Likert scale, 251
    questionnaires, 251-52
    semantic differential, 253
Mass communication theories, 72-96,
    102-10
    see also Communication theories,
        Mass communication models
Mass communications, 11, 13, 21-41,
    43-56, 74, 130-33, 183
Mass communication systems
    Federal Republic of Germany,
        131-32
    Japan, 132
    Nigeria, 132-34
    Soviet system, 130-31
    United States, 125-30
Mass media, see Mass communications
Mathematical Theory of Communication,
    14
Media codes, 260-338
    Journalism codes
        Canons of journalism, 260-61
        Code of ethics, 263-65
        A statement of principles, 261-63
    Motion picture codes
        Motion picture production code,
            266-77
        Code of self-regulation, 278-84
        The movie rating system, 284-92

Media codes (*continued*)
  Broadcasting codes
    Code of broadcast news ethics, 292-94
    Radio code, 294-311
    Television code, 311-33
    Code of the Comics Magazine Association of America, Inc., 333-36
    Public Relations Society of America Code of Professional Standards for the Practice of Public Relations, 337-38
Media Employment
  Mexican-Americans, 200-201
  Puerto Ricans, 200-201
  women, 216-17
Media ethics, 184-87
Media gratifications and utility theory
  see Uses and gratification approach
Media investigatory bodies, 187-93
  Carnegie Commission on Educational Television, 190-91
  Carnegie Commission on the Future of Public Broadcasting, 192-93
  Commission on the Freedom of the Press, 188-90
  National Advisory Commission on Civil Disorders, 186, 190, 204
  National Commission on the Causes and Prevention of Violence, 191-92, 195
  Surgeon General's Scientific Advisory Committee on Television and Social Behavior, 192, 219
Medio Communication, 10
  see also Communication process
Medium Is the Massage, The, 74, 82-83
  see also McLuhan, theories
Medium Is the Message, The, 74, 82-83
Message, theories of, 74, 80-82, 103
Mexican-Americans, 194-202
Minorities, 195-202, 203-15
Minority broadcasting, 198-99
Modeling and imitation, 106
Moscow, 130-31
Motion picture production code, 266-77
Motion pictures, early development, 146-47
The movie rating system, 284-92
Multistep flow, 75

  see also N-step flow; One-step flow; Two-step flow
Mutual Broadcasting System, 128

NHK, 132
N-step flow, 83
  see also One-step flow; Two-step flow; Multistep flow
Nairobi, Kenya, 117
Nanook of the North, 148-49, 154
National Advisory Commission on Civil Disorders, 186, 190, 204
National Association for Better Broadcasting, 229
National Association of Broadcasters, 229
National Broadcasting Company, 126-29, 216, 221-22
National Citizen's Committee for Broadcasting, 221-22
National Commission on the Causes and Prevention of Violence, 191-92, 195
New York Associated Press, *see* News services
News agencies, *see* News services
New services, 117-25
  Agence France-Presse (AFP), 117, 121
  Associated Press (AP), 117, 120, 121-22
  coffeehouses, 118
  Deutsche Presse Agentur, 117
  Havas News Service, 119
  Hsinhua, 117, 121-22
  International News Service, 121
  New York Associated Press, 119-20
  Novosti, 117
  Prensa Latina, 117
  Reuters, 117-18, 121-22, 185
  ROSTA, 121
  TASS, 117, 121-22
  United Press Association, 120
  United Press International (UPI), 117, 121-22, 185
  Wolff News Agency, 118
Nigeria, 6, 132
Nigerian Broadcasting Corporation, 133
Nigerian Broadcasting Service, 133
No effects theory, 76, 89

No Way Out, 158-59
Noise, 14
Novosti, 117
  see also News services

Objective theory of the press, 74
  see also Press, theories of
Observational learning theory, 92, 94,
  106
  see also Modeling and imitation
One-step flow, 75
  see also Multistep flow; Two-step
  flow; N-step flow
Opinion leader, 15

Pacific Broadcasting Company, 128
Parent-teacher association, 222, 229
Play theory, 76, 86-87
Power of the press theory, 74
  see also Press, theories of
Pravda, 131
Prensa, Latina, 117
  see also News services
Press, theories of, 73-74, 77-80
Prime time school television, 249
Public Broadcasting Corporation, 126
Public Broadcasting System, 129
Public Relations Society of America
  Code of Professional Standards
  for the Practice of Public Rela-
  tions, 337-38
Public television, 129-30

Quality Network, 128

RCA SATCOM, 45
Radio code, 294-311
Radio Corporation of America, 127
Red Lion Broadcasting Co., 171
Red Network, 127
Red Star, 131
Redundancy, 14
Reinforcement theory, 93, 95
Reproduction, 44-46
Reuters, 117-18, 121-22, 185
  see also News services
Roots, 129

ROSTA, 121
  see also News services

Satellites, 45, 135-42
Selective exposure, 50, 87
Selective perception, 102
Sesame Street, 13
Social categories theory, 75, 86, 90,
  92-93
Socialization, 208-10, 224-28
Social learning theory, 76, 89
Social relationships theory, 75, 86, 93
Social responsibilities theory, 74, 78
  see also Press, theories of
South Africa, 47
Soviet-Communist theory, 74, 78
  see also Press, theories of
Soviet system of broadcasting, 130-31
Soviet Fleet, 131
Soviet Ukraine, 131
State University of New York at Buf-
  falo, 96, 225
A statement of principles, 261-63
Stereotypes, 208-10, 212-16
Stimulating effects theory, *see* Aggres-
  sive cues theories
Systems theory, 14-17, 110
Surgeon General's Scientific Advisory
  Committee on Television and
  Social Behavior, 192, 219

TASS (Telegrafnoie Agenstvo Sovets-
  kavo Soiuza), 111, 117, 121-22
  see also News services
*Taxonomy of Concepts in Communi-
  cation,* 10
*Television and Growing Up: The Impact
  of Televised Violence,* 192
Television and the Public, 101
Television awareness training, 249
Television code, 228, 311-33
Television news, violence in, 223
  see also Television violence; Vio-
  lence theories
Television violence, 219-31
Theory of effects, 89
  see Effects, theories of
Thompson, J. Walter, 229
Trud, 131
TV Border War, 241-43

TV Factbook, 129
Two-step 'flow, 14-15, 75

Understanding Media: The Extensions of Man, 143
UNESCO, 254-55
United Church of Christ, 216
United Press International (UPI), 117, 121-22, 185
  see also News services
United Press Association, 120
  see also News services
Uses and gratifications approach, 76, 88-89, 106-107
Uses and gratifications theory, *see* Uses and gratification approach; Mass communication effects
United States Broadcasting System, 125-30

Values, 17, 86, 240
Vietnam war, 223
Violence profile, 221
Violence theories, 89-96
  see also Television violence

War of the Worlds, 104
WBAI, 229-30
WEAF, New York, 127
WESTAR, 45
WGY, Schenectady, 127
WJZ, Newark, 127
Wolff News Agency, *see* News services
Women in daytime serials, 212-13
Women in prime time, 214-16
Women's movement, 203-205

Xerox, 44

Yankee Network, Inc., 128